E.J. PRATT: THE TRUANT YEARS

DAVID G. PITT

E.J. Pratt:
The Truant Years
1882–1927

UNIVERSITY OF TORONTO PRESS
Toronto Buffalo London

© University of Toronto Press 1984
Toronto Buffalo London
Printed in Canada
Reprinted in 2018
ISBN 0-8020-5660-1 (cloth)
ISBN 978-0-8020-6563-6 (paper)

Distributed in the Atlantic
Provinces by Jesperson Press

ISBN 0-920502-39-3 (cloth)
ISBN 0-920502-37-7 (paper)

Canadian Cataloguing in Publication Data

Pitt, David G. (David George), 1921–
    E. J. Pratt : the truant years 1882–1927
    Includes index.
    Bibliography: v.
    Contents: v. 1. The truant years, 1882–1927.
    ISBN 0-8020-5660-1 (v.1: bound)
    ISBN 978-0-8020-6563-6 (paper)
    1. Pratt, E. J. (Edwin John), 1882–1964 – Biography.
    2. Poets, Canadian (English) – 20th century –
    Biography.* I. Title.
    PS8531.R3Z68 1984   C811'.52   C84-098758-7
    PR9199.2.P73Z68 1984

Unless noted otherwise, photographs were provided by Viola and Claire Pratt (copying in most instances by Robert D. Pitt, St John's): United Church Archives, St John's – The Methodist College Home; United Church Archives, Toronto – George Blewett, Lorne Pierce; The Thomas Fisher Rare Book Library, Toronto – Pratt in 1926, Pelham Edgar, William Arthur Deacon, Arthur L. Phelps; Victoria University Library, Toronto – 'The Three Rebels,' Pratt at Lake O'Hara, Pratt and Wilson MacDonald, Pratt and mother and daughter in St John's; Lydia Trimble Harrison – Lydia Trimble.

For
Marion
Ruth and Rob

'... endeared
To me by all the natural ties ...'

'What have you there?' the great Panjandrum said
To the Master of the Revels who had led
A bucking truant with a stiff backbone
Close to the foot of the Almighty's throne.
...
And the great Panjandrum's face grew dark –
'I'll put those chemists to their annual purge,
And I myself shall be the thaumaturge
To find the nature of the fellow's spark.
Come, bring him nearer ...'

                    E.J. Pratt, from 'The Truant'

Contents

Preface

N THE EARLY 1960s, on a sunny afternoon in late summer, an old man sat in a wooden armchair under a tree in Toronto's Edwards Gardens. Except, perhaps, for the dark grey Homburg worn slightly off the brow, there was nothing about his appearance to distinguish him from many old men who are not derelicts and sit under trees in city parks. He was ordinarily dressed: slightly rumpled suit, a bit oversized now for the frame beneath it; white shirt and dark necktie, waistcoat, watch-chain and fob across the midriff, ankle-high black leather boots. A crook-handle walking-cane between his knees was lightly held by one hand with the peculiar, uncertain grip of arthritic fingers. The pale, clean-shaven face, though thin, was only slightly wrinkled about the eyes and mouth, its pallor clearly that of one who has been housebound for many weeks. But the face was very much alive; the eyes alert, shining; the mouth humorous; the expression of the face that of one eager for anything which might distract his thoughts from the ills that in old age 'Put palsy in your touch,' 'dry / Your blood and marrow, shoot / Arthritic needles through your cartilage ...'

Almost any old man. But not quite. A retinue of attendants nearby, professional-looking and professionally busy, a battery of klieg lights and cameras, microphones strategically placed, proclaimed that he indeed was not any old man sunning himself before the sun went down. Obviously a celebrity, yet everyone was calling him by his first name, Ned. Treating him with great respect, almost reverence, they nevertheless all seemed to know him familiarly, and he responded in like manner. Everything was very casual and informal. Yet it was clearly an occasion, and he was obviously enjoying it with a mixture of amused embarrassment and keenly savoured delight.

The experience was not unfamiliar to E.J. Pratt. There had been many occasions in the past of which he had been the central figure: publishers' galas to signal the launching of fifteen books of his poems; autographing sessions in crowded Toronto bookstores; dinners in his honour as 'distinguished poet' reading his works from coast to coast; university conclaves at which more honorary degrees had been conferred on him than he could remember; banquets to mark the bestowal of more than a dozen medals for this and that, and the blue and scarlet ribbon of the Order of St Michael and St George of which he had been made a Companion by King George VI; as well as hundreds of dinners and parties, large and small, of his own hosting.

Such occasions were much fewer now, for he was old and unwell. But looming not far ahead was his eightieth birthday, and the man who was called Canada's unofficial poet laureate was to be filmed and recorded for a last public performance, one to be seen and heard by the largest of the many audiences to have seen and heard him during his forty years as a public figure.

What had brought him here? By what curious 'convergence of the manifold' (to use his own Hardyesque definition of Fate) – of manifold events and circumstances, accidents and ironies, tragedies and triumphs – did the Newfoundland outport boy become Toronto's Grand Old Man of Canadian Poetry? The answer, of course, lies in the story of his life. But biography is not a science; it is a species of history whose answers to such questions are not solutions to mathematical problems. There is no formula for the production of a genius, no recipe of quantitative ingredients, no set of given conditions, circumstances, experiences which, converging, necessarily produce the miraculous result. Yet while the process by which from time to time such things occur may be too mysterious, too complex and uncertain to reduce to the terms of a formula or the graphics of a blueprint, it can be observed, documented, and perhaps thereby understood.

It was some months before the memorable filming session in Edwards Gardens that I visited Ned Pratt for the last time, but I had first met him long before then, in 1946 when I arrived in Toronto to enter the School of Graduate Studies at the University. Eager to meet the only fellow Newfoundlander who until then had made a name for himself in the literary world, I promptly called on him in his office at

Victoria College where he was a professor of English. We quickly became friends. Unfortunately I did not manage to see him as often as I would have liked during my three years in the graduate school. I was in another corner of the campus and only occasionally ran into him when our paths crossed accidentally, or when in the vicinity of the College I dropped in on him at his office for a brief chat. After my return to Newfoundland to teach in the new university there, on visits to Toronto I would try to see him, and once was invited to a large, informal party where I saw for myself what so many have spoken or written of to me: Ned Pratt as the 'convivial centre of attention in a convivial gathering of friends, mostly males.'

Visiting him in January 1960, mainly to discuss with him a selection of his poems which I was editing (*Here the Tides Flow*), I broached the idea of a full-dress biography, which his brother, the late Senator Calvert Pratt, and I had already discussed. The idea had not, it seems, occurred to him, but he was not averse to it. 'But not until I'm gone,' he said, gazing a little wistfully into the fireplace. 'If, then, people are still reading my stuff, a modest volume might be in order – to set the record straight.' I did not argue the point, though I felt that there was no time like the present, and was certain people would be reading his 'stuff' long after he was gone. Though still mentally vigorous, he was already unwell, getting a little feeble, sitting in a dressing-gown, books of his poems nearby. I suggested, however, that a question-and-answer session might greatly help to set the record straight when the time came to write it. He readily agreed, and I came away late that afternoon with what proved to be one of the most interesting and illuminating items which my eventually voluminous files were to contain. The occasion proved, moreover, to have been timely: though subsequent correspondence passed between us, I was not to see him again.

I respected his wishes regarding a biography. Apart from recording interviews with some of his old friends and acquaintances and several family members, contemporaries of his who had known him long ago and who, I feared, might not be here much longer, I did very little toward the project until 1969. Unfortunately responsibilities of another kind prevented my pursuing it thereafter as sedulously as I should have liked. What I had hoped to accomplish by his ninetieth anniversary has thus taken until his centenary to do. But the delay has had its compensations: a number of important biographical items have come to light which were not in my files a decade ago.

There are both advantages and disadvantages in writing of someone who has recently passed from the scene. The most serious disadvantage is undoubtedly the preclusion of that kind of perspective and distancing of one's subject which only the passage of time can bring, something perhaps even more difficult to achieve when he was known personally to his biographer. I trust, however, that this circumstance has not prevented my viewing Pratt with objectivity and writing of him with candour. He would not have wanted it otherwise. On the other hand, as suggested above, an important advantage of contemporaneity with one's subject is the presence of many living witnesses, people who knew him well or had personal dealings with him of one sort and another. In this respect I have been very fortunate. Scores of such individuals have given invaluable help, lending or giving me letters and other personal documents, answering my questions, writing or allowing me to record their recollections and impressions of Pratt, and generally co-operating to assist me in my venture. I do not recall a single rebuff.

People have seen him in differing lights, portrayed him in differing ways, though certain common features have emerged from all the various portraits, memoirs, and recollections: the warmth and geniality of his personality, the kindliness of his nature, the strength and courage of his spirit, and the magnetic affinity of his character for anecdote, even for 'legend.' One of my chief problems, indeed, in writing of Pratt has been to avoid an excess of anecdotal embellishment; as an old friend of his observed, 'Ned Pratt was the sort of person to whom anecdotes stuck like barnacles to a barge.' And most of them I have found to be true. Even those that are not are revealing: that he was the sort of person about whom such tales were told and believed is in itself an illuminating phenomenon.

Though I have from time to time allowed old friends who knew him well and observed him closely and sensitively to help fill in his portrait, I have wherever possible let him speak for himself. Unfortunately extant letters and other personal documents of his are not voluminous. He kept no diary or journal, and no carbon copies of letters he wrote, most of which were in his often indecipherable handwriting. After much searching and inquiring I have turned up only about a thousand or so of his letters, long and short, to fewer than a hundred correspondents although he must have written many more.

His letters to his mother, for example, were all destroyed shortly after her death. 'How did I know that he was going to be famous?' was the hapless culprit's defence. Nevertheless, a fair sampling of his correspondence has survived, for which his biographer is duly thankful.

As these prefatory remarks may have suggested already, while throughout this biography I have tried never to lose sight of E.J. Pratt the poet – in the early years the potential poet – my main interest has been, very frankly, Ned Pratt the man, the unlikely Newfoundlander who came to be called Canada's greatest poet of his time, yet who wrote no line that can properly be called poetry until he was thirty-five years old, and who became a poet at all almost by accident. I must, however, hasten to add that I have by no means neglected his writing, neither his poetry nor his prose. To have done so would not only have been perverse; it would have defeated one of the main purposes of literary biography. Yet while frequently casting a critical eye on Pratt's poetical and other works, except for the longer, major poems and certain of the more significant prose writings (Pratt was a far more prolific prose writer than is generally thought), or where special circumstances seemed to warrant a closer look at some of the lesser ones, I have not undertaken extensive analysis, nor attempted to make what has been done exhaustive. His writing has, of course, been frequently used to shed light on the man, his personality, mind, and spirit. Moreover, set for the first time in its full personal context the poetry in particular has, I think, been illuminated and at times reinterpreted by the biographical facts and circumstances surrounding its origin and composition. The fact is, however, that quite apart from being an important poet, Pratt was, as I hope my book will show, an extraordinary person in other ways; as a friend of his remarked to me, 'Ned Pratt was large enough as a human being, interesting and unusual enough, to warrant having his biography written had he never published a line of poetry nor done anything else that the world regards as significant in human affairs.' I am almost inclined to agree.

In acknowledging my many debts and expressing my grateful thanks to all who assisted in making this book possible, I have only one regret: that a number of those who were particularly helpful, having died before this book could have been completed, will not know of my public acknowledgment of my debts to them. I shall, however, in the statement that follows include their names as though they were still with us, making no formal distinction between the deceased and the living.

I must begin by saying that I am particularly indebted and most grateful to Viola Pratt, widow of E.J. Pratt, and their daughter Claire for help of many kinds. Without their assistance and co-operation, this book, however imperfect it may be, would have been far less a book than it is, if indeed it could have been written at all. Not only did they grant me many hours of tape-recorded and other interviews, write many letters in response to my importunate inquiries, and direct me to many informative friends and acquaintances of Pratt's, but they also made freely available to me all the personal letters in their possession written by and to him, as well as other personal documents. I must add that they have in no way attempted to influence or direct the writing of this book, leaving me entirely free to interpret the record as I saw it, draw my own conclusions, and make my own mistakes.

Other members of the families Pratt and Knight who were very helpful include the following: Senator C.C. Pratt, the poet's brother, conversations with whom between 1959 and 1962 laid the foundation for the entire project; Florence ('Floss') Pratt, the poet's sister, who granted me several long interviews; Daphne Pratt House, the poet's niece, who allowed me to interview her and also supplied a number of valuable family documents, including memorabilia of her father, the poet's brother, James; Maud Pratt, widow of the poet's brother Arthur; the Honourable Mr Justice H.G. Puddester and his wife, the former Gwenyth Pratt, a niece of the poet; William Knight, jr and Dr Cluny Macpherson, cousins of the poet, both of whom granted me lengthy interviews and provided valuable documents.

Many others who lent or gave me letters and other documents, wrote me their personal recollections of Pratt, answered my queries by mail or in person, or allowed me to tape-record interviews with them, whose contributions assisted me in writing this volume are named in the relevant subsections of the general bibliography at the end of this book and are herewith gratefully thanked. I wish, however, to acknowledge here a special debt to the following: Esther Magoon Bailey, Margaret (Mrs E.K.) Brown, Douglas Bush, William Arthur Deacon, Sandra Djwa, Barker Fairley, Alison Feder, Northrop Frye, Lydia Trimble Harrison, Watson Kirkconnell, Carl Klinck, R.S. Knox, Adrian Macdonald, Gordon Moyles, Patrick O'Flaherty,

Desmond Pacey, Arthur L. Phelps, William H. Pike, Clayton Pincock, E.R. Seary, Samuel H. Soper, May Stevenson, Henry W.
Wells, Hager H. Whitney, Healey Willan, and J. Frank Willis.

Others whose assistance of various kinds, especially in making
essential documents available to me, I wish to acknowledge with my
thanks, are (or were) holders of various official posts. In the list that
follows I shall refer to them by the titles they held or the posts they
occupied at the time they provided assistance to me: Walter F. Butt,
Archivist of the United Church in Newfoundland; Agnes O'Dea,
Custodian of the Newfoundland Room in the Library of Memorial
University of Newfoundland; Margaret Williams and the staff of the
Library of Memorial University; the head librarian and staff of the
Public Library, St John's; the Reverend Glenn Lucas, Archivist of the
United Church Archives at Victoria College, Toronto; Lorna Fraser,
Head Librarian, and her staff at the E.J. Pratt Library, Victoria
College, Toronto; the head librarians of the Sigmund Samuel Library
and the Thomas Fisher Rare Book Library at the University of
Toronto; the staff of the Public Reference Library, Toronto; the staff
of the Public Library, Burlington, Ontario; Donald Redmond, Head
Librarian, and the staff of the Douglas Library of Queen's University,
Kingston, Ontario; Donald Gallup, Curator, Collection of American
Literature, Beinecke Rare Book and Manuscript Library, Yale University; Pamela R. Mason, Assistant Curator for Modern Poetry Special Collections, University of Chicago Library; Lyn Harrington,
National Secretary of the Canadian Authors Association; librarians of
the university libraries: Acadia, British Columbia, New Brunswick,
McMaster, McGill, Saskatchewan, and York; the Office of the Regis-
trar-General of Ontario; the Saskatchewan Archives Board; the editors of the following newspapers and journals: the Amherstberg *Echo*,
the Estevan *Mercury*, the London *Free Press*, the Montreal *Star*, the St
John's *Daily News*, the St John's *Evening Telegram*, *Saturday Night*, and
the *United Church Observer*; the Canadian Broadcasting Corporation,
Toronto.

To other institutions and individuals who rendered different but no
less essential kinds of assistance I also acknowledge a debt of gratitude:
the Canada Council for two short-term grants and a leave fellowship;
the Memorial University of Newfoundland for the grant of sabbatical
leaves and for other material assistance; members of the Department

of English Language and Literature of Memorial University for many kinds of support; Paulette Bradbury Evans and Cathy Pitt Murphy, secretaries of the same department, for typing assistance.

This book has been published with the help of grants from the Canadian Federation for the Humanities, using funds provided by the Social Sciences and Humanities Research Council of Canada, and from the Publications Fund of the University of Toronto Press.

I also wish to acknowledge with gratitude the expert advice and assistance I have received in the preparation of the manuscript of this book from Jean Wilson and Gerald Hallowell of the University of Toronto Press.

Finally, I wish to thank publicly the members of my family, who have been my constant allies: my daughter Ruth and her husband Gordon Francis, my son Robert and his wife the former Janet Miller, and my wife Marion, who helped more than she can know, not the least in her patiently tolerant acknowledgment of a truth once uttered by someone, that 'a biographer needs a larger table to work on than anyone else.'

All those whose assistance to me of whatever kind pertains only to the second volume of this biography (covering the remaining years of Pratt's life from 1927 to his death in 1964) will be mentioned in that volume.

DAVID G. PITT
St John's, Newfoundland

NOTE

No asterisks or numerals have been used to clutter the text with reference signals. Such information as is usually supplied by signalled footnotes, when not given in the text, as it often is, will be found at the end of the volume under Notes and References and Bibliography. Under the former, page-by-page references are provided for all major data and citations in the text, as well as, where necessary, subsidiary notes.

Certain portions of this volume previously given orally but not published are as follows: the sections on Pratt's early poems in Chapters 7 and 10; on *Rachel* and *Clay* in Chapters 12 and 14; and the section on *The Witches' Brew* in Chapter 19 were included in a paper entitled 'Toward the First Spike: The Evolution of a Poet,' read before a regional conference of the Humanities Association of Canada in Sackville, NB, on 11 October 1969. Portions of Chapters 17 and 18 constituted parts of a lecture entitled 'The Context of the Twenties: The Background of *Newfoundland Verse* and *The Witches' Brew*,' given at a session of the Atlantic Canada Institute in Charlottetown, PEI, on 10 July 1974. Portions of the biographical matter in Books I and II and sections of the critical matter in Book III were included in the annual Pratt Lecture given at Memorial University of Newfoundland, 2 April 1982.

Class picture: The Methodist College, St John's, *c*1893. E.J. Pratt is the short boy, third from left in third row; Principal R.E. Holloway is fourth from left in the front row

John and Fanny Pratt and children, c1895. Seated L to R: John, Charlotte, Floss, William, Arthur, Fanny; standing L to R: Edwin, James; reclining: Calvert (an eighth child, Nellie, was born the following year)

John and Fanny Pratt, formally dressed for presentation to the Duke and Duchess of Cornwall and York (later King George v and Queen Mary), St John's, 1901

'The Three Rebels': E.J. Pratt, centre, S.H. Soper, left, W.H. Pike, right; taken near St John's before they left for Toronto, September 1907

The Methodist College Home, Long's Hill, St John's, a co-educational residence where Pratt boarded in 1901–2. Girls were housed on the second floor, boys on the third

RIGHT E.J. Pratt, graduation,
Victoria College, 1911

BOTTOM LEFT George Blewett
(1873–1912), a friend and teacher of
Pratt's, 1909–12; drowned in Lake
Huron

BOTTOM RIGHT Lydia Trimble
(1890–1912), to whom Pratt was
once engaged; buried on her graduation day, 1912

E.J. Pratt at Lake O'Hara, ready to climb Cathedral Mountain, July 1913

Viola Leone Whitney (whom Pratt married in 1918) as a student at
Victoria College, 1913

The bride and groom, Toronto, 20 August 1918

Viola Pratt and daughter Mildred Claire, summer 1924

LEFT Pelham Edgar

BOTTOM RIGHT Arthur L. Phelps, *c*1922

BOTTOM LEFT William Arthur Deacon, *c*1922

Lorne Pierce

E.J. Pratt and Wilson MacDonald at the Muskoka Assembly, *c*1927

E.J. Pratt, his daughter Claire, and his mother on the verandah of her house in St John's, June 1925

E.J. Pratt, c1926

BOOK I: THE NEWFOUNDLAND PARSON'S SON
1882–1907

... fundamentals spun
From the umbilicus ...

1

Ancestral Roots

'What is his pedigree?'
'The base is guaranteed ...'

E.J. Pratt, 'The Truant,' 1942

HE NAME PRATT is well known in Newfoundland though it is not common, and its connotations are as much commercial and financial as literary and artistic. Of alien worlds perhaps, yet the Pratts of Newfoundland have but a single family tree, which sprang from a lone, transplanted Yorkshireman, John Pratt, miner turned Methodist preacher, who rooted himself in the rocky soil of Newfoundland more than a century ago.

When his third child – and third son – the future poet was born in 1882, John Pratt was in the second and last year of his pastorate at Western Bay, a year, as he recorded it in his 'Spiritual State Report' to his Church, in which 'we have been lifted up and cast down':

We have seen the cloud arise which gave promise of a shower, but adverse winds came from the world ... and scattered the clouds, and our hopes have been blighted ... Many professed to have got a deep plunge in the fountain, and we all expected a good work, but the enemy succeeded in scattering discord in the Church, which produced barrenness and death ... To see such a number go back to the world and such crowds of young people unconverted has caused intense grief of heart and flooded our eyes with tears, yet we are encouraged with the thought that the triumph of the wicked is short ...

The story had been much the same in all his annual reports since he had come to Newfoundland from Yorkshire in 1873, an overseas missionary for the Wesleyan Methodist Church. But though he could be 'cast down' and easily moved to 'intense grief of heart,' he was made of too stern a stuff to yield to despair: 'a lamb yoked with a lion' was how a former parishioner once described him. His early life in the lead mines of Swaledale and the coalfields of Lancashire, and a long indoctrination with the tough creed of North Country Methodism had given him the temper of mind and will to shape in the end a man who had about him, as his third son would later say, 'a bit of the saint and a lot of the martyr.'

Not a great deal is known of John Pratt's early life, though what is suggests that it was one of extreme poverty and hardship. His father, James (1792–1858), like his father before him, was a leadminer, who had worked most of his life in the infamous Old Gang mines at Gunnerside, a small village near the confluence of the Rivers Arkle and Swale in Yorkshire. In 1813 he had married sixteen-year-old Sarah Bell, who, like him, made her mark in the marriage register. In quick succession she had borne him four sons, all of whom had died in infancy. But five more children had soon followed, and these, somehow, had survived the malnutrition and epidemic ills which stalked the families of the chronically poor in the black days of the English 1820s. For James and Sarah had united their destinies under most inauspicious stars.

Two years after their marriage Napoleon's wars had ended at Waterloo, and behind the receding wave of war and its economic surge had come a deep and lingering trough of economic distress. Markets for manufactured goods vanished overnight, and harvests that yielded virtually nothing combined with the new Corn Laws to make destitution a way of life for thousands, especially in the north. At Gunnerside the price of lead, mainstay of the population, plummeted from £33 a ton during the war years to £23 in 1818, and to £13 in 1829. Miners' wages, never high, fell accordingly, and the rocky land yielding little more than poor hay which supported only poorer sheep there was virtually nothing else to fall back upon. Even the hay crops failed in the 1820s, and to intensify the general misery came outbreaks of cholera, typhus, and scarlet fever, to say nothing of the ever-present 'miners' complent' (tuberculosis) which readily thrived in lungs long damaged by particles of lead and dust from the mines. The mines, however, managed to keep going until the 1830s, and though wages remained pitifully low, and the hours of work long and dreadful, James Pratt managed somehow to pull the remnant of his family through this slough of distress. But he and Sarah had other sources of sustenance.

'In the vacant misery of such a life,' Trevelyan has written of these dismal times, 'two sources of consolation, drink and religion, strove for the souls of men.' The Pratts had chosen the consolations of Methodism. The Swaledale Pratts had been, in fact, among the first of Wesley's converts in that part of England. As early as 1743 he had ridden into the Yorkshire dales bringing his new, fervid gospel of spiritual salvation and social reform into lives long beleaguered by poverty, hard labour, disease, and despair. On subsequent conquests he had established his 'classes' and 'societies,' founding members of which in Swaledale had been the Pratts. Recording a visit there in 1761, he wrote in his *Journals*: 'I found an earnest, loving, simple people, whom I ... exhorted not to leave the church, though they had not the best of Ministers.' Whether the Pratts were among the leadminers, also mentioned by Wesley, 'turned out of their work for following this way' (the Methodist Way) is not known. If so they were also among those whom, writes Wesley, 'their old master was glad to employ again,' for the Pratts were leadminers for several generations after that. Whatever the circumstances of their initiation into the Methodist fold, the roots of Wesleyanism struck deep in the Pratt family. No tradition was more proudly maintained through all the vicissitudes encountered by generations of Pratts than their passionate allegiance to the Way. For years a sacred family relic was a chair from which Wesley had preached while on one of his periodic crusades into the Yorkshire dales.

Yet even the consolations of Methodism could hardly satisfy a natural aspiration for something better here and now. Accordingly, as things at Gunnerside went from bad to worse, James and Sarah Pratt and their five surviving children, sometime around 1830, crossed 'the Jordan of Yorkshire,' as the Swale used to be called, and made their way across the moors to Barnard Castle on the Durham side of the River Tees. Not that Barney-Cassel (as it was locally named) was much of a Canaan: few of the towns any more than the villages of the North flowed with milk and honey in those hard times. Nevertheless, James Pratt remained there as a 'labourer' for more than a decade, during which time three more children were added to his and Sarah's brood. A son was born in 1835 and a daughter in 1837. The birth of their twelfth child, though only the eighth to survive infancy, is recorded thus: 'Born 28 August 1839 in the Market Place, Barnard Castle, John, son of James Pratt and Sarah Pratt formerly Bell, labourer.'

The Pratts did not, it seems, remain long at Barnard Castle after John was born: no one of that name is reported there in the 1841 census, and the birth of James and Sarah's thirteenth child, Thomas, was recorded at Spring End, Gunnerside, in 1843. Sometime, then, between August 1839 and the census of 1841 the Pratts returned to their old home, so that not Barnard Castle but Gunnerside on the Swale, with its penurious farms and louring lead mines, was the home of John Pratt's childhood and youth. The old house they lived in, probably built around 1770 by James Pratt's father, was still standing in 1924 when E.J. Pratt tramped over the moors to visit Gunnerside: 'It took me until five p.m. to reach the place, all tuckered out, but all the inhabitants made a great fuss over me when I disclosed my identity. They took me to the house where he [John Pratt] was brought up, a house made of stone (in fact, all the houses here are made of stone), and over one hundred and fifty years old ...'

The Pratts remained at Gunnerside for at least the next fifteen years. James and his older sons went back to the mines, which had reopened around 1840, where they were joined in due course by the younger ones, including John. The mines were situated on the hillside some three and a half miles from the village. Every morning they made their way up the slope, toiled all day in the mines, and in the evening tramped back to Gunnerside. Having such demands on their time and energy, the sons of James Pratt must have had little chance to get an education while they were boys at Gunnerside. There was a good school run by the Methodists at nearby Muker, and it is probable that some of them were casual pupils there from time to time. But it is not easy to imagine how they could have mustered either the energy or the means for much continuous schooling.

James Pratt died at Gunnerside in July 1858, after eight months 'in a consumption.' John, Thomas, and their sister Sarah Ann (and her illegitimate son, Moses) were still living with him and their mother at the time. William (b 1826), who had married in 1848, also lived at

Gunnerside. But not long after this, the mine having failed again, they all abandoned Gunnerside and made their way to Kettlewell in Wharfdale, and subsequently to Burnley in Lancashire, where they worked for a time in the coal mines. Here the family gradually dispersed. Sarah Ann married, Thomas emigrated to New Zealand, and John went into the work of the Wesleyan Methodist Church. William alone remained in Burnley, where his mother lived with him until her death in 1876.

It is uncertain when John Pratt exchanged the miner's pick and shovel for the preacher's book and pulpit. It is probable that before leaving Gunnerside in the late 1850s he had preached there occasionally, for E.J. Pratt, writing of his visit there in 1924, reported seeing the old chapel where his father 'used to hold forth.' But it was probably at Burnley that he formally committed himself to the ministry. It is known that in 1870 he was a local missionary on the Blackburn and Rochdale circuits.

His nurture in the Methodist Way had, of course, begun long before. The early indoctrination of the young had long been a primary article of the Wesleyan creed, and we can be sure that James Pratt had not neglected its faithful observance. John Pratt's 'conversion,' the great spiritual climacteric which every young Methodist was expected to undergo, probably occurred during a spectacular revival kindled at Gunnerside in 1850 by an itinerant evangelist from the East Riding. A witness to the event writing to a friend in America remarked of the evangelist and his technique: 'He is rather an original character; goes about from pew to pew and gives most terrific descriptions of Hell.' If young John Pratt was indeed among the 'saved' on that occasion, the experience was not lost on him. He too in later years won a wide reputation for his evangelical techniques, and for great revivals urged to their fruition by visitations from pew to pew and terrific descriptions of Hell.

What formal training he had to qualify him as a Methodist probationer is also a matter for conjecture. It seems probable that like many another young candidate recruited in Yorkshire and Lancashire for overseas missions in the second half of the last century, John Pratt was a protégé of Joseph Lawrence, a well-to-do Methodist of East Keswick in lower Wharfdale. Here, in the late 1860s, he established an academy for the training of young preachers, particularly those in straitened circumstances. He had, moreover, made it his especial duty to recruit promising young men to be sent to mission fields in Newfoundland and Nova Scotia. John Pratt was almost certainly one of these. Whether or not, in the summer of 1873 he set sail from Liverpool, crossed 'the Gert Dub' (as the Atlantic was called in Swaledale), and a few weeks later was received into the Methodist Church of Newfoundland.

A four-year probationship being required of all candidates for Methodist ordination, he was first posted to Catalina, on the northeast coast of Newfoundland, where he soon acquired a reputation, which he never lost, for 'flaming evangelism,' and the nickname 'Boanerges' – son of thunder. Local church historians still refer to him as 'that Boanerges, fiery John Pratt.' In 1875 the Methodist Conference moved him to the St John's circuit, where he completed the remaining two years of his probationship. It was here, in the congregation of George Street Methodist Church, that he met and soon fell in love with Fanny, the petite and dark-haired daughter of one of the circuit's long-standing trustees, better known as a sealing captain and coastal skipper, William Knight and his wife, the former Charlotte Pitts.

E.J. Pratt knew very little about his maternal ancestry, if we are to judge by the vagueness of his revelations on the subject in a letter (1941) to a friend who had inquired: 'My mother was the daughter of Captain Wm Knight whose ancestry went back several generations of Newfoundland sailors to (I think) Devonshire. But as hazy origins smoke up nationalities I can only say or suggest Devonshire, certainly English not Welsh or Scotch or Assyrian.' His surmise contains an element of truth: both the Knights and the Pittses were of West Country stock. The former had come to St John's in the latter half of the eighteenth century, while the Pittses had immigrated to Bell Island from Exeter in the early part of the last century.

William Knight was born at St John's in 1815, one of the eight children of Michael and Rachael Knight. His wife, whom he married in 1841, was one of seven children born to John and Elizabeth (Picco) Pitts. John Pitts drowned in Conception Bay in 1825, whereupon his wife and children moved in with her sister, Fanny, married to John's brother James, who also had seven children. Thus, the fourteen brothers, sisters, and 'double cousins' were raised as one family, so that as time passed relationships grew rather blurred. But there seems little doubt that Charlotte Pitts, who married William Knight, was in fact the daughter of John, drowned in 1825.

Like many of his forebears William Knight had gone to sea at an early age and had taken command of his first ship while still in his twenties. This was long before steampower had come to either the coastal trade or the seal-fishery, so that his earliest and most hazardous years were spent in 'wooden-walls' and windjammers entirely at the mercy of 'tide and wind and crag.' Space forbids recounting here his many adventures and misadventures. Yet, unlike many who have plied the ice-and-rock-strewn coastal routes of Newfoundland, he survived them all and died in bed at St John's in his eighty-sixth year. But one of his exploits must be briefly described.

This was an expedition undertaken in the summer of 1859. In March that year he had lost a sealing vessel under his command, crushed in rafting ice during a violent storm off Cape Bonavista. Left thus without a command he was easily prevailed upon to skipper an expedition that summer which must at first have struck him as more than a little absurd: a voyage along the northeast coasts of Newfoundland and Labrador – in search of icebergs! Nor had the quest any scientific or commercial ends. On the contrary, they were purely artistic and aesthetic ones, for the expedition was organized and financed by the American painter Frederic Edwin Church, who sought the huge 'islands of ice' (as Newfoundland seamen used to call them) to sketch and paint. Accompanying him was a friend, the Reverend Louis Noble, who in 1861 was to publish an interesting and colourful account of the voyage.

The season was a good one for bergs, and the quest proved very successful. Wherever they sailed – through Notre Dame Bay, along the Great Northern Peninsula, and across the Straits of Belle Isle to Labrador – huge mountains, cathedrals, and castles of ice bore down on them. Often the little 'pink-sterned schooner' was driven so close to the gleaming, fretted edges that the great 'paleolithic faces' towered above them as they stood on the heaving deck. The artist sketched and painted, and Louis Noble wrote, describing in vivid and dramatic phrase every detail of the gigantic forms and their imagined history. In this he was most successful, presenting each iceberg as a thing almost alive and individual, with its own strange story, a creature of awful beauty, majesty, and power, which only the 'inveterate sea' could ultimately destroy. His book, *After Icebergs with a Painter*, was among those on John Pratt's shelves and was read by the family with understandable interest, for it chronicled a story of one of their own kin. E.J. Pratt was to find in it, too, as we shall see, the original of the great 'sea-cathedral' of his poem by that name, and the vast 'corrundum form' that destroyed the *Titanic*.

Nor were paintings by Church (and, in time, poems by Pratt) the only artistic fruition of this unusual voyage: the captain himself turned painter – and of icebergs! A letter to him from Church, dated 7 October 1859 from New York, informs him of the dispatch of a 'package of colours, paper, etc.,' the paper having been 'prepared for oil colours.' The painter adds: 'I shall be glad to hear from you at any time and of your progress sketching Icebergs.' Unfortunately, none of the captain's sketches has come to light. Nor is this the only evidence we have of his aesthetic interests and artistic skills. In 1853 he was awarded a medal at the New York Exposition for a 'very ingenious model of a sealing vessel in ice' which he had made and entered for exhibition. Clearly, the poet's grandsire was no conventional 'weazened tar' whose eyes 'had looked / On nothing but the whip of salt and rain.'

Captain Knight is, nevertheless, chiefly remembered in Newfoundland as a sealing skipper. For nearly forty years, commencing in the mid-1830s, he rarely missed the annual hunt, in command during most of the voyages, all of them made in sailing ships until 1869. But he had other interests. The seal-fishery is, after all, only a brief seasonal occupation. Yet, unlike most sealers when the hunt was over, he did not set out for the Labrador cod-fishery. Instead, for many years he engaged in the lucrative coastal-trading business, freighting out cargoes of goods from the mercantile houses of St John's to 'local merchants' in the scattered and isolated outports, returning with loads of outport produce in payment therefor: dried, salt cod and cod livers, seal pelts and seal oil, and cargoes of billets and lumber from the water-driven sawmills scattered here and there around the coasts. Indeed, the boom in the lumbering trade of the 1850s and 1860s led him in 1861 to embark on still another commercial venture: the establishment of a small wood-cutting and -sawing operation at Halls Bay in Notre Dame Bay.

By then the Knights had six surviving children – Allan (b 1845), Edwin John (b 1848), Fanny (b 1851), Archibald (b 1854), Sophia (b

1856), and a baby, Arthur William (b 1861) – all of whom and their mother Will Knight now herded aboard a small schooner and transported northward to an almost uninhabited part of the Island. Here, surrounded by the sea and virgin coniferous forests which came down to the water's edge, they built a house and a water-powered sawmill, and made their home for the next four years. Thus it was that Fanny Knight spent her early teens amid the isolation and privations of a classic pioneer outpost, where nomadic Micmacs were seasonal neighbours and the heart of life beat close to the ribs of Nature. Yet this was undoubtedly a better training ground for the future outport parson's wife than the easier, more sophisticated city environment could possibly have provided. But her mother, it seems, had no need or desire for this kind of Spartan regimen, as her letters to her sister in St John's suggest.

The letters shed interesting light on both the kind of person Pratt's grandmother was and the life his own mother led during her most impressionable years. Though generally good-humoured and ironic, the letters often record much to annoy and dispirit: the isolation and loneliness of the long winter siege ('shut up here in this gloomy place frozen in till the 17th of May and then the drift Ice in till this time [9 July 1862]'); the problems of servants and mosquitoes ('It is hard to expect a girl to remain in this place to be eat alive with flies'); the disappointment of being unable to visit St John's ('I shall have to abandon it for the present unless any kind Samaritan comes to keep house for me'); the ingratitude of neighbours, of which there were a few families ('I have had quite enough to do ... to attend the sick and making cures ... and not getting any thanks for it').

But there were other interests and distractions: a fire in which they lost many of their belongings; an Indian burial ('The Indians have just arrived from the country and one of their young women died in the camp and they are busy burying her today'); a nativity over which Charlotte and a neighbour's wife presided ('We did the business first rate'); trading with the Indians for marten skins from which to make boas for her sister and herself ('Please God when we meet we will have a laugh at what I parted with to get them'); dispatching the skins by William to St John's to be 'made up,' along with orders for other items of female attire ('You see I am going to be an old dandy'). But Charlotte's deepest feelings toward her wilderness prison are best expressed in this ironic plea to her sister: 'I hope you will try to see me this Summer in Purgatory.' Her poet-grandson could not but have admired her vivid sense of metaphor and apocalyptic humour.

The letters, I think, reveal Pratt's grandmother as a strong personality, intensely gregarious, a bit garrulous, but capable of turning a crisp phrase or a telling metaphor, preoccupied with the niceties of keeping a proper ménage, not especially religious or immune to the lures of personal vanity, and above all endowed with familial affection and a keen sense of ironic humour. Through his mother, who in many ways (not all) resembled her own, Pratt was to inherit some of the same traits.

Fanny Knight's years of frontier life, while a valuable experience no doubt, did not provide her an academic education. There were no schools in Halls Bay then, and though she attended classes at a parochial school in St John's before the northward trek, she never progressed beyond Standard 4 (about Grade 6 today). Even so, this was further than most girls advanced into the world of academe in the Newfoundland of more than a century ago. Her letters, like her mother's, show that she had mastered at least the rudiments of literacy and for a woman in those days in Newfoundland that was not a negligible achievement.

But whatever her accomplishments – or lack of them – the Reverend John Pratt found her both desirable and proper as the helpmate of a Methodist parson. Having paid her discreet court for several months, on 1 February 1876 he addressed her father a 'note' which read in part:

My dear Mr Knight

I hope you will excuse me for the liberty I am taking in sending you this note. You will have perceived before this time by my conduct that I have been and still am paying special attention to your daughter Fanny for whom I have special respect and love.

I should like to be treading on sure and honourable ground and to set my mind free and at rest I desire to have the consent of her father and mother ... I promise you ... that she shall have every comfort and attention that a Wesleyan Minister can bestow.

Can you please give me an answer ... tonight ...

I am dear Sir
yours faithfully
John Pratt.

It was simple, direct, respectful, and had the desired result. The laws of his Church forbade marriage before his ordination, but this obstacle was removed on 17 June 1877 and he and Fanny Knight were wedded at St John's on 4 July. He was then in his thirty-eighth year, his bride in her twenty-sixth.

Their first pastorate together was at Exploits, a sprawling marine circuit in Notre Dame Bay, where they spent three years. Two sons were born to them there, the first named for his grandfather, William Knight, the second for one of John Pratt's 'heroes of the Faith,' the famous British preacher of the London Tabernacle, James Charles Spurgeon. The boy was known as 'little Spurgie' until he was nearly a grown man.

In 1880 the Pratts were posted to Western Bay, contrary to its name in eastern Newfoundland, on the North Shore of Conception Bay, where their third child was born on 4 February 1882. The old parsonage in which he was born has long since been torn down, but the site was still vacant in the 1970s, and in the shallow excavation which had been a root cellar beneath the kitchen, old stonework and firebrick could still be seen. He was baptized on 20 April by the Reverend James Dove, pastor of the neighbouring circuit at Black-head, whose surname he was given along with the names of his mother's favourite brother, Edwin John. His full baptismal name was thus Edwin John Dove Pratt. A decade later, however, the Reverend 'Jimmy' Dove having fallen from grace in the eyes of his Church for some offence against it (smoking tobacco, perhaps, or taking a pinch of snuff?), John Pratt expunged the old patriarch's name from that of his son forever. As a boy he was usually called 'Eddie' and later 'Ed,' but never 'Ned' while he lived at home. That name, which eventually became the only one he was known by among friends and acquaintances, came gradually into use after he had left Newfoundland. It seems to have been first given him by one William Magoon, whom Pratt called 'Skipper Billy,' a Saskatchewan farmer with whom he boarded as a student minister in the West. Disliking both Edwin and John, Pratt adopted it himself and encouraged others to do the same. His official signature was always 'E.J.,' though he signed himself 'Ned' in letters to close friends, and sometimes 'Neddie' to very intimate ones. Apart from a few early poems and essays published by him as 'Edwin J. Pratt,' all his publications were signed simply 'E.J. Pratt.'

2

The Outport World

[Newfoundlanders] are a steadfast people, whose home is wild and bare in all but a few months of summer, and they are drawn very closely together by the necessity of mutual support. They have withstood together the fury of the Atlantic when it came in and washed the very coffins from their graves ...
E.J. Pratt to N.A. Benson, 1927

EWFOUNDLAND IN THE 1880s was still the Cinderella of the Empire, among the ashes where she was to languish, untransformed, for the next seventy years. She had been wooed at Charlottetown and Quebec, but had hesitated, demurred, and finally declined. The prospects had looked inviting to her intermediaries, but glib and ingenious champions of what they called independence had conjured up such messes of pottage, to be bought with such expenditures of sacred birthrights, as to persuade the tattered virgin, though not quite of one mind, to settle for the ills she already had. Cinderella had gone back to the ashes, to the hewing of wood and the drawing of water, the hauling of nets and the splitting of cod. Two decades later life went on much as it had done for two centuries and more. While elsewhere on the North American continent the primary struggle had been progressively mitigated by the fruits of technology and the growth of social and economic structures, Newfoundland remained a stubborn exception.

Unique in colonial histories, the Newfoundlander shunned the conquest of the land as an element alien, almost, to his species. For him the sea alone was his destiny, determining how and where he lived, and often how and where he died. As late as 1900, fish and fish alone (mostly cod, salted and dried) still supported four-fifths of a population that clung to the serrated coastline like sea-kelp 'rooted in the joints of rocks.'

It is hard to describe those anomalous, sea- and rockbound clusters of human habitation scattered round the coasts of Newfoundland and known as outports, especially as they existed ninety or a hundred years ago. Comparisons with small villages elsewhere are of little avail, for even the terminology of description breaks down. Such fundamentals as street, marketplace, park, hedge, or garden have little or no meaning in our context. All imply a certain ascendancy of the human mind and imagination over Nature. But in the old outport her reign was still virtually unchallenged. Her tyranny was so harshly imposed that mind and imagination could hardly conceive of her as anything but invincible.

The outports were what they were because each was the result of a kind of accident, one that may be described as an extraordinary concatenation of outrageous geography and equally outrageous history. A land far from attractive in many respects, where proximity to fishing grounds determined where colonists settled, ruled over – in so far as it was ruled at all – by myopic absentee autocrats who for centuries forbade permanent colonization, could scarcely have been settled in anything but a haphazard and accidental fashion. It is a wonder, indeed, that the outports ever happened at all, and that so many, having happened, managed to survive. Yet most of them did because so long as there were harvests of cod to be had there were those who came and stayed to reap them whatever the penalties and privations. Only the fish mattered. No 'founder' of a settlement cared very much that the ground he built his wooden house or shack upon was barren, wind- and rain-denatured soil, or even solid rock. Nor did he care that it was inaccessible except by sea. If its shoreline permitted him to raise a fishing-stage and flake, that was all he looked for.

All the outports grew quite unplanned, though usually facing the sea. Simple wooden houses, ranging from primitive one-roomed shacks to substantial but still plain two-storied dwellings, were perched higgledy-piggledy as the terrain allowed, wherever there was space and solid ground for a foundation. Between the houses were footworn lanes which passed for streets, giving access to the waterfront. For centuries no one dreamed of *building* streets or roads. The sea was street and highway enough. In time, where the hinterland permitted, mainly on the Avalon Peninsula, nineteenth-century governments built primitive dirt roads connecting some of the larger communities with one another and St John's. By the 1880s a winding narrow-gauge railway was also being pushed round Conception Bay and projected even farther afield. By then, too, a fleet of small steamships provided a desultory mail and passenger service (from June to November) to some of the more accessible outports. But such amenities as parks, playgrounds, libraries, and the like were all undreamed of, neither asked for nor provided. The churches, of course, moved in as soon as two or three families had gathered in one place, and when their respective flocks were large enough erected church buildings and small schoolhouses.

Most of the outports had a merchant or 'dealer,' the larger ones several. He was usually a general provisioner who was often also the chief fish entrepreneur for the community, supplying the fisherman and his family on credit, the debt to be paid in the currency of the product when it was harvested. In this way the merchant almost literally owned the fisherman, who was rarely if ever out of his debt, though he himself usually managed to prosper. His house and establishment were often the only symbols of economic stability and substance which most outports could boast in those days. A few had medical doctors, but they were rarities in all but the largest communities when Pratt was a boy. Fortunately most places seem to have raised up a tribal sage who could usually be relied on in any crisis. Pratt recalled with admiration many such outport 'characters': 'Every village had such an individual.' But other than the clergy and a schoolmaster or two, and a few such home-grown indispensables as a midwife and a blacksmith, who often doubled as a dentist, there were usually no practitioners of special skills. (Pratt used to recall being taken at the age of ten to have a tooth extracted by a blacksmith: 'I recovered fully in the process of time,' he wrote, 'and there was no bill.') The fisherman himself was Jack of all the other trades an outport had need of.

Despite his narrowed vision and the limits of his world, the Newfoundland outporter had his qualities. Stern masters had taught him the primary lesson of survival: while Nature takes care of the species the individual must take care of himself. But in the process he had also learned other lessons which help the human spirit achieve a certain dignity and independence. While he would never have thought of himself as 'heroic,' there is no doubt that he had learned the survival values both physical and spiritual of dogged endurance, tenacity, and courage. He had certainly learned the patience of both unanswered prayer and unfulfilled promise. If nothing else, his religion had taught him the first and his politics the second. He had learned as well the need to temper the steel of the spirit with charity and humour – the latter usually ironic. Irony he could hardly escape. It was all round him, in his situation and in his blood. It was in the paltriness of his reward for gigantic labours. It was in the very character of the sea itself, for was not (as Pratt was to put it) 'the bread of life' in its right hand, 'the waters of death' in its left? Tragedy, too, in the nature of things he expected, yet usually met with equanimity. Providence was rarely blamed or railed against. Yet he had no theology, and if his religion had any hold on him – in its stress upon the evanescence of the temporal, the virtues of submission to the Divine Will, or the hope of Heaven as the undisputed goal of life – it was rather as a kind of ready-made mythology that gave a modicum of shape and meaning to his life. Perhaps he can best be described as an optimistic fatalist: one who believes that what will be will be, but acts in the hope that it will be better, if not here then hereafter. It was probably not an unreasonable creed, life in the outport world being what it was.

Unlike many a frontiersman elsewhere, the outporter was fortunate in that at least he lived in a community. And because it was typically small and never populous it was a closely knit, self-contained social unit, a clan almost, made up of families bound together by common destiny, if not, indeed – as it often was – by common blood. However much the individual's survival might depend upon his own ingenuity and enterprise, he and his fellows were all in it together. In a very real sense, what befell one befell all. So it was that in the old outport, when Pratt was a boy if no longer, there often prevailed a spirit of comradeship and brotherhood that gave the outporter a sense of oneness with his fellows, of communication and communion, that cannot exist in quite the same way, if at all, in the larger, impersonal society, even the small one that is easily in touch with an 'outside world.' Nor is the dominance here of masculine terminology merely a matter of conventional usage. While women in the old outport, as

elsewhere, were valued for their unique personal attributes and benefactions, perhaps because the one hazardous, all-sustaining enterprise
of life, the constant warfare with the sea, was a man's and virtually his
alone, males constituted what was almost a clan within a clan, a closed
fraternity such as veterans of other kinds of wars still form elsewhere.
Most male outporters in those days, even in their teens, were, after
all, veterans of a kind. Their strongest emotional bonds were thus
with those who shared physically their own dangers and labours, who
knew without being shown or told what the other felt. Male bonding
is not, of course, an uncommon phenomenon, but in the old outport it
was almost the primary element of the social ethos. Pratt though never
really more than a peripheral outporter (to be enlarged upon shortly)
did not escape its pervasive influence.

Outport culture was very largely oral. While the slow spread of
elementary education meant that by the 1880s most outporters had
the opportunity of learning at least the three Rs, few actually did.
And many who learned to read and write as children forgot both by
the time they had become adults. For in the 'typical' old outport there
were few if any books. Public libraries were unheard of and the school
had only its tattered textbooks. There seemed to be little need for
literacy, though the outporter looked in awe upon a man of learning,
especially if he was also a great talker. For the average outporter oral
communication sufficed. A last will and testament could be made
orally to one's family in the certain knowledge that it would be executed to the syllable, a contract with merchant or shareman likewise.

But though letters were little needed or employed, speech was of
the essence in outport life. Where two or three were gathered, there
was the Word in the midst, incessant, abundant, exuberant, and often
omnipotent. The great talker was held in as high regard as the great
fisherman, sealer, or hunter. If he possessed the requisite powers of
invention as well as loquacity he need never have caught a fish or shot
a partridge or seabird to wear the laurels of a Nimrod. The great
story-teller, the joker or wag (or 'card'), the singer of songs, the oral
entertainer of whatever talent was always a lodestone wherever he
went, much sought after and a kind of hero, at least in the eyes of
males of all ages. If he also played a Jew's harp, mouth-organ, or
accordion so much the greater his celebrity; greatest of all if he was
also a maker of 'verses' recording local events: shipwrecks, bumper

catches, weddings, and so on. All local legendry and history was oral, 'stories handed down ... / From father to the son ... ' So also were the multifarious lores of the weather and the sea; superstitions, cures, and charms; and the songs and sagas of the past. None of the roles of the 'heroic' outport performer – great talker, maker of verses, teller of hyperbolical tales, card – was to be lost on Eddie Pratt when later he came to choose the masks he felt a need to wear in the outside world.

Life in the old outport, then, was not a mere existence. It had its forms of imaginative expression, its outlets for creative energies, its symbolic acts and rituals, its social pageants. These communities were, after all, offshoots of the primary Anglo-Saxon culture, isolated, suspended in time, but still part of the same ethos and tradition. Time and separation had wrought some changes – new accretions and modifications – in the language, the tales and the songs, the festivals and rituals of an earlier time, but they were fundamentally the same.

In such an environment as I have sketched here, surrounded by such qualities of life as I have tried only to suggest, eighteen of E.J. Pratt's first twenty-five years were passed, and the missing seven were spent in St John's, which in many ways was really outport 'writ large.' And there can be no doubt that these years left a lasting and vivid impression upon him, nor that he drew much that remained a part of him from the outport world he grew up in. Long afterward he described thus his debt and bonds to his outport world: 'Those first twenty-odd years of my life gave me a wealth of experience which will never be completely drained. In fact, it crops up in my work in the most unexpected places ... It is like an idiom or accent from which one could not and would not if he could dissociate himself.' He never tired of telling stories of outport life, and of memorable outport characters he had known, both unsung heroes and quaint eccentrics. He often romanticized the simple, hardy, primitive life of what he called 'the Newfoundland type.' He sometimes, too, conjured up a picture of himself when a boy as a 'typical' outport youth, a character whom he clearly admired: rough, tough, full of oaths and colourful braggadocio, 'heroic,' mischievous, a truant in more ways than one.

But it must be said straightaway that the self-portrait is largely if not wholly a fictive one. The circumstances of E.J. Pratt's early life made it impossible for him ever really to have lived the life of an authentic outport Newfoundlander, or to have known such a life as an actual participant rather than mainly as an observer, albeit a very percipient and sensitive one. The fact is, I think, of considerable importance in understanding and appreciating Pratt's perspective and perception of the outport world. It is a fact that largely accounts for the absence from his Newfoundland poems of any real identification with either the place or the people. He saw and knew, to be sure, a good deal of outport life; it could hardly have been otherwise: he was surrounded by it for most of his early years. But to think of him as having been a typical outport youth of the time he grew up in, one wholly bred in its ways, is quite mistaken.

The son of an itinerant, British-born Methodist parson, even when settled for two or three years in one place, was inevitably a very different species. For one thing, no matter where the family temporarily pitched its tent (Western Bay, 1880–2; Bonavista, 1882–5; Cupids, 1885–8; Blackhead, 1888–91; Brigus, 1891–2; St John's, 1892–5; Fortune, 1895–8; Bay Roberts, 1898–1900; Grand Bank, 1900–4), nor how warmly if deferentially the family was greeted by each new flock, the boy was always an outsider. Having no blood ties with the local clan, bearing an unfamiliar name, speaking a different tongue, wearing even a different dress, he could never have been accepted fully into the small, close-knit, and clannish community that the old outport was, even had his father encouraged his assimilation, something which he did not. John Pratt had very firmly fixed ideas about the perils, as he saw them, of his offspring's mingling too much with the denizens of 'the World of the Great Unsaved.' Even had his father not been John Pratt, the very fact of his birth into a Methodist minister's family meant that E.J. Pratt could never have been a full-blooded member of the local tribe. Only had he been born of the native stock, raised in one small village, and sent to sea, semi-literate at best, at the age of fifteen or earlier, could he have qualified for such membership. Furthermore, the chief controlling influences of his earliest years, shaping his mind, sensibilities, and personality during their most plastic time, were necessarily very different from those of most of his outport compeers. And besides, having no settled home, no sense of roots except within the family – where they ran very deep – he had little if any of the psychic and emotional attachment usually felt for a home town.

By the time he was old enough to loosen a little the parental reins and achieve a measure of identification with the outport community, Pratt's inner world had already taken on its primary configurations. Besides, he was off to work in St John's before he was sixteen. Later, in his early twenties, when he returned to the outport, first as teacher and then as probationary minister, though still in roles which set him apart, boarding in outport homes and mingling closely with the people, he would, indeed, come to know and experience the life in a way that had not been possible for him before. It is, I think, from these last five years of his life in Newfoundland that mainly derived most of what the 'old Rock' (a term he sometimes used with a mixture of mild affection and measured irony) meant to him in later years. Viewing it with more experienced and appreciative eyes, he was able to feel and understand as never before 'the throb of pulse and nerve' of the outport world, to know, even if still largely as an observer, something of what it meant to be an embattled and beleaguered outport Newfoundlander of nearly a century ago.

But although he may never have *loved* the old rock – I do not think he ever really did – and although having once found a new kind of life in a new kind of environment he had no regrets at leaving Newfoundland never to return, except occasionally to visit his mother while she lived, there can be no doubt that it continued to loom very large in his consciousness for the whole of his life. Nor can there be any doubting the sincerity of the admiration he often expressed for the courage and tenacity, the stoical hardihood and self-sacrificing heroism of Newfoundland outporters he had known. One cannot doubt, for example, the depth of genuine feeling expressed – looking back it is true from the romanticizing perspective of the lapse of many years and the distance of many miles – in such lines as the following:

[T]he impression derived from the Newfoundland scene is that the process of rescue is a normal part of life's routine. It is taken for granted, like the action of the heart-valves. Some of the sublimest deeds I have ever known did not get outside the local records. They are enshrined in more imperishable tissue. They have a beauty about them more than the fragrance of roses, more than the music of nightingales, and they are part of the spiritual heritage of Newfoundlanders.

It was, I believe, a heritage he valued, and though he cannot be said to have 'bodied forth' either the true mythos or the true ethos of that heritage, though at times he tried, I think he would have been a very different poet had he not been born, and grown up mainly, in the outport world of Newfoundland.

3

Childhood in an Outport Manse

My total recollection is a medley, the trivial and incidental joined with the
dramatic and significant.

E.J. Pratt, from 'Highlights in My Early Life,' c1949

IS PARENTS CALLED HIM 'the odd one,' and in several
ways he *was* rather different from his brothers and sisters,
four brothers and three sisters by the time John and Fanny
Pratt's family was complete in 1896. Whether or not his was
a 'different' temperament from birth, or one whose differences were
shaped at least partly by unusual circumstances of his early life is
difficult to tell – probably a combination of both, as is true of most of
us who are 'cast in a different mould.' A child of obvious endowments
of intellect, sensitivity, imagination, and a 'pertinacious streak,' he
was also, it seems, of less than robust health and physique. This
certainly was something which his parents impressed upon him quite
early in childhood, as well as the caution that as a consequence he had
to be 'very careful about himself and what he did.' There may have
been good reason for this but it appears to have been somewhat over-
played. Whether or not this was the case, from it mainly seems to
have stemmed a number of important psychological consequences.

A 'serious illness' some time before his sixth year – undiagnosed (as
often happened in those days of few and frequently incompetent doctors) but probably rheumatic fever – had left him a reputed heart
murmur. To aggravate his case, he was highly susceptible to respira-
tory infections, croupy as an infant, and as a child a frequent victim of
prolonged colds, bronchitis, and wracking coughs. His mother, one of

the originals of Angelina, the old nurse of a 1930 poem, whose reputation as an amateur nurse-cum-apothecary extended far beyond the manse, made him her especial concern. A busy but anxious soul, who enjoyed hovering round, fussing over, and plying with her medicaments the ailing and the comfortless, she found in Eddie, the delicate odd one of her brood, the perfect subject to deluge with maternal solicitude and dose with herbal remedies (concocted no doubt from the recipes her own mother had learned from the Halls Bay Indians): 'Liquids unnamed ... / And all most pungent and disquieting.' Since, however, he lived to be an octogenerian and enjoyed reasonably good health during most of his adult life, how 'delicate' in fact he was as a child is hard to judge. Yet in a time when tuberculosis stalked the outports like an ogre, his parents can hardly be blamed if they were apprehensive and protective, or their neighbours if they shook their heads and 'allowed that the young Pratt boy was going into a consumption.' 'I am sure,' he recalled many years later, 'there was plenty of old wives' gossip in Blackhead and Brigus about Parson Pratt's sickly boy. They probably thought I deserved it – as punishment for my unrepented sins!'

His 'sins' unrepented or otherwise must have been very few. He had little scope even for peccadilloes. At least until he was well into his teens, any inclination he may have had toward wayward behaviour was pretty effectively curbed by parental edicts of one sort and another. All the children – 'for the good of our immortal souls and proper Christian up-bringing' – were subjected to many edicts and ordinances both general and specific. But because of his reputed 'condition,' there were for Eddie even more stringent and unmanning interdictions, his parents denying him many of even the minor liberties allowed his brothers, forbidding him to join in their more strenuous sports, confining him indoors when the weather threatened, swaddling him in extra clothing when he was allowed out, cautioning him against this and that. It should not be surprising that the child who grew to adolescence in John Pratt's parsonage should have been, most of the time, a quiet, shy, subdued boy who acquiesced in his delicacy and his parents' decrees, shunned the roughhouse sports of his brothers and their friends, read his books and dreamed his dreams, and generated a profound and envious admiration which he never outgrew for tough and heroic characters, whom he longed to emulate but did not dare to.

This is not to say that he engaged in none of the diversions, the improvised games and pastimes, of his brothers and their companions: fishing for brook trout in the spring, playing in the warm waters of some shallow pond in summer, sledding and skating – amply clad – in winter. What he shunned above all was engaging in any roughly physical contest. Being small for his age (until in his early teens he suddenly began to shoot up) as well as 'frail of health' (to use the family terminology), and by nature unaggressive, even timid, he retreated from any embroilment in the rough-and-tumble body-contact sports of his outport compeers: fisticuffs, wrestling, scrimmaging, and similar contests in which young outport gladiators proved their toughness. But though he shunned participating in all such so-called sports, he quite enjoyed watching them from the side lines. Even involvement in an altercation that never got beyond words did strange things to his adrenalin. Consequently he began quite early to devise tactics of diplomatic retreat, tactics in which he became highly adept and which were to serve him well throughout his life. Inevitably taunts and scurrilous outport epithets branding him coward or worse were hurled at him, but he could not be goaded to respond. 'Peaceful debate between reasonable people' (to quote his brother Calvert) he could engage in with lively enjoyment and much skill even as a boy, and he was not averse to watching any species of confrontation however physical – from a safe distance. As Calvert observed (and many others have confirmed, including himself), 'Ned loved a good fight, as long as he wasn't in it!' It should not be surprising that such brawny, combative types as boxers and wrestlers remained among his life-long heroes, nor that images from the boxing ring should turn up fairly often in his poems.

In none of these idiosyncrasies was he ever to change. What he had to do, however, was to find a role, a persona or mask, or several masks, which while shielding and hiding the sensitive, insecure, and vulnerable core of his nature might also enable him to be, on the visible stage, an actor whom he himself could admire and who might win the admiration and approval of others. It would take time to shape a satisfying role and appropriate masks, but the verbal world, quite early, seems to have offered him his best hope.

A measure of vicarious heroism was no doubt supplied by his reading, especially as he grew older and a wider range of books came into his hands than could be found under John Pratt's roof. For, partly because of the constraints upon him, partly too because he loved to read, books and reading occupied for him as a boy much of the time and imaginative energy usually spent by the young in more physical and momentary pursuits. Not that he was a confirmed recluse, or even a bookworm, or that he was lacking in normal animal spirits. Yet from the time he learned to read, he did; he used to say that he was so young when he began to read that he could not remember when he didn't.

He was certainly reading before he went to school, though this is not surprising, since because of his delicacy he had nearly reached his seventh year before his parents allowed him to go. Many years later he recalled as one of the 'highlights' of his childhood the 'blustery day in January' (1888) when, heavily muffled against the wind and 'assisted by my two brothers, Will and Jim,' he made his way for the first time to the small, one-roomed schoolhouse in Cupids where seventy-four pupils were already enrolled under one harried master. Of him we know only that his name was Pearce, but Pratt did not owe much to his tutelage, the boy's one term there being brief and his attendance sporadic. In July that year the family moved to Blackhead, where his schooling began in earnest under John Moores, a native of the place and a man of solid attainments, from whom he quickly acquired a good grounding in the few basic subjects which the curriculum comprised. From these years probably dates the cluster of recollections on which he based the small picture of himself as a schoolboy, and of his mother, which appears in his poem *Rachel* (1917):

> ... With slate and pencil in his hand, the boy
> Would hurry through the sums the teacher set,
> Write out the copy for the morning class,
> While Rachel, with her knitting placed aside,
> Would make him read his lessons, hear him spell
> The words that at the bottom of the page
> Were grouped in lists according to their length.   (114–20)

The pedagogical routines, practised without variation for decades, are also well remembered, and the very format of the long-lived *Royal Readers* with their solemn, hortatory tales and melancholy verse.

The small parochial schools, though an improvement on what they had been, were still a dubious means to an uncertain end. Not all it is true were as bad as most, though as late as 1901 the Methodist school inspector was moved to observe in his report that his visitations to the schools often left him sick at heart, the plight of many of them still 'suggesting to the mind the famous inscription at the portal of Dante's Inferno, "Abandon hope all ye who enter here".' They provided, nevertheless, instruction of sorts in the three Rs and a few other 'useful' subjects, but only up to Standard 6 (about Grade 8 nowadays). When he came 'out' of Standard 6, if he ever did, the student's only means to higher learning was – if he was a Methodist – to attend the Methodist College in St John's, which offered studies up to the Associate of Arts Diploma (junior matriculation). This being an expensive undertaking and since few outport children ever emerged from Standard 6 – most had abandoned school by then, the girls to go into service, the boys into the fishing-schooners – only the scions of the few 'better' families ever migrated from the tundras of the outport school to the city groves of academe. As a consequence considerable status, even snobbery, attached to such a singular distinction as going to college in St John's. It was, however, one distinction that John Pratt had long since resolved his children should somehow achieve. His eldest son, Will, having completed Standard 6 with great éclat and a small scholarship at Blackhead in 1891, was sent to the Methodist College in September that year. All the other children but one would follow him in turn as they reached the same climacteric in outport schooling. The one exception was Eddie. He would eventually achieve the coveted goal, but by a more circuitous route and under a burden of gratuitous obligations. But that is still some years ahead.

The frequent inhospitableness of the Newfoundland climate decreed that much of the children's leisure was spent indoors. Though his brothers may have deplored such days, they were a boon to Eddie. In the relative security of the home, his father out making his endless pastoral rounds, and his mother quietly if apprehensively indulgent, he was free and eager to join in their improvised play. It was usually he, inventive, enthusiastic, and lively (when the cat was away), who assumed the role of impresario and ringleader. (Already he was choosing parts which he could play in safety.) Under his direction parsonage furniture became boats and ships, large, hooked floor rugs shoals and ice floes, and birch brooms from the kitchen oars and sealing gaffs. A quieter diversion was impromptu dramatics. All the boys were born actors, Edwin and Arthur (b 1886) being particularly adept at mimicry. 'They could,' Calvert assures us, 'take off anyone at all if they'd seen and heard him once.' Schoolmasters, local politicians, visiting preachers, outport characters, all became subjects of their irreverent, impersonated caricature, even their father once – in absentia. As Calvert recalled the last-named memorable jape, 'It was, of course, Ned's doing.' Mother, it seems, intervened in time to avert sacrilege, but 'it was lucky for Ned that it wasn't Father who caught him.' Mimicry was an art he never lost, practising it in later life, I am told, 'with devastating effect' on subjects – *in absentia* – whom he especially disliked.

These sequestered interludes were happy ones for all, but especially for Eddie. The boys played well together; compared with many other sibling groups they were unusually, almost abnormally, good friends, a closely knit and intimate fraternity, a little clan within the largely alien clan without. They shared each other's woes and triumphs, supported one another in family crises, conspired together in playful mischief, and sometimes allied themselves to mollify, even outwit, a displeased tyrant. Family accounts declare that 'there was never even a minor quarrel amongst the boys.' Except for the unhappy defection of the eldest brother, Will (to be mentioned later), it was a relationship that was never to change, despite the partings of ways which inevitably came as they grew older. For Pratt, his brothers, even more essentially than his books, were the props of existence in his early years. There is little doubt that it was from his early psychological dependence upon, and the satisfactions he derived from, the small, intimate sibling clan that arose his lifelong, deep-seated need for close, if few, fraternal friends and his compulsion to seek them out, selectively, and make them his surrogate brothers.

Though Eddie Pratt revelled in his interludes of indoor play, finding in them small outlets for his imagination and repressed energies, his reading nevertheless was his chief diversion and escape both as a child and as an adolescent. What did he read in those impressionable years? Unfortunately very few titles can be named with certainty, but some we do know. In addition to those faithful companions of British Victorian childhood, *Chums* and *The Boy's Own Annual*, which he never forgot as his earliest escape hatches, there were, from his father's small library, Aesop's *Fables*, an abridged *Pilgrim's Progress* and Bunyan's *Holy War*, Foxe's *Book of Martyrs* and 'a Life of David Livingstone.' Gustave Doré's illustrated edition of *Paradise Lost* was also there, but it was 'the pictures and not the poem that captured me then – the poem came much later.' W.H.G. Kingston's *Peter the Whaler*, won as a school prize by an elder brother, was probably his first experience of juvenile fiction – as well as of whales in a literary context. Later in his teens he read 'some of the novels of Captain Marryat' and Dana's *Two Years before the Mast*, and one summer, at Fortune, Carlyle's *History of the French Revolution* and George Grote's *History of Greece*. The Bible, of course, was prescribed at an early age, passages of especial import having been marked for memorization. John Pratt 'encouraged us all to read,' but it seems unlikely that he provided his children many books chosen to appeal to youthful tastes and imaginations. Eddie Pratt seems, however, to have got his hands on a fair number of books which an intelligent boy could read and reread with interest. 'Ned always seemed to have a book in his hands when he was a boy at home,' Calvert recalled long after. Reading anything other than his schoolbooks made him, if not unique, certainly something of an odd one among his companions.

All the family accounts of John Pratt consistently stress his strictness and sternness, and the firm authority with which he ruled his household. Yet he does not seem to have been by nature a hardhearted, unfeeling man: 'A lamb yoked with a lion.' But it is not hard to understand why the image of him most vividly etched upon his children's memories was that of the very religious man who in the home was 'lord and master whose word was law.' Most Victorian fathers were, of course, lords and masters, but not all were also evangelical pastors for whom the salvation of souls within their own homes was as great a responsibility as general behavioural training. This was a concatenation of Christian duties which John Pratt took very seriously. Even had he been inclined to regard as somewhat out-of-date the injunctions of Wesley's 'Hymn for Parents' – to show the child 'his lost estate,' to 'beat the pride of nature down,' and 'bend or break the rising will' – his church countered any such inclinations with frequent reminders.

His regimen for his children's moral and spiritual nurture was both Methodistic and methodical. From earliest childhood Pratt and his seven brothers and sisters had fundamentalist religious tenets and Puritan-Victorian codes of morals and conduct drilled into them seven days a week. 'We got heaven and hell drummed into us,' Pratt recalled. 'At seven or eight years of age, I listened to the actual crackling of the flames.' And he was being only mildly hyperbolic. Family worship, morning and evening, was a daily routine. All attended, no excuse for absence, not even illness, being countenanced. Sunday, of course, was a day of abstinence from all that could be considered worldly, for John Pratt was as staunch a champion of the Sabbath as he was a foe of Demon Rum. Most of his sermons sooner or later got round to 'abominations to the Sabbath': ball games, skating, picnics, open shops, 'pleasure trips by train ... as if people could not go to hell fast enough now-a-days, but must go there by steam ... Can you wonder that God made the sun so hot last summer ... that the City of St John's ... went off in a blaze of destruction?' (St John's was swept by fire in July 1892). Not that there was little to do on a Methodist Sabbath if one was so inclined. But everything that nature craved – playing, singing (except hymns), reading (except the Bible), and much else – was strictly forbidden, for the very reason that nature craved it. John Pratt's youngest daughter all her life remembered standing at the parsonage window as a child on a Sunday evening longing for the sun to set.

The primary and immediate object of his regimen was, of course, his children's 'conversion.' The parson who preached the necessity of infant salvation could hardly for tactical reasons alone allow his own small 'fruitage' of 'Adam's blighted tree' to remain for long 'ungarnered from the fields of Sin.' Accordingly, in due season, the seeds of grace long since well planted and 'watered with the dews of Heaven,' the little 'candidate for glorious bliss,' like any other, was required whether he would or no to make his way to the altar rail to kneel in penitential tears. It is not hard to believe that Eddie Pratt's conversion at the age of ten in the Blackhead church was something he was glad to have behind him. But its consequences remained. Not only was he henceforth expected 'to walk humbly in the Way,' which meant forswearing much that was dearest to a young outporter's heart, and – most imperative for a minister's son – presenting a model of conduct to his friends; he was also required to 'bear witness' to the depth and reality of his religious experience and the permanence of his conversion by testifying regularly at the Wednesday night 'testimony meetings.' This was by far the most agonizing of all the crosses which the Pratt children (and countless others) were called upon to bear as young 'sinners saved by Grace.' And of them all there is no doubt that Eddie suffered most. It is not unlikely that as much as anything in his childhood, perhaps more than anything else, the repeated experience of baring his soul in public under the watchful and critical eye of his father instilled in him the almost neurotic dread of public performance and display that haunted him for years. Recognizing it as a handicap, he later schooled himself to master it, and largely succeeded, but never wholly overcame it. 'Ned's congenital weakness of the gut' was how a college roommate later described the impediment, but it was far more likely a legacy of his Methodist childhood than of his nativity. To quote his sister Floss: 'That testifying business on Wednesday nights did more harm to us, and more to turn us against old-time Methodism than anything else we were made to do.'

What Pratt's feelings were at the time about all the many concomitants of his father's regimen are, of course, hard to determine. These were things he rarely talked of in serious moments in his later life. When he did, he loyally avoided any direct, personal criticism of his father for performing a role he devoutly believed himself called to fill. Pratt took pains to soften the lines of the stern countenance, to palliate the physical chastisements with such remarks as 'He never gave us a crack that really hurt,' and once to describe him as having 'a bit of the saint and a lot of the martyr about him.' More often than not his early Methodist upbringing was recalled in the character of whimsical, hyperbolic story-teller which he liked to assume, whose reminiscences were calculated to produce a comic effect or picture him in a roguish guise. In such a character he could joke about the 'endless prayer-meetings,' the humiliations of the backslider, the puritanical prohibitions on this and that, or, waxing metaphorical and hyperbolic, describe his own conversion as hearing 'the actual crackling of the flames,' and the fire-and-brimstone preaching as capable of lifting 'the congregation out of their pews by the most gorgeous descriptions of heaven, or else shake them under the planks by painting hell with colours never seen on land or sea.' Yet one senses, more acutely on some occasions than others, that beneath the whimsey and jocularity are disquieting if not painful memories, that the metaphor and hyperbole have a mordant warp, as for example in the following, still on the subject of preaching:

We ... would creep under the seats until the time came for the benediction. We could come out from our hiding [place] when we were sure the colours were dry. One might dispute the gospel truth of the message but no one could deny the power. It was a real heaven and hell we saw. The cinders were in our eyes on Sunday night. Only the morning put out the nightmare fires, and not always then ...

It seems certain that looking back he could find little if any use or sympathy for old-time Methodism's means to spiritual ends, or for many of the ends themselves. He especially detested its puritanical excesses: 'I *always hated* Puritanism.' But there is nothing to suggest that as a boy he was not as submissive to his parents' demands and ministrations as they could have wished. This does not mean, of course, that the inward response was necessarily accordant with the outward signs. But though 'Ned had a bit of rebelliousness in him,' to quote his brother Calvert, 'he kept it in – most of the time – for Mother's sake.'

Apart from that of nurse and apothecary, Fanny Pratt's role in the drama of her children's early lives has so far been only incidentally touched on. But like most mothers she was the primary gravitational force of their universe. Different in temperament from her husband – easy-going and unpunctilious where he was careful and exacting, lenient and forbearing where he was 'strict' and inflexible, soft-hearted where he was hard-headed – she inevitably had a closer, more comradely relationship with the children. Raised in a less rigoristic household than he, she was prepared to take her children for what they were, make allowances for their fallen natures, and generally overlook their innocent iniquities. Not that she was less convinced than her husband of the necessity for their proper Christian upbringing. But she lacked his fanatical motives and, while quietly supporting his aims, left largely to him the business of evangelizing, as she did the business of administering discipline. Nor was the latter something she strenuously urged. Only when a misdemeanour was adjudged to be 'downright sinful' did she hand the little miscreant over to his father;

more often than not 'she winked at our mischief, and with that twinkle she had in her eye let it pass, and covered up for us if she had to.'

It was thus a very subtle emotional bondage that Fanny Pratt exercised upon her children, and of them all Eddie seems to have been most securely caught. This was perhaps inevitable, he being the delicate one. He himself was very reticent about the relationship, but other members of the family confirm an unusually strong and tender attachment. This does not, of course, necessarily point to emotional or other psychological distortions. Yet there seems little doubt that the psychological umbilicus which bound him for so long to his mother did much to hinder the shaping of an emotionally secure and independent personality of his own. Long after he had left home, a strong compulsion to please her, respect her wishes, live up to her expectations of him, was to influence all he did – and did not.

This is not to say that his father had no important influence in shaping the kind of man he became. He did, and despite the daunting image John Pratt at times presented, I think it was an influence which helped to integrate and consolidate the boy's character around a centre which, though it remained a very private and vulnerable one, *held*. For the image of John Pratt which one infers from most of his children's recollections seems both incomplete and misleading. There was another, more worldly and perhaps more human John Pratt, one possessed of very earthbound traits. Ultimately this other John Pratt probably had a greater influence upon his children's values, on his sons' especially, and their goals than had either the 'flaming evangel' or the 'sainted father.' For his object, it is clear, was not only to turn them out all good Methodists. That indeed, but he had other, much more worldly, ambitions for them too. As his youngest son Calvert, who became 'the family Midas,' expressed it, 'Father had high hopes and ambitions for us and never let us forget it. I guess we owed him a lot, driving us the way he did.' Whether he included ambition and initiative among the Christian graces, they were certainly virtues which John Pratt spared no pains to nourish in his sons. In Edwin's case there is no doubt that by directing him toward tangible goals to be achieved by the exercise of will and independent personal action, his father helped, perhaps more than Pratt ever realized, to make a man of him.

'Higher learning,' by which he meant at least graduation from the Methodist College, was, of course, a sine qua non of John Pratt's formula for the 'honourable success' he envisaged for his children. But though his own early life had virtually excluded them, as it had all but the rudiments of formal education, he also set a high value on the 'refining' and 'improving' virtues of artistic and cultural pursuits – conducted, of course, within the bounds of Christian teaching and Methodist propriety. Early in their marriage he bought a small reed-organ for Fanny, who was 'musical' and could play it, so that she might teach the children the rudiments of music, perhaps make competent organists of some of them. She did her best. Under her tutelage all but one of her children became passable amateur organists, and Jim (Little Spurgie) a professional of sorts. Curiously it was Eddie who alone successfully resisted his parents' efforts to make him a musician. But perhaps because of his delicacy he was not strenuously urged. Yet he became very fond of music, and in later years as a listener was nearly as ardent a devotee of opera, oratorio, and symphony as he was a spectator of prize fights and wrestling matches. Alert to signs of early artistic promise, when the eldest daughter Charlotte in her teens began to manifest some talent for painting, her father, at far greater expense than he could afford, sent her off to St John's to study art and continue her music. Her success fell short of distinction, but he was very proud of her modest accomplishments, writing her often and affectionately to praise the paintings she had sent him, once requesting as a special favour a 'spring or summer' scene to 'remind us of Heaven.' He had probably expected at least some of the children to 'lisp in numbers,' since their mother – a woman obviously of many talents – had earned a considerable reputation as a 'poetess.' None of her work has survived, but she is said to have made many 'poetical' contributions to special events in the church, as well as 'little verses' for the edification and 'innocent amusement' of her children. But none of them, not even Eddie in his early years, showed any sign of having inherited her 'gift.'

John Pratt had a high regard for all the arts of language. Most preachers do, one supposes, the Word being their chief stock-in-trade. But he seems to have taken a more than ordinary interest in the refined and literary uses of language, something not lost on his third son. He was particularly emphatic in discouraging the children's acquiring the speech habits of the Newfoundland outport patois, which he regarded as *contra bonos mores* and, thus, a decided obstacle to the 'success' he envisaged for them. He seized every opportunity that arose to instruct them in the proper use of the Queen's English as exemplified by himself. Not surprisingly this was something which the children found 'very aggravating,' but 'it was no use to complain ... He hated us using outport lingo.' Despite his own early background, which had included illiterate parents, his use of the language, to judge from his extant writings (letters, 'circuit notes' to the press, Spiritual State reports, and sermons) was in general carefully correct. Interestingly too, and perhaps significantly as the father of a future poet, he often manifests a well-developed sense of metaphor, as a witness, for example, the highly figurative passage quoted from one of his reports at the beginning of Chapter 1. His sermons suggest also that he was not lacking a sense of humour, more often than not ironic.

It is apparent that on 'fitting occasions' (a favourite phrase of his) John Pratt could be the antithesis of both the flaming evangel and stern father, a sociable and good-humoured man, even temperately convivial and entertaining. Former parishioners of his from the 1890s still remembered more than seventy years later his fondness for Sunday School picnics. It was usually he 'in his shovel hat and whispy beard' who led through the village lanes the customary ceremonial 'march' of scholars, their homemade banners and pennants held high; who led them too, in his strong not untuneful bass voice, in the hymn they sang as they paraded to the picnic field. He seems to have warmed to any social event in his church's calendar, especially if it included a 'festive board' or 'sumptuous repast.' Not that he was a gourmand; he was, in fact, almost ascetic in the satisfaction of his own physical wants. His delight seems to have been almost wholly extra-gustatory, deriving from a combination of social, aesthetic, and symbolic values.

A formal congregational dinner of whatever sort, he especially enjoyed, casting him as it did in what a former parishioner called 'a stellar role.' Seated in the place of honour at the head table, he it was who called the company to be seated, signalled the feast to begin with an elaborate blessing, and rallied conversation and spirits with his 'innocent pleasantries.' Nor was the fact lost on his sense of occasion that such fêtes loomed very large in the drab lives of many of his flock.

Though hardly matching Pratt's 'apocalyptic dinner' of his poem *The Depression Ends*, a church 'time' (the local designation) nevertheless was a signal event in the life of the whole community. Everyone came whether or not he was in the habit of attending Sunday service or Wednesday testimony meeting: as well the 'gaffers and the stowaways' as 'the faithful, the elect.' For although there was usually a small charge, no one was turned away, and the indigent fed gratis – '... all the gaunt, the cavern-cheeked, / The waifs whose tightened belts declare / The thinness of their daily fare ...'

For an hour at least depression ended, and John Pratt, for the nonce 'a padre of high blood,' was the focal figure of it all. One cannot but wonder whether the small, subdued boy seated at a far table set apart for those permitted to be seen but not heard, secretly admired and coveted his father's brave role and the aura of munificence and magnanimity that endued it for a time with Prospero's magic. It was a role he would often fill in the future, but on a far different stage.

The Pratts though by no means well-to-do – what country parson ever has been? – were never really poor. They had, of course, a rent-free manse, fairly comfortably if inelegantly furnished, and a small kitchen garden where Fanny grew vegetables and raised a few chickens. A 'circuit horse,' usually ancient, provided the parson transportation on his rounds and manure for the garden. Unlike most of his flock, the outport minister also had a small cash income ranging between five and eight hundred dollars a year, depending on the catch and price of fish, though it was not always easy to collect. Most of it came from the pockets of the outport merchants, shrewd and worldly bargain-drivers six days a week, but on Sunday staunch pillars of Methodist respectability and economic integrity. The remainder came from the mites of the fishermen, who when no cash materialized in a bad season made their offerings in kind: a sack of potatoes or turnips, a bundle of hay for the horse, a half-quintal of salt cod, or, at least once (as Pratt remembered long afterward), a salmon. Often John Pratt had no choice but to sally forth in quest of his 'dues.' 'He hated it,' Pratt recalled. 'He'd come home worn out. But at supper he'd whisper to Mother, "I got two dollars today," or "I got four dollars," and then he'd cheer up. But we could see he hated it, begging for his dues.' Fortunately for him, having eight children, the Methodist Church maintained a Children's Fund from which each minister was paid a small sum per annum for each child under sixteen years. The philanthropy of relatives, chiefly Fanny's, and several well-to-do friends of John Pratt in Yorkshire also helped to dull the edge of necessity. Sometimes too there were benefactions from members of the congregation, such as that reported by John Pratt from St John's in 1894: 'Our ... congregation know how to make "life in a parsonage" bright with Xmas and New Year's gifts for the table, wardrobe, book-shelf and the nursery. Soon as the watchnight service was over, several of our young men ... presented to their pastor a very fine overcoat which is highly appreciated.' (One wonders whether the old coat that John Pratt could now discard was the same which at Brigus in 1892 had suffered almost the loss of a sleeve – with the wearer's arm inside – when attacked by the circuit horse objecting to his harness on a wintry Sunday morning!) Coal being scarce and expensive, firewood was supplied the parson by his flock, who bestowed it as a huge communal offering on a day set apart for the purpose and known as 'Hauler's Day.' The children especially enjoyed their treat of 'Hauler's Bread,' heavy with raisins, molasses, and spices, which Fanny baked in vast quantities for the occasion.

An unexpected windfall was always a memorable event. Whatever its source – a wedding, perhaps, that brought a few more dollars than the customary fee, though even this was not always forthcoming, many a long and solid union being sanctified 'on tick' – a 'celebration,' which meant a 'sumptuous repast,' was almost always its end. The Pratts 'loved an excuse for a celebration.' What constituted the bill of fare on such occasions no one apparently thought of recording. But at least it was a departure from their daily bread. This novelty and the Cratchit-like cheer and jubilation that prevailed, as Father relaxed a little the reins upon his frisky colts, sufficed to endow it all with 'Memories that the years could not corrode.' Edwin for one never forgot those festive 'spots of time.' Small wonder that in his imagination the sharing of a sumptuous repast, no matter how precarious its economic foundations, became for him the ultimate act in the symbolic rituals of friendship and hospitality, a kind of secular Eucharist effecting a mystical communion of kindred spirits.

Though such occasions were rare, the Pratts, as mentioned, were relatively well off by usual outport standards. Even so this meant the plainest of fare at table most of the time: molasses instead of sugar in tea that rarely saw milk; salt cod and potatoes or 'salt beef / And its eternal partner, duff' in monotonous procession, and oranges and apples only at Christmas – always a celebration, of course, for which the 'big merchant' usually provided a goose or pair of ducks. It meant for all the children homemade clothing, often homespun, handed down from child to child until time and wear took their irreparable toll. It meant few if any 'boughten' toys or sporting accoutrements, the boys making for themselves all such necessities of youth in an outport as trout-poles, jiggers, dog-carts, and sleds. (Edwin remembered as a highlight of his childhood that *his* first 'snow-slide' had been built for him by his grandfather, Captain Knight.) It meant slates to write on at school and at home, paper and lead pencils being luxuries the children rarely enjoyed. Pratt never outgrew the respect for paper he learned as a boy, his poems often being written on treasured scraps covered in minute script with pencil stubs barely long enough to hold. It all meant, as one of the brothers observed, 'a lot of making do and doing without, but it no doubt had its virtues as well as its vexations.'

4

To the City and Back

When I was about ten we went to live in St John's – for three years. I got to like it there and was sorry to leave ... After that we moved down to Fortune, which I never did like; no one in the family did ...

E.J. Pratt to D.G. Pitt, January 1960

N JULY 1892 the Pratts moved from Brigus to the Cochrane Street circuit in St John's. This was a considerable appointment for an outport minister. The three city circuits were the plums among Methodist pastorates in Newfoundland, but unfortunately for outport ministers they were not always regarded as illustrious or exalted enough to occupy positions of such eminence. It had come, therefore, as a very welcome surprise when on Christmas Eve 1891 John Pratt had received a call from Cochrane Street Church to its much-prized pulpit with its $1,000 stipend – all cash: no turnips, hay, or salt cod. There was more than the usual festive celebration in the draughty Brigus manse ('the coldest in the Conference') that Christmas season.

There was, however, little rejoicing on their arrival on 8 July 1892, for that very day the 'Great Fire of '92' razed half the city, including a large part of John Pratt's new circuit. His church on Cochrane Street miraculously escaped, as did the manse on Military Road nearby, but among the thousands left homeless or financially ruined were scores of his parishioners. For days the ruins smouldered, great charred hulks of churches and cathedrals, schools and colleges, great mercantile houses of Water Street, and the mansions of their proprietors. The houses of most of the homeless left no ruins, only heaps of ash. The

Pratt children were greatly impressed; Edwin for one never forgot the awesome sight. John Pratt too, though he viewed the holocaust as a judgment of God, was painfully distressed, but what affected him most was the looting of burning shops which had accompanied the fire. This was no act of God, but 'the evil covetousness of men.' Accordingly, and to introduce the kind of pastor who had come among them, on the following Sunday he delivered himself of a searing discourse that so kindled the hearts of those who heard him that next day huge quantities of the booty were surreptitiously returned, some of it, including a grand piano (so it is said), penitentially deposited on the steps of his own church. It was not for nothing that he was nicknamed Boanerges, Son of Thunder.

St John's in the 1890s, though already called a city, was really little more than a fair-sized town. Its population was less than 30,000 and life there, as in the outports, was still almost wholly dominated by the sea and its occupations. The large, landlocked harbour, with its quays, docks, and forest of masts, ringed by hills on which the town was haphazardly perched, was the heart of its existence. Its main street, Water Street, which followed the curving shoreline barely above high-water mark, was the commercial and economic solar plexus of the town – almost of the island – and the street's existence was born of and almost wholly nurtured by the sea. Here, whatever the season, mariners walked, or gathered on street corners and wharves; and seaborne cargoes rattled over the rutted streets in horse-drawn carts. Apart from its somewhat more cosmopolitan air, its greater bustle and busyness, and the generally wider horizons of its world, St John's was in many ways little more than an overgrown outport. Pratt was right when he said that while he lived in Newfoundland he was never out of sight, sound, and smell of the sea nor out of touch with people whose lives were of the sea.

What might have provided the Pratt children with their greatest contrast between city and outport life did not quite materialize during their first year in St John's. The Methodist College, an all-grade school, where they were to have enrolled, had been levelled in the Great Fire. With the building had gone its substantial library, musical instruments, Principal Holloway's laboratory and all its treasured scientific equipment, a fine auditorium and gymnasium, everything in short that had given the College much of its distinction. But it had not become wholly defunct. Makeshift classrooms were hastily constructed; the principal and his staff moved in, and classes began in September as usual. It meant, however, that despite his new city environment, Pratt completed Standard 3 that year amid physical circumstances not very different from those of the outport school he had left behind in Brigus. A year later the College moved into a new brick building and he was at last introduced to life in a large and modern city school. A class picture of him that year shows a short boy in a tweed suit, with neat hair and eager face, peering out among the generally bigger boys ranked behind their teachers and 'Professor' Holloway in his drooping moustaches and academic gown. Too young to be enrolled in any of Holloway's classes, Pratt was fortunate in at least one of his teachers that year, J. Alexander Robinson, a young Englishman and amateur poet (shortly to found and edit the St John's *Daily News*), who taught him English literature and introduced him to Latin. Many years later, reviewing *Newfoundland Verse* for his paper, Robinson would write of the 'brilliant promise' the poet had shown as a boy in his classes, but he must have been recalling other signs than formal academic records: none of Pratt's three years at the College then was especially notable for marks earned in examination papers. Perhaps the novelties of city life had proved too distracting for even a bookish outport boy.

Despite its still somewhat outport-ish character, St John's had its novelties and attractions for an outport boy. The fire had, of course, erased much that would have been of prime attraction: the fine, well-stocked shops of Water Street; many of the old, substantial, and imposing buildings, and much else. Yet much remained, and what had been swept away was soon replaced, so that before very long Eddie Pratt knew that living in town was much more to his liking than outport life for all it had to offer in other ways. Most of all, as he recalled it many years later, 'I was caught by all the marvels and conveniences provided by Science': electricity, the telephone, central heating, indoor plumbing, all of them amenities most outports would lack for many years to come. (His preference for city life, with its marvels and conveniences, was never to change.) But there were other things too he would long remember. In summer there was 'swimming in "The Hole" off "Sliding Rock" in Rennies Mill River' (actually a brook, which meandered through the countryside nearby), where he first began to learn an art in which he came to excel; and there were the boat races at Quidi Vidi Pond on Regatta Day, with bands playing, side-shows, and hawkers peddling trinkets, buns, and home-brew. Because the event attracted a large 'riffraff-ish mob,' the children were not permitted to attend, but it was only a short walk to a strategic hillside where one could view the spectacle and hear the band. In winter, when Quidi Vidi was a gleaming plane, there was skating for all – though not on Sunday. Eddie Pratt, well bundled against the stinging winds that rarely ceased to blow, was usually permitted this diversion, and in time became a very good skater. In late winter and early spring there were the departure and return of the sealing fleet, followed by 'Gargantuan meals of flippers.' A small lending library on Water Street was fondly remembered for providing a rather different kind of fare.

Undoubtedly his most pregnant memories were those of visits to his grandfather Knight, now retired from the sea and living with an unmarried daughter, 'Aunt Sophie.' (His grandmother had died in the year the Pratts moved to St John's.) Until now the boy had had little opportunity to know the old man. He was nearing eighty, but his memory was good and he liked to talk about his life at sea. When Pratt long afterward reminisced about 'the stories of old salts who knew life as it was in the sixties and seventies' they were mainly those of his grandfather. And there is little doubt that he was remembering the yarns of Captain Knight when in *Rachel* he wrote of his young hero's fascination for 'stories handed down': 'sagas of the Gulf of Labrador / The stories of the Banks, the travel lore / Of Ocean tracts ...' It is not unlikely that 'a secret ambition to go to sea,' which, it seems, he nourished for a time thereafter, sprang from the tales of this authentic ancient mariner. It is difficult to calculate how much the poet may have owed to him.

Pratt, as he said, was sorry to leave St John's when his father's pastorate there ended in July 1895. The experience had been good for an outport boy inclined to be shy and reserved, especially as a student at a spirited and demonstrative city school. It had brought him for the first time into the company of a fairly urbane, young élite – the College had a more or less exclusive clientele – moneyed (many of them), lively, extroverted, and largely unsaved. It had given him a glimpse of a very different world and life from those he had known. His status, too, as a parson's son had not the same significance or liabilities. In the larger, more impersonal population of the College, he had been just another boy meeting his fellows on common ground and in his own person rather than that of his father's son.

Had he, like his brother Jim that year, won a scholarship at the College he would undoubtedly have returned to continue his studies there. But having fallen short of that mark, he had no choice but to accompany his parents to Fortune, his father's new circuit, and return to the academic tundras of an outport school.

Fortune, on the south coast peninsula of Burin, was an utter change from St John's. Small, bleak, vulnerable, isolated, an archetypal sea-built and sea-girt outport, it was truly the most typical outport the Pratts had yet lived in. It was, partly at least, for this reason that the family did not like Fortune, though there were other reasons too. To John Pratt it was one of the most 'godless' circuits he ever served, where 'unbelief and indifference' prevailed, where his congregations were small, and few who came remained to be saved. (Once, at an outlying church on the circuit, his godless congregation turned violent, departing en masse during the sermon and pelting the building with stones.) To make matters worse, his term there was one 'of unequalled poverty and distress.' For all the family too, but especially for Edwin, though he would take away some triumphant memories of adolescent rites of passage, Fortune was forever associated with constantly recurring disasters at sea.

All Newfoundland fishing grounds are hazardous, but the Grand Banks, where most of the Fortune fishermen sailed, were (and still are) a veritable fisherman's graveyard. Whole crews were often lost in a single storm, sometimes all from one family. To John Pratt fell the hard task of breaking the news. It was a duty he performed well, but for all his tough exterior one he always shrank from. In later years Pratt numbered among his most vivid and painful memories the recurring Gethsemanes of anguish his father passed through as he steeled himself for each such visitation: 'I have never been able to forget his face.' Sometimes, whether for moral support or, more likely, to provide another exemplum of the tough creed he had to teach them, he would make one of his sons accompany him on his grim mission. This too was an experience Edwin never forgot. His poem 'Erosion' described something he had seen many times, the awful power of the sea in 'an hour of storm' to carve the 'sculpture of ... granite seams / Upon a woman's face.' It is not hard to understand why so many of his Newfoundland poems were written from the viewpoint not of mariners but of their anxious, anguished women, bereaved or fearing bereavement, or to appreciate the dilemma that troubled him for many years: 'We were brought up in a belief in the goodness of God and yet we had to reconcile tragedy to it.' It seemed to him looking back that 'We were always very close to death.'

It should not be surprising that nostalgic, romantic yearnings toward the sea – or nature generally – rarely occur in Pratt's poetry, not at all once he abandons his early, mistaken attempts to imitate the wrong models. Such yearnings are clearly alien to his Newfoundland environment and experience. Far more imaginatively immanent for him in later years 'than the fragrance of roses ... than the music of nightingales' was '... the struggle of ... men ... the pitched battle with the elements ... and the ironic enigma of nature ...' Small wonder that when he came to read him, Hardy's darkly clouded vision of the Universe should have struck him with a shock of recognition.

Pratt was now, in 1895, thirteen years old. His mother still kept vigilant watch over his physical welfare, his father likewise over his moral and spiritual. Nevertheless, it is apparent that the boy had reached a stage where he began to feel a need to participate more fully in the normal adolescent goings-on of the outport world. What he felt, it seems, was above all a need to prove himself something more than the quiet, timid-seeming youth whom a former schoolmate remembered only as 'a retiring, diffident sort of chap who wouldn't hurt a fly.' Deterred both by his own nature and his parents' nurture from winning his spurs in the usual manner of outport boys – as often in impious contests of verbal heroics as in feats of actual daring and prowess – he seems to have felt an urge to make at least a show of mettle. Physical confrontation still daunted him and always would and he had yet to learn the arts of verbal heroics. But somehow he had to prove, as much to himself as to the 'fisher boys' of godless Fortune, that he might, after all, be a 'tough guy' of sorts, the constraints upon him notwithstanding.

Unlikely as it may seem the medium he chose for his rite of passage was swimming. He may have done so, partly, because so few outport boys ever mastered the art. But it was also something he could practise on his own without competitors at his elbow. He was not, as we know, a total stranger to the water, but he now set out – at what cost of borrowed courage we can only guess – to make himself not only an accomplished swimmer, but possibly a high-diver as well. So successful was he that by the summer of 1897 he had made himself 'champeen' (his own word) not only among his brothers, already good swimmers, but of 'the whole of Fortune' as well. This was not perhaps a very remarkable feat in itself, Fortune boasting few good swimmers, but for the boy he had been it was nothing short of Herculean. Besides, he was now, to quote Calvert, 'the envy of most of his chums.' His swimming laurels paid him other dividends too: only because he was a good swimmer did he escape certain death by drowning when, unnoticed by his companions, he was once knocked overboard by the jibing boom of a speeding sailboat far from shore. They were triumphs he never forgot. Twenty years later in his semi-autobiographical poem *Rachel* he recalled them with obvious relish and in much vivid and evocative detail: 'the raptures of the morning swim ... the loud shout of defiance to the waves ... the zest of battle in the breakers.' He was probably not exaggerating greatly if at all either his skill or daring when he described how he

> ... ventured far
> Into the deeper channels, tried the stress
> Of surface currents and of undertow
> With lusty breast or side-stroke, or in view
> Of gazing mariners on a schooner's deck
> ... sprang from boom or bowsprit, diving full
> Into the azure bay with agile curve ...   (155–61)

Sometimes when on shipboard, to terrify and amaze his audience with further exhibitions of derring-do, he would scurry up the schooner's rigging to stand in triumph on the cross-trees atop the spars. His brothers and their friends would try to follow, but (in Calvert's words) 'Ned would reach the masthead when the rest of us would stop part way up.' Whether he dived from such a height we do not know, but it is not unlikely that he did, at least once.

They were all risky, foolhardy, improbable exploits, especially for a still undersized, not particularly robust boy – though he was outgrowing much of his earlier delicacy. But clearly they answered a deep-seated need: the need to compensate not only for inadequacies of physique and a natural timidity which made him shun the bodily contact of more obvious adolescent tests of valour, but also, perhaps most of all, for all the unmanning prohibitions and constraints imposed on him as the son of a Methodist parson, of John Pratt in particular. The point is worthy of more than passing note, for it was a need, conscious or unconscious, that he was never to be rid of, though he would try to mask it and, happily, often directed it into creative channels. A need to compensate – mostly, I believe, for legacies, real or imagined, of his childhood rather than any congenital 'weakness of the gut' – in various ways determined much of his behaviour all his life, in his poetry as well as out of it. In his poetry, his fondness for hyperbole, verbal and other kinds of heroics, his often obsessive preoccupation with brute strength, power, and sheer magnitude, and what some critics have called his 'juvenile delight in violence,' are more obvious examples of its manifestation. Outside his poetry it was usually, if not always, behind the truant role he often played in various guises, behind his penchant for fathering upon mites of fact elaborate, often hyperbolic, fictions, especially about himself in his early years; behind all that is epitomized in the remark of a long-time friend of his: 'With Ned, if something was worth doing at all, it was worth *over*-doing!' Questioned about his risky boyhood exploits he confessed that they 'used to *terrify* me, but I felt I had to do them – something no one else would do. A lot of that sort of thing went on, one fellow trying to outdo the other. I wasn't much good at other sports, but I was cham-peen swimmer and diver. *No one* could *touch* me there!' His answer, I think, both confirms the motives that prompted him and reveals something of the tenacious will that enabled him to act, a will unbroken, if a little bent, by a rather literal application of Wesley's mischievous 'Hymn for Parents.'

No matter that it was all an exhibition of compensatory behaviour, having required a summoning of buried reserves, it was an important psychological advance for the timid, retiring, diffident boy he had been. Being a champion of something also helped, no doubt, to establish for him a small niche within the circle of his outport peers. But there were still his father's rigid moral and behavioural codes to be

reckoned with before the whole-hearted social acceptance he seems to
have increasingly desired could be a reality. It was hard enough for an
ordinary outsider to break into the tightly drawn circle of the local
clan; it was infinitely harder for one presumed to be 'holier than thou.'
And in those days (it is much the same yet, I have no doubt) typical
outport youngsters whether saved or not were rarely paragons of
either Victorian propriety or Puritan punctiliousness. Yet most, if not
all, of the naughty delights and minor depravities which characterized
their life-style, the minister's son, under threat of Divine retribution
not to mention his father's walking stick, was expected to eschew with
stoical disdain. It was clearly not an easy burden of rectitude to bear
nor to escape from under. But small, discreet gestures of personal
independence could be made, and inevitably were, though more often
by the eldest Pratt brother than by the less refractory younger ones.
Nevertheless, as he grew older Edwin too, it seems, began to make
occasional, cautious forays into forbidden realms. What irreparable
damage, after all, could be done his immortal soul by a furtive smoke
behind a fish-shed now and then, a mug or two of home-brew in a
noisy foc's'le, a game of 'Devil's cards' in a darkened sail-loft, a little
awkward dancing at an 'Irish wedding,' even a little 'funning with the
maidens' now and then?

The last-named 'naughty delight' has, of course, a sexual connota-
tion. But the extent, if any, of Pratt's early sexual adventures is impossible to determine. During his years at Fortune, I am told, he had
several casual girlfriends, 'two Hazels and a Nellie.' But it is certain
that he was no youthful rake. Compared with many young 'fellers
from Fortune' (as the old song has it) he was a most unprofligate
sinner, if not an utter innocent. Friends who knew him then have
described him as a 'normally heterosexual' youth, but the most emphatically proclaimed of his parents' codes, reinforced by impreca-
tions called down from his father's pulpit on all fornicators old and
young, greatly inhibited any inclination to stray. That, and a strict
veto imposed within the home on any gratuitous syllable which so
much as hinted at human sexuality, impressed him with such a deep,
puritanical sense of the 'sinfulness' of sex that it haunted his conscience for years to come. It did not dampen his instincts, but it long
censored his mind, denying his poetry any scintilla of sexual passion

or consciously admitted erotic image. Any adolescent transgressions, if they ever achieved actual sinfulness, must have been acts of very troubled and guilty pleasure.

Pratt's last year at school in Fortune (1896–7) was, it seems, a troublesome one for both him and his parents. Unfortunately few details are known; but whatever the reason (or reasons), unable to settle down to his studies, he was soon getting into problems with the schoolmaster, 'a bit of a martinet.' It is not unlikely that, a precocious boy, he was simply bored by the repetitious, uninspired academic routines, and the dreary textbooks and subject-matter fed him day after day. Lines in *Rachel* describing his schooldays undoubtedly recall his troublesome year at Fortune, though nothing is suggested of *serious* misdeeds:

> ... Less was said
> Of boyish pranks and mischief that outlived
> The pickled strap and hickory stick, of deeds
> Of truant muscles feebly held in leash.
> When such reports came to his mother's ears,
> ...
> She took her son to task with serious looks
> And words that while they left no sting yet brought
> The promise made with solemn vows and signs
> Of good behaviour for the following day.   (123–34)

The picture is entirely credible. Much less credible, however, are the tales he sometimes told of 'many a school thrashing,' implying frequent and major misdemeanours. It is unlikely that his problems were ever serious enough to require such Draconian solutions. But, as we know, looking back he often painted himself as a boy in more dramatic if not lurid colours than the bare facts warranted.

Another of his tales from this time which, though probably embellished a little, I think we can believe, reveals that it was one of the martinet's favourite alternatives to the pickled strap and hickory stick that first drove a future poet to 'the extremity of verse.' This was the time-honoured expedient of standing young miscreants in the Dunce's Corner. It was an experience which Pratt, it seems, found especially humiliating, if not agonizing – 'like sitting in the stocks or the public penitent form.' Denied by parental edict the satisfaction of appeasing his outraged sensibilities in the colourful expletives and 'blasphemous clichés' of his classmates, he resorted to rhyme and metre instead. 'Much of this stuff,' he wrote more than a half-century later, 'was satirical and transitory.'

The result, however, was of some importance for I enjoyed the experience of a boyish retaliation, heightened by the fun my classmates got when I read the lines, and I soon realized that there was something about rhyme and rhythm which acted as a very superior substitute for the blasphemous *clichés* which easily fall from student lips ... There was a quality about a really well turned line which gave me a great internal satisfaction.

But the satisfaction was not to be sustained. Apart from one or two similar 'lampoons' (as he called them) reputedly written during a year in residence at the Methodist College Home, his next venture into verse, also 'satirical and transitory,' was not to be made for more than another decade.

Whatever internal benefits he may have derived from his literary excursions, his more formal schoolwork seemed to derive none at all. In the published examination results (for all candidates in Newfoundland) his name stood almost at the bottom of a very long list in 1896, and in virtually the same place in the following year. All his classmates at Fortune stood well above him, and one was a scholarship winner. What was the reason for such fiascoes? In view of his early scholastic promise and triumphs yet to come an answer is not easy to give. There was, clearly, no lack of intellectual capacity or ability. There were, it is true, his expanded interests and preoccupations in the secular and unacademic world of the youthful companions with whom he had now begun to mingle more freely, his greater concern to identify himself with their life-style, their attitudes, and ambitions. Yet neglecting his studies for whatever reason seems unlikely for one intent on going to college, the essential, next rung of John Pratt's 'ladder to honourable success.' But had Edwin himself any such intention or desire?

He told me once that as a boy at Fortune he had had 'a secret ambition to go to sea ... like most of the other fellows I knew'; on another occasion elsewhere he stated that he had in fact gone to sea for a time in a fishing-schooner on the Grand Banks, implying that he had once been a member of a fishing crew. I have found nothing to support the statement, which I very much doubt. It is most unlikely that his father would have permitted his being a Bank fisherman even for one voyage. To John Pratt all fishing-schooners were 'dens of vice' where 'religion is slain daily.' (Some years later Pratt did make a fairly long voyage on a schooner, but as a passenger. He was later, no doubt, as he sometimes did, rewriting the record as he wished it had been.) Heroic dreams of a life on the ocean waves are, of course, another matter, and very probable for a none-too-hardy youth who had visions of being a tough guy some day. In *Rachel*, his young hero's defying his mother and going to sea against her wishes is almost certainly retroactive dream-fulfilment, which is another form of rewriting the record. There is little doubt that he had dreams, waking and sleeping, which took him far away from the Methodist manse and the Fortune schoolhouse. None of this, of course, necessarily explains the academic disasters of his early and middle teens, but it may suggest something of the restless, even restive, truant spirit which seems to have overtaken him, making life in the school at Fortune 'stale, flat, and unprofitable,' and the prospect of being sent to College, to follow thereafter some suitable calling, an unexhilarating goal to aim for.

What suitable calling John Pratt may have had in mind for his third son is not apparent. Not unnaturally it had been his hope that at least one of the boys would follow in his footsteps. To give him his due, he preferred to parental coercion a free-will choosing in response to a distinct call. Not that he was averse to using the thumb-screws a little if that became necessary. But there is nothing to suggest that Edwin was yet being viewed as potential ministerial timber. Family tradition has it that Jim had been his father's choice to inherit the mantle. A steady, conscientious youth, deeply religious and a good musician, he alone of the boys had from childhood exhibited the qualities of mind and temperament to have fitted him for the role. But by 1897 it was becoming increasingly apparent that his candidature would not materialize. Having taken his Associate of Arts Diploma at the Methodist College the previous year, he was already launched on what proved a sharply rising trajectory in what his father called 'the commercial life.'

Not that John Pratt had any settled antipathy toward such an occupation, nor toward any respectable calling with 'prospects.' He sometimes – rashly, perhaps, since much of his income depended on their good will – castigated the merchant from his pulpit for 'coveting an evil covetousness': 'God's woe will find him and pillage his nest' of 'ill-gotten wealth.' But he was not so unrealistic as to proscribe altogether the commercial life, nor deny the value of having men of substance in one's congregation. On the contrary, he insisted that provided the businessman's motives were 'fenced round and guarded by right, justice, truth, honesty,' not only was he exculpated but blessed 'in setting his nest on high.' As for Little Spurgie, though he had eschewed the Cloth he had no doubt reclaimed a degree of his father's favour by uniting himself with George Street Methodist Church and joining its choir.

But the same cannot be said of his eldest son, William. He too by then was launched on his way, but as a newspaperman, a profession which John Pratt regarded as neither promising nor quite respectable. A brilliant but headstrong and difficult boy, he had already caused his parents much mental and emotional anguish. Growing restive and at last rebellious under his father's 'evangelization' and other impositions, and having graduated from the Methodist College in 1895, he had struck out on his own, taking almost the first job that came his way and, in effect, leaving home and the Methodist fold for good. Some time later (after a 'violent quarrel' with his mother, I am told, though details are lacking) he emigrated to the United States and thereafter, until his 'tragic' death in 1924 (to be mentioned briefly later), virtually disappeared from the family records.

As for Eddie, the odd one, he too must have presented his parents a problem in the summer of 1897. He had passed his Standard 8 – barely, but passed it; College in St John's was the next normal step, and though he had won no scholarship his father could have managed to send him there nevertheless. As a result of three good years on a relatively lucrative city circuit, John Pratt was better off financially than he had ever been. Besides, his two elder sons were now through College and at work, no longer charges on their father, and there was no other child than Edwin on the threshold, nor would there be for several years to come. Yet he did not go to College that year, but went to work instead, the only one of John Pratt's eight children to cut short his schooling to take a job.

His own explanation in later years was that he had had to earn his way through College. But the story hardly stands up to scrutiny. For one thing, as just noted, his father was far better able to finance him than he had his brothers; for another, prevailing wages for boys of fifteen precluded his saving a penny. John Pratt, in fact, had to subsidize the boy until he established himself in some suitable calling. But what actually occurred to launch him into the workaday world at fifteen is not entirely clear. According to Pratt's cousin, Cluny Macpherson, the boy's dismal academic record during several years – his decline had set in as early as 1894–5 when he was still at school in St John's – had convinced his father that higher learning was not for Eddie and that he had better aim for goals that might be reached by a different route. In Macpherson's words, 'His father reached the conclusion that Ned was an academic washout and simply wrote him off and told him to get a job.' It is not unlikely. To John Pratt higher learning was an investment, and he was not one to gamble recklessly. The only other explanation seems to be that having lost all interest himself, the boy refused to remain at school any longer. (I am inclined to accept Macpherson's explanation: had John Pratt insisted, he would have gone to College then, interest or no.) In the light of Pratt's subsequent academic successes either explanation seems strange and ironic. It is perhaps not surprising that in later years the actual reason for what happened should have been cloaked in tales of having to earn his way to College.

5

Commerce and College

I've often tried to assess the value of those three years. What would there be,
taking the assets with the liabilities? I'd be *in the red*!

E.J. Pratt to J. Frank Willis, 1961

HEN IT WAS DECIDED that Edwin Pratt, aged fifteen, should
leave school and go to work, there was no thought in anyone's mind, least of all John Pratt's, that he should be
fobbed off with some dead-end job. What his father wished
for him was a position, one with prospects, if possible an apprenticeship in some respectable, commercial firm where he might in time
work up to a comfortable situation, perhaps a partnership. And so it
came about – at least in part. Enquiries by his father, assisted by
Fanny's brother, who was in business in St John's, shortly produced
the desired result. Sometime, then, in the late summer or early
autumn of 1897, Edwin Pratt became a junior apprentice in the dry-
goods firm of W.A. Sclater, Water Street, St John's.

His mother made him ready – somewhat reluctantly, even tearfully
one gathers from family accounts – and he was put aboard the coastal
steamer. Apart from brief holidays with the family, he was leaving
home for good. (It is not unlikely that in *Rachel* his young hero's
parting from his tremulous mother [405–10] recalls his own home-
leaving.) A few days later his uncle accompanied him downtown to a
building on the corner opposite Queen Street, known as Sclater's
Drapery. (With a new facade and other renovations it was still standing and in use as a shoe store more than eighty years later.) It was a
grim, three-storied, brick building, with large Roman-arched win-

dows which extended upward from the second to embrace the third floor as well. The display windows on either side of the front door were crowded with cloaks and mantles, caps, hats, and footwear, as well as large bolts of cloth, and what were delicately called (he later learned) 'ladies' furnishings.' Inside, the ceiling-high shelves were equally crammed with more of the same, and the counters piled high at either end. They were shortly ushered into the presence of the elder of the two Sclater brothers who owned and ran the establishment, who wasted no time on needless ceremony. 'He looked me over,' Pratt recalled, 'and said, "Eighty dollars for the first year, a hundred for the second, and a hundred and twenty for the third".' That was all. He was hired, indentured for three years. He was on his own, a man of business.

He had a dreadful time at Sclater's from the start. To learn the business from the ground up, he was given a multitude of tasks and the title 'cash-boy,' since his chief responsibility was keeping check on receipts, making change, and ensuring that the contents of the cash-box tallied with the sales slips. But though exacting, that was the least onerous of his duties. Entrusted with the front door key, he had to arrive each morning in time to fire up the stove, sweep the floors, take down the shutters, and open up for business to begin at nine o'clock. During the day, besides his duties as cash-boy, he was expected to keep the fire going and, when business was brisk, to help out at the counters. At day's end, which might be as late as eleven o'clock, having first made sure that the cash tallied, he had to damp down the fire, put up the shutters, lock the doors, and tramp home in the darkness of the unlighted street. Aunt Sophie Knight, with whom he boarded, lived on Leslie Street, an almost vertical incline in the west end of town, a mile or more from Sclater's. Once home, having to rise at seven, he could only fall into bed to recoup his energies for the long, busy, repetitious next day.

To make matters worse for Pratt, Sclater made no allowance for either the inexperience of youth or the infirmities of the flesh. Minor errors were seized upon and inflated into major disasters; accidental breakages were deducted from his wages; being late to open up one morning, having overslept, he was punished by being forced in future to tramp round to the boss's house to fetch the one and only key, which Sclater thenceforward kept in case of future dereliction; com-

ing down with measles and near collapse, he was ordered to show up
for work at night, ill or not; when the younger Sclater borrowed $10
from the till, Edwin was accused of theft and only escaped dismissal,
or worse, by the timely appearance of the culprit, who blithely admitted having helped himself to a loan which he had forgotten to report.

In later years, when Pratt talked of those unhappy days at all, he
preferred remembering occasional episodes that could be viewed in a
less painful light. One he often recounted with great merriment concerned a dramatic confrontation with an amplitudinous client, whose
demand for a 'medium' corset he had boldly countered with a suggestion that 'extra large' seemed nearer the mark. Reprimanded by the
boss, to whom she made voluble complaint, Pratt had promised to be
more discreet if somewhat less 'helpful' in future. As a result, he
wrote, 'I learned a little finesse in suggesting bust measurements –
and established a reputation for conservative estimates.' But though a
source of subsequent merriment, even a justifiable indiscretion was no
doubt far less risible at the time.

'I hated every minute of it,' he would declare with much bitterness,
looking back on his 'three lost years.' His succinct summation, 'I'd be
in the red!,' was unquestionably correct. His chief liability was loss of
time, three years of his youth spent in monotonous, sterile drudgery,
with scarcely a moment when he had either the opportunity or the
energy to meet friends, or go swimming, or even to read. Imprisoned
in Sclater's cramped and cluttered shop, hot and airless in summer,
cold and damp in winter despite his ceaseless efforts to keep the fire
going, with the constant clatter in his ears of the horse-drawn carts in
the cobble-stoned street, he could hardly but have hated every minute
and longed to be free of it all.

The only possible asset was that for the first time he was largely on
his own, freer than he had ever been to let his personality shape itself
from within, relatively unconstrained by the need to reflect his
father's image. Aunt Sophie, under his father's instructions, ensured
that he went to George Street Methodist Church every Sunday and to
class-meeting fairly regularly. But he no longer lived in the unrelieved
and oppressive atmosphere of daily evangelization. In the commercial
world of Water Street he was not a parson's son, just another boy
making his way in the secular world, neither insulated by a special
role nor exposed to special attention because of it. It was a rather

different society he lived in, too, from that of the close-knit, personal outport, an environment of indifference and impersonality, in which he was thrown wholly on his own resources. Yet, for one whose life had been sheltered and protected, whose personality had been largely overwhelmed by that of a domineering parent, such an experience was probably, in the long run, an asset of no small value.

An experience of a different kind was the arrival in port on 28 March 1898 of the ill-fated *SS Greenland* with her cargo of frozen bodies. Forty-eight of her sealing crew had been lost in a blizzard on the ice-floes; twenty-five bodies only had been found and these were brought home for burial. It was Sunday afternoon, and Pratt was among the crowd that lined the wharves and hillsides as the ship steamed slowly in the Narrows, flags at half-mast, sirens stilled, bearing home her ghastly freight. He was present too next morning – all employees were given a day off – when two mass funeral services were held, one in the Anglican cathedral, the other in Gower Street Church nearby. Nothing escaped him. More than two decades later he recreated in *The Ice-Floes* the story of the tragedy in vivid detail, and in 'The Toll of the Bells' the emotions evoked by the sombre obsequies. 'No part of the whole ritual,' he wrote a half-century later, 'that made up the formal part of the services seemed able to the same degree to bring home to our hearts as did the bells the solemnity and desolation of the tragedy.' 'I was only a boy at the time; but it is an ineffaceable memory.'

But there was little else from those lost years that he did not wish to forget, and nothing else it seems that found its way, directly at least, into his poems. After three years, still in the red, he decided at last to break out, convinced that if he was to have a satisfying future he must have a better education. He had fulfilled his contract, so that there were no formalities to quitting. He simply went in one day (some time in the spring or summer of 1900), announced to his employer 'I'm sick of it; it's a dead end to me,' and left. The Pratts had just moved to Grand Bank from Bay Roberts, where they had gone after leaving Fortune in 1898. He decided to join them there, at least until he had had time to ponder his future.

Pratt did not remain at Grand Bank for long, but what occurred during that time is of crucial importance. Had it not happened it is hard to conjecture what course his life might have taken thereafter.

For when he left home again in the early autumn he was off to the Methodist College to resume his interrupted education, but committed to offering himself as a candidate for the Methodist ministry!

What led him to make such a crucial commitment is simply if somewhat improbably explained. By the summer of 1900 John Pratt was a sick man, stricken with the illness that would eventually kill him. But the prospect was dimmer than ever that any of his sons of their own volition would take up his work when he was finally forced to lay it down. Edwin had abandoned his prospects in business and now wished to return to school, to College, yet quite lacked the financial means to do so. His father offered to provide him the means if he would make a commitment to become a candidate for the Methodist ministry. As Cluny Macpherson succinctly phrased it, 'Old John saw his chance and offered Ned a deal. It was as simple as that. I know Ned *never* wanted to do it, but in the circumstances he had little choice.'

Yet it must have been an agonizing decision for the boy to make; as Macpherson says and Pratt himself repeatedly declared, 'I never, never, never once wanted to go into the ministry.' There is no reason to question his disavowals, and very good reason to accept them. Long before his mind was clouded by religious doubts, scenes from clerical life viewed too closely and too early, its austerity if not penury, its moral rigorism, its 'recurring Gethsemanes of anguish,' had all, it seems, been enough to dampen any early inclinations he may possibly have had. But more important, I believe, was that a preacher-pastor – a John Pratt – did not fit the self-image Edwin already visualized, nor did the role answer the kind of persona he had already begun to shape for himself. In short, the part was out of character for Edwin Pratt as he saw him and wished him to be seen. Once he had accepted the part he would try to play it out faithfully for as long as he could. But in doing so he was to retard the severing of his impeditive umbilical cords and thereby retard his full self-realization for years to come; to plague himself with many frustrations and a sense of guilt at his eventual but inevitable dereliction; to misdirect and dissipate his energies and delay the flowering of his genius for nearly two decades. The educational asset which accrued to him from his deal was unquestionably one of great value; the pity is that it could not have been had at a lower and an uncontractual cost.

Unfortunately we do not know all the details of what passed between him and his parents during his days of decision, after his return like the prodigal, having wasted – though hardly in riotous living – three years of his youth as well as his father's substance. Was there a family row? Did Boanerges mount the rostrum? Did Fanny Pratt melt into tears, as she often did to effect persuasion? What other pressures were brought to bear upon him? There is little doubt that his mother's role was crucial. His father's being unwell must also have added weight. Yet it was a momentous commitment to make, one fraught with many implications, moral and otherwise. One can only assume that in making it Pratt either believed that his misgivings, if not outright antipathy, would disappear in time, that he might grow into the role, even generate some enthusiasm for it, or, as seems more likely, counted on some stroke of Fate – his father's death perhaps – to release him from his bond before it fell due. He was still only eighteen, and could not become a bona fide candidate until he was at least twenty-one. But whatever his feelings in the matter may have been, he yielded to the parental blackmail and went off to the Methodist College in September financed by his father and with his blessing.

Enrolled in the newly instituted Intermediate Grade, he registered in all the courses he was permitted to take. It was a substantial program, but he seems to have tackled it with enthusiasm. His first-term marks were not spectacular, but they were respectable, and in the final papers in June he came sixth in his class, only Latin and Scripture history barring him from an honours average. In the following year, as a candidate for the Associate of Arts Diploma (junior matriculation), he maintained a good record throughout the course, and in the final examinations (set and marked by the University of London) took second place in the College and third place in Newfoundland. His marks in chemistry being the highest in the Island, he was awarded a scholarship but was made to relinquish it when it was learned that he was beyond the age limit of eighteen years. But scholarship or no, it was an excellent year's work, especially for someone who had been written off as an academic washout.

Having a personal, if not a vocational, motive to make up for lost time, he had quickly recovered his early habits of study and application. But though some of his classmates would remember him when a collegian as a 'quiet, reserved, studious, young fellow,' who 'preferred to be left to himself and his books,' it is certain that he was not wholly a bookworm or a hermit. Another classmate recalled the Sunday afternoons when, 'mooching' from Sunday School (attendance was required of all inmates of the College 'home' where Pratt lived during his second year), he and Pratt would roam LeMarchant Road in quest of whatever unSabbatarian fun they could find. Others describe him as 'the life of the party' when a crew of kindred spirits gathered in one of their rooms for occasional soirées of high-jinks and temperate conviviality. (Whether or not minor accidents sometimes resulted, the College accounts show that Edwin J. Pratt was charged 'thirty cents for breaking a jug,' a debt promptly paid by 'Rev. J. Pratt.') He also maintained a moderate interest in the 'more civilized' athletic sports, particularly cricket, a popular College game in the days when most of the masters were British.

Chief of the British masters at the College was Robert E. Holloway (glimpsed earlier in his gown and drooping moustaches), principal and head teacher but usually called 'Professor,' a title he disliked because (to quote him) 'a very large number of those who affix it spell it "proffessor".' Pratt left the college with rather mixed feelings toward the man, a former British grammar-school master, severe disciplinarian, and plague of all idlers and bluffers. But he never qualified his admiration for Holloway the teacher, particularly of science. He taught several subjects, but science was his forte and his passion. He believed that the true dawn of the new scientific age had yet to appear, and was determined that his students would be ready for it and perhaps contribute to what was to come. His hope proved not entirely vain: one of his pupils that year was Robert William Boyle, who was to become a renowned physicist, co-inventor of sonar, and a close friend of E.J. Pratt, who consulted him on technical details when writing *Behind the Log*.

Though he had studied no science before, Pratt was enthralled by Holloway's classes and soon became his top pupil; but for his ministerial commitment he might well have followed 'Billy' Boyle into a career in science. Holloway finding Pratt both apt and inquisitive took an especial interest in him, allowing him complete freedom of the laboratories and lending him books from his own library, including some, such as those of T.H. Huxley and Herbert Spencer, which because of his public role as custodian of Methodist doctrines and

morals he could not openly admit to owning. Here for the first time
Pratt encountered, with excitement and fascination, the theory of
evolution and its religious and ethical implications (heresy and ana-
thema to his father), a complex of ideas which was to engage his mind,
at times exhilarating him and at times tormenting him, for many years
to come and to appear in one form and another as a recurrent theme in
many of his poems when at last he began to write.

Holloway was also deeply interested in electrical phenomena, X-
rays, photography, and their application to what are now called com-
munications media and to the treatment of disease. He purchased the
first X-ray machine in Newfoundland and for a time provided the
medical profession of St John's with its only X-ray service. Patients
were X-rayed in the College laboratory, students acting as techni-
cians. 'To see through an opaque object,' Pratt wrote, 'was a marvel
like listening for the first time through a telephone or hearing the
reproduction of a voice on the gramophone.' (Both the telephone and
the gramophone were novelties to outport boys.) Holloway was also a
first-class photographer, of natural objects and landscape especially,
and taught his students all he knew of the art, instructed them how to
develop their own pictures, and how to mount slides. An avid astro-
nomer too, he often took his students out at night to study the stars
and learn their names. From him and his nocturnal forays Pratt derived a life-long interest in astronomy and a quite respectable compe-
tence. His calling the stars and constellations by name in many of his
poems required no checking in textbooks. In Holloway's classes, indeed, originated Pratt's abiding fascination for science and technology, which was later to have profound effects upon his thought,
sensibility, and vision as a poet.

His most memorable scientific experience during this time was undoubtedly the visit to St John's in December 1901 of Gugliemo Marconi, inventor of wireless telegraphy, to perform his climactic experiment on Signal Hill. Excited himself by the invention, Holloway
arranged for his class to visit the Colonial (Legislative) Building,
where the young Italian was conducting his final tests. For Pratt, as he
wrote long afterward, 'to see Marconi in person' was 'like coming into
the presence of Diety': 'This was shattering enough ... but it was only
a prelude to what occurred next day ... [I]magine the thrill of the

following morning when the newspapers headlined the statement that Marconi had bridged the Atlantic ... with wireless telegraphy!'

Many years later Pratt recalled having been present on the Hill when the historic first signals were heard, and that he had to be made by his mother to wash the hand that Marconi had shaken. But both 'recollections' were fanciful inventions: only Marconi and his assistant witnessed the great event and Pratt's mother at the time was far away in Grand Bank. Nevertheless he could truthfully write that he had never forgotten 'the sensation' of being 'in close to the actual discovery, as it were, the last lap of his achievement ... That morning will always remain one of the big moments of existence.' But his excitement did not arise merely from witnessing a marvel of science. The boy who knew so well the tragedy of disaster at sea was able to feel very keenly the immense human significance of what he had seen. As he expressed it elsewhere, 'Wireless had ... given a richer meaning to the phrase, "the brotherhood of the sea".' A decade later the *Titanic*, ironically, went down in almost the same longitude as Signal Hill, a victim (partly at least, as Pratt saw it) of a man's blind 'trust in science' to prevent 'the grosser human calamities.' Yet Marconi's invention remained for him one of man's greatest conquests over one of his greatest foes, not the sea merely, but isolation – 'night and space and the silence' – a state in which life is, almost if not wholly, without form and void. All his life, both as man and as poet, Pratt manifested an extraordinary interest in the many forms and functions of human communication, from speech and gestures, signs and symbols, 'flashlights and echoes,' to the most sophisticated electronic devices developed during his lifetime. Later he came to view the ideal form of a human society not as a corporate mass in which individual identity is swallowed up and individual consciousness submerged, but as a kind of telegraphic network or nervous system, in which each individual is a station or cell, discrete and inviolate, the quality of whose life depends, however, upon the signals sent out to and received from others. ('For only such culture [of hate] could grow in a climate of silence.') He was to give many talks in which this is an underlying theme, and write many poems in which the idea is present, either explicit or implied. There can be little doubt that these early experiences of the new miraculous techniques of communication, set in the context of the life he had known in the isolated, cellular, almost incommunicado outport, where life often literally, physically, hung on a fragile thread of communication – or was lost for lack of it – helped him in no small measure to his later views.

Pratt greatly admired Robert Holloway as a pedagogue, describing him as 'one of the most remarkable teachers I have ever known, and one of the most gifted and thorough ...' He owed him much, not only for opening to him the world of science and its humane and civilizing possibilities, but also for his perceptive and imaginative teaching of English literature. These were debts that he acknowledged often. But he never forgot or forgave Holloway's bullying, insensitive treatment of the weaker, slower, more backward members of his classes, especially the timid, quiet youngsters just out of their outport homes for the first time, whose spirits were no match for the master's sarcasm and threats, let alone his punishments. Pratt was older and, besides, was one of Holloway's model pupils; yet his blood would boil as he watched the young victims quail and squirm under 'the Professor's' cruel and unjust bombardments. He would remember with especial bitterness Holloway's treatment of a young boy, sickly and academically backward, whom Pratt had spent long hours tutoring for a crucial oral test. Though well prepared by his tutor, the boy had collapsed under Holloway's barrage of sarcasm and taunts, finishing a tearful failure, to be administered discipline in the usual fashion. Pratt was outraged, but though he must have been tempted, it was not in his nature to play Nickleby to Holloway's Squeers. But his sense of outrage then was nothing compared with his feelings when a few weeks later the boy died of the consumption that had been sapping his spirits for months. Pratt laid the tragedy to Holloway's charge and never forgave him. He vowed that should he become a teacher he would use far different methods to lead his young protégés to Pierian springs.

He was soon to have an opportunity to make good his vow. In no hurry to become an active candidate for the ministry, and being besides under the customary age for admission, graduating from the Methodist College in the spring of 1902 he decided to be a teacher for a year or two. With his College diploma he would qualify at once for a Second Grade Teacher's Certificate, which required only that the candidate having passed the intermediate grade, 'be able to read with fluency, ease and expression, and to recite at least thirty consecutive lines from any Standard Author.' The salary would not be munificent, but at $300 per annum it would be nearly half his father's after thirty years in the ministry. Some time then in the spring of 1902 Pratt applied for a certificate and a teaching post. Both were shortly forthcoming, the latter being that of headmaster of the two-room school at Moreton's Harbour.

6

Teaching, Preaching, and Peddling

The little villages lived to themselves. In such a place ... I taught school for
two years ... A teacher was often called on to perform all kinds of tasks ...
E.J. Pratt, from an unpublished script, c1951

ORETON'S HARBOUR, situated on New World Island near
the head of Notre Dame Bay and forty miles by sea from
the closest railway point, lived very much to itself. Pratt's
two years there were to be lived in the most complete isolation from family and friends he was ever to experience. But though
during his first few weeks, bereft for the first time of all familiar faces,
he experienced awful pangs of loneliness, his pedagogical duties, in
addition to all kinds of other tasks, soon left him little time to dwell on
distant scenes and absent friends.

His schoolhouse, a frame building which had once been a church,
was divided across the middle to form two classrooms. In one of these
a young woman of the place (Georgina French) taught the lower
grades, while in the other he taught Standards 4, 5, and 6. He had
twenty-seven pupils in his first year, twenty-nine in his second, to
whom he was expected to teach, besides the traditional subjects,
bookkeeping and school management, both of which he loathed. Consequently he largely ignored them, leaving his pupils to get them up
on their own. Instead he gave them classes in astronomy, and sometimes (like Mr Holloway) took them out at night to study the stars and
learn their names. In the end his pupils did poorly in bookkeeping and
school management, but quite respectably in everything else. Five of
his candidates passed the Council of Higher Education examinations

in his first year, and nine in his second. His tale in later years that 'the whole caboodle failed' and that he turned in a 'complete list of naughts' to an irate schoolboard was pure invention.

He was kept very busy in his first year. Besides his teaching he had much reading and other preparation to do for the London Matriculation Examinations for which he had registered. Yet he found opportunity to visit neighbours and make friends, so that he came to be favourably well known in the village and long remembered by former pupils as a quiet, likeable young fellow, a bit shy but friendly, 'more like one of our own than a college-educated boy.' He especially enjoyed going down to the wharves and fishing-stages to watch the men at work and talk to them. Whaling was then a considerable industry at Moreton's Harbour and this particularly interested him. He was fascinated by the whales that were towed into the harbour to be moored belly up until they were taken to the factories. 'I used to row around the whales some of which were 70 to 80 feet long.' One former pupil remembered his taking the class down to view an unusually large specimen and tell them 'about its anatomy, and habits of life, and how far it had probably travelled.' Though he did not know it then, the seed of *The Cachalot* had probably been already sown.

His pupils generally liked him, remembering him as interesting, imaginative, and very fond of telling stories. But he was *not* a good disciplinarian so that his classroom was often noisy and disorganized. Yet no one recalled his using the pickled strap and hickory stick. He usually had complete order and attention when he read or told stories, or when holding forth on a subject he really liked, such as literature or history, especially the latter: 'He was very fond of describing battles, making them come to life. He could spellbind us then.'

In the summer of 1903 he took passage for St John's, where he wrote the London Matric Examinations. Then he went home to Grand Bank to be with his family for a time – with his father for the last time. John Pratt's illness had steadily advanced, and he was now suffering much, though still struggling to perform his regular pastoral duties. When Pratt left at the end of August to return to his school, he knew that he would not see his father alive again. But he left, it seems, with the satisfaction of having shown his father that he might be ministerial timber after all. According to his sister Floss, Pratt's first sermon from a pulpit was delivered that summer at Grand Bank

before his gravely ill father. 'Father was almost overcome with pleasure ... I'm sure he had no doubts after that about Ned going through
with the ministry.' But whether Pratt himself had banished any of his
own misgivings is much less certain.

Returning to Moreton's Harbour he learned that he had passed the
London Matriculation papers with high honours and was now quali-
fied to enter a university. He was very pleased and promptly wrote to
the Methodist College asking that his name be added to its list of
London matriculants. 'I got through,' he added, 'wholly and absolutely upon the strength of the 1902 and previous year's grinding.'
But, curiously, he declined the opportunity to acquire a First Grade
Teaching Certificate. This required a year's teaching service, which
he had done, but it also required his passing a test in elocution.
Painfully timid, as he was for many years when called on to perform
before an audience of potential critics, he refused to undergo the
ordeal (whatever it may have entailed), preferring to complete his
teaching in Newfoundland with the lower certificate and the smaller
stipend.

'A teacher,' he observed long after, 'was often called on to perform
many tasks.' But some of his at Moreton's Harbour seem to have been
wholly self-appointed. Two of these must be briefly mentioned, illus-
trating as they do the practical, bold, even rash initiative he could
sometimes take in matters that moved him deeply whether to anger or
compassion. A paradoxical mixture on the one hand of diffidence and
unassertiveness, and on the other of an impulsive, sometimes exaggerated and self-willed boldness, he might shun a test in elocution for fear
of a critical appraisal, yet throw himself into something that roused
his spirit or capricious enthusiasm where the risks were far greater.

The first of the two episodes mentioned involved few risks beyond
the possibility of a curt rebuff, but it did demand a certain boldness
and directness of approach. This was to find a medical doctor, their
first, for the villagers of Moreton's Harbour. Until then if one was
needed either he was fetched by boat – by dog-team over the ice in
winter – from Twillingate, a dozen miles distant, or the patient was
taken there by the same means. Having witnessed during his first
term there several deaths which might have been prevented by proper
medical care, Pratt decided that the villagers had waited long enough.
Writing to the Medical School of McGill University, he laid the case

before them, accompanied by an interesting proposition: 'Every person in the place, sick or not, will pay four dollars a year' to any doctor willing to take on the job. Before the following year was out, thanks to Pratt's initiative, Moreton's Harbour had its first resident physician.

The other was rather different and much more daring, this, no doubt, lending it a certain attraction for him. A ship had grounded off the harbour and its cargo and fittings had been raided by 'wreckers,' a species of pirate not unknown in Newfoundland even in the twentieth century. Pratt's deep sense of fair play outraged, and the nearest law officer being at Twillingate, he decided to act in the name of Justice. By means of 'surreptitious sleuthing' – mainly, one gathers, eavesdropping and simple observation – and a public enquiry at which he 'took testimony under oath,' he managed to provide enough evidence to enable a constable when he at last arrived to make a number of immediate arrests. A properly constituted court at Twillingate concluded the affair with several convictions. But ironically – and unfairly, many believed – the young amateur detective-magistrate was merely reprimanded by the Bench for administering oaths without a commission.

One wishes more particulars of this curious incident were known, but these are all, a careful search of the local court records – admittedly incomplete – yielding in fact no mention of it whatsoever. But the tale, which Pratt himself often told – no guarantee, of course, of its complete authenticity – was corroborated for me after Pratt's death by his friend Clayton Pincock, who had been a teacher in Twillingate at the time and who remembered the incident 'very clearly.'

Tasks of a different nature were soon to be thrust upon him. Early in January (1904) his mother wrote to disclose that his father's illness had finally forced him to abandon all his pastoral duties and that he was now bedridden, calmly awaiting the end. The news, though not unexpected, was all the more distressing for Pratt because he could not be with his mother at a time that was 'terribly harrowing' for her. But his response was to throw himself into another arduous enterprise that left him little time to brood.

Partly to prepare himself for his prospective new vocation, but mainly, one suspects, to provide his father an assurance that the promise made him would be kept, Pratt applied for and was granted a Local Preacher's licence. Though still a full-time teacher, for the next six months he was also in all but name (and stipend) curate to the pastor of Moreton's Harbour. It was to be a very busy time for him: conducting Sunday services, preaching occasional sermons, and generally assisting in the work of a large circuit, besides his normal teaching duties. But he was glad to be busy.

John Pratt died at Grand Bank on 15 March. Pratt could not go home, but his three sisters were with their mother, and Jim had made the trip from St John's when it was apparent that the end was near. Three days before his death, unable to rise, John Pratt dictated to Jim a last message 'To my Congregation.' A curious document, almost an *apologia pro vita sua* in brief, it inscribed in burning characters the faith and courage of a man who had never wavered in the face of the most daunting disappointments and excruciating bodily torments. But the suffering borne for months had been nothing compared with 'the rapture and the joy' he had known, confident that 'I am going to Heaven ...' He lamented that despite his ceaseless efforts few hardened Grand Bank hearts had yielded to God's grace, but he fervently hoped that the harvest would yet come: 'I want to meet in Heaven hundreds of souls for whom I have seemed to labour in vain.' He gave instructions for his funeral in Grand Bank and burial in St John's, and bade his congregation a cheerful farewell, 'a subject of the saving grace of God, who died in the certain hope of a resurrection to eternal life.' He managed to sign it with his own hand; as instructed, Jim read it from the pulpit at his funeral. Reading it one may understand more clearly what Pratt meant when he said: 'He had a bit of the saint and a lot of the martyr about him.'

Having been unable to attend the funeral in Grand Bank, Pratt determined to attend the burial in St John's, mainly, one suspects, to be with his mother. Notre Dame Bay having frozen over firmly that winter – 'the coldest in memory' – he had no difficulty making the trip by dog-team to Lewisporte, where he took a train to St John's. Ironically, however, the severe winter had for the first time in decades filled Placentia Bay with massive, close-packed ice. As a consequence the ship bearing his father's body (accompanied by Fanny, Jim, and Charlotte) took eight instead of the usual two days to reach St John's, having been twice reported in danger of foundering. Pratt, who had waited out the anxious vigil at Aunt Sophie's, was on hand to meet his mother and take delivery of his father's body. Ten days having elapsed since the man had died, the funeral service in George Street Church was held with great dispatch. Due respect and honour, nevertheless, were paid the 'sainted fallen warrior.' So many of his clerical brethren delivered themselves of such handsome tributes to the 'bold and fearless preacher of Righteousness,' who 'courted no man's smile' and 'feared no man's frown' that, sitting in a front pew with his mother, the young prospective candidate for the same vocation must have wondered whether 'his sainted father's mantle' might not be more than he could bear.

The funeral over, Pratt and his mother parted once more. All that passed between them during his short visit is, of course, not known, but if he had hoped that his father's death might release him from his promise, his hope had been groundless. Not only did his mother insist that the pledge must not be broken; she insisted that his candidacy be initiated at once. Whether or not he attempted to resist is also unknown. But one suspects that in the face of her grief and her expectations of him, he resigned himself to what must now have seemed his inescapable destiny. In any event, immediately upon his return to Moreton's Harbour he placed his name before the Quarterly Official Board of the Moreton's Harbour Church requesting the Board's recommendation of his candidature to the Twillingate Methodist District at its spring meeting. That he delayed resigning his teaching post until late June suggests that he may have clung to a fragile hope that either the District Meeting or the June session of the Conference, which had the final power to accept or reject, might possibly decide against him.

If such had been his hope it proved a vain one. Whatever may have been his own doubts about the fateful step he was taking, the Twillingate District Meeting had none. The minutes of its sessions in May 1904 contain the following auspicious entry:

Edwin John Pratt is recommended by the Quarterly Board of Moreton's Harbour as a suitable candidate for the Ministry. Converted at 10 years of age at Blackhead under his father, about five years ago he felt a distinct call to the Ministry. He has read and will keep the Rules of Methodism, believes our doctrines, and is determined to employ all his time in the service of God. He does not take snuff, tobacco, or strong drink; is in sound health of body and mind, is not in debt, and is not engaged to marry. He has been an accepted Local Preacher for six months and is 22 years of age. Unanimously recommended.

Though a curious if not ironic caricature of the much later, un-Methodistical Ned Pratt of Toronto, the sketch is clearly that of an exemplary candidate for Methodist holy orders in 1904. The Conference could not but accept the recommendation, and by late June Brother Edwin Pratt had been formally received as a candidate on trial, and posted to the first circuit of his mandatory three-year probationship: at Cupids-Clarke's Beach as assistant to the Reverend William Harris for an annual stipend of $302.

This was familiar territory; his father had been stationed here nearly twenty years ago and Pratt himself had started school at Cupids. On familiar ground and among old friends he might have been expected to have passed his initiatory year not unpleasantly. This, unfortunately, was not the case. His superintendent pastor though not an old man was unwell during most of the year, so that a far more onerous burden than was his due fell upon the young assistant. The circuit, besides, was large and scattered, comprising four churches far apart. Often he had to preach three times on a Sunday and walk fifteen miles, frequently in the vilest of weather, to complete his round of pulpits. It was a baptism of fire, especially for one who despite his sterling testimonials could hardly be described as an unreluctant recruit. It is certain that nothing he experienced that year brightened the prospect which lay before him.

Something which brightened his spirits that autumn was news of his pupils' successes at Moreton's Harbour. When the Public Examination results were announced in late August he learned that all his candidates had passed, several with distinction. He was very pleased, and wrote his top pupil a long letter of congratulations, concluding with some fatherly advice: '[G]o on, continue to study as you have in the past and there won't be much chances of failure with you. A girl that keeps to her work and doesn't put pleasure and amusement before it will always succeed. Don't fail to write this return mail ...' The hortatory, sermonic style is almost his father's. He would seem to be slipping easily into his new role; or, at least, he was getting its lines.

Preaching and visiting were not his only duties. Baptisms, marriages, and burials also fell to him from time to time, though as he often confessed he was 'very uncomfortable' performing any of them. Burials he found especially distressing, though he was to acquire the reputation of 'a wonderful funeral man.' Baptisms, it seems, sometimes distressed him in a rather different way, though one he described many years later was certainly not typical:

I was called on to baptize a baby girl. I took the infant in my arms and asked the father the name. He said Jecholiah. I had a hazy notion that the name came from the Old Testament. Two or three relatives objected, and the father answered sympathetically, It's Jecholiah after her aunt Jeck. Well, any other names? Yes, it's Jecholiah Pratt ... The middle name was in honour of me. I managed to stutter through the baptismal formula and the ceremony was over after an unusual amount of water was sprinkled on the poor infant. But the girl survived the ordeal.

Needless to say no such name appears in the relevant baptismal records, confirming one's suspicions that the inventive raconteur of a later time has here been at work. But as was often the case his harmless travesty would seem to contain a kernel of truth. A letter in my possession (written in 1968) reads in part: 'I was the first baby he baptized at Portugal Cove when he was a young probationary minister. He asked my parents to name me after one of his sisters, but as they already had chosen a name they liked very much, he could not get them to change it, so he asked them to have the second name of Pratt added, so I became "Lillian Pratt".' And this is confirmed by the records. Though some of the personal, often humorous, anecdotes of his later years were wholly but guilelessly fictive, most of them, I find, were fathered upon at least a mite of fact. He has left no account of a typical wedding, though the marriage registers show that not a few nuptials were 'Solemnized between ... In the Presence of ... By me, Edwin J. Pratt.'

For all the levity with which he sometimes recalled his probationary ministry, its first year at least was no laughing matter. The levity is itself a clue to the real nature of his memories: he consistently laid his painful ghosts by making them figures of fun. While the actual state of his mind and emotions during his first strenuous year is hard to gauge, all the evidence indicates that he was very unhappy much of the time. Not only were the physical demands upon him extraordinarily heavy, especially for one who had never been robust, but the daily strain of performing tasks that required commitment and dedication, as well as convictions which he did not feel, was hardly conducive to either mental or emotional well-being. It is not surprising, therefore, that before the winter was over he suffered 'a species of breakdown.' Too few details of its nature are known to yield a precise diagnosis, but it seems to have been a combination of physical exhaustion and neurasthenic depression. Miles of walking in all weathers, late-night hours of studying (to master several theology texts on which all candidates on trial were examined each spring), to say nothing of the dietary deficiencies that were normal mid-winter concomitants of outport poverty, could not but have taken their toll of his health. A heavy cold that left him a nagging cough aggravated his condition – and prompted among his parishioners unfounded rumours of incipient consumption. But there is little doubt that the general depression of spirits he also experienced was mainly due to the prospect of what lay ahead for him in a role for which, as he often said, he was not cut out, and which so far had been, in the main, a continuing ordeal of body and spirit, but to which he felt irrevocably committed.

Wisely he decided to take leave of his post for a while, and in early April packed up his theological tomes and took a train home, 'home' being a house on Hamilton Avenue, St John's, where his mother now lived with Jim and Calvert and their younger sisters, Floss and Nellie. There his mother's familiar regimen of medicaments and her ample if hardly luxurious table, and above all a period of relaxed inactivity seemed to work wonders for him. Before long he was slowly on the mend, helped also in a different but no less vital way by visits paid him by a wise and kindly friend of the family, their minister at George Street Church, the Reverend Walter Dunn. To him Pratt confided his doubts and misgivings about his calling and his future, and Dunn, it seems, was able to help him settle his mind and shore up his faltering resolve. By early May he was more or less his old self again and ready to submit to his required theological inquisition. As it happened, Dunn was one of the examiners that year and, no doubt, was not unduly demanding. In any event Pratt easily passed the test.

His restoration to health of both body and mind seems to have been complete. The experience, nevertheless, had been an unnerving one, not only raising spectres of future lapses of resolve, but also reviving anxieties concerning his earlier physical delicacy, planting fears in his mind that (in the words of his sister Floss) 'the old idea that he wasn't long for this world might be true after all ... But he came out of it all right.' So it seems. A few days after his inquisition – held on 7 May – he returned to Clarke's Beach to complete the remaining five weeks or so of his incumbency there.

By late June he was back home again, this time to attend the annual District and Conference sessions, held that year in St John's. The extent of his recovery may perhaps be inferred from his accepting a rare but demanding honour bestowed on him by the Conference Executive: an invitation to be among the clergy chosen to preach from City pulpits during 'Conference Week.' This was an honour very rarely conferred on young probationers, one usually reserved for seasoned veterans and grave dignitaries from Canada. But that year, whether because the name still bore a lingering evangelical magic, or because young Brother Pratt had already given it a lustre of his own, the name of the Reverend E.J. Pratt appeared twice in the list of chosen preachers. Thus on the evening of 20 June he preached at Gower Street Methodist Church and on the morning of 25 June at George Street. Fanny Pratt was in both congregations and it is not hard to imagine how she felt, seeing her 'little preacher boy' (as she was to call him for years to come) fully restored to health, in his father's role, and standing where his father had often stood. (John Pratt's second posting in Newfoundland had been as an assistant minister to the old St John's Circuit, which had then included the two churches mentioned.)

Conference that year (1905) happily transferred him from Clarke's Beach to the Bell Island-Portugal Cove circuit, where he was to remain for the two years left in his probationship. It was a very welcome change for Pratt: not only was it a less demanding circuit under a healthy superintendent minister (the Reverend Anthony Hill), but Portugal Cove being only ten miles distant from St John's he was able to visit his mother and family much oftener than before. His accommodation to the ministerial life at Bell Island was, it seems, equally happy. References to 'my young colleague' by Mr Hill in his annual reports suggest that 'Bro. Pratt' left nothing to be desired as a minister. Reporting to *The Methodist Greeting* in March 1906, Hill wrote of him: 'I think it safe to say that the mantle of his sainted father has fallen on him. He is a good preacher and well liked. He is one of those who is more like "to wear out than rust out".' Hill's perception of the 'sainted father' in the son would seem to be confirmed by his being one of two evangelists invited to a rally held that month at George Street Church, St John's. The 'brethren,' we are told, 'did good service.'

Pratt's term on the Portugal Cove-Bell Island circuit was made especially agreeable by the many new, congenial friendships he formed both in the Cove and on the Island. Long afterward he continued to write old friends appreciative letters recalling pleasant times gone by. One on Bell Island whom he remembered with especial affection was a Mr Willis Pike, whom he called 'Uncle Billy,' in whose home he was an almost nightly visitor. A hearty, genial man with a wife to match (and three little girls to whom Pratt became deeply attached), Pike kept a good table at which the lean, young probationer was a frequent guest. During his penurious student days in Toronto he often recalled – with regret that they were no more – his many 'feasts' at Uncle Billy's: platters of 'mussels and pigs tongues,' and mounds of 'cabbage ... boiled in pork.' 'They don't know how to cook things like that up here' (in Toronto), he would lament. 'If you ever do get a bit of cabbage it is no good because it is not boiled in pork.' Once at Uncle Billy's there was a 'duck supper' of which, he wrote, 'I eat [sic] so much that I could hardly get home afterwards. I saw hobgoblins and ghosts all night in my sleep after it. Oh! these were good times.' So memorable were Uncle Billy's duck supper and its consequent nightmare that twenty-five years later they provided the matter for a short comic poem, 'The Pursuit,' which he published in *Many Moods* (1932).

Pratt's second year at Bell Island was the last of his probationship. Having survived his three years on trial he was then ready for his formal studies in arts and theology at an 'approved' university. But it was all too apparent to him that though his church could be counted on to pay his tuition – the normal policy – he would still need more money than he had managed to save, even to survive for one year at university. And so was born the first of many schemes by which he would try, though not to make his fortune, at least, as he used to put it, 'garner a little extra gink [ready cash].' Of them all the first was the most unusual, certainly the most unlikely for a Methodist preacher, yet not, perhaps, for one who had been a victim of illnesses medicated with many home-brewed nostrums. His scheme – not in any roguish sense – was to make and peddle a 'wonderful cure' not only for 'lung troubles but all the most diverse diseases.' The 'secret recipe' had been given him by his landlady's husband, whose father, it was alleged, had been cured of tuberculosis by 'a potion which he had manufactured out of spruce tops, wild cherry bark and the rind of fir trees plus sarsaparilla.' Since 'such a concoction was not on the market,' Pratt decided to make good the deficiency, providing his customers a humanitarian service and himself a little extra cash.

According to his own oft-repeated story, which must be discounted for imaginative embellishment, though its essential facts are independently corroborated, he brewed his lung healer himself while still on circuit at Bell Island. Discreetly going out at night under cover of dark, he gathered his herbal ingredients in a large sack. These he boiled in a bark pot (used by fishermen for barking sails or nets) – a veritable witches' cauldron – provided by his host, until he had reduced them 'to a vile concentrate.' A St John's druggist supplied him on credit several gross of four-sided bottles and a quantity of sarsaparilla. A local printer provided the labels, bearing not only the name 'Universal Lung Healer,' but directions in English, French, and Italian, to catch the eye of foreign seamen along the St John's waterfront, where his brother Calvert working as a wharfinger's helper was to act as his local agent. Pratt in later years, regaling his friends with accounts of the unlikely enterprise, which became the pièce de résistance of his reminiscences, sometimes enhanced the original formula with 'a powerful tincture of Barbados rum.' But his friend W.H. Pike (no kin to Uncle Billy), who accompanied him on his peddling expedition that summer, insisted that if the mixture contained any 'Barbados' it was 'blackstrap molasses rather than rum.' According to Pike, 'It was mostly water, though Ned at the time was quite convinced that the base was highly curative.' As a lung healer it was, of course, quite as 'useless and worthless' as one of its self-styled 'victims' described it to me in a vituperative letter written more than sixty years later. Yet no laws were broken. Pratt had often seen in the daily papers far more extravagant claims made for the medicinal properties of Winston's Balsam of Wild Cherry and Paine's Celery Compound than ever he made for his Universal Lung Healer.

As things turned out his need for any profit from the sale of his nostrum was to be much greater and more urgent than he had originally foreseen. But the background to this exigency must first be briefly sketched.

Pratt's two closest, probationary-ministerial friends during this time were W.H. (Billy) Pike, and S.H. (Sam) Soper. Former Methodist College classmates, they had been received together as candidates on trial in 1904 and had kept in touch with one another during the intervening years. (Pratt had exchanged circuits with Soper for a preaching vacation at Carmanville in the summer of 1905 and with Pike at Glovertown in 1906.) The three had already decided that when the time came they would do their advanced studies in arts and theology at Wesleyan College, an affiliate of McGill University in Montreal, rather than at Mount Allison University in Sackville, New Brunswick, or at Victoria College in Toronto, the other approved Methodist institutions. Their preference was no random vagary; strange as it may seem, it was prompted by Wesleyan's growing reputation for theological liberalism, several members of its faculty having, in fact, already been branded heretics by some of the Methodist hierarchy. Chief among these 'heretics' was George Workman, who more than a decade earlier had first brought 'higher criticism' to Canada from the University of Leipzig and had since published several 'scandalous' books on the subject. Victoria College had rid itself of him earlier and he had since been under a cloud at Wesleyan but had managed to retain his post there. Victoria had thrown open a few windows since, but still lagged far behind Wesleyan as a 'liberal' college. Mount Allison, however, remained securely in the traditional, conservative fold, being regarded, therefore, by most of the Methodist clergy, particularly in Newfoundland, as the only safe nursery for their theological neophytes.

Pratt and his two friends were well aware of the attitude of their Conference toward the new theology and Wesleyan College, and their choice may have been made, partly, as a challenge to the grey-bearded, reactionary 'panjandrums' who then ruled the Methodist Church in Newfoundland. But not, it seems, wholly for this reason. Not that any of them had yet drunk very deeply of the new heady wines of radical theology; they would soon have been 'dropped' by the Conference had they done so, or at least allowed any dram of the new distillation to taint the pure waters they must dispense from their pulpits. But it seems they were alike in their desire, to quote Pike, 'to know what was being said, to examine it for ourselves, and to be free to choose what might be shown after all to be the truth.' Of Pratt this seems to have been particularly true. To quote Soper:

Even before Ned went to university, he had developed a very inquiring mind ... Once he got the idea that the traditional theology might not have the whole truth ... he became obsessed with the desire to find out what the whole truth was ... It was natural that a man like George Workman, that radical of radicals, would have attracted him. So we made up our minds that we would go to McGill.

Conference that year met at Grand Bank in late June, but Pratt, Soper, and Pike did not attend. For one thing, they were too busy filling pulpits left vacant by the exodus to Grand Bank. (Pratt's sermon in George Street Church on the evening of 30 June, the last he was ever to preach in Newfoundland as it proved, was, ironically, an exposition of a text from St Paul: 'I have fought a good fight, I have finished my course, I have kept the faith.') As it turned out it was just as well that they had not attended Conference. Most of its sessions were devoted to a concerted assault on the 'new' theology, and as mere probationers their presence would have done little to stop the passage of a motion declaring Wesleyan College 'out of bounds to all further candidates from Newfoundland.'

The fiat was not wholly unexpected; what was, however, was an 'order' by Conference that 'Bros Pratt, Pike, and Soper shall attend Mount Allison University for their advanced studies.' This, undoubtedly, as they suspected, was a deliberate reprimand for their having already chosen Wesleyan, as well as, perhaps, an attempt to smother incipient heterodoxy in the ranks before it became rampant. But it meant that for them Victoria College was also out of bounds. 'We were incredulous,' Pike recalled. But what might they do? They decided that open rebellion was their only means of redress! They would not beard the panjandrums further by defying the express edict and betake themselves to that den of error, Wesleyan College. But neither would they be ordered to Mount Allison. Victoria College, then, it must be. It was a calculated risk: they might well be dropped forthwith, forfeiting the tuition allowances they so badly needed. But they were prepared to take the gamble.

And so, instead of Montreal, Pratt found himself facing toward Toronto. By a curious and unexpected 'convergence of the manifold,' as he later defined Fate, the whole course of his life was to be wrenched into directions he had never dreamed of following, and with consequences he could not possibly have foreseen. What his life might have been had he been permitted to follow his original plan we can only conjecture. But from what we know of him and his early experience of the ministerial life and his attitude toward it, it seems unlikely that he could ever have settled down to such a life, at least not in Newfoundland, whether or not he had gone to Montreal. What is, however, a virtual certainty is that had he not gone to Victoria College and not come under the spell of Pelham Edgar, its extraordinary professor of English literature, he would never have been a poet. A strange assertion perhaps, but subsequent chapters will show, I believe, that it is substantially true. The Methodist Church in Newfoundland by meddling with a young probationer's plans may not, perhaps, have denied the Church a great preacher, but it undoubtedly helped to give Canada one of its greatest poets.

Having chosen to defy their church, whose financial help might well now be denied them, Pike and Pratt found themselves in greater need than ever of additional funds. Soper having private means, his future was relatively secure, however Conference might adjudge their unprecedented crime. But Pike and Pratt had no recourse but to find ways of providing for themselves. Pratt already had a stock of lung healer on hand, Calvert having assisted him in the final stages. His plan had been to peddle it only along the St John's waterfront, but the new crisis impelled him to consider a wider market. So it was that when Pike secured an agency from a St John's photographer to take family portraits in Notre Dame Bay, Pratt, laden with samples of his nostrum, decided to join him. By extolling its miraculous virtues to outport retail merchants, he hoped to write enough orders (which Calvert would fill later) to reap himself at least a modest profit.

The pair set out in mid-July and it is doubtful whether a more unlikely brace of commercial travelers had ever set foot before in the Newfoundland outport. 'There we were,' to quote Pike, two Methodist preachers, one trying to persuade penniless families that they simply *had to have* family portraits done, and the other trying to convince debt-ridden shopkeepers that a stock of wonder-working medicine on their shelves would cure all their ills, both physical and financial. I felt like a crook, but Ned I think convinced himself that he was really a species of medical missionary!

Pratt at least looked the part, having raised himself a set of handsome moustaches and bought a new black suit, which he wore with a high collar, light tie, and a watch-fob and chain across his waistcoat. Beside him, Pike (to quote him) 'looked like a poor relation.'

Travelling by train to Lewisporte, they embarked on the *SS Clyde* and headed up the north side of the Bay. For six weeks they travelled from outport to outport, in and out of small bays and coves, and called at many of the island settlements which dot the ragged coastline. Pike, despite his qualms, took portraits and pocketed some orders; Pratt exhibited his wares and also wrote orders – cash in advance, as Calvert had advised him. How many orders he actually sold is not known, but the number must have been fairly substantial: he returned to St John's in September with 'well over $300' in his pocket, more than his entire salary for a year as a dispenser of the Word of God.

For the student of Pratt the writer, perhaps more important than the financial aspects of the venture – though these ensured that he would go to Toronto whether dropped by the Church or not – is a long essay which he took time off to write between calls on customers. Submitted to the St John's *Daily News* under the title 'A Northern Holiday,' it was published on 23 August to become, so far as can be discovered, his first publication.

The essay hardly signals a new luminary in the literary firmament, but it is a competent piece of amateur craftsmanship in light prose. In two distinct parts, it first describes, somewhat rhapsodically, the natural delights encountered on a voyage among the islands of Notre Dame Bay. But despite its generally effective use of language and imagery, his description is undistinguished by matter of particular interest or originality. Its second part, however, in which he moves from description to narrative, and from a mood of contemplative wonder to one of fanciful, often hyperbolic, humour, is much more lively and interesting, even perhaps prophetic of things to come. Its unlikely subject is 'the ubiquitous mosquito,' the large, northern, insatiable variety known in Newfoundland as the 'nipper.' Having painfully discovered that the inlets of Notre Dame Bay were a fertile habitat for this 'rattlesnake of Newfoundland,' Pratt proceeded to exploit the torments it may visit upon the unwary traveler as well as the latter's usually futile attempts to defend himself. To illustrate briefly, here is a portion of his closing paragraph, in which the weary combatant finally sinks 'into a deep slumber':

At 12 o'clock or so a mysterious sensation gradually rouses you to a dim consciousness that your blood supply is running rather short, and the first thing that strikes your awakening senses is that ominous buzz, revealing the terrifying fact that the enemy is in possession of the fort. For an hour or so that noise will continue around your ear, approaching and receding, making your nocturnal condition considerably worse than that of Tantalus in your frenzy to 'get at 'em.' Then when one finally settles on the face your hand comes round like a twelve inch shell and thunders down on the bitten spot with a fiery force which a trained pugilist would envy, and then you strike up the first chord of the Dead March in Saul in honor of the passing of a blood relation.

It is all a bit of gratuitous fun, but Pratt's relish for it is very evident, as is also a natural flair for exploiting the comic possibilities of both language and event (even more apparent in several further similar ventures in prose to be looked at shortly), suggesting that perhaps poet Pratt was, after all, a Leacock manqué.

Back in St John's by early September, Pratt could now prepare for his journey to Canada, leaving his patent medicine days behind him for good. Calvert would have many orders to fill, but stocks were already on hand. It was Pike's recollection that the brothers had 'laid in more than six gross one-pint bottles of the stuff.' What Calvert had not foreseen was that he would also have complaints from irate customers, mostly retail merchants, who found that the bottles broke with the onset of frost. ('It was mostly water.') Whether complaints about its medicinal shortcomings also came to him is not known. But not all who credulously bought the nostrum were prepared to laugh off its many unfulfilled promises. Unlikely as it may seem there were living as late as the latter 1960s Newfoundlanders (a people clearly as notable for length of memory as of days), who still recalled Ned and Cal Pratt as 'unscrupulous young men,' who, capitalizing on the almost endemic prevalence of tuberculosis on the Island, 'planned a hellish scheme' to put themselves on the road to success. More than sixty years after the event, one 'victim,' whose young brother had died despite his parents' investment in the cure, wrote bitterly in a letter to me: 'Young Pratt was ambitious – nothing this side of Hell would stop him in his upward climb ... The so-called cure was bought by distressed, anguished parents, and so young Pratt went on to university and on to fame on the death rattles of my kit [sic] and kin ...' Strong words! But it is doubtful that Pratt ever knew that such callous offences had been laid to his charge, or even dreamed that anyone might have reason to do so. Once questioned on the point, he denied that he had ever received any complaints. But when he was far away in Toronto there was little anyone could do.

Unaware, then, of any rumblings, Pratt and his two friends – Soper had joined him and Pike at St John's – set their sights on Victoria College. On 18 September, their worldly treasure strapped round their waists (characteristically alive to dramatic potentialities, Pratt had insisted that 'as a precaution against thievery' their funds be converted into gold specie and sewn into stout canvas money-belts) 'the three rebels,' at a cost of $30 each for a 'saloon passage,' embarked on the SS *Bonavista* for Montreal.

It would be many years before Pratt saw again the Atlantic or the rockbound shores of Newfoundland. As if conscious of the historic parting and determined to make it a memorable one, the elements before nightfall erupted in the most violent storm to assault the battered Island in many years – 'the Great September Gale of Nineteen-Seven.' No part of Newfoundland escaped and several ships were lost with all their crews. Fortunately the *Bonavista* had passed 'the weltering tide-rips off Cape Race' before the full fury broke, but the voyage that night and next day was an ordeal of seasickness and tempest which did not end until the old ship finally punched her way into the calmer waters of the Gulf of St Lawrence. It was Pratt's first encounter on shipboard with a genuine Atlantic hurricane and he never forgot it. Twenty years later in *The Roosevelt and the Antinoe* he recreated it with all the detail and immediacy of a recent first-hand experience. (It may well have been recalled, less successfully, ten years earlier in *Rachel* – not only the storm, but the widowed mother sitting anxiously at home [ll. 428-78].)

Their discomfort was soon forgotten in the excitement aroused by the new vistas which constantly opened before them as the ship moved up the river toward Quebec. To quote Pike:

Ned was enraptured by all he saw. He had never been out of Newfoundland before, so that everything was new and fascinating ... I remember that as we hove in sight of Quebec City and neared the steep cliffs on which were the historic 'plains' [of Abraham], he crept carefully out on the bowsprit as far as he could safely get, searching the cliff for the famous path up which Wolfe had climbed ... That was typical of Ned. The first sight of something new and stirring transfixed him. He'd gaze at it with intense concentration, letting the feelings it aroused sink into his memory and its image stamp itself on his mind. But, oddly enough, a second view was usually unnecessary – superfluous – for him. Once he had it, I think it was his forever. He didn't need a second look!

Pike is right. This was a trait of Pratt's often remarked on by others. One good look at Niagara Falls, the Rocky mountains, a prairie sun-set, was all he needed to have them forever. His visual memory seems to have been highly developed and very efficient.

The trio's memorable voyage ended next day at Montreal, where they took a train for Toronto. Thus came E.J. Pratt to the city where he was to make his home for the rest of his life.

    ... your sergeant-major Fate
    Will catch you ...

BOOK II: THE WANDERING SCHOLAR
1907–16

... Perambulated ... through prisms ...

7

Undergraduate of Victoria College

When Ned came ... to Toronto to attend University he was lean, gangling
and different. His speech had what seemed an Irish lilt in it. He was both
more innocent and far shrewder than the typical undergraduate of those
days; he was another of 'those queer Newfoundlanders' ...

A.L. Phelps, *Canadian Writers*, 1951

HE 'QUEER NEWFOUNDLANDER' just cast ashore in Toronto may have been somewhat a fish out of water, but not,
it seems, for very long. In the words of his fellow 'queer'
expatriate, W.H. Pike, 'Ned quickly fell in love with
Toronto – and never fell out!' With a population then of a quarter
million, Toronto was hardly the metropolis it is today. Yet compared
with St John's, one-tenth its size, parochial and insular despite its
cosmopolitan airs, the Queen City with its teeming, heterogeneous
life, its forest of great buildings, spires, and chimneys, its parks and
theatres, and omnifarious shops, was to him 'like a dream come true.'

Victoria College having no residence for men, the 'three rebels'
(dubbed thus in Methodist Conference circles at home) decided to take
digs together, and looked for a suitable rooming-house close by. They
shortly found one on St George Street near University College, where
they installed themselves, in reasonable comfort though hardly luxury, in two small bed-and-breakfast rooms. Soper, who could afford
it, took one room to himself, Pike and Pratt shared the other, but as
'blood brothers – figuratively speaking' (to quote Pike), as well as
'brothers in Christ,' they lived as a single ménage. Breakfast being
provided, they ate dinner, always at noon, in a small restaurant

nearby, where ten meal tickets could be had for three dollars. Gas jets in their rooms enabled them to prepare a light supper at home, as well as that most necessary of repasts to a Newfoundlander, a hot 'mug-up' at bedtime. 'We have everything like that here,' Pratt wrote Uncle Billy Pike, but 'OH for a roast duck or a dish of pigs tongues.' In the days ahead he often longed for outport delicacies now no more. 'They don't know how to cook things like that up here in Toronto.' But 'they' could be forgiven, 'as I can get all the fruit I want at a low cost.' Toronto's ignorance of Newfoundland's cuisine seems, however, to have been its only failing in his eyes, and as time went on the queer Newfoundlander became reconciled to alien viands besides fruit – the latter always a treat to one who had seen oranges only at Christmas. In the following year they moved to somewhat larger quarters on Czar Street (later renamed Charles Street West) adjacent to Victoria College, where they conducted their ménage much as before.

Soon after the trio had settled in for their first term they had written the Newfoundland Conference to confess their rebellion, adding a prayer that they be forgiven and their tuition allowance paid in the customary fashion. But many weeks passed without a reply. Accounts fell due, then overdue, and the Dean threatened summary expulsion. Just when they had reconciled themselves to the dreadful necessity of calling on their Yonge Street banker, before whose astonished eyes they had earlier emptied their laden money-belts (he had 'bitten each gold-piece to make sure it was real'), the long-awaited letters arrived. The Conference, having adjudicated the 'unprecedented case' at great length, had reluctantly forgiven them, at least to the extent that their fees shortly would be paid. They were much relieved, but the prospect of returning to the work of the Methodist Church in Newfoundland had already become 'exceedingly distasteful.' None of them, in fact, was ever to return to Newfoundland, except to visit. But though they would still have to snatch at every pecuniary morsel that turned up, tuition fees assured and financial pressures to that extent relieved, they could now settle down to the full enjoyment of university life.

From the start of his university studies Pratt was clearly, in Soper's phrase, an 'unusual student.' Reminiscing about his freshman days, Pratt once said that, ignorant and naïve, 'knowing nothing about the big, bad world' other than the price of fish, he had 'come up to the College with knees trembling.' He was, of course, engaging in fanciful leg-pulling, what he sometimes called 'codology'; he was far more cognizant of the world than his whimsey implied. Any tremors he may have experienced were rather those of expectation and excitement than of apprehension. 'I am sure,' S.H. Soper declared, 'no one ever embarked on university studies with higher hopes and greater expectations than Ned did.' He went on to describe Pratt as a student thus:

He was probably the most brilliant, certainly the most unusual, student of his time at Victoria. He had, at the outset at least, the almost naive conviction that his courses would open doors not only to knowledge – facts, data, enlightenment – but to *truth*. I think it can be said that Ned Pratt set out on a kind of *quest*, which had as its goal nothing less than Truth – with a capital T! He'd already come to doubt whether his father's Methodist faith had all the answers to the 'ultimate questions.' And he wanted to know the answers. He was almost obsessed with this. I am sure he realized that the truth might turn out to be a rather bleak affair, but that didn't deter him. He believed you *must find the truth*; if you sweat mental agony to find it, it is still worth the pains ... Many thought him a strange student, especially for a theologue – and I suppose he was!

A strange student, especially for a theologue! Many of his classmates before very long were, in fact, calling him 'sceptic if not agnostic,' some of them wondering aloud 'how heretic Pratt made out with his Sunday sermons.' (He found it necessary, almost from the beginning, to do supply preaching for small fees whenever the opportunity arose, usually on small rural circuits near Toronto, and continued to do for many years.) But though no sermon from his student days is extant, the evidence of former parishioners on the circuits he served and of fellow theologues who knew him best suggests that his preaching was as traditional and orthodox as his 'sainted father' could have wished. Whatever he himself may or may not have believed, he seems to have had no desire to unsettle his rural congregations. It is doubtful whether during his student days, if at all, he was ever actually either a sceptic or an agnostic in any usually accepted sense of the words. The term humanist, admittedly vague, probably comes closest to describing him then, for what he sought and hoped to find in his university courses was that spirit of free enquiry which usually characterizes the

humanist's approach to truth. Inevitably he was to know disappointment and disillusionment. Yet seeing himself as venturing on a quest
for Truth was doubtless an admirable, if to some of his fellow students a strange, attitude of mind in which to embark on his university
studies.

He had little choice of courses in his first year. Disregarding his
London Matriculation Diploma, for which he had expected to receive
advanced standing, the College made him complete the usual freshman curriculum. But he seems to have lodged no protest. Writing to
Uncle Billy, he declared, 'I am very fond of the work. I am taking an
Arts course and like it immensely.' He came through with A standing
in all subjects but mathematics.

His second year saw him initiated at last into the disciplines he had
expected to be his chief doors to Truth: philosophy and theology. But
it was soon apparent to him that his theology courses at least, most of
them given by conservative 'old-time professors,' were unlikely to
offer him anything very new or profound. That he did not, to quote
Soper, 'quit Theology in spite of his family commitments,' was because among his professors he found one 'of a very different intellectual breed from the others.' This was George Blewett, a young Canadian scholar, appointed to Victoria's Chair of Ethics and Apologetics
in 1906. Blewett's 'excitingly unorthodox approach to age-old problems' did not cause Pratt to revise his general opinion of theology at
Victoria, but it soon showed him that even in that discipline there
might be avenues to Truth which he had never dreamed of exploring.
Apart from Pelham Edgar, whom Pratt was not to encounter in the
classroom until his last undergraduate year, George Blewett, for good
or ill and despite the relative brevity of their association (he drowned
in 1912), was probably to have a more important influence on Pratt
and his subsequent history than any other of his university teachers.

As a student at Victoria in the 1890s Blewett had taken an honours
degree in philosophy, which in those days, as for several decades to
come, also embraced psychology. And this branch of the discipline
had become his primary interest and specialization, in particular the
then 'new' psychology: the scientific, experimental, laboratory-con-
trolled investigation of mind and mental events fathered at the University of Leipzig in the 1870s by Wilhelm Wundt. It had been intro-

duced to the Department of Philosophy at Toronto in the following decade and by the mid-1890s was well established there as one of the major 'schools' of psychology, supported by an extensive program of study and research, well-equipped laboratories, and the energetic direction of August Kirschmann, former student and colleague of Wundt.

No detailed exposition of Wundtian psychology can, of course, be given here, but because of its importance for Blewett and in time for Pratt, at least a glance at its main features is probably necessary. Briefly stated, what Wundt had done was to bring the scientific methods and experimental techniques of the physical sciences to the analysis of the contents of consciousness; in other words, to shift the context of psychological study and research from the orbit of philosophical, speculative studies to that of scientific, empirical experimentation and analysis. The task of the psychologist as Wundt and his school saw it was to isolate and identify the simple elements out of which the compounds of consciousness are constructed, and to discover the laws by which both the elements are compounded and the compounds integrated to form structured, unified wholes. Once this was done it was possible to account for, predict, and even manipulate all mental events, including the so-called 'higher' mental activities such as those involved in moral and aesthetic judgments. It also, of course, reduced all psychic activity to physical elements and largely mechanical processes. As we shall see, it was, partly at least, Pratt's gradual recognition of the full import of the mechanistic implications of Wundt's system that eventually led to his defection from psychology.

For Blewett, who seems to have overlooked the implicit mechanism of the new psychology, its chief attraction – as it was to be for Pratt initially – was that it offered the possibility of a fruitful marriage between science and the humanities, religion in particular. As a recent commentator on Blewett writes:

[He] saw the analysis of a person's faith-consciousness as an extension of the science of mind ... Already an evolutionist ... he maintained that there is a continuity between the enterprise of science and the vision of faith. The search for truth is a quest for the *unities* that underlie apparent diversity – and he believed that science and religion were only *apparently* diverse ... that an understanding of nature is preliminary to but not different in kind from an understanding of the human mind and ... of God. The physical sciences, psychology, and theology form a continuum.

A convert to the new psychology, but a man with a religious mission, Blewett had gone on to graduate studies in Wundtian psychology, as well as in philosophy and theology, first at Wurtzburg, then at Harvard, Oxford, and Berlin. When he returned to Victoria at the age of thirty-three, he already had an international reputation for original, even revolutionary, scholarship – as well as a passion to convert to his new gospel all who sat at his feet.

Pratt, already a convert to 'the enterprise of science' and dubious about the traditional theology of the old-time professors, was fertile ground for the new seed. The notion of a union between science and religion he found especially attractive. It was thus not long after his first encounter with Blewett in the classroom (September 1908) that, to quote S.H. Soper, 'Ned was caught by Dr Blewett's excitingly unorthodox approach to age-old problems of ethics and faith.' Before the academic year was out Pratt was quite convinced that the most promising way to the truth he sought was George Blewett's way. His registering that autumn in the honours philosophy program, with psychology as his special area, was an expression of that conviction in practical terms.

Pratt's faith in the Faculty of Theology, restored somewhat by his work with Blewett, was shortly reinforced by a contentious appointment to a newly-created Chair of English Bible. The appointee was George Jackson, a liberal Scottish theologian who had served for a time, most of it in the midst of controversy, as minister of Sherbourne Street Methodist Church in Toronto. (That Blewett's appointment had caused little stir was due, it seems, to his being Canadian and, more important, to his not being known as a 'Higher Critic' of the Bible.) Not surprisingly, the conflict which for weeks swirled round Jackson's appointment, dividing not only the College Board but the Methodist establishment itself, 'delighted and exhilarated' Pratt and his two fellow rebels. In a smaller arena they had already pitted themselves against the same reactionary antagonist and fought to a not unsatisfactory draw. Now the battle was joined by weightier forces in a larger field and with a much larger issue at stake: 'For us,' to quote Soper, 'especially for Ned, it was Truth itself on the scaffold.' As members of a controversial Bible class Jackson had conducted at Sherbourne Street, they knew their man and joined his party from the start, none, it seems, more enthusiastically than Pratt. But there was little they could do on their own to support Jackson's cause. When, however, at a conclave of theology students, many others of like mind hoisted his colours, student opinion soon became an important element in the affray, and may well have helped to determine the outcome. Pratt expressed his approval by promptly enrolling in Jackson's course. But it is probably true that few of his 'radical interpretations of Genesis, the concepts of myth and allegory he applied to the Bible, and the many other "modern" approaches he took to the Scriptures,' were startlingly new to Pratt. In the words of Soper, 'Ned had already groped his way to many of these conceptions himself.' What was new and exciting to him was to have found someone who formulated them in a cogent and convincing manner and offered them as valid ways of reading the Bible and of approaching religion in general.

But most of his other theology courses – apart from Blewett's – seem to have had little or no attraction for Pratt. Often he simply cut classes, swatting up the syllabus from Pike's or Soper's notes, or showing up in class to sleep through lectures that bored him. Psychology was a different matter. It is true that he often found 'exciting ... stimulating, and soul-searching' his more traditional courses in philosophy, which seem to have covered almost everything from the Greek philosophers down to the contemporary, including 'huge doses of Thomas Hill Green's Idealism' and Bergson's 'Creative Evolution,' given, he wrote, as 'the "antidote" to Darwin's naturalism, though the serum worked on some of us and not on others.' Nevertheless, 'it was Psychology with its emphasis on experience – Wundt, James, and others ... that most impressed me in undergraduate days.' As he later diagnosed himself, 'It seemed to me then that the new Psychology, the new science of human nature, was the only genuine and certain road to the truth about man ... I was very naive.'

In time his naïveté would be fully revealed to him, as he came to realize that the empirical-experimental methods of Wundt and his school's science of physio-psychology were no more productive of the answers and solutions he sought than were those of pure abstract reason. But the revelation did not come overnight, and for many years he wrestled with concepts and theories that grew less and less congenial. Yet his quest, which became a search for himself and the goals of his life, took him through the time-and-energy-devouring processes of four university degrees and into years of desultory, self-defeating labours, personal anxieties and frustrations, continuing poverty, and increasing dissatisfaction with both the results of his quest and the direction of his life. It was, partly at least, his failure to find what he sought in the rationalistic and scientific academic disciplines to which he had given himself that sent him back to the humane insights and imaginative illuminations of literature, of poetry especially, to find at last a satisfying anchorage. Afterward he looked back on the decade 1910–20 with almost the same chagrin as he did on his three lost years in Sclater's shop. His long peregrination meant that by the time he had found himself, and his destiny, Pratt was nearly forty years of age.

After a mostly anonymous and sequestered but busy first year, his academic successes in the spring of 1908 brought him a degree of notice beyond the immediate circle of his special friends. In October that year he accepted his first public role at Victoria: treasurer to the 'Bob' Committee. As such he had his picture in the undergraduate journal, *Acta Victoriana*: a sober-looking young man in high collar, white waistcoat, and white tie. The annual Bob was an institution peculiar to the College. It had been started in 1874 as a Christmas benefit for a much-loved janitor, Robert Beare (hence its name), and had grown from its original conception into a public occasion for lively entertainment and high jinks, the only officially sanctioned frivolity at staid Victoria. In the following year Pratt also assisted the Committee in writing scripts for its farcical skits, in some of which he caricatured certain professors of theology, and played several parts on stage.

Literary farce and frivolity having caught his fancy that year, he wrote and published in *Acta* (May 1909) a long farcical extravaganza in verse. Entitled 'A Poem on the May Examinations,' it is his first 'poem' of which we have any actual knowledge, but it can hardly be seen as marking the dawn of a poetic career. A single shot in the pre-dawn darkness, it was not followed by another until five years later; even then the darkness will be barely touched with a dim illumination. This was not a serious attempt to write poetry, or even verse; merely some high jinks in metre dashed off as a joke on himself and his classmates, very much in the spirit of the Bob, which undoubtedly prompted it. But it is worth looking at briefly.

Consisting of twenty-five heptameter quatrains, it is a bit of mildly satiric doggerel describing the carnage wrought by examinees upon the various subjects of instruction in the annual Armageddon known as the 'Finals.' The metre is often rough, though never (I think) resistant to scansion, and lines are sometimes hard to read with any sense of rhythm. The humour is often strained, the language generally prosy, almost completely devoid of metaphor and similar poetic figures. Once only is there a metaphor which anyone knowing the later Pratt might spot as possibly Prattian: a reference to history as 'tempered well / In a millenium's furnace ...'

And yet, interestingly, there are intimations here of the later poet – the comic, ebullient, irreverent poet of *The Witches' Brew*, for example. That poem would certainly seem to be foreshadowed by one of this 'poem's' chief devices: the incongruous juxtaposition and ironic distortion of historical worthies: Alexander fighting 'Spanish rebels' and driving 'old Caesar's veterans from the frontier'; the 'fiery Plato' managing to stay sober until Carthage has outlasted Rome'; 'the noble Phidias' hanged for his verses along with his cousin Xenophon, the victor of Marathon; and other travesties of history. *The Great Feud* too may be seen looming ahead: the early poem is, after all, a kind of 'dream of Armageddon,' characterized by a certain hyperbolic whimsicality, crude though it may sometimes be. It is, moreover, a very spirited 'truant' who in the last half-dozen stanzas delivers a perhaps not unjustified assault upon a panjandrum whom theologues had yearned to dethrone for generations: 'notorious Hebrew,' prerequisite to all diplomas in theology. Here, to illustrate briefly, are a few lines from the closing scene as the detested victim is dragged to his doom:

Dire was the punishment imposed for conduct mean and base,
Beghadkhephaths and Degheshes were thrown right in his face,
Around his neck the Athnak yoke was tied secure and fast,
The paper with the crimes were read before he breathed his last.

No tear was shed, no sigh was raised, save only of relief;
No pitying theologue gazed on with tear-stained handkerchief,
No groans came forth, but from the prisoner crouching in full dread
As Pe Nun verbs and gutturals were aimed straight at his head ...

Across the scene let fall the curtain, spare the cultured eye ...

It is good advice. After all, this was hardly a serious attempt to write poetry. And yet, there is *something* about it –

Notwithstanding the farcical character of his first 'poetic' effort, Pratt's literary talents were soon recognized by his fellow students, who that year appointed him one of *Acta*'s two 'Locals' editors, responsible for campus news. In the following year (1910) he was elevated to the post of Literary Editor and 'Class Prophet.' Another photograph of him that year as an *Acta* editor shows a thin-faced, thin-lipped, unsmiling, intense, ascetic-looking young man, still fortified by a high collar, white waistcoat, and tie.

Also that year, in October, Pratt's second formal prose essay was published in *Acta*. (His first appeared in 1907 in the St John's *Daily News*.) Entitled 'A Western Experience,' this was a narrative essay recounting, faithfully on the whole, some of the adventures of his first summer (1908) as a student minister in Saskatchewan (to be described with quotation from the essay in the next chapter). A light-hearted, somewhat hyperbolical tale, again with many Leacockian touches, it shows that the flair for both the narrative form and the comic exploitation of language exhibited in the earlier essay was no passing whim. Compared with his recent poem it is a far more accomplished work, suggesting that his literary future might well have turned with equal success in the direction of prose.

He was at last beginning to master what Soper called 'Ned's congenital weakness of the gut,' by which he meant mainly the qualms with which in those days Pratt usually faced a public audience. Haunted by it, whatever its origin, he had characteristically set about schooling himself to master it, much as he had done as a boy to change the image of a weakling, if not a coward, into that of a daring swimmer and diver. A certain boldness of presence, besides, was a sine qua non for a crusader 'on the ramparts of sin,' to use a phrase of his father's. His years of teaching and preaching had helped a little, but it would be many years before he did not shy from 'throwing himself to the public wolves.' To the end of his days, in fact, he never contemplated a performance in public, not even a reading of his poetry, without moments of at least mild trepidation. In small groups of close friends on the other hand, he was usually the focal figure, whether of serious debate or of light-hearted amusement, uninhibited and (one must believe) at ease, though even there he preferred playing a role to appearing wholly in his own person. Taking to the boards as he did at the 1909 Bob must have demanded a kind of grim determination not very different from the forced bravery that had impelled him up a schooner's rigging to dive, even as it terrified him, into the frigid waters of Fortune harbour.

So also did his going out for public speaking and debating, as in the autumn of 1909. It was a logical choice of weapons. For all his diffidence toward mounting the podium, he was already a very good speaker, fluent, articulate, having good voice quality and production, and using the language carefully and effectively. He had wholly escaped the inhibiting legacy of an excessively outlandish outport tongue. His years in St John's and the influence of his mother's brogue-ish St John's speech had given him a mild infusion of that city's quasi-Irish accents, what a friend of his undergraduate years recalled as an 'Irish lilt,' which he was never to lose completely nor try to lose. (He sometimes pretended to be of Irish extraction.) But the influence of his father's moderately educated British tongue and his strict surveillance of his children's every utterance had saved him from the worst of the old outport's speech habits – miscellaneous mutilations, slurrings, illiteracies, and other barbarisms – which in those days of extreme outport isolation and endemic illiteracy often made the outporter at large a breed apart. What colourful 'Newfoundlandisms' (as distinct from barbarisms) characterized Pratt's vocabulary he took pride in and used whenever he could. If it is true that speech shows the man, he had no reason to fear lest he appear badly. Yet, according to Pike (and Soper agreed), 'every oratory or debating contest of Ned's that year was preceded by a spell of pure funk ... But in the end he would go and do it all the same' – and, in the opinion of his critics it seems, do it very well. In the contests held at the end of the autumn term, he carried off the Union Prize for oratory (*Acta* reported it as 'one of the best contests held for some time, and the winning speech was ... excellent'), and in the following year was one of the two debaters chosen to carry Victoria's standard into battle against McMaster University in the debating finals. Pratt and his co-debater did not win the coveted shield, but one feels sure that he won what was of more value and satisfaction to him.

His diffidence toward public exposure did not affect his cultivation of new friends, except to make his need of them all the greater. Pike and Soper were, of course, his most intimate companions during his early years at Victoria College. But Pratt while remaining loyal to them was not content to limit his circle of friends to fellow islanders. Having acquired few if any of the common traits of an insular personality, which often hinder an easy rapport with outsiders, he was not at a disadvantage often experienced by many of his outport compatriots. In a small group, even of relative strangers, he was, besides, characteristically extroverted, good-humoured, conversable, even a bit garrulous, fond of innocent jokes and (usually) hyperbolic stories. So it was that almost from his arrival at Victoria, with nothing to hinder and much to favour the process, his circle of friends – rather, perhaps, of friendly acquaintances – began to grow. His actual, authentic friends – close, familiar, brotherly – were always very few, limited to those only with whom he felt a particularly strong psychic affinity, with whom, to quote Pike, 'he could feel at ease and at home.' He was very adroit at shucking off – tactfully – any to whom he felt no especial attraction; it was an art he never lost, would, indeed, perfect as the years passed.

As an undergraduate he acquired many friendly acquaintances, some more intimate than others. His class biography (in the University Yearbook) later declared: 'His friends are legion.' But scarcely any were ever surrogate brothers. Fred Hetherington of St Catharines, Clarke Locke and Leopold Macaulay of Toronto, John Line, another Newfoundland theologue though British-born (later a professor of theology at Victoria College) to name a few, were all good friends and were to remain so for many years. But other than Will Pike and Sam Soper, only one of his undergraduate classmates seems to have been admitted to the inner circle, but he was to remain there for more than half a century. This was Arthur Phelps, Ontario-born but another Methodist student minister and a son of the Methodist manse. Destined, like Pratt, to flee the preacher's pulpit for the professor's

podium and the poet's bays, he was for many years to play as important a part in Pratt's life as any friend he ever made. (William Arthur
Deacon, a student at the College during Pratt's first two years there,
and a prominent friend of sorts at a later time, was never more than a
casual acquaintance then.)

While these friendships and acquaintanceships – all of them male –
were important to Pratt, for a period of several years even more
important, though hitherto virtually absent from the records of his
life, was a different kind of relationship which probably began during
his second undergraduate year. Typically reticent about whatever
touched his innermost feelings, he rarely spoke of Lydia Ella Trimble
in later years, burying the bittersweet memory of his first real love for
a woman (other than his mother) in some recess of his being which he
opened to no other eyes – like the strongbox of personal treasures he
kept beneath his bed for years. But there is no doubt that the experience was profound, and its effects lasting, especially of her sudden,
tragic death four days before she was to have graduated in 1912. Pratt
had had several girlfriends during his adolescence in Newfoundland,
but nothing had come of these friendships. He fell genuinely in love
with Lydia Trimble.

She had been born near Essex, Ontario, but had moved with her
family to Red Deer, Alberta, whence she had come to Victoria College in 1908. She was only eighteen – eight years younger than
Pratt – and a beautiful girl, as her portraits show and people I talked
with who had known her affirmed, popular with her classmates, who
elected her to several high student offices, and not a few of whom
among the men fell in love with her at first sight. But it was the 'lean,
gangling, different' student from Newfoundland (as Phelps described
him) whose attentions she returned with equal affection.

How soon it was after she came to the College that Pratt began to
keep her company is uncertain. Both Pike and Soper believed that it
was during her first year there, probably in the winter of 1909, when
they were living with Pratt on Czar Street near Annesley Hall (the
women's residence at Victoria) where she lodged. It is also uncertain
when they were engaged to be married, though it is known that they
were. (Except with 'special permission' of the Newfoundland Methodist Conference Pratt could not marry until he had been ordained.) It
was, clearly, no brief or shallow infatuation. Yet though it went on for

at least three years, not a great deal can be told about the romance, for very little about it was every recorded or, it seems, recalled in conversation. Not only was Pratt himself virtually silent on the subject in later years; his friends too who had known about it and its tragic ending did not revive the subject while he lived. During the lengthy session I had with him, much of it on his early life and student years, he made no mention of Lydia Trimble, and not having heard of her then, I asked no questions. Pike, Soper, and Phelps remembered her well and Pratt's 'absolute enchantment' with her, but their recollections were mostly general ones: of his taking her to concerts at Massey Hall, sometimes to church at Sherbourne Street (perhaps to hear George Jackson), on occasional outings to 'the Island' (in Toronto harbour), and of their strolling hand in hand under the trees in Queen's Park – the normal mating rituals of students in love in those tranquil times. Only the following anecdotal vignette by Will Pike provides a slightly more intimate and (one can readily imagine) not untypical glimpse of Pratt in love:

I don't think Ned had ever been in love before, but he was absolutely enchanted with Lydia. And no one could blame him. She was a beautiful child – fresh complexion, natural, innocent-looking, and a lovely disposition to go with her looks ... During the last year I was there with him – I left in 1910 – they were almost inseparable. At times I used to wonder if he wasn't seeing too much of her for his own good – and her's – because they both had heavy courses, and Ned was doing various jobs, to earn a little cash, besides. But for the strict curfew at Annesley, he probably wouldn't have kept up [with his studies] ... I remember many little incidents about them, but this one I'll relate, because it was so like Ned, when he got absorbed in conversation and lost all track of time and his surroundings. One night when he was out with Lydia he didn't come home at the usual time. Sam and I waited up for him a while, and finally turned in without him. About two a.m. or maybe later, we were awakened by Ned just getting in. His boots were all muddy and his clothes were a bit of a mess. 'What happened?' I asked, 'Where've you been?' 'Got lost,' said Ned. He never did have any sense of direction and often got lost in Toronto even in daylight. 'Where?' I asked him. 'Well,' he said, a bit sheepishly, 'Lydia and I went down in the Don [River] Valley and couldn't find our way out. We were lost, just rambling around, for hours. But for Lydia we'd probably be there yet!' Sam and I couldn't help laughing.

But Ned was very worried, because Lydia had missed curfew and was probably on the carpet. But it was all his fault, he said ... That was so very like Ned Pratt! There is no doubt that they were very much in love, and would have got married if things had turned out differently ... It was very sad.

It was clearly a strong and serious attachment, one that, I think, both broadened and deepened – and darkened perhaps – the view of life which Pratt brought to his work as poet.

The conclusion of this tragic-romantic episode will be told in due course. But another very different kind of relationship, of which at least the seeds were sown during this time, must detain us now. For although it was not to grow into a full-blown friendship for some years to come, it was to be the most important Pratt ever formed. This was with Pelham Edgar, Victoria's already celebrated Professor of English.

Because Edgar taught only French during Pratt's first two years at Victoria and was on leave in 1909–10, it was not until his last undergraduate year that he was able to take classes from 'the Great Cham of Vic.' But though Pratt would long remember his first lecture from Edgar – 'It is engraven on the tablets,' he would declare, though his recollection of its alleged subject underwent several changes with the passage of time – he was not 'to know Dr Edgar *personally* until after graduation.' Nor would Edgar himself remember the young Newfoundland theologue among his host of virtually anonymous students that term. 'When I really knew him first,' Edgar recalled long after, 'he was attached to the psychology staff in the University of Toronto.' Yet even before Pratt's memorable first lecture from Edgar, the man himself, an exotic figure glimpsed from afar, an original personality conjured up in his imagination by innumerable tales and anecdotes in constant circulation, had already become for Pratt an object of admiring curiosity if not of secret hero-worship.

Though still in his thirties and only a few years at Victoria, Edgar was already a species of legendary figure both within and without the University. Unlike most of his colleagues at Methodist Victoria, he was not a non-conformist, nor was he either a son of the rural working class who had dragged himself up by brains and hard work or the scion of some Toronto cleric – graduate in any case of Victoria – as the typical Methodist don at the College in those days usually was.

Besides being High Anglican (Pratt once described him whimsically as a 'Pagan, or, what is the same thing, a High Anglican'), he was also, for a Canadian, 'high-born,' a son of Sir James Edgar, prominent member of the Ontario Bar, politician, sometime Speaker of the House of Commons, and his wife, the daughter of an old and aristocratic Toronto family, authors both and historians of note. Born to wealth, gentility, social prestige, and the tastes and graces that usually go with them; accustomed from youth to move among the haut monde of Toronto and Ottawa, to dress, dine, and talk in their style; knowing his way about the exclusive clubs and drawing-rooms of both cities as well as he did his father's wine-cellar and library; educated at Upper Canada College, University College (Toronto), and Johns Hopkins, he was in origin, breeding, and background as unlike the usual Victoria College appointee – plebian, teetotal, puritan – as one could possibly imagine, in many ways a swan among ducklings if not a Triton among minnows. His appearance suited his patrician background. Tall, slim, erect, with fine features, fresh complexion, a dark mane of hair and large moustache, carefully and modishly dressed, he might be seen (in Pratt's undergraduate days at least) striding down from his home on Elgin Street, swinging his cane, and leading his inseparable terrier on a leash to be tethered to his desk while he lectured. His lecturing pose, paraphernalia, and eccentricities were already legendary when Pratt arrived at the College. As he later wrote:

We had heard that there were preliminaries indispensable to his lectures, his cap and gown and his reading stand; that he had a way of wrapping himself around the lectern when he was reciting which resulted in a disastrous sartorial disarray, and that no matter what the subject of the lecture was he always concluded by reciting Shelley's Ode to the West Wind ... My interest in the first ten minutes [of the lecture] was taken up altogether in watching his wrestling bout with the lectern ... At the end of the hour I heard for the first time adequately intoned 'O wild West Wind, Thou breath of autumn's being.' It had such an effect on the class that any one of us might have looked out from the window of Room 19 and seen not Queen's Park but a storm on the Mediterranean.

Elsewhere Pratt wrote:

He had a method of interpretation peculiar to himself. He assumed, without affectation, the idiosyncrasies of the writer he was expounding, passing from Wordsworth, through Shelley and Keats, to Tennyson, Browning and Arnold ... Next to Shelley I should say it was Arnold who taught him his basic cadences. In fact it was very easy for Pelham Edgar to don the Victorian apparel and speak in the grand manner with its high seriousness and subdued melancholy.

To this, B.K. Sandwell, another longtime friend of both Edgar and Pratt, added the following:

The justness of [Pratt's] observation will be at once apparent to those who recall the tall, austere, and aloof figure which he presented in any gathering where he was not inclined to relax – a figure which was far too magnificent to give any suggestion that here was a man who could be the life and soul of a not-too-large poker party composed of the kind of people he liked ...

As Sandwell suggests, with the passing years Edgar mellowed, relaxing considerably his patrician austerity and reserve, but retaining a certain aura of 'magnificence' and distinction which set him apart from Pratt's other friends and colleagues.

No one in Pratt's previous experience had presented in the flesh either an original personality like his or an image of a kind of life and world that he had hitherto only read or dreamed of. And while the personality fascinated him, there seems little doubt that, at the beginning at least, it was the life-style and the social and cultural world that Edgar symbolized which had the strongest attraction for Pratt. To quote Arthur Phelps, who witnessed the attraction and watched the early friendship grow,

Ned's eyes would shine with a faraway light when he talked about Dr Edgar in those early days. But it was not merely his teaching, though he gloried in Edgar's classes. To Ned he was, even then, a sort of *beau ideal* of the 'good' life in this world. And it is easy to understand why. He was erudite, but in an easy, unpompous way, a true gentleman-scholar. And he had class and style, a bit of the cultured aristocrat about him, but an aristocrat of the imagination and intellect as well as other things. And besides he was in those days, by academic standards, fairly well off, so that he could afford a bit of style and luxury in his life. Ned saw all that and he *loved* it, and wanted it himself. The instinct was in his nature really – and, of course, it didn't jibe with Methodist holy orders ... Pelham Edgar represented what might be called Ned's passion for the *full life* – of the cultivated mind and imagination, the feelings and senses, and the social and economic circumstances that go with them, or ought to ... What Ned eventually did and became had, I think, a lot to do with these deep-seated desires and inclinations. That was where Edgar came in – certainly at the beginning, and I daresay much longer than that.

That was where Edgar came in, though what he represented was alien to almost everything Pratt had known before. Yet, however engendered, the attraction was there. Some years were to pass before Pratt did more than admire Edgar from the anonymity of the student throng, but already, as early as 1910, the magnet was tugging firmly at the needle.

Despite his rather full extracurricular calendar – writing for *Acta* and the Bob, participating in debates and similar activities, and above all paying court to Lydia Trimble – Pratt's academic record did not suffer noticeably. When in June 1911 he graduated with the Bachelor of Arts degree, he did so with First Class Honours and a silver medal (for standing second in his class). His success is all the more remarkable when one takes into account that besides the distractions mentioned above, much of his time was occupied with merely surviving. During his first year and a half or so, while his savings held out (mostly proceeds from the sale of lung healer), he lived in relative comfort of both body and mind. But thereafter, despite his Church's payment of tuition fees, summer 'vacations' wholly devoted to miscellaneous kinds of wage-earning, mostly in western Canada (to be looked at in the next chapter), as well as various odd jobs on and off campus during term, he was often barely able to get by. In such straits was he, for example, in the winter of 1909 that he was reduced to living on two meals a day, one of which was provided him as a part-time waiter in Simpson's restaurant on Yonge Street. So destitute was he, in fact, that, learning of his plight, a group of his better-off classmates banded together to make a collection of funds on his behalf. Greatly embarrassed at being the subject of a charitable campaign and vigorously protesting his self-sufficiency, he refused at first to accept the well-meant gift, but eventually agreed to a private and unpublicized bestowal.

It is hardly surprising, especially in view of his early medical history, that the circumstances of his life told at last on his health. The inadequacies of his diet, the exertions of his enforced wage-earning, the pressures of his all-important academic workload, perhaps too the new emotional tensions of a burgeoning love affair, brought on that spring in the wake of the May examinations another 'breakdown' not unlike the one he had suffered five years earlier at Clarke's Beach. Doubts about his calling may not have been a factor now – though they may have been – but it appears that his condition though mainly physical (anaemia, underweight, and severe headaches) was aggravated by mental and emotional stresses. Fortunately, his classmate, Fred Hetherington, came to his rescue, inviting Pratt to spend a holiday in St Catharines. He accepted the invitation and accompanied Hetherington to his parents' home, where a pleasant month of proper diet, rest, and relaxation in the sunshine of Ontario's vineyard country restored him, fully it seems, to health. It added little flesh to his bones, but by July he felt he was ready to take up a summer's labours once more.

8

Westward Ho!

I had often wished very strongly to see a little of the vast prairie stretches that lie on the other side of the Great Lakes, and as it was not altogether practicable ... to take the trip out there for the gratification of that personal wish, I entered quite enthusiastically into the plan of employment by which the student services could be distributed throughout Saskatchewan and Alberta. Estevan, in the southern part of Saskatchewan, and not far from the international boundary became my objective.

E.J. Pratt, from 'A Western Experience,' *Acta Victoriana*, October 1910

THE METHODIST CHURCH'S mission fields on the western prairies were perennially undermanned. Many of them would have seen no preacher at all if young student ministers in the East had not been willing to spend three months in summer traversing many square miles of prairie, visiting hundreds of scattered, scarcely accessible farms, and preaching on Sundays in any schoolhouse, shack, or farm kitchen that could be appropriated for the purpose. Some students it is true preferred more lucrative jobs in more comfortable, less challenging surroundings. But Pratt in the summer of 1908 had no difficulty deciding where he should go, though, as his account of his 'Western experience' cited above suggests, it was as much the call of the West itself as of the pulpit that lured him there.

Alberta and Saskatchewan had become provinces in 1905, but were still thinly populated and undeveloped. Immigrants were needed, and to attract them large advertisements in the public press offered free homesteads 'to every man of 18 years of age, able and willing ...' One such had caught the eye and impulsive imagination of Edwin Pratt. The Church might be his ostensible, ultimate goal, but there was no law, human or divine, which forbade his being both a fisher of men and a tiller of the soil. The notion was, clearly, a novel and unlikely one for a scion of a race whose back was congenitally turned against the land, for someone who had no drop of agrarian blood in his veins. But this, undoubtedly, gave the idea part of its piquancy; the rest was provided by the promise of riches to come. He whose family had never owned a square foot of land (even his father's grave plot was 'borrowed') or a roof over its head which was not owned by someone else, now, it seems, looked to the possession of land as a possible first step toward changing the old pattern. In the spring of 1908 when he chose the West as his 'objective,' Pratt was already determined to try his fortune as a prairie landowner, though, to be sure, as an absentee landlord for most of the time. (I cannot believe he ever envisaged himself as some have thought, as a permanent prairie settler, riches or no. Arthur Phelps saw in him a potential 'lord of the manor.' No doubt, but not in the remoteness of a western, frontier prairie, especially as it was in those still pioneering days. I think his dream was rather of riches to be garnered there, but enjoyed in other, more congenially populous places.)

He set out in mid-June. The Canadian Pacific Railway was running 'Homeseekers' Excursions' twice weekly during the summer, and Pratt quite properly took advantage. Even so, a return ticket for the two-and-a-half days' journey to Estevan cost him $40, which he had to borrow from the Methodist Mission Board. Travelling in a coach crowded with expectant 'homeseekers,' he must have felt, as Pike remarked recalling 'Ned's enthusiasm and hopes when he set out,' like 'a true pioneer going out to open up the Great West.' (Pike himself that summer, having lesser though perhaps more realistic dreams, went to New Brunswick to peddle magic lanterns.)

As Pratt soon discovered, that part of Saskatchewan which was his destination, though still very much a frontier, had already been fairly well opened up. Having had rail connections for more than a decade, much of the area had been settled, if thinly; most of the arable home-steads had been taken and passable dirt roads connected them with Estevan and other railway points. Travelling, at least, would be easier there for the young circuit-rider than had he gone farther north or west. But prospects were dim for the would-be landowner who hoped to avail himself of the free land grants which the government had offered. Still, cheap land could be had by those who were able to buy.

At Estevan he was met by his Superintendent Pastor, who gave him his 'plan of campaign,' as well as 'an abundance of data, amongst which geographical facts, racial characteristics, broncho eccentricities, and the fundamentals of the Methodist Discipline, were all combined in one bewildering confusion.' The broncho data, he soon learned, were intended to introduce him to a singularly idiosyncratic animal answering to the name of Jack who was to be his travelling companion on circuit. By an ironic stroke of Fate, of all the 'mission horses' in the West, Pratt had, it seems, been consigned the most ill-favoured equine beast ever to be pressed into the service of the Church. As he described him, in a rather colourful account published two years later as 'A Western Experience,' Jack was no beauty:

Nature had designed him in a freak of architectural genius for a wild, nomadic life upon the plains and not for the purposes of civilization. He was short, thickset, and of very disproportionate build. His hind legs had so far outstripped their front competitors in length that the result of this congenital infirmity was to slope the back in the direction of the head at such an angle as to give a prospective rider considerable nervous uneasiness ...

No less unnerving than his appearance was his temperament, characterized, among other eccentricities, by a deep-seated aversion to being harnessed to a buggy. This whim soon resulted in such hair-raising escapades on the part of the novice driver that he shortly abandoned the vehicle in favour of a saddle. This mode of carriage too was not without its initial perils. Pratt wryly reconstructed his equestrian initiation in a diverting passage from which I quote – mainly to illustrate his management of comic prose narrative:

I had ridden five miles [when] I was confronted by a very sluggish slough too long to ride around, but narrow enough to render the passage apparently easy ... The broncho hesitated to go across. Sure-footed though he was, he declined the prospect of a burial in soft mud ... I coaxed him a little, then gave him a touch of the spur ... and after a little more urging Jack condescended to place his forefeet in the water. Then sank several inches in mud. I felt sorry now that I had urged him in; so did he, for the next moment, without any warning beyond an indignant snort, his head suddenly dropped, those long hind legs of his shot up in the air like a flash, and I suddenly learnt much more about analytical geometry, the path of a parabola, and the properties of curves than I had ever learnt at the university ... I managed somehow to extricate myself from the bed of the slough, and when I had regained some composure I saw my broncho munching the grass by the bank. I went up to him. He made no resistance, showed no concern, but looked at me with every feature stamped with cool and placid innocence. The only severe derangement I sustained was a serious dislocation of vocabulary which, had Noah Webster or Samuel Johnson been present, would have occasioned a very animated discussion upon the orthodoxy of verbal hybrids. I got into the saddle and rode home ...

But his baptism rites were now at an end: 'It proved afterwards to have been the only mishap of that nature for the summer.' Thereafter Jack and his master, having learned a proper respect for each other, formed an inseparable partnership, soon becoming a familiar and usually welcome sight to the far-flung homesteaders.

His prairie circuit was real enough, but the Methodist mission to which he had been posted was non-existent. Having only recently been settled, the territory west of Estevan had not yet been gathered to the fold. Pratt's job was thus to organize a rural mission field in a vast region to which as yet no church organization had come. It was a formidable task, especially for a tenderfoot, but it does not appear to have daunted him. Like a military commander in the field, he set out to implement a careful plan of campaign. 'I spent the first three weeks,' he wrote the Mission Board (8 July), 'exploring the country to find out the chances of establishing a good Mission Centre ... I visited all the homesteads within a radius of 20 miles and arranged for three [preaching] appointments every Sunday.' As headquarters for the mission he decided on Turner, situated fairly in the centre of the farming country he had been sent to 'Methodize,' and chose as his pied-à-terre the farmhouse of one William ('Billy') Magoon, who was content both to board the preacher and allow his house to be used for Sunday services.

Sunday, of course, was his busiest day, described thus in a letter to the Mission Board:

The morning appointment is at Shires about 7 or 8 miles South. I hold service in a large shack, then drive home to Magoon's and hold afternoon service at that place, after which I drive across the country about 20 miles and take the third appointment at the small town of Hitchcock on the railway line. The meeting there is held in the school-house, and the congregation has been growing continually until last Sunday night the building was filled ...

During the week he travelled even farther afield, visiting scattered families, conducting prayers in the farm kitchens, baptising infants, and burying the dead. His father would have been immensely proud.

Despite the variety and multiplicity of his duties, the summer passed quickly and, on the whole, pleasantly. The work was familiar, but everything else was a new experience, the kind of 'adventure at the outposts' he could throw himself into – until the novelty wore off. (Once, in fact, proved to be enough: he never tackled a prairie mission again.) He was also fortunate in his choice of lodgings. The Magoons found him a congenial boarder, though somewhat eccentric in his demands for quiet and privacy when he wished to read; this was new to a prairie homestead but they respected his wishes. He liked Magoon, who soon became and remained his good friend – in spite of occasional mild scoldings provoked by Pratt's neglecting Jack's animal needs at the end of a day's travels: more used to boats than bronchos, he sometimes simply 'moored' Jack in his stall and forgot him until next day. Before long Magoon, the first, it seems, ever to do so, was calling him 'Ned,' and he, reverting to a familiar outport habit, named his forthright host 'the Skipper.' To Magoon's two little girls he was 'Uncle Ned' for many years, sending them books so inscribed. Magoon taught him to pitch horseshoes, and when work in the fields and other chores were done – in which Pratt sometimes joined him – they would often play until the prairie sunset had faded from the sky.

In spite of his labours and other diversions he had not forgotten his plan to take a homestead. His travels, however, had soon shown him that there was not an acre of unclaimed arable land in the district. And it was just as well: to acquire title to free land one had to live on it for at least six months in three consecutive years, break ten acres each year, and build 'a habitable house.' He could not have satisfied the legal requirements without quitting university and this he had no intention of doing. He decided, therefore, to look for a homestead that had already been worked which he could 'buy' from a legal title-holder. And so he did. With the help and advice of Magoon and a small down payment borrowed from him, he took mortgaged posses-sion of a quarter section (160 acres) already broken, situated a few miles west of Turner, and made the Skipper his partner and manager. Since Pratt could not come west for seeding or stay for harvesting, Magoon would 'cultivate, seed, harvest, and market the crop – share and share alike.' It seemed a good arrangement. Actually it was as hare-brained as any of the many schemes on which he was to nourish great expectations in the future. When the following spring Magoon wrote him requesting a hundred dollars for seed, Pratt had no re-course but to borrow the money from Pike, who cashed an insurance policy, and to whom he gave as 'security' a scrawled note for 'ten acres of land and a share of the crop.' Sixty years later the note was still in Pike's possession – and still unredeemed.

Because of his 'breakdown' in the spring of 1909 Pratt did not go West that summer. Instead he accepted a six-week 'summer supply' appointment to the Bridge Street Methodist Church in Belleville, Ontario. Facing a large, more-or-less urban congregation was for him a new and rather daunting assignment, but the experience served him well in his continuing regimen of intestinal self-discipline. Nor was it unsatisfying to return to Toronto at the end of August with 'around $100.00 clear profit' to show for his summer's labours. Fortunately too, for his agrarian investment in Saskatchewan returned him noth-ing. The season in the west was a bad one and the crops consequently poor. Magoon barely managed to meet the mortgage payment and put by a small sum for next year's seed. Farmer Pratt collected nothing and Pike's loan was carried forward intact, the $100 clear profit being his only reserve against the expenses of another academic year.

By the spring of 1910, however, the lure of the West, to which was now added that of Lydia Trimble, who had gone home to Red Deer for the summer, was tugging him thither once more. But having no desire to repeat his experience as a circuit-riding preacher, he volun-teered to 'campaign' for the Young People's Forward Movement, a Methodist missionary organization begun in 1894 by Dr Frederick Clark Stephenson, medical missionary and evangelist. The Move-ment's summer field work of education, recruitment, and financial canvassing was carried on by student volunteers, who were paid an 'appropriate remuneration' for their services. It would not be lucrative employment, but it would take him West again. (He used to tell an amusing tale – bearing all the hallmarks of Prattian apocrypha, but repeated by Christopher Love in his memoir of Stephenson – of how during a 'trial run' staged by Stephenson on the corner of Yonge and Dundas streets in Toronto, Pratt almost wrecked the campaign by 'hammering home' with 'a fine flourish of rhetoric' how small a sum would feed 'a Chinaman' on rice for a day. He had been expected to stress how *great* an amount the Movement needed to carry on its good works. Duly 'chastened' by Stephenson, he was nevertheless chosen as a summer campaigner.)

The full extent and exact nature of his exploits that summer are unclear. It is known that he stopped off at Turner to look over his farm, which Magoon had sown in flax, and was pleased with the early prospect of a fabulous crop. From there he went west to Red Deer and seems to have spent some weeks campaigning for the Movement in that neighbourhood. Later he appears to have returned to Saskatchewan and canvassed the region round North Battleford. But his full itinerary cannot be uncovered. Many years later he told a magazine reporter (whose story was repeated by others) that for a time he was billeted with a farmer who allowed him to earn his keep by cleaning out pig-pens, driving the farmer's binder, and servicing his far-flung rural mail route! But this has a familiarly fanciful aura about it. Financially, however, he fared no better than before, and again had to borrow his passage home. Nor did his fabulous crop materialize; in fact, his farm barely broke even, returning him nothing.

Undiscouraged, the following year (1911) he again decided to try his fortune in the West, partly no doubt because Lydia would again be at Red Deer. This time he totally abandoned religious for strictly secular, commercial enterprises, and before the summer was over had dabbled in a number of ventures, none of which (almost needless to say) reaped him any profit. His chief enterprise, and his ostensible reason for going west that year, was (as he used to say) a 'literary' one: to solicit orders for a substantial tome called *The Standard Dictionary of Facts*.

He made his headquarters at Red Deer, where, having acquired an old Planet bicycle, for the second time in his life he took to the road as a travelling salesman. The immediate neighbourhood having already, it seems, been well saturated with the dictionary, he decided to try more distant fields. Piling his bicycle aboard a train he headed westward, to the region of the Athabasca River. In his own words many years later, 'I visited most of the homesteads on the Athabasca River. [One suspects some exaggeration here.] Everyone was so glad to see me, and so good to me that it was the hardest thing in the world to pull the prospectus out of my pocket and try to sell the dictionary. I felt like a swindler, so I often didn't ...' Even when he did write an order, remorse, it seems, often countervailed any policy of cash in advance: 'I found, at the end of each visit, I just couldn't bring myself to broach the subject of money when they had been so hospitable to me.' He was obviously not destined to be wealthy.

Another venture that summer proved even less remunerative. Heading back east in August, he stopped off in Regina to visit his uncle, Allan Knight. Learning that the Regina Exhibition was about to open he decided to apply for a refreshment concession. His uncle (whom Pratt for some undisclosed reason disliked) advised him against the venture, but the advice went unheeded. Securing a licence to operate, he set up a booth, bought a supply of hams, mustard, bread, and ice-cream, and opened for business. Had his booth been covered, or the heavens not deluged the earth day after day, he might at least have recouped his expenses. In the end he had no recourse but to hand out most of his soggy sandwiches gratis, consoling himself with the knowledge that at least 'good food had not gone entirely to waste.' It was the old story once more repeated. When the time came for him to move on eastward, he was compelled, much as it galled him, to 'touch' Uncle Allan for the price of a ticket to Toronto.

Nor was this all. The weather that had devastated his sandwiches had not helped his crops. One week-end he had gone down from Regina to visit the Magoons and see how his flax was faring. Disembarking from the train at Hitchcock he walked the fifteen miles to Turner where the Magoons warmly welcomed him. But his agricultural prospects, he found, were far less cheering. It was his last visit to Turner: as Esther Magoon recalled the occasion, 'After we took him back to the train, we never saw him again.' What harvest there was that year did not even cover the mortgage payment, and when the full dismal reckoning was known he decided that he had had enough of farming. Finding a venturesome soul willing to take over where he had left off, he signed over his equity in exchange for two small houses on Atlas Avenue, Toronto. That was the end of his dream of wealth in the West, but it was also the beginning of a new one: of riches in Toronto real estate. But that is another story.

9

In Search of an Anchorage

So rich his wit; his heart, how tender;
His mind profound; his body slender.

S O RUNS THE EPIGRAPH that heads the brief class biography of 'Ed' Pratt in *Torontonensis* (the University yearbook) for 1911. It is not an unapt epitome. The biography
goes on to mention his 'many academic distinctions,' including a scholarship in philosophy, a prize in the English essay, and
the Union Literary Prize for oratory. It continues: 'He revels in story-
telling, and one of his greatest joys is, surrounded by a group of his
chums, to thrill them with imaginary hair-splitting [*sic*] adventures ...'
The picture is not an unpropitious one: the zealous story-teller surrounded by an appreciative audience of his friends. But unlike most of
his fellow graduands he is vouchsafed no predictions of future eminence, in fact no prognostications at all.

Yet this is hardly surprising. For in spite of all his academic successes and distinctions, his wit, intellectual profundity, and so on, Ed
Pratt (as he was still generally known) at the end of his undergraduate
life, twenty-nine years old, a 'sceptic' (or 'agnostic') who still preached
a Christian gospel, a prospective clergyman who hatched hare-brained
schemes to make his fortune, a psychology student who won prizes
for writing and public speaking, 'a queer Newfoundlander' who had
already won the West, must have been an enigma to even his closest
friends. Committed to a calling he knew he was not cut out for,
conscious of instincts which did not jibe with Methodist holy orders,
conscious too of unusual capacities and energies even if still uncertain

of their real nature, he must at times have been very much an enigma to himself. Prognosticating his future was something which it is doubtful even he would have ventured in 1911.

What conclusions if any he may have reached about the direction of his life, or what plans, however tentative, he may have formed when in the autumn of 1911, back from the West with another tale of woe, he registered for graduate studies at Victoria we do not know. But however he may have envisaged his future, he signed up in September for a Master of Arts degree in philosophy and psychology, with, of course, theology as an inescapable addendum.

At least he now had a modicum of financial security. He had rented his newly acquired houses on Atlas Avenue – though these were to prove greater liabilities than assets – and been appointed a class assistant in psychology. Having these resources, supplemented by occasional week-end preaching, he was able to move from Czar Street into slightly better quarters on Cumberland Street (north of Bloor in Yorkville), still within easy walking distance of the campus and the small office he was provided at University College. (Pike had already left Victoria; Soper remained but had moved into other quarters in the previous year.)

Pratt plunged into his graduate studies with apparent enthusiasm, aiming, despite fairly demanding duties in the psychology laboratories and his intensifying courtship of Lydia Trimble, to complete his Master's degree in a year. He and Lydia would then graduate together, she as a Bachelor of Arts and he as a Master. With his characteristic flair for the unusual, he chose as the subject of his thesis 'The Demonology of the New Testament in Its Relation to Earlier Developments and to the Mind of Christ.' His supervisors, it seems, thought his subject a strange one, but they approved it, and he threw himself into the fray with New Testament demons with his typical relish for anything that fully captured his interest and imagination. At the end of his labours he submitted a curious and original document which earned him his degree with high standing in the spring of 1912. At the same time he also won a small scholarship for Old Testament studies. But none of these was for him the most memorable or crucial event of the winter and spring of 1912.

How far his plans for marriage with Lydia Trimble had proceeded is uncertain. A niece of hers (and her namesake) assured me that not

only were they engaged by the autumn of 1911; they already looked
forward to marriage in the near future. This would seem to be positively confirmed by a minute of a Special Committee of the Newfoundland Methodist Conference (January 1912), which recorded that
the Committee had considered two requests from students at College
for 'permission to enter into matrimony prior to their ordination.' One
had come from 'Bro. J. Pratt [sic], student at Victoria College,
Toronto.' Soper had successfully made the same request during the
previous year, but Pratt's request seems to have been denied. The
Minutes record no decision taken, only that 'These requests were
considered at some length.' But the Committee having also recorded
its grave concern about 'the increasing frequency of this request' and
its responsibility to 'maintain a firm policy in this important matter,'
the inference is that both requests were denied. In Pratt's case, this
would seem to be substantiated by his applying shortly thereafter to
be transferred from the Newfoundland to the Alberta Methodist Conference. This request *was* granted him, but with the penalty of having
his three probationary years expunged from his record of pensionable
service in the Church. In the Newfoundland Conference Minutes of
1912, Pratt's 'ministry' is recorded as having begun only in 1907, the
year of his rebellion and arrival in Toronto. It would seem that to the
Newfoundland Conference 'Bro. Pratt' had become a 'non-person.'
His choosing Alberta is, of course, explained by the fact that Red
Deer was now the home of Lydia Trimble. It was into the Red Deer
Methodist District (now called Presbytery) that he chose to be transferred in the winter of 1912. Though he never served on circuit there,
his name remained on the Red Deer rolls, as a 'minister not in pastoral
work,' until two years before his death, when it was finally removed –
in rather curious circumstances.

His failure to win the Committee's approval may have had other
important consequences, for some time thereafter the engagement was
broken off. Whether in fact the Committee's action was the cause, or
what the exact circumstances of the case were is unfortunately unclear. But other more tragic events were soon to make the matter
irrelevant. Lydia fell gravely ill, a victim of what was still known as
'galloping consumption' (a rapidly progressing and highly fatal type of
miliary tuberculosis). In apparent good health shortly before then –
her graduation photograph taken earlier that year is a picture of

health – with appalling suddenness she was dying. She was taken to the Cottage Sanitarium at Gravenhurst, a hundred miles north of Toronto, in Muskoka, but her case was hopeless from the start. Pratt went up to visit her, but how often we do not know; she was undoubtedly closely quarantined. She died on 3 June at the age of twenty-one and was buried four days later. It was Convocation Day at Victoria College, and since she had all but completed her course of studies before falling ill, she was awarded the Bachelor of Arts degree posthumously. Pratt became a Master of Arts on the same day.

How profoundly and for how long Lydia Trimble's death affected Pratt is difficult to determine, especially in view of the broken engagement and more especially in view of his characteristic reticence about anything that touched him deeply. That he was almost stonily silent about it in later years is perhaps the most telling testimony we have of the depth and acuteness of his feelings. It was a strong and persistent trait of his to bury within him whatever affected painfully his deepest emotions, to bear it in silence even among those closest to him. The emotional quick of his nature was very near the surface, making him acutely vulnerable both to the experience itself and to the scrutiny of others. All the cardinal emotions affected him deeply; had he allowed himself he could have wept very easily ('Tears were often very near the surface,' says his daughter Claire). But he seems to have had a horror of being seen as tenderly sensitive, of being thought womanish. Much of his gregarious sociability and boisterous good humour was, I believe, an armour – rather than a mask – worn to cover and shield an inherently sensitive and private spirit. In him that part of the inner self where, to quote Wordsworth, 'we all stand single' was very jealously guarded and carefully shielded from both violation and scrutiny. All of this inevitably affected his poetry. But one would greatly err to mistake emotional continence for emotional frigidity.

The testimony of those who knew him best during this time of crisis, Soper and Phelps in particular, is that he was, to quote the former, 'profoundly affected, but carried it off with heroic grimness.' Male grief in the outport, after all, was characteristically dry-eyed. 'He was devastated,' said Phelps, 'but few would have known it. I did, because I was privy to a lot about Ned that no one else ever knew.' Yet however deeply he felt, it was not in his nature – for all that one could see – to brood over or repine at what could not be changed. As Soper put it, '... there was a resiliency of life, a vitality about him. He accepted – or seemed to accept – this tragedy in the spirit expressed so – "It is very hard, but the human family has got to endure".' Yet there is no doubt that it left its mark upon him, helping with the other personal griefs and calamities still to come to focus his mind and imagination upon the riddles and ironies of life and death. The tragic-ironic strain so prominent in much of his work was not the legacy only of a boyhood 'lived always under the shadow.'

Death would touch him closely and often in the years – even months – ahead. Before that fateful summer was over, while he served as summer supply preacher at Streetsville, he learned that his much respected and admired professor and mentor, George Blewett, had drowned in Lake Huron while on holiday with his family. He and Pratt had not been closely intimate friends, as Pratt and Edgar were to be, for Blewett, unlike Edgar, was a 'shy, retiring, restrained' man. But their association had been much more than the usual one between professor and student. Blewett was only eight years older than Pratt, in whom, besides, he had taken an especial interest as (in Soper's phrase) 'a sort of kindred intellectual spirit.' Victoria College for Pratt would not be the same without him. But, as Phelps observed many years later, recalling a meeting with Pratt not long after it happened, his feelings 'were more of anger than grief – anger at the injustice and unfairness of things that a man of such brilliant promise should have been snatched away, *wantonly* ... He'd say sometimes, clenching his fist, "the *bloody purblind doomsters!*" No wonder he felt an affinity for old Hardy.'

Phelps is, of course, right; he felt at times a very strong affinity for 'old Hardy.' It would not have been surprising had his 'philosophy' been closer to Hardy's than it was. There was much in his experience to supply the ingredients of pessimistic determinism. As we shall see, some of the darker philosophical interpretations of the scheme of things were to haunt him – and his poetry – for many years.

What Soper called his resiliency and vitality sustained him well in the days following Lydia's death, and by July he was ready to face the summer as supply preacher at Streetsville. The circuit's minister, the Reverend T.W. Leggott, was pleased with him and asked him to continue as an 'occasional supply' during the fall and winter. Pratt agreed to go out on week-ends as needed, returning on Sunday night to his busy University schedule.

A busier schedule is hard to imagine. Promoted in September that year from Class Assistant to Fellow in Psychology, he now had a full complement of duties in the laboratories, besides innumerable scripts to mark and projects to examine, though not yet any actual teaching. But with his occasional preaching as well, he had more than enough to fill his time. Yet, having already learned the therapeutic value of a busy life, he chose to add the studies leading to the Bachelor of Divinity degree. This was not necessary for Methodist ordination, but it might be an advantage when the time came to take a regular circuit posting.

This was not a prospect which had brightened for him as its realization had grown nearer. But he had not dismissed it as a possible if not probable destiny. There were still, after all, his mother's expectations to be considered. She must long have wondered when her little preacher boy, now thirty years old and six years in college – twice as long as the average theologue spent there – would at last take his final vows and settle down as a proper pastor. Had he and Lydia married perhaps he might have done so despite his distaste for the role, but one very much doubts it. Certainly a pastorate in Red Deer Presbytery was now unthinkable. By doing occasional 'pulpit work' he was in a sense keeping faith, but there is no doubt that his enthusiasm for it was as feeble as it had ever been. In any case, he decided that should he complete his BD program by the spring of 1913, he would at least request ordination. But it is highly unlikely that he entertained any thought of then taking a regular circuit appointment. Perhaps eventually, but not yet. But what other possible options were open to him? In 1913 there seemed to be only one: a university appointment in psychology. His enthusiasm for the new science still ran high; and besides, the universities were full of ordained clergymen 'on leave to engage in educational work.' George Blewett himself had been one.

Ironically enough, before another two years passed the prospect of a lifetime in the psychology laboratories and lecture rooms would have as little attraction for him as that of a lifetime in the preacher's study and pulpit. But it was fortunate for him that in 1913 he had at least an alternative anchor for his restless interests and energies. He needed anchors of one sort or another, emotional or intellectual, physical or metaphysical. It was one of the great ironies of his life that most of his prime of manhood when creative energies usually run strongest was passed in a state of anchorless drift or, at best, of uncertain steerage.

He still pushed on toward his degree in divinity, but there is no doubt that he now saw the practice of psychology as his best prospective escape-hatch from the ministry, perhaps also as his best prospect for a satisfying career. More than this, and therein lay its chief attraction for him, psychology still seemed to promise him answers which his quest for Truth had so far not provided. When in the winter of 1913 he wrote and published a long essay entitled 'The Scientific Character of Psychology' (*Acta*, March 1913), he seemed quite confident that psychology, using 'a new method which is Scientific in its very foundation,' now possessed the means 'to understand human nature in its manifold phases' and 'to find solutions of questions that are as old as the history of human thinking.' Though still 'only in its pioneer stages ... it has the strength and vigor of youth, the faith and hope of a great future development.' Its possibilities were 'soul-stirring.'

The essay is an interesting and revealing document. Not only is it a professional, at times almost clinical, manifesto of the new breed of scientific psychologist whom Pratt admires and of which he already sees himself one; it is also for him a personal profession of faith. As such it reveals something of the degree of his devotion to 'the Science' (as he calls it) at the time of its greatest attraction for him, the excitement and enthusiasm it arouses, as well as of the peculiar intellectual bent that inclines him toward it. At the same time it also, I think, gives a brief glimpse, unwittingly no doubt, of that other side of Pratt's consciousness, of his sensibility, which prompted him to repudiate almost everything the new psychology represents, its ends as well as its means.

The truth is that Pratt was a man with one foot planted in each of two different worlds. It might almost be said that his was, as it were, a dual or split sensibility, divided between the appeals and fascinations of the scientist's ordered but amoral universe of 'mathematical certainties' and 'clock-like mechanisms,' and those of the philosopher-poet's moral but untidy universe of mysterious imponderables. It seems apparent indeed that it was this very bifurcation of sensibility that prompted his attraction to the new scientific psychology at all. For, as his essay makes very clear, his passion for the Science is motivated not only by Pratt the scientist's implicit faith in what he believes is the 'secure and scientific basis' of its 'empirical conclusions,' but also by Pratt the humanist's deep and genuine interest in the 'territory' which psychology undertakes to explore and chart, 'human nature in all its manifold phases.' As he sees it, unlike the natural sciences, whose aims and methods he approves but which deal only with matter and energy, with man only as physical organism, psychology addresses itself to human experience, to man not as thing (or animal) but as human being. On the other hand, unlike philosophy, ethics, and theology, whose human concerns he also shares, but which deal only in what he calls 'guesswork and airy deductions,' the new psychology is factual, concrete, and empirical. By bringing the mathematical certainties and clock-like mechanisms of the one to the exploration and charting of the territory of the other, psychology unites the best of both worlds in what can be a true and fruitful marriage. His mentor, George Blewett, once had the same dream.

Throughout most of the essay, a cogent and convincing if at times somewhat over-enthusiastic 'defence and illustration' of psychology, there is nothing to prompt one to doubt his total commitment to it. Stressing its absolute dependence on actual data, its scrupulous exclusion of presupposition, its techniques of analysis and classification, and its use of apparatus and exact experiment, he shows that psychology is able to study, analyse, and explain scientifically the whole 'great complex unity of Experience.' Nothing in human experience is beyond its scope or capacity. The 'nature of Thought,' 'the emotional side of life,' 'individual and social morality,' 'the nature of moral judgment,' 'the basis of the distinction between Right and Wrong,' even the hitherto sacrosanct 'realm of Aesthetics,' all fall within its legitimate territory.

It is only when he pauses to take a second look at the implications of psychology's intrusions into aesthetic experience and the emotional side of life that any mote of doubt may be detected in his otherwise clear-eyed vision of the Science's bright future. His ostensible purpose is to anticipate objections which might be raised by some sceptical soul, but one gets the feeling that he himself, or part of him, is the real sceptic, that the other side – the 'truant' side – of his nature is not quite comfortable with the 'equations' and 'metric curves,' the 'mechanical appliances' and 'empirical conclusions' of the scientist's world. He writes:

it might well be objected that ... there are many important conscious processes that will forever baffle and escape the exactitude of mechanics. What about the soul thrills which the artist experiences as he gazes upon a grand panorama of natural scenery? Are you going to bottle up the spirit of Beethoven or of Wagner, and draw metric curves around the sonatas and symphonies, nocturnes and arias? Is the lyric to be placed upon the dissecting table, and the stately march of the Epic robbed of its majesty by measuring out the length of its strides and counting the number of its steps? And worst of all unhallowed attempts – what laboratory is going to fetter with its mechanisms the *Grande Passion* and explain its moods and its fancies, its attractions and repulsions, in terms of equations and logarithms? No experimentee has yet been found so devoted to the interests of Science that he is willing to give an exhibition before the eye of his experimenter.

The tone is that of a whimsically ironic dismissal and he goes on to assure his reader that 'even if the Emotional side of life eludes the tangible test of apparatus, that does not deprive it of the possibility of Scientific treatment.' Nevertheless, it is difficult to suppress the suspicion that, unwittingly perhaps, he is voicing objections, even doubts, which, though not yet clamant, are his own.

Resuming his confident posture, he reaffirms psychology's claim to be called a science and ends with a salute to 'the modern Spirit of Progress,' under whose banner it marches boldly forward accepting 'hard but honest toil as the only path to success.'

The essay undoubtedly marks the pinnacle of what Pratt later called his 'naïve' commitment to the new psychology. Within a year – by the winter of 1914 – he had already begun openly to backslide. It is true that the atmosphere of bickering and animosity gradually pervading his department helped to hasten his defection. But that it should have begun so soon probably confirms our suspicion of incipient misgivings even as he writes in the winter of 1913. As suggested above, his problem – if *problem* is the best word – seems to have lain in what I have called his split sensibility, which pulled him in opposite directions at once: toward the terra firma of the scientist's regulated world of the quantifiable and controllable and the terra incognita of the humanist's and artist's labyrinthine world of 'mysterious imponderables.' All his life he was subject to the contrary attractions of these two 'lode-stones of truth.' Nor did he ever wholly reconcile them. Already they have muddied the waters of his religious convictions and 'tangled up ... the compass' that was to have guided his quest for Truth. In time they gave rise – for which perhaps we may be thankful – to many of the major tensions, ironies, and paradoxes of his poetry, and the curious ambivalences of thought and feeling which more than one puzzled critic has remarked on. But of this, more later. It may, however, be apropos as we leave his essay of 1913 to note that his poem 'The Truant,' written nearly thirty years later, is essentially a debate – still, I think, without a clear winner – of a fundamental issue raised first, if somewhat obliquely, in this ambivalent essay. In the poem the Panjandrum, who represents (among other things) the scientist's view of man and the universe, is thus one face of Pratt himself, and the Truant, who represents the opposing view, is thus Pratt's other face.

But in 1913 he felt he had, for the time being at least, an anchorage in psychology where he could be happy in his work, despite the increasing ground swell of unpleasantness around him (a result mainly of personal jealousies and professional rivalries among his colleagues). Yet his emotional nature craved the stimuli and distractions of close companionship, which no one in his factious department supplied. More than ever he needed friends. Lydia Trimble was dead, her memory fading – or being buried. Most of his other friends, both ecclesiastical and secular, had graduated and gone. Arthur Phelps remained and was still a good friend, but he was busy with postgraduate studies and pastoral duties on a suburban circuit. But friends he must have, and before very long a new one had become, in so far as his limited free time permitted, a frequent companion.

She was Viola Leona Whitney, a member of Victoria's class of 1913, whose father owned a farm at Atherley (near Orillia), Ontario. In many ways she was not unlike Lydia Trimble, pretty, unaffected, warm, and possessing a fine and lively sense of humour. She was also an excellent student and a gold medalist, and had already demonstrated a considerable literary bent, having contributed many essays to *Acta*. Pratt had met her casually before Lydia's death; she and Viola had been friends as fellow boarders at Annesley Hall. By the spring of 1913 he and Viola had become fast friends. Before another year was out they were engaged to marry.

In spite of his many duties and the distractions of a burgeoning courtship, Pratt's studies in divinity flourished, and in the finals of 1913 he emerged, ironically, as the top student in the BD program. Not only did he win a prize, a bursary, and a scholarship (worth a grand total of $75), but also the Sandford Gold Medal for 'general proficiency in the whole B.D. course.' (This was not, it seems, a trophy he prized for its extrinsic significance: a few days later he pawned the medal for $17 in cash to spend on a 'glorious dinner' at the Queen's Hotel for a 'crew' of recent emigrés from Newfoundland!)

No obstacle now remained to postpone any longer his fulfilling the final term of the contract made nearly fifteen years earlier. Accordingly, on Friday, 13 June 1913, in Central Methodist Church, Toronto, he 'was received into full connexion' and on the Sunday following was ordained by the Reverend Dr James Smythe, Principal of McGill's Wesleyan College, whose portals he had not been permitted to enter. He was now in very fact the Reverend E.J. Pratt, clear in conscience that his 'bargain' had been kept.

What, one wonders, did the solemn ritual of ordination mean to him at the time, and afterward? Not surprisingly he is quite silent on the subject. Most ordinands (I am told) view it as a great spiritual climacteric in their lives, confessing to a sense of consecration, of being set apart, of 'spiritual community with the ages,' and, even in an unmystical communion like Methodism, a 'mystical sense of the Divine Presence.' Lorne Pierce, a close friend of Pratt's in later years, who himself underwent the same experience ('a marked moment in my life') wrote in 1955: 'It must have had a profound emotional effect [on Pratt] at the time, and must still return to him in his greatest and best moments, for he had known the laying on of hands at ordination, and ... the fact of the emotional crisis would remain, and the command to "Go and preach, etc. ..." the old ritual of all ordinations.' Pierce believed that he could see 'the latent priest in the poet.' He may have been right. But whether the actual ritual of ordination was in fact an emotional crisis for him at the time in the manner that Pierce suggests, or that it would return to him 'in his greatest and best moments,' is more doubtful. Ordination had hung over him like a Damoclean sword for so long that any emotional effect he may have felt was more likely to have been a feeling of relief, if not of release.

More memorable for him in later years was a triumph of a far different kind, yet one that perhaps dramatizes the sense of deliverance and flow of spirits he experienced that summer. This was a mountain-climbing expedition, another of the improbable adventures which crop up from time to time in Pratt's history, contradicting in its rashness and impetuosity the deep strain of cautiousness that was actually in him. Hitherto he had shown no particular interest in mountains, in fact had scarcely seen any, and mountain-climbing as a sport or hobby was as much beyond his means as it was foreign to his interests. And yet, perhaps, in the light of his hazardous boyhood exploits aboard the schooners at Fortune, one should not find it too preposterous that the notion of scaling a mountain at least once should have caught his still boyish fancy.

The prime mover in this fresh adventure was another new acquaintance of his, a member of Victoria's History Department, C.B. ('Charlie') Sissons, one of whose hobbies for some years had been (and continued to be for another quarter-century) mountaineering. Sissons that year was organizing an expedition to the Rockies with the object, in addition to his personal satisfaction, of qualifying new members for the Alpine Club. Admission required their conquest of a substantial peak and payment of a substantial fee. Pratt, who by some unlikely chance had 'a couple of hundred' uncommitted dollars, decided to join, and in mid-July set out with the expedition for Banff, travelling thence to Lake O'Hara, where the Club held its annual camp.

His ascent of Cathedral Mountain, some 10,000 feet high, was accomplished on 21 July in the presence of Sissons and his new wife (they were actually on their honeymoon), two other tyros, and Conrad Kain, the famous mountain man, whom Earle Birney later commemorated in a stirring poem. Sissons refers to the climb briefly in his *Memoirs*: 'On top we ... encountered an electric storm which literally made our "hair to stare." We found it amusing rather than frightening. Our ice-axes we put in a heap and let them sing away.' But though Pratt climbed his mountain and had the satisfaction of becoming a bona fide alpinist and receiving a button to wear in his lapel to prove the fact, he was quite unable to raise any real enthusiasm for the 'sport' of mountaineering. 'It was,' he wrote, 'the first real mountain I ever climbed, and the last. I realized through the stiffness of my joints next day that mountains were meant to be looked at not climbed.' But the experience seems not to have been lost on him: from its vantage-point nearly forty years later he would sketch the Rockies in *Towards the Last Spike* (1952) with the same slightly ironic pen:

> Terror and beauty like twin signal flags
> Flew on the peaks for men to keep their distance.
> ...
> The Ranges could put cramps in hands and feet
> Merely by the suggestion of the venture.
> They needed miles to render up their beauty,
> As if the gods in high aesthetic moments,
> Resenting the profanity of touch,
> Chiselled this sculpture for the eye alone.   (987–97)

During the following winter he wrote and published a long and entertaining account which he called 'A Rocky Mountain Experience' (*Acta*, March 1914). But it was characteristic of him, of his sense of the incongruous in human aspirations and achievements, that he did not choose the story of his triumphal, if physically taxing, ascent. What he chose to tell instead was of an ignominious fishing expedition which he and another prospective alpinist had undertaken, mainly to postpone their day of judgment. 'There is no logic,' he had reasoned, 'that compels a fellow to die before his time. Five thousand feet of a drop to-morrow evening might be a painless way of getting rid of life's sorrows, but I prefer the end to come later.' Written in the quasi-Leacockian style he had used in his tale of Jack, the Western broncho, the story is given almost entirely to the farcical fishing trip. It is an unlikely memento of an alpine adventure, but Pratt rarely chose the obvious. Besides, fishing was in his blood; mountaineering was not.

September saw him back in Toronto, installed now as a Demonstrator in psychology. This small promotion gave him added responsibilities for the laboratories and the conduct of many of the exact experiments which the Science required: experiments and demonstrations in colour-discrimination, visual contrasts, after-images, binocular vision, optical illusions, and many other 'psycho-physical' phenomena. Most of these required his using various 'ingenious mechanical devices' and exercising considerable mechanical skill. Unfortunately such skill was not contained in his repertory of talents; in fact, as he admitted with ironic amusement at his own expense, in the laboratory he was a 'veritable menace':

My most vivid memory of my laboratory aptitudes was the way I smashed up the prisms and lenses and coloured discs. I don't think I ever started a motor to illustrate color combinations without sending the discs all over the room in a thousand fragments as the motor whizzed at a million revolutions to the minute. The class always ducked when I started the motor to do a demonstration with them ...

Old students of his with whom I talked confirm that he was only mildly exaggerating. His increasingly manifest ineptness in the laboratory undoubtedly would have soon shattered the illusion that he could have been a successful scientific psychologist even if he had still wanted to be one. His superiors, however, seem to have clung to the illusion much longer – or perhaps in wartime had no more likely recruit available – for he was performing in the laboratories (and smashing up apparatus) for more than another five years.

Whether or not prompted by the growing suspicion that his employment by the Department of Psychology was unlikely to be permanent, Pratt decided that autumn to enrol again as a postgraduate student: in the doctoral program in philosophy. The rolls of the Methodist Church still listed him as a member of the Red Deer Presbytery of the Alberta Conference, 'left without a station at his own request,' but he was already hoping that there might be a place for him in some university department, though preferably *not* in the discipline of experimental psychology. Philosophy, or even theology were possible alternatives, but it seems that English literature did not cross his mind. Whatever, it might be, he was well aware that a doctorate in something was often a helpful if not an essential passport to a university appointment with prospects and security.

Adding to his labours that autumn, he agreed to accompany the Reverend T.W. Leggott when he moved from Streetsville to Mount Albert (north of Toronto) and to continue as an assistant supply for another term. (The following year, however, Pratt returned to his old haunts at Streetsville.) He had grown fond of the Leggotts and they of him, inviting him to the parsonage during his week-end visits when he made himself very much at home and became a good friend of the Leggotts' teenage daughter. (Many years later she recalled him sitting 'with his stockinged feet in the oven telling stories of his boyhood and a Newfoundland dog he had once had.') By a curious coincidence the girl was to marry a young Englishman, William E. Collin, who would one day write the first full-dress study of the poetry of E.J. Pratt.

The poetry of E.J. Pratt! So far in this chronicle we have not seen a great deal of it, for so far he has written almost none. But he will soon begin. In the autumn of 1913 (or early winter of 1914), growing more and more disillusioned, frustrated, and unhappy in psychology, at the invitation of his new girlfriend, Viola Whitney, then deeply immersed in the study of pedagogy at the Ontario College of Education but already concerned for his well-being, Pratt decided to seek an 'oasis' (as he later called it) to which to escape from his 'Sahara.' The oasis, as it happened, was a small, informal poetry class which met on Monday evenings at Victoria College under the tutelage of Pelham Edgar.

10

Oasis in the Sahara

I certainly cannot lay much claim to precocity. Fortunately there are no records to the effect that, 'This was written at six years of age, this at ten, this at thirteen'!

E.J. Pratt, 'My First Book,'
The Canadian Author and Bookman, Winter 1952–3

AS WE ALREADY KNOW, fortunately or unfortunately, Pratt is right: there are no such early records. In fact there is so little evidence of 'poetic promise' in the early life of E.J. Pratt, almost the first half indeed, that one may be forgiven should he wonder whether this is in fact the life-story of a major poet – or *any* poet for that matter. Even the verse lampoons which late in life he talked of having written as a schoolboy may well have been merely retrospective fiction. The reading of poetry, too, seems to have had no especial attraction for him in boyhood and youth. And both Pike and Soper were quite insistent that apart from one crude effort in verse during his second year at Victoria, he neither wrote poetry nor read it (outside his literature textbooks) during their undergraduate life at the College. What recreational reading he had time for seems to have run entirely to prose, mostly recent fiction, his favourite novelists being Hardy, Conrad, Jack London, and Conan Doyle, to all of whom he became addicted and in time owed a variety of literary debts.

As we have seen, his early excursions in writing were almost all prose. His early prose, moreover, what little there is, is very good. Whether Pratt ever seriously considered journalism as a profession is not known. But there seems little doubt that during his undergraduate years he felt a strong urge to use his pen, at least as a satisfying pastime if not yet as a medium of imaginative and emotional deliverance. His prizes in English essay and oratory, his laurels in debating, his reputation for 'hair-splitting' tales are all suggestive of latent talents striving for an appropriate outlet. All of this is undoubtedly worth noting, yet one would be very hard-pressed to prove that it betokens a poet. As late as 1914 anyone at the University of Toronto compelled to speculate on a literary future for Pratt could only have seen him, possibly, as a writer of prose. Even that would have seemed very unlikely. If he had any poetic inclinations in those days they were well disguised.

There was little or nothing in the air to rouse poetic instincts even where they existed. Toronto especially, in the decade before the Great War, could hardly be said to have pulsated with poetic excitement and activity. A general malaise, in fact, seemed to have settled over literary, especially poetic, creativity throughout Canada since the turn of the century. The other arts flourished in reasonable health; commerce and industry blossomed abundantly; towns and cities burst their boundaries; and the spirit of a vigorous young giant was already bidding fair to make Laurier's prophecy come true, that the twentieth century belonged to Canada. But hardly in the realm of literature, certainly not of poetry. A number of prose writers, mainly of fiction, produced competent work, some of it very good of its kind: Sara Jeannette Duncan, Ralph Connor, Norman Duncan, Theodore Goodridge Roberts, L.M. Montgomery, and a few others. But in poetry there was virtually nothing. Archibald Lampman was dead. Charles G.D. Roberts had gone abroad to live, and was to publish nothing new in verse for nearly twenty years. Bliss Carman too lived mainly in the United States, publishing little of interest or significance for many years. And Duncan Campbell Scott, after his daughter's sudden death in 1907, published no more until 1916. All four continued to be read, but the tradition they represented having run down had little about it now to stir new talent into vigorous and original creativity. Nor had anything else appeared to take its place. There were other publishing 'poets' in Canada, even in Toronto, but they were, with a few exceptions, the declining progeny of the Group of the Sixties, an issue slowly dying off from the combined effects of imaginative sterility, emotional inbreeding, and intellectual virginity. A quick survey of the contemporary contents of J.W. Garvin's *Canadian Poets* (1916) will show what is meant.

By 1914, it is true, the new noises being heard and the new techniques being tried abroad – by Ezra Pound and the Imagists, for example, and the poets who were now finding a public through the pages of *Poetry* (Chicago) – were beginning to attract the interest of a few Canadian poets. The new modes were still rather tentative and experimental, and when they did show up in Canadian wares – in Arthur Stringer's *Open Water* for instance – were so misunderstood and inexpertly used as to cause most young poets who encountered them with interest in *Poetry* to shy away from using them in a Canadian context. It would be a long time before even the technique of vers libre would be tried without apology and defensiveness by Canadian poets. In the English departments of Canadian universities, poetry was still mainly the British 'Masters,' ending with Tennyson. Here and there a few recent Americans were thrown in for the sake of catholicity. But most undergraduates, including those at Victoria College, heard very little about 'modern' poetry in their classes until the 1920s.

Pelham Edgar's poetry class had no official status or formal organization. Described by him as 'a group of younger professors at Victoria' who had asked him 'to talk to them on poetry,' and by Pratt as 'a post-graduate class where a half a dozen of us including my old friend Arthur Phelps met every Monday evening to study 19th century poetry,' it had begun meeting (so far as can be determined) in the early autumn of 1913. Phelps, still working in postgraduate studies, had been as he put it 'a charter member' and later recalled having invited Pratt to join the 'little conclave.' Perhaps so, but it was Viola Whitney who actually introduced Pratt to Edgar's group, of which she was, at Edgar's personal invitation, the only female member. (She had been his star pupil in her graduating year and he had spotted her potential gifts.) Pratt, willing to try any antidote to his academic miseries, agreed to go along; at least it would be a diversion from psychology, its bickering exponents and recalcitrant apparatus.

There is little doubt, however, that it was the prospect of his foregathering with Pelham Edgar – seeing him, hearing him, perhaps meeting him socially – that as much as the need for a diversion or the pleasure of Viola's company prompted Pratt to join the poetry group. The magnet had never ceased to pull at the needle, but no opportunity had arisen until now to permit an actual response. Before many sessions had passed, however, what went on in the class had become for Pratt almost if not quite as great an attraction as Edgar himself. His being the prime mover and presiding spirit provided an interest and excitement which otherwise would certainly have been lacking; but soon the reading and study of poetry for its own sake had become for Pratt as great an enthusiasm as psychology had ever been. As he put it, 'that hour became for me the oasis in the Sahara.'

For the first time he began to read English poetry with a genuine interest, and soon a genuine appreciation. Until then he had known little more than 'the usual anthologized pieces in the textbooks,' but soon Edgar had him reading 'large portions of Wordsworth, Keats, Shelley, and Tennyson we had never heard of before,' and making the acquaintance for the first time of Browning, Arnold, and Swinbourne. In this way, he wrote, '[Edgar] was continually shaping and modifying our tastes, changing neutrality in the case of Shelley and Matthew Arnold into a glowing enthusiasm, and what may have been a tepid regard for Keats into a lasting and fervid admiration.' Before the winter was over the 'class' had become a virtual workshop for would-be poets. As Phelps observed, 'When Pelham Edgar read and talked about it, poetry and the *practice* of poetry seemed to become the noblest and most necessary occupation in the world. So we all tried to become poets!' Phelps himself was the first to succeed and was soon publishing quite respectable verse in *The Canadian Magazine* and other journals and papers.

Pratt's progress was slower, but not because he lacked the enterprise or courage to begin, and begin with characteristic élan. According to Viola Pratt, he announced 'quite casually' one day, early in 1914, that he was about to write 'a long epic poem.' Until then, though she had known that he was a member of Edgar's group, she had had 'no inkling that he was the least bit interested in writing poetry.' She dismissed his projected epic as 'another of the stories with which he liked to tease and mystify people,' and thought no more of it – until he appeared one evening a few weeks later, the finished epic in his hand, and proceeded to read it to her. 'It was,' she recalled, 'the *craziest* thing ever written, absolutely *idiotic*!' Suppressing her amusement she listened attentively until he had ended, then released her feelings in such gales of laughter that he could not but join her: 'His poem was perfectly ludicrous. I only wish I had saved it. But all I can remember from the whole business was a "gory, dripping dragon." But that was typical of it. And when Ned read it to me, he saw how silly it was ... Afterward he just pitched it away or burned it.' A pity. The hints that survive intrigue and tantalize, suggesting a native mythopoeic strain in Pratt's imagination that his subsequent apprenticeship to poetry – or his fiancée's laughter – effectively suppressed for many years to come.

Fortunately his ignominious début did not discourage him. However it may have come about, Edgar had awakened something in his soul, ignited a fire in his imagination, which he was not about to let be extinguished by a single fiasco. It was characteristic of him, as we know, that when his fancy had been captured by something that truly interested him, especially if it presented a challenge, he could be quite fanatical in his determination to master it. As his old classmate, Leopold Macaulay, once remarked, not unaptly if somewhat inelegantly, 'If Ned took a real interest in something he went overboard for it; if he took no interest he was a dead fish. There was no middle ground for Ned!'

And so he persisted, trying his hand now at shorter, less ambitious pieces, taking them to Edgar for his comments and advice. But if the poems he soon began to publish in *Acta Victoriana* were typical of those he took to Edgar – they were no doubt the best of his efforts – one can readily sympathize with Edgar for failing to spot a burgeoning genius straightaway. They were hardly promising pieces, imitative, conventional, self-conscious, though they generally exhibited a certain skill in the rudiments of prosody and a not unmusical ear. So profuse are most of them in the 'thee-ing' and 'thou-ing' and the 'faded decorations' which Pratt the critic later damned as 'the surest sign of amateurishness, of literary inertia and incapacity,' that they might almost have passed for parodies of what another critic described as the 'airy-fairy fifth-rate stuff' that filled so much space in Garvin's anthology and *The Canadian Magazine*. But one should not, perhaps, be too critical; after all, as he put it, 'I was just testing my wings to see if there was any locomotion in them. I wasn't even sure that I really wanted to take the plunge – and perhaps end up with a broken neck.'

One hesitates to quote from this early verse, but it does convey some impression of how far Pratt had to go before he could be considered a full-fledged poet. I shall, however, forgo an extensive sampling. Here, for example, are two of the five stanzas of 'Wind of the West,' the earliest of his serious attempts at verse to be published (*Acta*, June 1914):

Thou Wind of the West, beloved of the Ocean,
Shepherd of peace to her wild-wandering fears,
Claimant of Heaven to maiden's devotion
And sweetest of music to mariners' ears!
        To-day does thy chorus ring
        Soaring on azure wing
As homeward the sailor his ship proudly steers.

This morning I woke to the Dawn's tender breaking,
And sped to the window that fronts on the lea
To hear thy soft pinions all-tremulous, shaking
The silver ringed tassels from clover and tree;
        In a rose scented aisle
        Thou didst linger a-while
To vow to fulfilment this message to me.

And here are three of the eleven stanzas of 'The Sea-Shell' (written, it seems, about the same time as the foregoing, but not published until several years later, having been submitted for inclusion in an American anthology of student verse, where it eventually appeared):

Thou silver shell that liest near
    The pebbled margin of the sea
Bidding sunbeams reappear
    In opal-cintured tracery!

...

Whence came that myriad-voicéd stream
    Within those coral veins – that flow
Of murmurous melody whose theme
    Swings round a rapture, and a woe?

...

> But list! What notes are these that fall
>   In broken music wildly strange,
> Like Autumn answering Winter's call
>   To seared embrace, that soon must change ...

Such verse is so remote from the E.J. Pratt we know best, so fragile, romantic, feminine, so tremulously elegiacal, that it might well have been written by another person, by almost any of the 'sweet spinners of dreams' then plying their delicate looms in Ontario alone. Even when he writes directly of the sea, in a poem entitled 'The Sea' (*Acta*, December 1914), the manner and effect are much the same, the thee-ings and thou-ings and faded decorations only slightly less obtrusive:

> Tell me thy secret O sea,
>   The mystery sealed in thy breast,
> Low breathe it in whispers to me,
>   A child of thy fevered unrest ...

– and so on for seven more stanzas in the same vein. The sea gets in to be sure (as is true of the two preceding poems), but it is not the Newfoundland Atlantic. One does not apostrophize and personify *that* sea in these terms – if at all. This is a literary and conventionalized sea, and the novice poet is speaking with a literary and conventionalized voice. He is writing from books and magazines – not very good ones at that – rather than from his own experience, a legitimate enough apprenticeship really, though one wishes he had chosen other models.

He soon would, for an important result of Pelham Edgar's tutelage was that the wide and attentive reading in the major British poets which Pratt was now doing, really for the first time, began to open his mind and imagination to more substantial resources of language and imagery. Inevitably he soon fell under their spell too, and in the verse he wrote during the next three years or longer it is easy to spot echoes, borrowings, and imitations of his British models, Shelley and Wordsworth in particular, for he still had much to learn about the processes of poetic assimilation and re-creation. Still running a decade or more behind the usual progress of a rising poet, he was in his thirties undergoing the kind of apprenticeship that most young poets serve in their teens and early twenties.

So far, not so good. But at least he had tested his wings – if not yet *soared* 'in the high region of his fancies' – and had found that he enjoyed the experience. He was, after all, as he once described his early, fumbling flights in verse, 'only playing with words – only *words*.' Yet this, perhaps, on reflection, is the only proper genesis of poetic creativity: a passion for words, for hunting them out, pursuing and capturing them, finding them 'sweet / for their own *sakes*, a passion, and a power' (as Wordsworth described his own very similar initiation). For words are not merely the poet's medium, not only the element he moves in, but also the wings he soars with and the energy that drives them. So that Pratt in these early years of his apprenticeship, a true amateur of words, in his affaires d'amour with those of other poets, and above all in dreaming up and bodying forth, Pygmalion-like, his own Galateas, unenchanting if some of them seem to us – 'opal-cinctured tracery,' 'sombre-suited solitudes,' 'choral wavelets silvering,' and many others – was, perhaps, engaged in something as necessary to becoming a poet as anything else he might have done. A passion has its dangers, of course, especially for the ardent but unwary tyro – and Pratt, I fear, was one for many years; for a passion may obsess and blind, displacing judgment, taste, and objectivity. Nevertheless, it is probably true that no one was ever a poet who was not at first seduced by 'only words.' The secret, of course, is, having discovered their spell, to break it and cast one's own. This was something that took time to learn and practice to make perfect. But he had to experience the passion and the pleasure first.

The outbreak of the Great War in 1914, a rallying call to almost everyone who penned a rhyme in those high days, did not help Pratt's development as a poet. It is true that it gave the eager amateur who would never be anything more something to write about other than maple leaves and 'the way a grasshopper cocks his legs while jumping on a cabbage-leaf,' as Pratt characterized the typical interest of the 'typical' Canadian poet. But for one who though a tardy entrant in the race had the capacity to mount on wings, given the right conditions of 'lift and carriage,' the emotional and imaginative ambience of war, especially in those days before the irony of experience had shattered the romance of innocence, hardly provided the best conditions. Nor did the plethora of verse evoked by the War, at least on the 'Home Front.' (The War of course, eventually helped produce dramatic and radical changes not only in war poetry but in most of the literature of the Western world. But it took time for the changes in attitude, feeling, and technique to filter into Canadian poetry. E.J. Pratt assisted the process, but by then the War was long over.)

The War's retarding Pratt's development as a poet had nothing to do with any notion of his enlisting. This was something he never so much as toyed with. As we know he quite lacked the psychological capacity to submit to the kind of commitment that soldiering demands. Indeed, in his verse at least, he tried at first to ignore the War. But once the tragic drama began to unfold and the notion grew into a conviction that freedom, justice, truth, and all the other noble abstractions were indeed hanging in the balance, it was almost inevitable that he should have joined the mounting chorus, though he was late in giving it his 'full measure of devotion.' Unlike many others he did not with the opening guns leap into print with calls to the colours ('Come up and serve your King, in this his needful hour ...') or effusions of patriotic bathos ('O Britain, these are thine / These are thy heroes true / Who seek the distant battle-line / To die for love of you!'). Of such he was never guilty, neither of such naïve responses nor of such banalities of expression. Nowhere does the antique notion, *dulce et decorum est pro patria mori*, occur in his poems. (Actually he was a pacifist, both by instinct and by conviction.) Unfortunately, despite the modest progress he was making in the technique of verse and the discipline of language, impelled at last to join the national outpouring as the war struck nearer home, he committed in many of his war poems a host of literary sins that are almost as bad.

Signs of modest progress are already apparent in the first of his published war poems (probably also the first to be written), a sonnet entitled 'Unseen Allies' (*Acta*, May 1915). It is quite free of the kind of faded decoration which had caught his fancy earlier. Avoiding most of the current clichés both verbal and emotional, he views the War in historical perspective as part of an age-old struggle for freedom waged by its champions from Drake and Cromwell down to Nelson and Wellington. He concludes as follows:

... The present issue stands
In aim confederate with the gallant past:
Across the bourne of Time we join our hands
With serried hosts. Behind our lines are massed
Battalions of a memorable age
Whose deeds emblazon Freedom's valorous page.

The thought is not new, the diction studied and bookish, but echoes of Milton and Wordsworth (even a phrase lifted intact from Tennyson) pall less than others we might have heard.

As if still reluctant to join the swelling chorus of war poets, he turns to Wordsworthian nature in his next poem, 'By the Sea' (*Acta*, October 1915), more appropriately entitled 'Evening' in *Newfoundland Verse* (1923). (Since the poem contains nothing whatsoever of the sea, the original title, if not a purely gratuitous gesture toward his own maritime origins, may have been suggested by Wordsworth's 'It Is a Beauteous Evening,' almost certainly the poem's begetter, whose locale *is* 'by the sea,' and which Pratt's subsequent title appears to echo.) Pratt's poem was written, in fact, while he was visiting the Whitneys that summer at a cottage on the Severn River near Georgian Bay. Hager Whitney, Viola's brother, recalled its 'première' as having taken place on the river in a rowboat, which Ned at the oars abstractedly rowed round in a circle as he recited. In the poem, another sonnet, he attempts (apparently) to express a Wordsworthian sense of the spiritual refreshment and fulfilment that come in moments of tranquillity in Nature's presence. The poem begins firmly enough, the poet's eye sharply on Wordsworth: 'So calm the air, the sunset's dying beat / Wafts slowly to me from the distant brim / Of silent waters ...' But thereafter it collapses in a welter of vague abstractions, confused emotions, tangled syntaxes, muddy and unrealized imagery, and banalities of diction more typical of the Canadian than of the English Romantics.

Two more brief war poems followed, but little need be said of them. Bearing the cautionary titles 'The Sacrifice of Youth' (*Acta*, December 1915) and 'Dead on the Field of Honor' (*Acta*, June 1916), both replete with studied infelicities – 'verdurous blooms,' 'grinding griefs,' 'bleak defiles of duty,' 'Glory's paeans,' 'cloistered grief' – they are probably best forgotten. Perhaps himself recognizing that such verse was somewhat less than memorable, he wisely published no more for nearly a year. Besides, his extra-poetic activities – teaching, preaching, doctoral researches, and sundry other ventures – were devouring more and more of his time.

But he had not abandoned his new avocation or suspended his training in its practice. Though he also seems to have written little during his absence from print (at least until the late autumn of 1916), under Pelham Edgar's wise and sympathetic mentorship, in many diverse and often subtle ways, of which Pratt himself was, perhaps, not always fully aware, his nurture and education as a poet were proceeding steadily.

The fact is that by 1915 his escape to Edgar's oasis had come to mean far more to Pratt than attending classes devoted to the reading and study of poetry, or even a workshop for would-be poets. It had come to mean also a close personal relationship with 'the most remarkable man, the most deeply versed in literature, and one of the most humane I ever met.' For although it had not been until Pratt joined Edgar's little circle that either had really come to know the other, once they had done so a lively rapport had soon been kindled between them. Pratt's enthusiasm for the meetings and his boyish eagerness to try his hand at writing verse; a curious coincidence of temperaments and, in many things, of tastes as well; Edgar's warm response to Pratt's engaging personality, unaffected manner, and wry good humour; and, it seems, Edgar's early recognition of Pratt's 'brilliant mind' (the phrase is Edgar's), had quickly combined to establish strong bonds of understanding and respect between them, and soon of friendship and affection as well. Although the relationship had begun as one largely between mentor and protégé, before the poetry group disbanded (apparently in the spring of 1916) Pratt had been fully accorded an equal place in the inner circle of Edgar's elect.

His awareness of Pratt's possibilities seems to have dawned very early in their friendship, long before Edgar could have had what he later called 'proof' from Pratt's verse that he possessed the makings of a genuine poet. By some instinct Edgar seems to have sensed that within this odd psychologist-cum-clergyman who dabbled in verse there were hidden sources of unusual energies awaiting only release and direction, energies of which Pratt himself was not yet fully conscious. Sensing this, it seems, and aware of Pratt's growing unhappiness in psychology and his need for other, more liberating interests, Edgar went out of his way to ensure that Pratt had other fare, as he put it, to 'nourish my mind besides textbooks' in psychology. 'At almost every meeting of our little group,' Pratt recalled long afterward, 'he had a parcel of books to lend me, and sometimes a book to *give* me,' in this way broadening Pratt's still limited knowledge and uncertain appreciation of literature, as well as, in his words, 'administering an antidote to the venom that Smith and his crew were trying to pump into me.' (W.G. Smith, of whom more later, was a professor of psychology, Pratt's overseer in the laboratories, and later his doctoral supervisor.) The antidote was also one which when at last Pratt fully succumbed to the war fever that raged in Canadian verse until the War was long over, helped to save him from some of its worst excesses.

What all this reading matter comprised, over a period of several years, we do not know in detail. But if Pratt's recollections more than four decades later are reliable it was 'numerous and varied ... mostly works of poetry and drama, and some prose, critical stuff as well as fiction.' He recalled poetry by Masefield, Bridges, Kipling, Hardy, and 'the celtic twilight Yeats'; plays by Shaw and Galsworthy, and fiction by Wells, Conrad, and Arnold Bennett, the last of whom 'Pelham had once met ... somewhere and highly recommended.' (Edgar had met Bennett in Florence in 1910, when, he learned later, he had been somewhat dubiously immortalized in a brief, rather ambivalent sketch in Bennett's *Journals*: 'Lounge suit, dirty brown boots; dégagé; small piercing eyes ... an impatient man ... probably suffers from some intellectual arrogance ...')

Besides sharing selected authors with him through their works, Edgar also shortly began to share with Pratt more randomly-chosen authors in the flesh. Literary 'celebrities,' national or international, who happened to be visiting Toronto, were usually during the course of their visits invited to Edgar's house to small, informal conversazioni, to which, in honour of the visitor, he also asked a selection of the Toronto writing fraternity and a few university friends. From 1916 or 1917 Pratt was often among them.

Who they all were whose acquaintance he thus made in those early days we do not know. Most, invited like him to meet the visitor, were, of course, Toronto writers, relatively minor figures in Canadian literature. (Toronto, curiously, boasted no major author in those days.) But among the more celebrated visitors, we do know the names of a few: Stephen Leacock (an old classmate of Edgar's at Upper Canada College), Bliss Carman (by whom Pratt, it seems, was at first 'puzzled,' but on better acquaintance became very fond of: 'He could sniff a joke a mile off,' Pratt once wrote of him), and the then regnant poet in Canada, Duncan Campbell Scott. Pratt's introduction to Scott was recalled in a letter to me by Barker Fairley who, a year or so after his appointment to the German Department in 1915, was a guest at one of Edgar's evenings when Pratt was 'presented.' 'Ned,' Fairley wrote, 'read some of his verses' – probably portions of *Rachel* – and Scott was 'greatly impressed ... This must have been almost the beginning of [Pratt's] publicity.' Another attendant – no 'celebrity' yet but pushing – whom Pratt met at least once at Edgar's about this time was a strange, dark, Italianate man, who entertained the company with 'some clever sleight-of-hand.' His name, Pratt had good reason to remember later, was Wilson MacDonald.

How important these occasions were to Pratt in directing him from other goals he might have sought and toward a life in letters and academe is difficult to tell. They were probably not decisive factors, but they undoubtedly helped to attach a certain attractive, even lustrous, aura to a kind of life and avocation, if not profession, he seems already to have been hungering after. He sometimes said that 'poetry opened many doors' to him, and he had in mind – among other things no doubt – doors to friendships he would not otherwise have made. Though not all he met at such gatherings remained his friends, or even friendly acquaintances, there seems little doubt that the opportunity offered him to rub shoulders with Pelham Edgar and with even minor celebrities gave him a sense of having at least one foot in a door which, he already hoped, would someday open wide for him.

Many friendships Pratt formed both within and without the University were stepping-stones to the larger and fuller life he desired. But it would be wrong to impute to him the motives usually ascribed to the social climber. He did not use a friendship as a means to an ulterior end. The conversation and stimulation it brought him, the fellowship of mind and spirit, were ends enough, and often he found them in other company than that of a social or intellectual élite. Nor had he any desire to be a social renegade, to rise above his origins because he despised them. His blood was that of mariners and miners, and he was, I think, proud of both facts. His contempt for the snob, the assumer of airs, the pompous and the pretentious, was very great. On the contrary, his affection and compassion for the down-trodden and the down-and-out – 'The shabby ones of the earth's despite / The victims of her rude neglect' – were sincere and lasting, and never gestures of condescension.

Yet he would have been less than honest had he affected to dismiss as unattractive, undesirable, ungratifying to his sense of the fitness of things, the physical and spiritual amenities which go hand-in-hand with social and material advantage much oftener than with their antitheses. His great apocalyptic dinner of *The Depression Ends* (1932) was, after all, the largess of a lord, a royal feast of nectarean wines and ambrosial foods, served under 'myriad-diamond' roofs and glittering candelabra. No 'white / Self-pinched, self-punished anchorite ... unto this feast shall ... come / To breathe his gloom.' With proper ritual all shall rise

> and hold
> Their glasses to the light a minute
> Just to observe the mellow gold
> And the rare glint of autumn in it.

These are not the gestures of one to whom dinner is merely a means to a satisfied belly; they are rather those of a man to whom the bounty of the table, the beauty of the glass, and the rituals of gracious, though hearty, dining are values both aesthetic and humane.

Saying that it was only after Pratt settled in Toronto that he began to reach after and grow into this kind of life is not to imply that a change in habitats suddenly began to transform the image and instincts of a duckling into those of a swan. For all his self-depreciatory descriptions of himself as a 'raw youth' and a 'rough and unpolished greenhorn,' Pratt was never a bumpkin or a 'bay-noddy.' What roughness covered his diamond core was never deep or abrasive. It is true that some years passed before 'the natural gentleman of learning and parts' (as a later acquaintance once described him) would come to rub shoulders with (though never really to displace) the open, earthy, unvarnished, 'shrewd and innocent' Newfoundlander in him. Yet the instincts were there which impelled him toward a new, expansive, stimulating, creative kind of life, here and now, in the flesh, in the mind, imagination, and spirit, such as no penurious and circumscribed outport existence, for all its basic values and endowments of other kinds, could possibly offer him. His never returning to the Newfoundland ministry was due far more to such inner drives and appetites than either the autocracy of the Newfoundland Methodist establishment or any dissenting views he may have held on certain Methodist doctrines. But in 1916, for the struggling thirty-four-year-old graduate student, part-time drudge in psychology, and sporadic week-end preacher, who made an occasional hobby of playing with verse, such a life as his instincts impelled him toward was still a long and difficult way off. Even if he dreamed of it, his dreams must have been very vague and improbable. That poetry might be his open sesame was hardly yet even a dream.

Yet, whether he was aware of the fact or not, he had already taken an important step, perhaps several steps, toward realizing his dreams, however vague and improbable. For the disbanding of the poetry group was far from being the end of his friendship with Edgar. It was in fact but the beginning. Although for the next four years (1916–20) Pratt was busy in his several Saharas, he kept in touch – and far more frequently than by attending occasional literary evenings – with his kindly if often critical patron. Sometimes he called on him with new verse to be scrutinized before it was sent along to *Acta*, sometimes with new poems he had already confidently published, hoping for words of approval from Edgar. 'Pelham was always forthright in his remarks,' Pratt would recall, 'even when he knew I was squirming underneath. I didn't always agree with him at the time, but I usually realized later that he was right.' Edgar, for his part, though he confessed that in those early years he had seen little promise of Pratt's later achievements, seems to have had no doubt that the possibility of later achievement existed. Though generous to help and encourage young writers, he was not one to squander his energies on obviously hopeless cases. Pratt for all his slow and erratic progress was clearly not among these. He remained, in fact, Edgar's favourite protégé, to be helped and encouraged, supplied with books, sustained and counselled, fed at his table (in more senses than one), and at last, to use Edgar's phrase, 'rescued from Psychology' (and the Methodist ministry), and given a place at the master's right hand. 'I owe so much to him – friend and critic,' Pratt wrote a quarter century later. The debts were many and great, but none was greater than the one he owed Edgar for helping, far more perhaps than either realized, to make a poet of E.J. Pratt.

11

Tangential Steps

He ... like an undomesticated slattern,
Walks with tangential step ...   E.J. Pratt, 'The Truant,' 1943

That time in Psychology was ... the worst ... I ever had ...
                              E.J. Pratt to J. Frank Willis, 1961

RATT WAS NOW teaching and 'demonstrating' psychology almost full time. When not thus engaged he laboured on his doctoral dissertation, mostly at night. But financial need also compelled him to continue as an occasional supply preacher on week-ends as required, first at Streetsville with its four dependent churches, and then at nearby Trafalgar. During the summer, usually in August when the University was not in session and the regular minister was on holiday, he was responsible for all pastoral duties, living on the circuit full time, except for occasional mid-week visits with Viola Whitney at Atherley or at the summer cottage they used on Georgian Bay.

His boarding-mistress during these years (1915–18) was a Mrs Stevenson, in whose home he became almost a member of the family. Her daughter, then in her teens, on whom he made 'an indelible impression long before he became a national figure,' has written a brief but illuminating account of the young scholar-preacher in those days of his pastoral peregrinations. In one of the few intimate portraits we have of him at this time, she has written, in part, as follows:

He was tall and lanky, but paid very little attention to his personal appearance. My mother often had to suggest tactfully that he comb his hair, brush his clothes, or polish his shoes before going to church to preach. He was always very grateful when she did so. Having four churches, he had to hire a horse and buggy to travel on Sunday, which was a busy day for him. The strain was very apparent. But when the day was over he was a different person. Often after church in the evening a group of young people would gather at the house to sing around the piano. He would join us and, on occasion, become the life of the party. I remember very clearly two of his favourite 'acts.' One was entering the room as a drunk: he could be very realistic. The other was sitting with a flourish at the piano and imitating Paderewski playing the 'Dead March in Saul,' done with great body-bending, swinging of arms, and lifting of hands high above the keys. When he was in the mood his performances were the cause of great hilarity.

During August when he stayed the whole month with us, when he wasn't visiting his parishioners he spent most of his time writing. But sometimes he would offer to go out and hoe potatoes in our large vegetable garden. We were always very amused when he did this, because we knew that only a few 'hills' would get hoed. Most of the time he was leaning on the hoe deep in thought. I am sure that many of his early poems were conceived in our potato patch, or in our hammock under the chestnut trees ... My sister and I stood in awe of him, because he seemed to us a great scholar and a deep thinker. When he moved to Trafalgar he asked to stay on and board with us ...

Viola never went with him on these preaching assignments. He refused to permit her. Only once, when he preached in Toronto one evening, did she see him perform in a pulpit. She agreed that it was not his proper métier.

Nor was the role of businessman, at least in real estate. Yet his continuing need for funds combined with his unquenchable 'fancy for business' (to quote Viola) drove him to dabble in commercial ventures so long as his 'optimistic fatalism' prompted the dream of better things ahead. He had rented his two houses on Atlas Avenue, but he soon found that frequent repairs and refurbishing consumed so much of his small return, and the necessity of finding a succession of tenants was so great a nuisance, that being a landlord was hardly worth the bother. Hearing one day (to quote Viola again) 'of a wonderful bit of property in a downtown location,' he arranged 'a trade.' The deal completed sight unseen, he went down to inspect his new property. To his horror he found it a 'worthless patch' adjoining a large abattoir.

Learning of someone who owned a property in North York but who wanted a downtown site, he again offered to trade, and became the owner of a substantial property which might have proved a valuable investment had he developed it. What in fact became of it in the end is unclear from the records, though it is known that Pratt still owned it in 1932, when some enterprising speculator offered him two New-foundland dogs in exchange. Only Viola's intervention forestalled the rather inequitable bargain, which Pratt, it seems – reminding one of Goldsmith's Moses at the fair – would happily have made. But the acquisition of the North York property was by no means the end of his early speculation in real estate.

That his next venture proved to be much more successful was mainly due to his having a partner whose business acumen was, it seems, a natural gift. An old schoolmate from Pratt's years at Cupids and the Methodist College, Robert LeDrew had recently settled in Toronto where he had joined a brokerage firm. Equally impecunious and eager to prosper, they formed a partnership in a new real estate venture, convinced that in spite of Pratt's recent débâcles real estate was still a promising investment. With the help of another friend of Pratt's, Walter Brown (in philosophy at Victoria College and after-ward its President), they secured a plot of land on Kenworthy Ave-nue, 'away out in the sticks' off Danforth near Victoria Park. Just how or why Brown helped them is uncertain, but five or six small houses (Pratt himself later was unsure precisely how many!) were built there in the name of the Pratt-LeDrew partnership. 'Ned was also very vague about how they got built,' Viola recalled, 'but they did get built.' The houses were heavily mortgaged and were to liquidate the debt out of their rental income. This time the business of renting proved less onerous and more profitable than before. The partners were still active, if hardly wealthy, landlords at the time of LeDrew's death in 1919, when Pratt fell heir to his friend's interest in the property. During 1916–18 the two lived in one of their Kenworthy houses, managing much as Pratt, Pike, and Soper had done nearly a decade earlier.

But if his exploits in real estate brought him certain minor satisfac-tions, his work in psychology brought him fewer and fewer. It was not merely that his mechanical inaptitude made his laboratory work an almost daily crisis, nor that life in a disharmonious department was less than congenial; his whole perception of psychology, at least as it was mainly pursued in his Department, had undergone critical changes since he had written of 'the Science' as the great, new pathfinder to Truth. More and more often as time had gone on, the truant side of his nature, the visionary-idealist-humanist side, which was now in the process of turning him poet, had risen up in rebellion against the impersonal, detached, abstract character of experimental psychology and the coldly clinical, dehumanized pursuits of its proponents, the 'mechanistical psychologists' (as he later called them), who dominated the Department. Most of them, to quote him, 'were determinists,' adherents of the extreme variation on 'Wundtianism and [its] mechanisms' known as 'structuralism,' formulated and propagated at Cornell University by E.B. Titchener. Titchener's vast, four-volume work, *Experimental Psychology*, was the 'monumental textbook' round which most of the undergraduate work in the Department revolved, and W.G. Smith ('a man,' so Pratt described him, 'who could out-swear Beelzebub'), chief instructor in Psychology, was a dedicated proponent of the Wundt-Titchener system and methodology. August Kirschmann, former student and colleague of Wundt, was still Director of the laboratories. The syllabus included the theories of certain other psychologists, but Wundt and Titchener remained the presiding deities in the Department during most of the time Pratt was there.

Titchener's psychology was founded on Wundt, who had been his teacher, but unlike him Titchener excluded all philosophical concerns from his conception of psychology. For Titchener, to quote a recent commentator, 'psychology is a pure and general science':

It has no practical aims. It does not exist to discover means for improving human performance, to correct human infirmities. It is not ... aimed at helping to cure 'mental illness,' improve educational methods or assist in solving human problems ... It is impersonal, detached, abstract ... strictly empirical in its methods ...

In many ways of course such a conception was not far removed, if at all, from much of Pratt's 1913 essay, in which he had adopted an almost identical stance, and which clearly had been influenced by Titchener. But it was, especially in such things as its utter rejection of the 'detest[ed] "theological" concept of a soul or ego, controlling and organizing our reactions from some inner centre,' a very long way from George Blewett's conception of the 'new' psychology as 'a continuity between the enterprise of science and the vision of faith.' As his 1913 essay showed, Pratt, in his quest for Truth under mentors who had replaced Blewett after his death, had gone far beyond anything Blewett had envisaged by a marriage between science and the humanities, theology and philosophy in particular. The truant, despite the nagging misgivings of which the essay had hinted, had gone wholly over to the Panjandrum's camp and been taken captive. But he was not long there before it began to dawn on him that fruitful unions rarely occur in captivity. The marriage which he – and Blewett – had envisaged the new psychology as making possible, if not inevitable, was, he now realized, less than even a friendly acquaintanceship; rather, very often, a state of open hostility.

The addition to his duties in 1916 of classroom teaching, of which he was assigned more and more as members of the regular (junior) staff enlisted and went overseas, did not help to reassure him. At first he had welcomed the opportunity as a distracting change from his unhappy laboratory experiences. But 'lecturing or trying to lecture' in experimental psychology merely confirmed his dislike for it. He found, indeed, as he put it, that 'though I had to teach Wundt, I *hated* Wundtianism and [its] mechanisms.' The same seems to have been true of much of what had been his earlier persuasion. It is not surprising that there were many times when he felt 'a deep wish' for 'a whiff of idealism.'

Lacking the interest and motivation, he was hardly an inspired, or inspiring, teacher. In his later years in the Department, having pleaded with Dr Abbott, one of his old professors and the Department head, for something closer to his current interests, he was assigned courses in philosophy and a 'special' course in psychology designed for the School of Social Work. As a consequence he finished his career in the Department at least with flags aloft if not conspicuously flying, and a reputation among his students as 'a lucid, interesting, and personable lecturer.' But until 1918 most of his work continued to be in experimental psychology, expounding Titchener's textbook and, after a fashion, performing Wundtian-Titchenerian experiments and demonstrations.

He was kept on in laboratory work mainly because in wartime there were few if any replacements who might have done any better. Nevertheless his work was tolerated rather than approved and as time went on evoked increasing criticism from his superior, the master of maledictions, 'that man [W.G.] Smith.' Bungling experiments and breaking apparatus were humiliating enough, but having his incompetence proclaimed and himself chastized in front of his class was a mortifying ordeal: he was, after all, a man of more than thirty years of age. Yet this he often had to endure from Smith. As a former student of Pratt's would 'well remember,' 'W.G. Smith regarded him as an impractical dreamer, if not an utter nincompoop, and let his assistant know exactly what he thought of him.'

Besides this personal vendetta, Pratt was inevitably, as time went on, caught up in the general ferment of ill-will which pervaded the Department during most of his time there. Years later he recalled it with painful bitterness: 'That time in Psychology was one of the worst times I ever had. There wasn't *one* fellow who even *liked* another. They were all doing this –' and he whipped a forefinger across his throat, emitting as he did so an exquisite imitation of a snickersnee in action, adding, 'You could almost hear the blades!' It is hardly to be wondered that he should have longed for some congenial oasis where he might permanently encamp. Queen's University offered him a post in its Department of Philosophy, but he declined it. For one thing, though the atmosphere would undoubtedly have been very different at Queen's, his teaching duties would have been much the same. For another, he was anxious, now that it was in its final stages, to complete his doctorate. But most important, one gathers, was that he had become too deeply attached to Pelham Edgar and all that their association had come to mean to him to tear himself away from Toronto, even to settle in nearby Kingston.

What part was played in his changing perception of psychology by his new-found interest in poetry and humane letters generally, and the new kind of life it was already opening to him, is impossible to say with certainty. But one suspects that it was a significant part. The intellectual and imaginative world of Edgar and his circle, so utterly different from the world of his daily life in psychology, supplied needs and fed hungers, emotional as well as intellectual and imaginative, of which his 'Sahara' (the metaphor was well chosen) seemed to know nothing. Their very climates were zones apart; in one an atmosphere of creative warmth and recreative geniality prevailed, in the other the chill dispassion of men who lived by ingenious devices and clocklike mechanisms, to say nothing of the smoulder of barely suppressed hostility. A flaw, besides, in a metric line was far less critical than one in a 'metric curve'; and if an observant critic pointed him out the first, he was far more tolerant than any critic who pointed him out the second. If by chance the former swore occasionally, he was certainly no match for Beelzebub. There seems little doubt that his new avocation, both in itself and in its subsidiary rewards, played a significant part in revising his notions about psychology, both as an academic interest and as a possible profession.

Not that he had lost interest in the subject altogether. But the direction of what interest he retained had changed. The scientist in him still believed that scientific methods and techniques could be used successfully in many areas of human experience and behaviour. But having abandoned his naïve hope that the Science might unlock some of the larger riddles of human life, he now looked more and more toward concepts and techniques which might help to solve specific problems of individual human beings.

He revived an earlier interest in Functionalist psychology, to which he had been introduced and by which he had been briefly attracted as an undergraduate before being seduced by the more 'scientific character' of Titchenerian psychology. Functionalism, which had sprung up under John Dewey and J.R. Angell at the University of Chicago toward the end of the century, was basically anti-Titchenerian. Tracing their descent from Darwin and William James, the Functionalists were 'scientific' psychologists of a sort; but whereas the Titchenerians were primarily concerned with the 'impersonal, detached, abstract ... strictly empirical' analysis of the *content* and *structure* of consciousness, the Functionalists stressed the *function* of mental activity in enabling the individual to adjust to his environment and hence survive in it. Having a primary concern for individual differences – intelligence, perception, motor activity, and others – Functionalism was in effect a psychology directed to ends specifically excluded by the school of Titchener as lying beyond the bounds of a 'pure science': 'improving human performances' and 'correcting human infirmities.' Since these were matters in which Pratt was becoming increasingly interested as more and more he sought justification for his own work in 'social and humanitarian' results, the Functionalists and, in particular, one of their chief mentors, William James, who had long been and would continue to be one of his own intellectual lodestars, were especially congenial allies.

By a fortunate chance Pratt was shortly provided an opportunity to pursue these interests in a very practical way, something which so far he had been unable to do. This was the result of his Department's being invaded in 1915 by a most unusual personality, a young medical doctor-cum-psychiatrist named Clarence ('Clare') Hincks. Pratt did not come to know him until the following year, but once he did they soon became good friends and remained so for many years.

Hincks had graduated in medicine in 1907 and had gone into private practice in Toronto. There he had soon found himself so deeply involved in the personal problems and emotional ills of his patients that he had little time left to maintain a regular – and paying – medical practice. Taking postgraduate courses in psychiatry at the Faculty of Medicine, for which he felt a growing need, also reduced his hours of labour and his income. But his unusual talents were not overlooked. In 1912 he was appointed Medical Inspector of Toronto Schools and in 1915 Psychiatrist to the City Health Department. These appointments, however, intensified his desire for greater knowledge, less of the medical than of the *human* aspects of mental health. This it was that sent him to the Department of Philosophy in 1915 where he registered in some psychology courses and in the following year met E.J. Pratt.

Both sons of the Methodist manse, the two were strongly attracted to one another from their first acquaintance; similarities of background and upbringing gave them close bonds of sympathy and understanding. Soon Pratt had been indoctrinated with two of Hincks's strongest convictions: that mental health is a primary aspect of health per se, and that the chief concern of the mental hygienist must be the child, on whom the conditions which cause mental illness have not yet done their worst. Convinced that intelligence testing was a vital first step in both diagnosis and treatment, Hincks now enlisted Pratt's help in modifying the Binet-Simon Tests for use on Canadian children, intelligence tests never having been used in Canada before.

Pratt did his best, though the full extent of his contribution to this project is unknown. By 1917, however, the psychiatric clinic recently set up at the Toronto General Hospital by Dr C.K. Clarke, Dean of Medicine at the University, was sending children and sometimes adults to the Department of Philosophy (which still embraced psychology) for mental tests which no one outside it was yet qualified to conduct. Even there, apart from Hincks, the only competent administrant was not a regular member of faculty but (to quote Hincks's wife, then his assistant) 'a mere underling by the name of Pratt.' Soon, 'with the skill of a professional,' Pratt was teaching the psychiatric assistants who accompanied the children how to conduct the tests themselves. At last he began to feel that his years of training were being directed toward worthy ends. His new, though quite unofficial, occupation also provided him a new interest which, with the more personal satisfactions of his friendship with Hincks, proved to be a salutory antidote to the vexations of life in the Department of Philosophy. Without them and in spite of the other attractions the University still held for him, including his deepening friendship with Pelham Edgar, it is doubtful whether Pratt would have stayed on there to finish his doctorate.

His work on his doctoral dissertation, which continued intermittently from 1915 to 1917, might have been expected to bring him a measure of solace and relief. But this was not the case. For the man appointed to supervise his research was none other than Professor W.G. Smith. To make matters worse, his subject, Pauline eschatology (St Paul's doctrines of 'last things'), was not Smith's forte. He was a good psychologist but no specialist in eschatology, and suspected (according to Phelps) that Pratt had chosen the subject deliberately to embarrass him.

This seems as unlikely as Pratt's assertion in 1954 that 'the subject was not of my own choosing.' (His published thesis became a great embarrassment to him in later years, as students and critics began to delve into his published record, and he made many disclaimers of any personal attachment to the work or any special significance to be read into its subject.) Nor was the University in 1915 in the habit of thrusting subjects of research upon unwilling candidates. There is little doubt that the choice was his own, made because it combined a valid and respectable subject for detached, scholarly inquiry with a very real and long-standing personal interest. As Viola observed, 'The subject of "last things" was one that had gripped Ned's mind long before he wrote that thesis. He was well aware how much in our religion hangs on it.' His motives for a choice of subject seem to have run much deeper than a desire for a little personal revenge on W.G. Smith.

Eschatology was hardly a concern of the new psychology: the phenomena that came under its ken were of a much more this-worldly and measurable nature. On the face of it, then, his subject must have seemed an unlikely one for a candidate in a 'scientific' discipline. But, in fact, his researches were not primarily addressed to a speculative problem. For he chose an approach to his subject which enabled him to pursue a personal interest while strictly maintaining a detached and critical point of view, applying analytical methods, and achieving a more or less scientific end. Thus, the purpose of his study of ancient eschatological beliefs, both Pauline and earlier, was not, as his introduction made clear, to test their objective truth. It was rather to determine by critical analysis how 'various controlling ideas ... regulated and inspired ... people,' producing the 'thought-content of a succeeding age.'

But for the chronic antagonism between him and his supervisor, Pratt would probably have enjoyed his eschatological pursuits. But Smith was determined to play the schoolmaster, though his pupil was a colleague nearly his contemporary in age. During the early phases of his work, when Pratt read and made notes in Victoria College Library, there were few opportunities for recrimination. But as the work advanced, and drafts of chapters had to be examined *viva voce*, skirmishing became inevitable. Pratt, who had no relish for argument (except as a neutral bystander), received his criticism with courteous restraint. But as the project neared completion, and his final drafts continued to be mauled for minor flaws, he could no longer forbear taking up the cudgels in his own defence. When Smith exhausted himself of faults to find with the substance of the work – it was in fact a meticulous, carefully organized piece of work – he set himself up as a literary critic. Pratt, who took pride in his prose, had tried to write with somewhat more verve than is possible in the cool monotones of academic dispassion. But Smith, who prided himself equally on his scientific detachment and plain speaking, would have none of it. Roused now to righteous wrath, Pratt fought back. 'I'd tell him he was trying to pauperize the English language by cutting out all the finest words,' while Smith 'would go over to the window and shake with anger.' Time and again, Pratt would go home 'feeling sick' after another row with his mulish adviser. Small wonder that before the job was finished, he would come to loathe Smith with a rare intensity, and the dissertation almost as much.

There were many crises that brought him to the verge of giving up in frustration and despair. But his streak of stubbornness surfaced in time to save him from capitulation, and in the end bore him through. His *Studies in Pauline Eschatology* was finished at last, examined, and approved, and he was awarded the degree of Doctor of Philosophy at the May convocation of 1917.

The thesis, which was published later that year, is a model of logical, orderly, scholarly discourse, carefully documented, fortified with voluminous and impressive charts and tables, and attractively and lucidly presented. Despite Smith's fiats to avoid the literary and 'stick to facts,' the style is personal, the vocabulary rich, the prose rhythms easy and natural. Its matter, too, is solid and authoritative, and astonishingly wide-ranging. Nothing, it seems, in pagan-gentile, Judaic, or Pauline mytho-theology on his subject escaped his net – at least in so far as a layman can tell. Especially interesting for students of Pratt the man of letters is his sensitive response to and appreciative understanding of Paul's language: his metaphoric and analogic phraseology, his figures of speech drawn from everyday usage. Much space is devoted to minute and penetrating studies of metaphors which have become the hieroglyphs of Christian thought, but whose original meaning and force have been lost in the unthinking usage of many centuries. Whole sections are given over to what is essentially a poet's imaginative critique of the prose-poetry of an impassioned scholar who had a compelling message to deliver to common people. The poet-humanist side of Pratt has, at times at least, clearly prevailed over the scientist. Perhaps Smith had his reasons.

Pratt was not especially eager to publish the thesis and lived to regret that he allowed himself to be persuaded by members of the

Faculty of Theology to take his manuscript down to William Briggs, publisher for the Methodist Church. Briggs agreed to publish on payment of a substantial fee, which Pratt, having been assured that the sum would be recovered 'several times over,' somehow managed to raise. Published in the late autumn of 1917, the book was well received by theologians and favourably reviewed in *The Christian Guardian* (30 January 1918). Describing it as an 'exhaustive' study 'carried out with painstaking care and completeness,' and the author as one of 'the younger men ... whose work is adding to the fame of the university,' the reviewer went on to hope 'that the success of this first literary adventure' might 'lead to further work from his hand.' But, not surprisingly, the book had little appeal for the public at large and most of the 500 copies printed went unsold. For years afterward Pratt was to be painfully reminded of his lost investment by frequently encountering copies, priced at a few cents each, among the promiscuous piles of unwanted tomes heaped on the remainder tables of Toronto book shops. It was not until January 1932 that Ryerson Press (successor to William Briggs) finally disposed of its remaining stocks in a manner graphically suggested by the following correspondence between Pratt and Ryerson's editor, Lorne Pierce:

Dear Ned:
    The stock department are loath to consign your PAULINE ESCHATOLOGY to the Eschatological incinerator without your written say so. Will you please be good enough to give me your written authority.

Sincerely yours,
Lorne

Dear Lorne,
    You are most welcome to consign these Eschatological monstrosities to the everlasting flames where they should have gone in the first place. I burned some fifty copies of them seven years ago and the house has remained hot ever since. I calculate that twenty tons of coal was saved thereby. This is your authorization to give them a hasty and fiery dispatch.

Ned.

It was, of course, a defensive and therefore exaggerated response. The book was much better than he pretended to think. What irked him no doubt was the memory of his naïveté in having paid to have it published in the belief that people would buy it.

For most of eighteen months the greater part of his 'spare' time had gone to the writing of his dissertation. His poetry had inevitably been neglected, but his Muse had merely been sent into temporary exile, not banished for life.

> There still remains that strange precipitate
> Which has the quality ...

BOOK III: THE YOUNG POET 1916–23

... The sunlight in Apollo's eyes ...

12

Stirrings of New Notes

... The stirring of new notes ...
Pulsing their way into ... life. E.J. Pratt, *Rachel* (1917), 601–2

My first long poem [*Rachel*] written 40 years ago was never published ... [but]
privately printed ... for personal and non-commercial distribution ... It is
the most 'Newfoundland' poem I ever wrote ... I should rather have it published first in your Newfoundland collection [*Here the Tides Flow*, 1962]. As a
first long poem it is a bit amateurish and if you thought it advisable, you
might edit it ...

E.J. Pratt to D.G. Pitt, February 1958

LL TOO MANY of Pratt's memories of Newfoundland were
already linked with tragedy: 'We were always very close to
death.' It was, therefore, an ironic coincidence that he
should have been in St John's – his first visit since he had
left Newfoundland in 1907 – during one of the darkest weeks in its
history, the first week of July 1916. On 1 July at Beaumont-Hamél in
France, during the infamous 'July Drive' which had opened the
bloody Battle of the Somme, the Newfoundland Regiment had been
all but annihilated. At the end of his brief visit Pratt would take away
with him fresh memories of tragedy as painful as any he had already
laid away from the days of his boyhood and youth. By then few
families in the Island had been left untouched by the long lists of
dead, wounded, and missing which for days filled the public bulletin
board at the St John's General Post Office. Many victims were his old

schoolmates, and several (through his mother) his distant kin. But most heart-sickening of all had been finding the name of his brother Arthur among the 'wounded in action.' As it turned out his injuries had not been critical, but several days were to pass before the dread of a tragic sequel was lifted from their hearts.

Pratt had travelled to St John's for the wedding of his youngest brother Calvert, now comfortably established in business. He and his fiancée, Agnes Horwood, had invited him not only to attend the wedding but to assist in the marriage ceremony. This as an ordained clergyman he was entitled to do without any legal formalities, and he did. Though the unforeseen events of that dark week inevitably cast a pall upon the family and their friends, the marriage took place as planned on 6 July, the Reverend E.J. Pratt assisting the presiding clergyman. Unfortunately for him, his summer preaching duties at Streetsville soon called him back, and after another brief visit with his mother he returned to Toronto.

Only one short poem of his refers directly to the events of the first week of July 1916: the bitterly ironic 'Before a Bulletin Board (After Beaumont-Hamél).' But there is little doubt that it was his 'ineffaceable memory' of those grim days which more than anything else persuaded him to surrender at last to the emotions evoked by the War and commit his pen to 'the Cause.' Fortunately his capitulation was delayed long enough for him to begin, late that autumn when his dissertation was finished, his 'most "Newfoundland" poem' – also his first – and his most ambitious venture since the abortive 'epic' of 1914. Though memories of the first week of July undoubtedly helped evoke some of his most inglorious verse, his Newfoundland visit of 1916, by prompting not only his first Newfoundland poem but his first narrative poem of any kind, as well as one of his most personal, proved on balance, I think, to have been more fortunate than disastrous after all.

Rachel: A Sea Story of Newfoundland in Verse tells the tale of a widowed mother and her only son and the tragedy which befalls them as a consequence of the boy's choosing a life at sea contrary to his mother's wishes. The poem was conceived, Pratt wrote, as 'a Wordsworthian narrative in the manner of Michael,' referring, of course, to Wordsworth's 'Michael: A Pastoral Poem,' the story of a domestic tragedy not unlike that told in *Rachel*. But, also like 'Michael,' Pratt's poem is much more than a story told for its own sake. Like Wordsworth, using the story as form rather than as substance, and substituting New-foundland outport for English Lake District characters and setting, Pratt attempted an imaginative recreation of his boyhood world in the general manner in which Wordsworth often recreated his. *Rachel* is thus a very personal poem, a rarity in Pratt, and far more personal than merely drawing on memories of the outport world at large. Closer at times to *The Prelude* than to 'Michael,' the poem is in fact (as seen from brief excerpts used earlier) in many particulars a picture of himself and his early life. The relationship described between mother and son bears many resemblances to his own. His youthful fantasies of a life at sea are undoubtedly reflected in his young hero's yearning for such a life; and the boy's rejecting his mother's plans for him, to follow the sea instead may also reflect – consciously or not – his own already settled resolve to choose a life other than that his mother had set her heart on for him. Rachel herself, widowed mother, daughter of a mariner lost at sea, is clearly modelled on Fanny Pratt, doting and over-protective, whose maternal grandfather was drowned in Concep-tion Bay and whose paternal grandmother was named Rachel. John Pratt undoubtedly supplied the model for the village clergyman, whose 'high duty' it was '"To break the news" / ... when the storms / Had spent their fury on the coast ...' and 'comfort stricken ones' in 'low, assuaging tones.'

The poem was indeed very different from anything else Pratt had yet written, in fact from anything else he ever wrote. In time he consigned it to his limbo of personal ghosts, another 'thing' from his past to be 'buried' with all its 'amateurish flaws and puerilities,' its imitations of 'Wordsworth at a low level.' Yet, though the poem is admittedly only a partial success (but a greater one than his dis-claimers imply), for the student of Pratt's development as a poet and his progress toward poetic autonomy and self-discovery, *Rachel* is by far the most interesting and illuminating of all his early poems.

For one thing, it shows that in 1916–17 he was capable of writing much better than he had been, better in fact than he would in much of the verse to follow. It is true that *Rachel* occasionally lapses into bor-rowed banalities; sometimes too the language is flat and prosy, a result, as he himself saw it, of his initial Wordsworthian aspirations. But in general the difference between *Rachel* and any of his previous poems, especially in the texture of the verse, is so startling as almost to suggest that it had been written by a different poet. In a sense it had been. Until now, as we have seen, he had been largely 'playing with words – only *words*,' mostly those of other poets, a useful enough kind of exercise for an apprentice. But the apprentice who wishes to be a master craftsman must eventually relinquish his dependence on others, act freely on his own, be his own poet. Until now Pratt had rarely if ever done this, mainly because he had found no firm ground of his own to stand on, where he could feel comfortable and confident, fully in control of his materials and of himself. Following paths well worn by others, he had been led into places where neither imaginatively nor temperamentally did he belong. As a consequence he had tried to be the wrong kind of poet, writing poems that were only nominally his. What he had chosen to write about in *Rachel*, even though he had set out to do it in the manner of Wordsworth, gave him for the first time the kind of both matter and milieu (imaginative as well as physical) necessary to being his own kind of poet: a story which, if fictional, was nevertheless real, familiar to his experience; characters who already existed in his own mind; a setting which he knew from first-hand knowledge. Going back to the life and world he had known, determined so far as possible to be true to his familiar Newfoundland materials, he found that he had little choice but to discard most of the acquired paraphernalia he had been using, the stale images, the gratuitous epithets, the stock gestures, and false values. The idiom of Wordsworth was no better. Freeing his imagination and sensibilities, if only temporarily, from the unreal world of the Canadian and other Romantics, he found that he could when he tried use an explicit, realistic vocabulary, adopt a tough imaginative stance, use a hammer and chisel instead of a brush and palette. The world he was describing was, after all, one of deeds, actions, kinetic energies, hard substances, harsh sounds, and almost overwhelming visual dimensions. It was hardly matter for 'verdurous blooms,' 'cinctured tracery,' 'slumber-laden skies,' 'sapphire-bosomed swell,' or 'reverent hush.' Adjectives now were few, almost always essential, and usually simple descriptives. His substantives were concrete, sensory. But it was his verbs and verbals that were most striking and most Prattian: verbs of physical often violent action became the primary elements of most of his lines. The description which opens the poem is a very good example of his new style and mode of attack:

Piercing the rugged coastline for a depth
Of sixty miles in-rolled the giant bay,
Forming small harbours in its winding course
With narrow inlets, creeks and shallow coves,
Here following a rough unyielding shore
That broke a-main the Atlantic's power, and there
Curving with widened sweep into a mile
Of rising headland where, with favouring winds
A ship might ride at anchor, but so slight
The shelter in the heavier seas when gales
From contrary quarters raged upon the land,
That human hands by dint of arduous toil
Had countered Nature's sternness with long lines
Of shielding ramparts pushed out from the beach ...

It is not brilliantly original writing, but the style has both a firmness and suppleness, a concreteness and particularity, which have not hitherto appeared in Pratt's verse, suggesting also for the first time the kinetic and tactile qualities of his later more characteristic style. He had written nothing remotely like it before.

It is obvious that the more objective and concrete his materials the more comfortably and successfully he worked with them. Although he had been mistaken, as he himself later realized, in trying to be a Wordsworthian story-teller, the most successful parts of *Rachel* are those which are purely narrative or narrative-descriptive. When he flounders it is usually when he tries to convey emotional responses or to suffuse the narrative with romantic pathos. This is something at which he is clearly not at ease and therefore not adept. It is largely a matter of temperament, of psychology. Lyric verse, even what may be called 'impersonal lyric,' troubled him for many years, though he mastered it once he learned to find 'objective correlatives' for his emotions. Even so, most of his lyrics have a firmly maintained discursive shape and order, narrative, descriptive, expository, or dramatic.

Story-telling, or any objective mode that could be treated discursively, detachedly, was a different matter. A story assumed an audience, was by its nature a contract with a public, a social not a private event, a public performance and not, as he once put it, 'a psychological release for the poetic patient.' But, his personal idiosyncrasies aside, it should not be surprising that Pratt, product of a mainly oral culture in which the story-telling entertainer-historian was a kind of hero, by instinct himself a born actor, and by training and self-discipline an orator of sorts, should have found the narrative an ideally congenial form. It was to be his forte, satisfying most nearly his creed that the artist and audience are complementary.

In retrospect *Rachel* can also be seen as a kind of blueprint for much of Pratt's later work both lyric and narrative. We have, for example, in the person of Rachel the prototype of all his bereaved and anguished women whose husbands, lovers, or sons have gone to sea. Foreshadowings of such poems as 'Newfoundland,' *The Ice-Floes*, 'The Ground Swell,' and 'Erosion' are easy to detect, as well as many having no direct association with Newfoundland. One section of the poem (210–33), containing a 'high recital of heroic deeds / Wrought out upon the Ocean's troubled face,' sets forth an uncannily prophetic catalogue of most of his major narratives. There seems to be little doubt what kind of matter was already stirring his imagination.

Rachel was finished in the early summer of 1917 while Pratt served his customary stint as summer supply on the Streetsville circuit. On 5 July he wrote Viola that he had just finished the poem and was sending her a copy. He was also sending one to Pelham Edgar, on war service (briefly) at Camp Kapuskasing in northern Ontario. It was Pratt's first major poem and Edgar's verdict would be crucial. Its details are, however, unknown, but Pratt's recollection long afterward was that Edgar 'was very encouraging – thought it my best so far, very promising, and so on.' Edgar also, he recalled, 'made suggestions for improvement, which I always planned to do, but never did so far as I remember.' What attempts, if any, Pratt made to have the poem published at the time we do not know. Running to nearly 600 lines, it was too long for magazine publication, and in those days, especially in wartime, slim volumes by unknown poets were rarely taken on by publishing houses except at the author's expense, a proposition he rejected later when he tried to publish his second major work. But *Rachel* was at least *printed* before the year was out, thanks to the initiative of his friend, Robert LeDrew.

Living then with Pratt in one of their Kenworthy houses, LeDrew had watched and encouraged the poem's progress throughout its gestation. From the time he had first read lines by Pratt, he had been convinced of his genius; and *Rachel*, as a poem which evoked a world even more essentially his own than Pratt's, was to him its crowning achievement. Clearly, the poem deserved a wide audience. Knowing the obstacles to normal publication, he suggested a private reading to 'a group of friends.' So came about the first of the many 'premières' of new poems which Pratt gave for his friends during the next thirty years. LeDrew, it seems, included among the company his fiancée's brother-in-law, a well-to-do businessman who was visiting from New York. Prompted, one suspects, by LeDrew the man requested a copy of *Rachel* and, to quote Pratt, 'the next thing I knew he had a limited number [about 500 copies] printed in New York in soft covers and without the name of either printer or publisher,' or, he might have added, author. So it was that E.J. Pratt's first 'book' of verse was in fact a pirated edition, anonymous, undated, unrevised, and unproof-read, 'distributed just among friends.'

His friends, it seems, were 'generally enthusiastic, especially around the campus.' But in spite of its favourable reception and Edgar's encouraging verdict, rereading *Rachel* a year later Pratt decided that he himself 'didn't think much of the poem.' But by then he was planning, if not already writing, a new 'opus' which he hoped would be much more substantial and mind-revealing. Edgar, after all, as Pratt well knew, was a strong advocate of getting ideas into poetry.

Meanwhile, even before he was done with *Rachel*, Pratt had fallen victim to the war fever. Apart from finishing that poem and beginning his new opus, which was partly about the War, he wrote almost nothing but war verse for nearly the next two years. Unfortunately the lessons learned and the improved skills exhibited in writing *Rachel* appear to have had almost no effect on these poems, certainly not on those he wrote and hastily published between the winter of 1917 and early 1919. A few contain some passable lines, but others include many of the worst he ever published. On the few occasions when he diverted his mind from the War, the verse, on the whole, was much better. But it was, perhaps, inevitable that preoccupation with so emotional and provocative a subject as the War, as it continued to drag on and more and more of his friends and old classmates joined the ranks of the Fallen, should have beclouded the judgment and subverted the sensibilities of one still largely innocent of the exacting disciplines of poetry. Undoubtedly, too, having a particular audience in mind – the war poems he published all appeared in *Acta* – had its effect upon him. By contrast, a few years after the War, when the feelings it had generated had ceased to be so immediate, and he had more fully mastered the skills of his craft, Pratt published in *Newfoundland Verse* (1923) some of the best Canadian poetry to come out of the First World War.

(It should be noted that in *Newfoundland Verse* these war poems are grouped, along with a few that had appeared earlier, under the general heading 'Flashlights and Echoes: From the Years of 1914 and 1915.' From this it has usually been inferred that they were written much earlier than in fact they were. It is doubtful that any is earlier than 1917. The quality alone suggests a much later date for most of those published there for the first time. Some may well be late revisions of poems written earlier, 'Before a Bulletin Board,' for example. Others were clearly written not long before they appeared in *Newfoundland Verse*. 'Come Not the Seasons Here' is such a one. The obvious explanation for the misleading heading is that 1915 is one of the many printer's errors in the book. Pratt's heading was apparently intended to read '1914 and 1918' or '1914 to 1918.' In other words, these are his poems about the War, whenever they may have been written.)

Most of the fugitive pieces he wrote and published between the winter of 1917 and the autumn of 1918 (bearing such titles as 'The Seed Must Die,' 'The Greater Sacrifice,' 'The Great Mother,' and 'The Wooden Cross') may be passed over without comment. They do nothing to enhance his reputation, nor do they shed any significant light on his progress in the craft of poetry, except to show that for its sake the Great War could not end too soon. Yet while this is true of most of these poems, a few are interesting and significant enough to warrant at least brief comment.

'For Valor' (*Acta*, October 1918), despite many obvious echoes from his reading and a quantity of high-flown writing, is a curiously interesting poem, and better than most of the others, mainly because though the War has prompted it, it is only peripherally a war poem. Pratt had already used its chief motif – really its theme – two years earlier in 'The Sacrifice of Youth': the contrast between the life of quiet ease, whose reward is a mere gratuity, and that of heroic adventure, whose 'crown' is *won* in arduous battle. The theme, which he seems to have had a special fondness for and would use again, was one he had often heard expressed in vivid terms in a popular prayer-meeting hymn of his boyhood, Isaac Watts's 'Am I a soldier of the Cross?':

> Must I be carried to the skies
>   On flowery beds of ease,
> While others fought to win the prize
>   And sailed through bloody seas? ...

In similar metaphoric terms but far more detail, Pratt now makes it the basis of an elaborate religious allegory, clothed at times in a language which approaches the rhetoric of evangelical passion.

The poem begins with a long, meandering paragraph, replete, not inappropriately perhaps, with Romantic reverberations – Wordsworthian 'confluent harmonies,' Keatsian 'wine of mist and beaded foam,' Shelleyan 'nurslings of the hills' – in which he describes the peaceful, easy life of a mariner who sails only 'inland seas' – obviously a Great Lakes sailor. Then follows a vivid account of the contrasting life – clearly of a Newfoundland mariner – whose destiny it is

> To sail with thrice-reefed canvas, chartless gulfs,
> When stars have left their spheres, and the moon's rays
> Are swallowed up i' the void; when chaos broods,
> When rising seas have swept away the stanchions ...

– and so on, through a dramatic extravaganza of perils braved. But the poem does not end there: it goes on to present a vision, almost apocalyptic in nature, of the apotheosis of embattled man. Not only, Pratt proclaims, is the life of militant struggle 'nobler far' than that of 'flowing ease,' but the struggle itself is the redemptive ordeal by which, if he braves it, man may realize his latent divinity, become fully Man at last, 'Emerging from the clod, redeemed':

> ... This, this!
> Is to bring forth refined gold, nay more[,]
> Create a metal rarer than the gold,
> ...
> The birth-stamp of the human spirit, – This
> Is to outstrip the angel, put on God ...

The poem has many flaws, but it is a landmark of sorts. In it for the first time we meet full-face the poet of muscular action and, if only fleetingly, of the 'vigorous, virile' line (to use favourite terms of his later reviewers) whose image stamped much of his best poetry to come. The poem's statement too is of particular interest. Not strikingly original, it nevertheless embodies a conception of life and values not fundamentally different from that which informs much of Pratt's mature work. One wonders, of course, how far its fairly explicit Christian affirmation is his own, rather than that expected of a clergyman-poet in wartime. Nevertheless it is interesting, and perhaps significant, to find it here, even if only as a species of allegorical metaphor.

Apocalyptic consummations between war and religion are also featured in three poems written late in 1917. By far the best of these, 'Ode to December 1917,' probably because of its length (nearly 200 lines), was not published until it appeared with minor revisions in *Newfoundland Verse*. But it is the most original and experimental of his war poems, using a variety of metrical and stanzaic forms and based on a single extended metaphor that recurs frequently in Pratt: the cycle of the seasons (in both landscape and seascape) as representing the cycle of human life and the changing landscape of mind and emotions as they pass from the winter of war and despair to the springtime of peace and hope. Even as revised the poem is still a repository for many poeticisms from the latter-day landscape romantics. But it is apparent that Pratt is learning at last to avoid the purely gratuitous and ornamental uses of imagery and figurative language. The following lines, for example, were already part of the early version sent to a friend shortly after it was written:

Fled are they all,
The flowers and the birds,
In vain we call,
With cries too dumb for words;
The fragrance and the music gone,
The fire of sunset, flush of dawn,
The water-lily in the lake,
The robin's love-song in the brake –

All these are fled and gone,

...

Gone like the memory of a dream,
A rainbow hovering o'er a stream;
And we, of nature's joys bereft,
Are with her darkening shadows left
With gray upon the sea,
And driftwood on the reef,
With winter in the tree,
And death within the leaf.

It was not new, but it had scarcely been done better in Canadian verse.

It is, therefore, all the more astonishing that 'The Largess of 1917' (*Acta*, February 1918), obviously written at about the same time, should have turned out to be so bad. Parading a profusion of verbal banalities – 'the lifted wand of heaven's skies,' 'the passionate blush / Of damask rose,' the 'crystal shores' (of Heaven), the 'virginal white' and 'trembling vestments' (of snow on trees), 'God's martial hosts advancing, angel-psalmed,' to docket a few of them – it is as maudlin and sentimentally preachy a poem as he ever wrote. And he was thirty-six years old when this was published!

Yet he was *capable* of better things – when he let himself forget his parochial audience, third-rate models, and above all the War. Though his poetry had so far shown little sign of the fact, for some time now he had been reading, occasionally, Harriet Monroe's *Poetry: A Magazine of Verse*, the revolutionary little journal of 'modern' poetry published in Chicago. But, perhaps deterred by the more conservative expectations of his *Acta* readers, he had so far not ventured to experiment in the usually unconventional modes of verse he found there. But early in 1918 he decided to permit himself a modest excursion into Imagist territory. The result was undistinguished, but it showed that he could, when he tried, write with economy and minimal dependence on borrowed rhetoric. Originally entitled 'The Angler,' it was published, significantly perhaps, not in *Acta* but in a new, mildly radical University magazine called *The Rebel* (March 1918):

Dawn!
Gold-minted;
The monarch of the morning,
Awake;
Shadows withdrawn,
A sheet of glass rose-tinted,
The lake!
Splash!
A coral ring,
Studded with rubies and agates and gold,
Finely wrought out;
A vision of a silver flash, –
Lost! Was it a grayling,
Or a rainbow-trout?

He seems to have thought well of the poem, including it five years later, with minor revisions and the title '?', in *Newfoundland Verse.*

It was hardly a daring foray, but at least he had ventured on new ground. But not for long. Soon he was back in the old domains again, where, for all his public saw of him, he was virtually stalled for the next twelve months. It should be said, however, that in his new long work, *Clay*, by then in progress, he was for the most part eschewing the worst of his old sins, and by mid-1919 had succeeded in washing them away from almost everything he wrote. Traces of the old influences reappeared from time to time, but their domination had ended. Apart from a bombastic valediction to Kaiser Wilhelm ('Amerongen,' *Acta*, January 1919), the poems he published in 1919 are in most respects the best, the most original, of any he had yet committed to print. 'The Hidden Scar' (*Acta*, June 1919) is simple, direct, restrained, and quite free of decorative trimmings. 'In Memoriam' (*Acta War Supplement*, autumn 1919), a pair of commemorative war sonnets written for the occasion, lured him, predictably, into several brief lapses, but it is still the best war poetry he published before *Newfoundland Verse.* 'A Dialogue by a Stream,' an experiment in colloquial realism, shows that he was indeed making a conscious and deliberate effort to break still further away from the influences that had held him for so long. Undoubtedly because the poem used a daringly emphatic 'damn,' it was published not in *Acta* but in *The Rebel* (December 1919), such a term being much too strong for Methodist palates in those days. This surmise would seem to be confirmed by his replacing 'damn' with a quite innocuous term when, as 'Overheard by a Stream,' the poem was published in *Newfoundland Verse* by Ryerson Press, a Methodist firm. But 'big fool' had neither the authenticity nor the passion of the original expletive.

The last of what may be called Pratt's juvenilia appeared in *Acta* in January 1920, a single fifteen-line stanza entitled 'Blow! Winds, and Roar.' Apart from the closing lines in which he managed a relatively restrained elegiac effect, it is not especially noteworthy for either its merits or its faults:

> ... Along the tide-swept shore,
> The mornings break, the evenings fall,
> Night comes, and in the cliffs above,
> The sea-gull answers the fledgling's call
> But he – who was my life, my love –
> Returns no more.

As is so often true of Pratt, the speaker is, presumably, a woman. He published nothing more for nearly a year.

13

Matrimony and Other Diversions

One of the best things that ever happened to Ned Pratt was his marrying
Viola Whitney. Up until then he was just drifting hither and yon with every
tide that rose and fell. He had no settled way of life, no regular job, no actual
goal in life. And this was bound to militate against any real creativity. But
after he got married all that began to change ...
A.L. Phelps to D.G. Pitt, June 1967

PRATT'S DOCTORAL DEGREE had been conferred in June
1917. His major academic goal having been thus achieved,
the ostensible reason for his continuing in the Department
of Philosophy no longer existed. But what should he do?
His feelings toward the prospect of a permanent future in the Department had not changed, but there was nothing else in view. The Methodist ministry was still open to him, but his attitude toward that was
likewise unchanged. The old dilemma was still with him. In the end
he found he had little choice but to hang on with Abbott and Smith,
hoping like Micawber that something would turn up. By now he had
grown used to being in limbo; another year or so would not matter.
Being able to remain in Toronto, which he had long come to love, of
which he now felt himself almost a native son, among the friends he
knew so well and whose companionship was so essential to him, was
sufficient to salve the pains he might have to bear as a consequence of
staying on in his malcontent department.

He was still going out for a month in summer and on occasional
week-ends at other times to preach in Streetsville, Trafalgar, Clarkson, and elsewhere in that neighbourhood. While there he would

sometimes contrive to slip away with notebook and pencils to draft a stanza or two of verse. Former parishioners I talked with, or who wrote me about him, recalled his going off to the woods on a Saturday afternoon to write poetry. Sometimes, too, they recalled far different engagements from those with the Muse. An octagenarian in Clarkson vividly remembered fifty years later the Reverend Dr Pratt, in his 'pulpit clothes' and with 'devilry in his shining eyes,' eagerly usurping the duties of chief excavator and dynamiter to blast an eight-ton boulder out of existence.

Though less productive, perhaps, of grist to Pratt's poetic mill, his work in Mental Hygiene also continued. More and more closely as time went on he allied himself with Clare Hincks and C.K. Clarke in expanding the work done at the University for the Psychiatric Clinic at the Toronto General Hospital. Sometimes, too, Clarke conscripted him to conduct tests at a clinic which he had set up as an adjunct to the Toronto courts. This was usually work Pratt did not particularly relish, for it often entailed unpleasant encounters – with convicted murderers, for example, in the cells of Don Jail – though he later recalled them with retrospective humour and, one suspects, a degree of exaggeration. But having performed the chore fairly often for some months, after one exceptionally unpleasant duologue behind bars he persuaded Clarke to relieve him of any further such responsibilities.

But he had no qualms about throwing his support behind a new project launched by Clare Hincks in the winter of 1918. This was the creation of a Canadian equivalent of the American National Committee for Mental Health established a few years earlier by Clifford Beers. Hincks and his colleagues were convinced that without some such national organization little could be properly accomplished in Canada for the prevention and treatment of mental illness. Hincks called on Beers for advice and support, but it was mainly Hincks himself, preaching the cause like a Methodist evangelist, who roused the necessary interest and gathered the necessary funds to make possible a national convention in Ottawa during April that year. He was very pleased with his success but remained apprehensive that opposition, which was far from slight or silent, would kill the project even before it began. Feeling the need above all for moral support, he asked Pratt to accompany him and Clarke to Ottawa. Pratt gladly agreed to go, and when on 26 April 1918 the meeting convened it was he who seconded the historic motion which established the National Committee for Mental Hygiene (later the Canadian Mental Health Association). Despite all the multifarious interests which ensnared his time and attention in the years ahead, Pratt remained a sponsor and advocate of the Association's work till the end of his life.

But his immediate involvement with Clare Hincks was far from over. His National Committee established and girding itself for battle, Hincks now turned once more to projects nearer home, in Toronto. Convinced that the most serious and compelling problems in mental health were those of the young, he proposed that the City of Toronto establish a new post in its Health Department, a directorship of mental health, a post to be filled by a trained psychologist who would work mainly in the city's schools. The Council agreed and offered him the job. But Hincks was too deeply involved in his work at the clinic and in plans for his new National Committee to accept. In declining the offer he proposed an alternative candidate: Dr E.J. Pratt. The Council, it seems, was pleased to endorse the proposal, and Pratt though somewhat diffident agreed to take the post. So it was that, in the words of Dr John Griffin (later Director of the Canadian Mental Health Association),

Ned Pratt became the first Mental Hygienist to be employed by any municipality anywhere in Canada to work primarily with children in the schools. His job was to go around the city testing children who were suspected of being retarded or having learning difficulties, and from this has developed the very effective work of special classes, courses, and other provisions for the mentally retarded now organized throughout the country. Pratt was the pioneer, and laid the groundwork on which the present programmes were built ...

Thus, though virtually forgotten since, the unlikely fact is that Pratt not only played an important part in the history of Canadian literature; he also played a significant one in the history of Canadian medicine.

His new job was not lucrative, intended as a part-time post for a psychologist regularly employed elsewhere, but it meant that he was now sufficiently well-off to get married at last. He and Viola had been engaged since 1914 and the relationship had not only survived the prospect of an indefinitely delayed marriage, but had grown stronger and closer. The uncertainty of his future and the meagreness of his income, as well as the obligation which Viola felt to repay her parents for her own education, had caused a continuing postponement of their marriage. Now, however, their prospects were more sanguine. Small though it was his new stipend nearly doubled his income, slightly increased also by his promotion that year from demonstrator to instructor in psychology. On the strength of these improvements he and Viola decided to postpone their wedding no longer.

They were married on 20 August 1918 by the Reverend J.F. McLaughlin, one of Pratt's old professors at Victoria. Robert Le-Drew, whose health had been failing for some months, had long been chosen groomsman. Unfortunately his illness (Hodgkins disease) had worsened rapidly during the summer, compelling him to enter hospital, but he would not permit a further postponement on his account and Pratt asked Clare Hincks to accompany him to the altar. Unable to afford an expensive honeymoon, the newlyweds borrowed a cottage in Muskoka, where in spite of 'myriads of mosquitoes' they passed 'a quietly pleasant week' broken only by Pratt's departure on a brief visit to LeDrew's bedside. The Hinckses' oft-repeated story that Pratt's entire nuptial luggage consisted of 'a small dilapidated briefcase containing three books and a toothbrush' is unverified by Viola Pratt's recollections.

Back in Toronto, established in a small apartment on Dupont Street, Pratt gradually began to settle into more or less conventional domestic habits, although at the age of thirty-six he was hardly likely to be made over by a wife. Wisely she made few attempts to change him. Having had few resources to spare on dress, he had grown indifferent to clothes, usually dressing carelessly, even sloppily. Viola soon took his wardrobe under her supervision and before long had him dressing fairly neatly if somewhat less comfortably, but he was never noted for sartorial distinction. She early abandoned trying to keep him in proper headgear, topcoat, and overshoes, for he had a habit, which persisted, of coming home in someone else's, usually much more worn than his own and always ill-fitting. (Sometimes the effect was quite startling, deserving an entry in Viola's diary: 'Ned arrived with a little black fedora, which made him look like a brisk undertaker. His own nice shabby grey hat will now be misfitting someone else.') What he did not exchange he simply left behind: toothbrushes, umbrellas, shaving-brushes, pyjamas, and much else – abandoned in hotels and the houses of friends wherever he went.

As a handyman about the house he was quite unhandy, but he fancied himself a gardener, spending many hours happily grubbing away in whatever small patch a Toronto backyard afforded him. Later, at the summer cottage he acquired in Bobcaygeon, he raised some very good squash, strawberries, and 'Irish Cobblers' (his term for all potatoes). He also fancied himself an expert chef, and enjoyed presiding at the kitchen stove or, more especially, an outdoor barbecue. The verdicts of his friends varied widely on the results of his culinary enterprises, but there is no question about his enthusiasm for them. The business of dining and the rituals of the table became, indeed, a life-long preoccupation. Though his appetite was not great or his tastes exotic, he coveted the reputation of being a good host. Viola soon learned to expect unexpected guests, for he early acquired the habit of inviting friends, and sometimes total strangers, 'up to the house for a feed,' and they rarely declined his genuinely warm invitation. He usually did not bother to warn his wife by telephoning. His fondness for playing host led to more munificent occasions – receptions, parties, dinners large and small, and sometimes an 'apocalyptic banquet' – for which in time he became widely celebrated in Toronto and beyond. But for some years yet his means were too meagre to permit many such fêtes.

Viola soon learned, however, that he had other tastes which he could afford to indulge, if circumspectly. Though he played no musical instrument (except the piano a little) and could not sing, he was fond of music. Accordingly he soon bought a small gramophone and invested in a single record, the sextette from *Lucia di Lammermoor*, which he played over and over until it was worn down to a tuneless cacophony of scrapes and scratches. Other operatic selections were added in time, of which 'the more melting arias of Verdi' (to quote one of his friends) quickly became and remained his life-long favourites, followed closely, and curiously enough, by *The Dead March in Saul*. Though his early education had excluded them completely, he soon became a passionate devotee of the opera and symphony, indulging his devotion by regular attendance at Massey and Convocation halls, by slowly building a fine collection of gramophone records, and later by regular listening to radio concerts.

Among the many other things that Viola Pratt soon learned about the man of contradictions she had married, what amazed her most – 'It appalled me when we were first married, though I got used to it in time' – was his addiction to the sport of boxing. For years he rarely missed a prize fight of any consequence staged in Toronto, and frequently made his way to contestants' dressing-rooms afterward. One of his long-cherished memories was of meeting Gene Tunney and shaking his vast hand. When fights on film arrived at Toronto movie-houses, he was usually among the first to view them; later, when radio and then television brought them into his home, he rarely missed a broadcast. 'I've a passion for fights,' he once admitted to a reporter who had heard strange rumours about this most unpugnacious of men. 'They hold a tremendous fascination for me. I love to read about them and I never miss one.' His curious passion is, of course, most obviously diagnosed as another form of behavioural compensation. But it is not unlikely that it was also a gesture of defiance toward another of the many prohibitions of his Methodist youth. In any case it is not surprising that imagery of the ring occurs fairly often in his poetry.

Arthur Phelps did not exaggerate when he spoke of Pratt's marriage as 'one of the best things that ever happened to him.' Its economic foundations were, to be sure, precarious, and the added responsibility of supporting a wife, and soon a child, intensified the pressure he felt to secure his future. Yet having a settled home for the first time in more than two decades gave him an anchorage whose physical comforts and emotional if not economic securities went far to countervail the other uncertainties of his life that remained. (It is not surprising that his writing soon reflected the benefits of at least a modicum of orderliness and tranquillity in his life.) Viola, moreover, was an ideal companion for one long accustomed to going his own way, indulgent toward his whims, amenable to his habits, amused more often than annoyed by his eccentricities. There were times when her patience was heavily taxed and her good humour brought almost to the point of souring, but her understanding of his temperament and sympathetic tolerance of his foibles preserved the vital fabric of what was, despite the trials and near tragedy which later beset it, an essentially happy union. Before very long, like Samuel Johnson (to whom he bore certain behavioural and temperamental resemblances), Pratt developed a taste, if not a need, for the peculiar emotional and intellectual stimulants found only at a club or similar resort, becoming in time a confirmed habitué. His home, nevertheless, was his ultimate refuge, his cloister and castle, where he might, as he wished, retreat behind his closed doors or throw them wide to all who might come.

As time passed and his means improved (a little), his doors were opened more often and more widely, each of the succession of houses he occupied becoming a veritable hospice-cum-salon for all whom his fancy adopted. Since many of these were young writers, and sometimes artists of other species, still struggling in obscurity and often penury, needing the support of a patron and mentor (as he himself had found in Pelham Edgar, on whom his own role was closely modelled), the part he played in the literary and artistic life of Canada in the second quarter of the twentieth century was far more than that of a major actor upon its stage. Behind the scenes and in the wings he was in many ways no less active and perhaps more influential. Many years later Lorne Pierce (whose friendship he made in the 1920s), writing of the marriage of Pratt and Viola Whitney, observed: 'The home they established together belongs to the history and legendry of the arts and letters of Canada ... the influence of that fire-side upon our times is beyond measure ...' As we shall see, Pierce was probably not far off the mark, if at all. But in 1918 Pratt was still very much in need of a patron of his own. Fortunately he had one, who would shortly 'rescue' him from the last 'Sahara' still barring his passage to the green pastures now in sight.

As it turned out, his new work for the Toronto City Health Department proved to be, initially at least, far less an arid drudgery than he had feared. For one thing, he found that the nature of the project had been changed. Instead of making widespread visits to the Toronto schools to investigate reputed cases of mental defectiveness and retardation, at the suggestion of C.K. Clarke, the Health Department and Board of Education had agreed that he should first conduct a 'vitally necessary pilot project': a comprehensive 'psychological survey' of the entire population of a single public school. The findings of such a survey, it was argued, would make possible a far more enlightened approach to future action than existing knowledge then permitted. He was pleased with the change, since it set more specific goals for his task, more clearly defined its terms of reference, and confined his activities to a single locale and his contacts to a single group of students and their teachers.

Western Avenue School, Toronto, was chosen as the site of his pilot project, because (according to the official records) 'it was of an average social status, with an enrollment large enough to furnish a basis for reasonable generalizations, and moderate enough to be effectively handled by one investigator.' Embracing a total of nearly 700 children, the survey was to be 'the most intensive piece of work of its kind ever attempted in Canada,' the results of which when published would provide 'useful material' for 'boards of education and other interested bodies and individuals throughout the dominion.' Stated briefly, its object was to correlate measured intelligence quotients with such things as academic ratings, general school behaviour, nutritional history, family background, and, where they existed, physical stigmata, and emotional problems. It was clearly an ambitious and thorough survey, requiring much patience, professional skill, and time-consuming labour. But though he still had his duties as Instructor in the Department of Philosophy, Pratt threw himself into the work with the enthusiasm that a new challenge characteristically evoked.

Though they kept him ceaselessly busy, he seems to have enjoyed his visits – made whenever his teaching and laboratory schedules permitted – to Western Avenue School, enjoyed working with the children, conducting his tests, recording and tabulating his findings. Not only was the work new and challenging; it also gave him a sense of participating in a useful humanitarian endeavour. His training in psychology was at last being directed toward problems surrounding 'human performances' and 'human infirmities.' But the added strain eventually began to take its toll of both his physical and emotional reserves. By the end of the academic year, the job still only half done, he was already finding the project a heavy burden.

To rob him of the relief he might have found when the University term ended in May (1919), he allowed himself (tempted, no doubt, by the extra fee) to be conscripted to give an eight-week course at the School of Social Service. The course, a special one and the first of its kind in Canada, had been devised by Clarke and Hincks for nurses and other institutional workers who were being increasingly con-. fronted with the peculiar mental and nervous problems of War veterans returning from the battlefields of Europe. Though he was not one himself, Pratt, we are told, was regarded by Clarke and Hincks as 'the only person in the whole of Toronto competent and understanding enough to provide this unique service.' As if that were not sufficient, when the special course ended in late June he again succumbed to the lure of a further small emolument and agreed to teach a four-week course (8 July–8 August) in 'Psychology: General and Special' at the University Summer School for Teachers. Preaching that summer at Clarkson and Sheridan ensured that his week-ends were equally busy.

It would not have been surprising had his verse been wholly neglected during these crowded months, but such was not the case. Though his left-over time and energy must have been very limited, most of it seems to have been spent on his writing. To quote Viola, recalling those early months of their marriage:

When the spirit moved him – and it did quite often, even when he was so busy – it made no difference who was around, or what was going on, Ned was off to his room to write. He'd say, 'I got a new idea for another poem today,' or 'I thought of a way to fix up the one I messed up last week,' and he had to get it down before he lost it again. I didn't see much of him when he got caught up in something he was really intent on ...

But she was not complaining. It is obvious that he was fortunate not only in having an oasis to escape to from his multifarious Saharas, but also a wife who understood his need to escape and did not attempt to prevent his doing so.

Nevertheless, by the autumn of 1919, still frantically striving to keep his many irons in the fire, he had come to realize that he could not remain much longer on the ceaseless whirligig to which he had bound himself. But what could he do to escape it permanently? Despite his experimental débâcles in the laboratory – which had grown fewer with the passage of time – a permanent post in psychology was there for the asking. But though his feelings toward the Science had been softened a little by the satisfactions he had derived from his recent activities, the thought of a lifetime in a department that was still, and promised to remain for some time to come, 'a bear-garden of Kilkenny Cats – if you know what I mean' made him 'sick to the heart.' Yet it was clear to him that he would have to choose something, and very soon. Once again it was Pelham Edgar who came to the rescue.

14

Storming Parnassus

'Clay' was a philosophical poem – a lyrical drama so-called done in 1918 [actually 1918–20]. I had high hopes of this at the time but on looking at it soberly later I concluded that it was exceedingly dull and verbose ... I salvaged a small section of it – the conclusion – and there it is [in *Newfoundland Verse*] ...

Yes, the conclusion ... did represent my viewpoint and still does – *more or less*. I can never see nihilism behind any struggle ...

E.J. Pratt to E.K. Brown, 1942

UCH OF WHAT TIME Pratt was able to snatch from his busy schedule between 1918 and 1920 was occupied with the 'opus' which he had been contemplating since the winter of 1917–18. Postponed while he paid 'Honor's tribute' to 'the Fallen' (and duly belaboured 'the Foe'), it was finally begun, it seems, during the Christmas holidays of 1918. This ambitious undertaking was a 'philosophico-lyrical drama' that he called *Clay*, less than one-fifth of which he ever published, as 'A Fragment of a Story' in *Newfoundland Verse*.

Pratt often referred to *Clay* as his first long poem, curiously omitting all mention of *Rachel*. He would then proceed, in that mood of ironic self-mockery which he liked to indulge in when recalling in later years his early endeavours to realize high and earnest ambitions, to give a totally fictitious description of the poem, calling it a five-act play in the Elizabethan manner, full of carnage and bloody exits. It is indeed written in a more or less dramatic form, in three 'acts' and eight 'scenes,' but it can hardly be called a play, Elizabethan or other-

wise. It has no plot, and no external action except for what is reported, and that is very generalized: storms at sea and wars on land.
True, it is written mainly in blank verse, but, the long polemical
monologues being freely interspersed with rhymed lyrics, the 'play'
bears closer resemblance to *Prometheus Unbound* and *The Dynasts* than
to Elizabethan drama. The characters, of which there are five, are
static and wooden, differentiated only superficially by what we are
told about them or by the philosophical and religious views they
represent. They are actually closer to allegorical personifications than
to human personalities.

But there is no doubt that Pratt intended *Clay* to be a magnum
opus, quite unlike and vastly superior to anything he had done so far.
Many years later, describing his 'high hopes' for the 'drama,' he wrote
as follows:

I started out most ambitiously and with a cock-sure confidence that I would
storm Parnassus ... I was consumed with a desire to write a philosophico-
lyrical drama in which all I had learned and taught in philosophy and psychology would be presented to the public in a verse composition. I spent two
years upon it, which really meant two summers and two Christmas vacations ... [The poem was begun in late 1918 and finished, apparently, in the
summer of 1920.] It was full of theories and reflections of theories, ethical
maxims, philosophical truisms, bald, very bald generalizations – practically
the whole cargo of the department of philosophy and psychology as it existed
twenty years or so ago in the University of Toronto ...

This, though partly true, is also exaggerated and misleading. Needless to say, there was much in philosophy and psychology at Toronto
which does not appear in the poem. Yet it does reflect much that his
reading in nineteenth-century and contemporary philosophy and psychology had thrown together in his mind. If *Rachel* was a personal
poem in that it drew on his childhood memories and experiences, *Clay*
in a very real sense was even more personal in that it attempted,
though in the objective and impersonal form of a drama, to sort out,
piece together, and give rational and coherent form to a chaos of
philosophical, religious, and ethical notions which had been churning
around in his mind for a decade or more.

The 'play,' set in Newfoundland during the Great War, is in the form of a series of philosophical colloquies interspersed with 'mood' lyrics. There are three main characters: Julian, an old man of the sea, for whom life has long since extinguished all traditional religious belief; his young friend, Merrivale, 'a traditionalist,' who still clings to the old creeds of a revealed religion; and Thaddeus, 'a seer,' who traverses a middle ground in quest of a faith which will resolve the baffling contradictions all too apparent in the record of human history and the spectacle of incessant conflict between man and nature, and man and man. At the beginning of the 'action,' which is spread over three years, Thaddeus like Julian is also deeply influenced by the grounds for pessimism and scepticism which he sees all round him. But unlike Julian his mind is not closed to other 'evidences.' A seeker for 'the Truth' – and therefore identifiable with Pratt himself – he must examine both sides of the ledger, and in the end frames a simple, heroic philosophy of life, not unlike that expressed in the recent shorter poem 'For Valor,' which affirms the 'higher meaning' and 'ultimate values' of life, a 'view' which Pratt declared many years later to be 'more or less' his own.

But although this may be true, it is Julian nevertheless who constantly occupies centre-stage, whose dark view of life and the Universe is given fullest and most emphatic (one may almost say enthusiastic) exposition, who is given most of the best lines, and whose arguments come closest to conveying conviction. Disappointed and disillusioned by tragedy and 'ruined hope' in his own life, as well as by the record of human folly and evil, Julian has lost all faith both in a rational cosmic order and in the moral progress of man. Acutely sensitive to human suffering and still capable of deeds of great compassion, he nevertheless can find no evidence in the record of human evolution and history from which he can infer anything but a mindless, haphazard, 'Sterile progression ... where each life repeats / The racial circuit, and finds unrepealed / The acrid law by which its parent died.' He can conclude only that

A gambler's been at work upon this job,
Or else a journeyman that did not learn
His trade too well, and left somewhere a flaw,
Spoiling a nobler plan ...

Like Hardy in *The Dynasts* (a poem which almost certainly influenced the writing of *Clay*), Julian is acutely aware of the irony inherent in an evolutionary process of which the end result is (in Hardy's words) 'the intolerable antilogy of making figments feel.'

Drawing thus the bleakest conclusions from Darwinian naturalism, Julian surveys both the natural and human worlds to find only 'Hell's jungle-statutes' reigning wherever he turns:

> ... everywhere that human feet
> Had trod he saw the Satyr's hoof; a core
> Malevolent inhered in life; the ape
> Was grinning through men's eyes and teeth ...

Everywhere man and nature are locked in 'deadly feud,' the outcome of which is unaffected by any manifestation of either justice or compassion. Such a spectacle can only confirm his deepest pessimism concerning whatever Power may control the Universe:

> ... What Father, this,
> Who cares so little for his children's fate,
> That though he holds the sea within his hands,
> He pours its floods upon their heads, lets loose
> His lightnings, blasts and stalking pestilences,
> Although, it's said, that by his name's great power,
> They could be held, mute, harmless, near his throne,
> Chained to its pillars ...
> Who calls him Father; hears his Shepherd's voice;
> Knows him as Friend, Physician, Master, King?
> The subject's head falls crushed within the wheels
> Of some immaculate law ...
> A sufferer calls in pain,
> In the lone watches of his couch, and hears
> No answer save the leaden brush of wings
> Against the window-pane ...
> Name you him, Father?
> God? No. Rather a Potter with some clay.

Nor does Julian find less reason for despair when, leaving the divine aside, he turns to the purely human world. For the record of human 'progress' shows neither evidence nor promise of any significant melioration of man's lot vis-à-vis either nature or his fellow man. For Julian the failure of technology to tame 'Dark Nature's minions,' which still 'break from the leash of law' as they have done from time immemorial, proves the hollowness of material progress; and the ever-recurring ravages of war are proof abundant that 'moral progress' is equally illusory. Above all, he sees in the failure of Christ's mission ('as failed / He has with the momentum of the years') the final proof that there is little hope for man's salvation here or hereafter:

> There was a hill once climbed, on which the world
> Had built a warrant for a grander faith,
> A hope more excellent. A cross was raised,
> And at its foot a river ran whose fount
> Welled from the noblest veins that ever bore
> Imperial tides. This was the last great stream;
> The hill – the final altar of the world;
> The tender hands upraised in death had made
> High intercession, closing once for all
> The scourge that bled the heart, scourging the soul ...
> O broken reed! O spirit! trebly-crushed
> By the barbed insult where the iron failed,
> By dreams o'ershot and courage spent for nought;
> Still are the stones laid and the shambles spread,
> The candles lighted and the censer swung,
> And crosses! ... In cluttered heaps they rise,
> Stacked pile on pile, until they twist and sag
> The rivets on the bolted doors of God;
> And Calvary – is but a peak that flared
> An evanescent torch whose light was quenched
> In a red mist of sweat, and man's tired feet
> When once they scale the summit must, in shame,
> Re-walk the bloody gradient to the grave.

(Despite his later dismissal of the poem as 'dull and verbose' – and much of it is – such a passage alone shows very clearly, I think, that the E.J. Pratt we know best, the passionate ironist, the master of the spare, controlled, taut line and the evocative image, is already close at hand.)

So far – and the 'play' is three-fourths over – Julian has had the best of the argument, although Merrivale (supported by two minor characters) has put up a fairly spirited defence of Christian orthodoxy. But now, three years having elapsed since the events of the opening scene, the initiative passes to Thaddeus. He has fought his way through the labyrinths of the doubters and pessimists and has emerged at last into the light of a new 'faith,' which he is ready to defend as vigorously as Julian will oppose it. The new faith, which we can pretty safely assume to represent the rational synthesis to which Pratt's 'quest' had led him by 1919, is founded on a simple conviction that the human spirit, whatever its origin and destiny, is something more than a manifestation of merely physical energies, something, therefore, which neither Darwinian naturalism nor scientific material-ism can account for. The grounds for this conviction he finds mainly in man's unique capacity for deeds of heroism, self-sacrifice, compas-sion, and love which neither mere mechanisms nor rational beings programmed for mere survival can possibly evince. He cites as evi-dence the self-sacrificing ministrations of nurses on a battlefield; a shipwreck in which 'a slim girl' gives up her place in the lifeboat to 'an aged woman / Unnoticed in the crowd'; a 'lad' who 'struck out in the storm without a star' foredoomed to lose his life attempting to save another's. 'No life,' he is convinced, 'however craven at the face,' but finds 'a courage stirring at the core.' Thus, he believes, 'The ground-work's there to build a structure on.'

The old apostate, not surprisingly, is quite unmoved:

> ... Enswathe it as you may
> The skeleton will grin and mock the hand
> That touches it.

But Thaddeus too has his reply:

> No. Lime and ash tell not
> The story of the struggle. Causes lost
> Awhile on earth, at stake or cross, try out
> On new arenas fiercer qualities.
> They are reborn in the air; they storm
> The souls of men; find homes in thunder-peals;
> Are hitched to lightnings. Slain, they rise again

With such forged temper that they turn aside
The opposing edge of armouries of steel.
And every life that guideless though it seemed,
And blinded to the sockets, joined
The losing issues swings again to play
With falcon vision and its speed of wing,
A winning game.

The poem continues through several hundred more lines, but this is its high point. This is the climax of the debate, the most positive affirmation which Pratt can make – at least at this stage in his wayfaring. In the end Julian remains not quite convinced, though wavering:

... there is a knocking in this clay, –
A restless flame, – something that, if it could
Would leap the grammared confines of slow speech,
And give the echo to your dancing words.

The poem is long, too long, and sags under the sheer weight of its 'prose meaning.' Pratt makes a conscientious, and sometimes successful, effort to relieve the burden by clothing his meaning in the effects and accessories of poetry, but all too often that coalescence and mutual transmutation of elements which is the essence of poetry does not occur. Yet where he succeeds in achieving this, as he does, for example, in several of the passages quoted above, the lines are surprisingly effective, rising at times to levels of near sublimity (for example, the lines beginning 'There was a hill once climbed ...' already commented on briefly). But in general the poem all too obviously has what Keats described as 'a palpable design upon us,' something which as he well knew, and Pratt was learning, is inimical to poetry's being 'great and unobtrusive, a thing which enters into one's soul ...' The very nature of what he set out to do in the poem almost inevitably foredoomed much of it to be dull and verbose.

His later assertion that it contained 'the whole cargo of the philosophy department' may be an exaggeration, but it is evident that he has sampled a large portion of its manifest. Few of the ideas are original, most being commonplaces of the great confrontation between religion and its many recent assailants and revisionists which Pratt had long encountered in his university studies and reading. Yet *Clay* is not quite the unpoetical hodge-podge which he would later declare it to be. Though my brief summary can scarcely have suggested the fact, it has a kind of unity and pattern, and, as noted, occasional passages that reach the heights of poetry. Several of the brief interspersed lyrics are among his best war verse: for example, 'Now let the earth take ...' and 'Snowfall on a Battlefield.'

What is most interesting about *Clay* is, of course, its dramatic portrayal of Pratt in conflict with himself, that side of his consciousness which inclines him to assent to the rational, coldly logical findings of scientific naturalism in contention with that other side which resists such assent and looks instead for grounds to believe that the Universe comprehends a moral order and that Man is more than clay. The poem is thus in a very real sense a recapitulation of his troubled quest for final answers, which by 1920 at least led to a clearing in the jungle if not yet to the high ground of a final vantage-point. There is no doubt that he intends the optimistically affirmative faith voiced by Thaddeus to constitute his primary message to his reader. Even so, the elaborate and reiterated asseverations of Julian's scepticism, the poetic care and attention he devotes to them, his making Julian not only his chief character but also the best developed, the most clearly conceived, suggest that despite the poem's contrary conclusions, somewhere in the back of Pratt's consciousness there remains a lurking suspicion that Julian may be right. The faith expressed by Thaddeus is, after all, a kind of rational compromise, and it can hardly be without significance that whatever case the poem makes for Christian theism (through Merrivale and his friend) it is the least convincing of them all, giving no place whatsoever to the Incarnation nor to any doctrine of human immortality.

Yet the view of man and human life which, despite the weight given at times to contrary arguments, the poem ultimately affirms, and which Pratt later declared to be his own, is neither pessimistic nor determinist. Whether or not man's origin or his destiny is in the hand of a benign Deity, he is much more than either animal or automaton. This alone is sufficient to confirm Pratt's declaration of assent, for the most fundamental characteristic of human nature as he sees it is man's constant refusal to conform to nature, to be a docile member of the 'cosmic ballet.' Product though he may be of natural processes working mindlessly through mechanisms of survival and self-preservation, he nevertheless spurns his origins, turns truant from his very nature, to manifest compassion, self-sacrifice, and love. Unlike the clay which humbly submits to the potter in Isaiah (46:9 and 64:8, from which Pratt takes the title of his poem), the clay which is man resists the turning of the wheel and through the exercise of imagination sets out to usurp the potter's role. Man is far from perfect; the irrationality and self-destructiveness of war are proof of this: the ape still grins through men's eyes and teeth (as Julian phrased it). But man has come a long way. Clearly grounds exist for hope that he will yet 'climb the sunlit peak.'

As I have suggested, and as Pratt's words to E.K. Brown confirm, the views here expressed remained largely unchanged for Pratt throughout the years. They were developed more definitively and much more memorably twenty years later in 'The Truant,' but they were virtually the same. When, in his letter to Brown, Pratt adds that the 'conclusion' of *Clay* represents his 'viewpoint ... *more or less*,' he has in mind his subsequent conviction of human immortality, which gave it a new dimension later – as we shall see. Nevertheless the view of man expressed in this early, laboured, often unsubtle and infelicitous poem forms a major part of the bedrock on which is founded the vision of life that informs most of Pratt's later poetry.

There is no doubt that writing *Clay* was very important to him. For nearly two years he wrote almost nothing else, and he was not exaggerating when he later wrote that he 'had high hopes of it at the time.' With publication in mind he had a number of typescripts made, some of which he passed round to close academic friends, including Pelham Edgar, to learn their views on his new opus. They were not enthusiastic. 'I remember now,' he recalled long after, 'their attempts to say something nice about it without betraying their critical integrity, but I detected a sober undercurrent of scepticism, a mood of "This will never do," although it wasn't so bluntly articulated.' He hoped, nevertheless, that a publisher might think better of the poem. Accordingly he took his manuscript – forty-one single-spaced pages – down to William Briggs (later Ryerson Press). But Briggs was equally unenthralled. He would publish the poem, but only if the author was prepared to subsidize the venture. Wrote Pratt: 'As my salary then was so low that it wasn't taxable, I said – No.' He was very disappointed; the poem was to have been his first real publication as a poet, his first bid for recognition beyond the campus.

Convinced of his failure he decided to obliterate the poem forever. His account of what happened next – somewhat embellished, no doubt – is as follows:

I went home that evening [from William Briggs's office] and piled up the typed copies of *Clay*, and I said to my wife – 'I am going to burn them.' She replied – 'If you think you must, all right ...' All the hopes of two years crashed, and I shall never forget the effort of will as well as of the fingers when I tore the tremendous manuscript to shreds in all its copies and sent them into the flames. It was like the strangulation of a child ... The only thing in the world that really wanted that poem was the fire ... When I recovered from my bereavement with the passage of time, I asked myself what was wrong. I discovered that Mrs. Pratt, unknown to me, had salvaged one copy. I re-read the poem this time like a stranger with a cold critical eye ... I came round to the conviction that philosophical and ethical insights whenever they find their way into poetry should be emotional renderings of experience actually lived or imaginatively grasped.

Though *Clay* had been accounted a failure and though his disappointment was great, the venture had not been entirely lost. From it he had learned something important about the art of poetry. The experience had also taken him through a refiner's fire from which he emerged, I think, not only a better poet but also, in some ways, a different man.

15

A Port at Last

I left the department of Psychology in 1919 [actually in 1920] and immediately entered English at Victoria ... I took the job with a mixture of enthusiasm and timidity as I could not lay claim to any highly specialized knowledge of English – that subject being rather a hobby than an academic pursuit. I had, in other words, 'to get it up.' Pelham was a Prince in every sense and had one blind eye for my limitations. He gave me the Elizabethan period, Sidney, Hakluyt, and the crowd, and Shakespeare and a lot of generalized survey work. I owe so much to him – friend and critic.

E.J. Pratt to E.K. Brown, 1942?

WHO FIRST HAD the unlikely notion of appointing a clergyman-psychologist to teach English literature is uncertain. Pratt himself credited Pelham Edgar, who 'made me the offer one day – out of the blue,' an offer which he had accepted only with 'grave misgivings and much trepidation.' Arthur Phelps, however, in 1967 would 'distinctly remember' that it was Pratt who first proposed 'his transfer from Psychology,' suggesting that Edgar 'give him a try,' and promising to 'withdraw quietly if he made a fizzle of it.' Edgar himself wrote in 1942 of having 'rescued Pratt from the Psychology Department,' but did not add whether the inspiration was his or Pratt's – or, indeed, someone else's. Not that it matters. What does is that the transfer took place, profoundly and permanently affecting the whole future course of Pratt's life both as man and as poet. Had it not occurred it is impossible to imagine what his life might have been. There seems little doubt that Canadian literature would have known him, if at all, only as a very minor poet.

However he may have been prompted, Edgar decided to act. He never regretted his decision. 'If I have any claim to immortality,' he wrote in 1942, 'the justification lies there.' He was well aware that Pratt was no literary scholar, but there were compensating factors which evened the odds: 'I would not admit that I was taking a gambler's chance. I freely granted that Pratt's training had been in philosophy and not in English. He might be lacking in some of the elements of exact scholarship but his mind was brilliant and his humanity abounding.' But there is no doubt that Edgar was motivated far more by a desire to rescue a struggling poet from an inhospitable climate than merely to add a brilliant mind to his department.

Pratt's transplantation was not at first as clean and complete as he would have wished. The College administration agreed only to an experimental, part-time appointment: if he could find another part-time post elsewhere in the University, he might test himself as an English instructor for a few years, a regular appointment being contingent on the outcome of his probationship. It was not an ideal resolution, for he was still condemned to leading a kind of amphibious existence, divided between two academic disciplines and two professional loyalties. But it was at least a start in a promising direction.

Finding himself a second part-time post presented no problem. The quality of his work for Dr C.K. Clarke in the special course for nurses he had taught in the summer of 1919 assured him a place in the Department of Social Service as long as he wished it. To ensure him a pied à terre at Victoria College Edgar arranged that two-thirds of his teaching was in English at the College, an arrangement which entitled him to office space and a desk under Edgar's roof and official recognition as a junior member of his Department. By the spring of 1920, both parts of his 'joint appointment' secured – 'Lecturer in English (Vic) and Lecturer in the Department of Social Service (U),' so the University calendar described him – Pratt was already looking forward in high spirits to a future whose long-settled clouds seemed to be lifting at last.

He would have preferred spending his free time that summer preparing himself for his new profession. Unfortunately for him his 'psychological survey' of Western Avenue School was unfinished. His individual studies were done, but his findings still had to be analysed and his report written. This was to occupy most of his 'spare' time during the summer of 1920, leaving him little opportunity for anything else. But at least before his new work began the old had been finished, and his report submitted to Dr Clarke and the Boards of Health and Education.

It was a substantial document, fully detailing all aspects of the survey, fortified with statistical tables, charts, and case histories, and concluding with proposals for future action. While it may be difficult for a layman to judge its real value, it was seen by Clarke and his colleagues (to quote one of them) 'as a work of utmost importance, a major milestone in the history of research and treatment of mental illness in Canada.' Such a verdict would seem to be confirmed by Pratt's being invited that autumn to address the Toronto Academy of Medicine on the subject of his report. Though by then he had re-signed as mental hygienist, he accepted the unusual invitation, and on 21 October 1920 delivered before a full meeting of the Academy a brief but solidly informative and, as befitted his new profession, highly readable paper entitled 'Mental Measurements as Applied to a Toronto School.' The august Academy, we are told, 'was greatly impressed.' (The following year the results of his work reached an even wider public when his Academy paper was published in *The Canadian Journal of Public Health* [Vol. XII, 1921] and a somewhat longer version, 'The Application of the Binet-Simon Tests ... to a Toronto School,' appeared in the April number of *The Canadian Journal of Mental Hygiene*.) It is clear that he had proved himself a competent research psychologist after all – given the kind of project in which he could engage with some conviction as to its value. It was obviously work he might have continued with great success. But though he had derived certain satisfactions from it, he seems to have had no regrets about quitting the job and devoting himself to something totally different.

Pratt was fortunate during his first, fumbling year of trial and error to share his office with a young teaching fellow who had just gradu-ated with Honours in English and was then a candidate for the Master's degree. Douglas Bush, later to become a Harvard professor and an international scholar and critic, proved exactly the mentor whom the novice required in that crucial year of his initiation. Pratt besieged him with questions, picked his brains, and sometimes bor-rowed his lecture notes. Bush, who remained a good friend of Pratt's throughout his life, recalled the time of their joint tenancy with affec-tion and some amusement:

As an everyday office mate, Ned was of course his jolly self ... I'm sure his classes were lively and illuminating in essential ways, though I don't know that Ned's hold on English Literature was ever very firm ... I remember his being disturbed – though not for long – when, in what connection I forget, I remarked that the 'Dear child' of Wordsworth's Calais sonnet was W's illegitimate daughter: he had told his class that she was another and later daughter.

But that was a minor point. Nevertheless, Bush's surmise, that Pratt's hold on his subject was never very firm, is generally substantiated by those who have told or written me about his work in the lecture room, though they also agree with Bush that his classes were lively and illuminating in essential ways.

The following account of Pratt as a teacher of English literature, provided me by a former student of his who was a freshman in the 1920s, is generally typical of those I have been given:

The course was a survey of English poetry, beginning with the ancient popular ballads and continuing to the end of the nineteenth century. One thing that impressed me right from the start was the way Ned Pratt established a rapport with the class. His enthusiasm and his enjoyment of literature immediately carried over to the rest of us. He had no prepared lectures that I can remember. He'd come into the classroom with a few notes which he seldom consulted, and read a great deal, pausing now and then to make some critical comment on what he had read. His voice was not very strong nor very resonant, but he had a sure sense of rhythm. And he had a very expressive face, so that when he read a passage – one of his favourite passages – his face would light up and this would electrify the whole class. We all enjoyed hearing him read; it was a great experience for us. We had never heard a poet reading poetry before – and here he was! It did something for us all. After nearly half a century I can still hear him, and see him in my mind's eye, as he read 'Sir Patrick Spens,' 'The Twa Corbies,' and some of the other ballads. I can't imagine even the dullest clod listening to Ned Pratt reading 'Sir Patrick Spens' without becoming excited about poetry.

As an English professor he was never erudite or pedantic – placed no emphasis at all on English scholarship. He never referred us to any scholarly journal. In fact, we never knew such journals existed – nor did he in all likelihood. He would occasionally mention a critical work, which he thought we might look up in the library, but these were mostly standard criticisms.

He put all the emphasis upon the texts themselves. He wanted us to understand the prose selections. In prose he was particularly excited about William Morris's *News from Nowhere*. Of course, Morris was entirely unknown to almost everyone in the class, but he had caught Pratt's imagination. He was especially interested in Morris's socialistic ideas, and the work that he did for the working-class of England. I remember Pratt stressing this again and again ...

It is an entirely credible portrait of Pratt the professor.

He was happy at Victoria College from the moment he installed himself behind a desk – the surface of which was soon lost from sight for thirty years – in the second-floor office which became his kingdom. Besides the civilized and congenial atmosphere of a small, closely-knit university community, he welcomed especially the opportunities his new life brought him to make new friends. Robert LeDrew, who had been his boon companion and literary ally for nearly three years, had died in 1919, and his death had left a large and painful void in Pratt's life. Clare Hincks was still, and would remain, a good friend, but his multifarious duties and interests had continued to grow so that Pratt saw less and less of him as time went on.

His need for congenial friends and companions was very great. And yet, as we know, the number of those who were really privy to his intimate thoughts and feelings, his inner, private self, was small and select, not more perhaps than a half-dozen or so. But these were the props of his existence. Even the presence of strangers about him was more welcome than solitude. Alone, his spirits soon declined and he became introspective, brooding, and unhappy. His creative powers flagged. Though he needed seclusion, or at least freedom from interruption, during the throes of composition, and though he was extremely sensitive to the least sound when he wished to be quiet, he nevertheless liked having people nearby, whose presence he was aware of – provided they made no noise – and who would be, as often happened, a ready audience on whom to try out what he had just written. The new friends he soon made at Victoria College were therefore as essential to his literary creativity as to his emotional sustenance.

At the College, Pelham Edgar was, of course, and remained the foremost among his intimates, the 'dearest of personal friends' as well as his 'honoured chief.' But there were others too who soon became almost as vital to his personal and social well-being: John Robins (then in German but later to move into English), Harold ('Hal') Bennett (Professor of Latin, afterward Principal of the College), J.W. Macmillan (sociologist, labour mediator – in which role Pratt would sometimes accompany him as an assistant – and avid golfer whose favourite partner Pratt later became), and others as time went on. But chief among his new friends at Victoria in the early twenties was undoubtedly W.H. (Hubert) Greaves and his wife Cornelia, to whom in later years he felt he owed a debt for happy memories, friendly counsel, and widened vistas of life almost as great as he owed to Edgar.

Greaves was a tall, large, hearty American of private means, and a natural entertainer both in his classes and out. Endowed with the brand of hyperbolic humour and the expansive personality which Pratt admired, as well as being a 'marvellous host,' he attracted Pratt (and he Greaves) from the moment they first met. Soon Greaves had become one of his most intimate friends and another model for the new 'life-style' he was still striving to cultivate. It is not surprising that visiting Hubert and Cornie in their handsome, spacious, elegantly appointed house 'upon the Humber's crested dome,' or at Cragmoor Farm, their summer retreat near Kingston, became for Pratt one of the happiest of oft-repeated experiences. As Professor of Public Speaking at Victoria College, Greaves was also an accomplished orator, public reader, and 'dramatic recitalist.' Declaiming scenes from Shakespeare with appropriate flourishes and gestures was his forte, and a favourite pastime in which Pratt sometimes joined him as an enthusiastic if less accomplished 'second.' Sometimes, at Cragmoor, these performances were executed in the open air, one of which – Pratt having donned a vastly oversized, bright red sweater belonging to Greaves – caused rumours to spread that madmen were at large in the neighbourhood!

Pratt's failure – though he tried very hard – to rival his master as a dramatic recitalist did not diminish his admiration or fondness for Greaves, nor his ambition to emulate him, if not as a public at least as a private entertainer and host. Here again Greaves provided him another example. An avid cardplayer, of poker especially, he soon helped to expunge from Pratt's mind the long-implanted notion that the 'devil's cards' of his Methodist childhood were but the vulgar diversion of unregenerate blackguards and wastrels. Enlightened by Greaves, he savoured again, for the first time since he had played an occasional clandestine game in an outport sail-loft, another of the delights forbidden by his father's church. Though he never played well – his most 'scrutable' face usually betrayed his hand – he enjoyed the game, and would often host a match himself, chiefly because it brought together a 'crew' of his favourite friends in an easy, relaxed, comradely atmosphere. When a few years later Greaves returned to the United States, Pratt was 'quite desolated' for weeks. It is not surprising that one of the few poems he ever addressed to a friend was inscribed for Hubert Greaves, 'In a Beloved Home (To W.H.G.),' first published in *Newfoundland Verse*. The poem, a sonnet, ends with the following evocative lines:

<blockquote>
... – a home, the heart of friends,
  The company of the past; a fragrant briar;
    All these were ours, for in the hearth's rich glow
  Even Hamlet came and brooded on the fire.
</blockquote>

Half a lifetime later Pratt recalled with nostalgia their many happy times together.

Almost as important as his new appointment in its effects upon both his private and his social life as well as on his poetry was another event which occurred during his first year in the Department of English at Victoria College: his acquiring a piece of land and a summer cottage at Bobcaygeon on the Kawartha Lakes. Situated about eighty miles northeast of Toronto and a lovely region, quite unspoiled in those days, Kawartha was a favourite locale for city-dwellers whose means permitted them the modest luxury of a 'summer place' relatively close to home. Arthur Phelps, then serving a Methodist circuit at Greenbank (north of Oshawa), had taken a cottage there in 1919 and had been singing its praises ever since both in conversation and in verse. The following spring, visiting Phelps and his wife Lila at Greenbank, the Pratts were taken in the Phelpses' ramshackle car over the winding, tree-shaded country-road to 'the little town ... amid the Kawarthas' (to quote Phelps's Bobcaygeon 'Sketch'). The Pratts too were 'immediately captivated,' as Viola recalled: 'Ned was so entranced that he decided then and there he was going to have a lot and cottage at Bobcaygeon. And when later the one next door to Art Phelps went on the market, he arranged to get it for us ...'

So it was that in the summer of 1921 Pratt and his family – a daughter, Mildred Claire, had been born to them in March – took possession of the cottage where they were to spend at least parts of their summers, and occasional week-ends at other times, for the next fifteen years. They had no car, nor would have one for some years to come, but there were two trains daily from Toronto and once he had reached his 'country estate' (as he sometimes jokingly called it) Pratt had no wish to travel further afield. To quote Viola again: 'Ned *loved* the place, which surprised me at first, because he wasn't the type who ordinarily enjoyed "roughing it in the bush." He hated the mosquitoes – and we surely had *lots* – but he devised ways to combat them, and after a while he didn't mind so much ... It was really a delightful spot, right on the lake, surrounded by trees, mostly cedars, with a clearing out back that we called the Glade.' Though it was more than his income could comfortably bear – as he soon discovered – his Bobcaygeon 'estate' was an investment he never regretted. In the years ahead it returned him many dividends, not only in physical and emotional restoration, in the enlargement of his social circle, and in the enhancement of his reputation as a weekend-host, but also in opportunities for creative relaxation that would not otherwise have been possible. It is true that in time Bobcaygeon generated its own distractions, as well as new pressures, especially financial ones, upon his time and energy. Yet there is no doubt that but for his retreat Pratt's middle years might have been hardly more productive of poetry than his early years had been.

It is not surprising that he looked forward to his first summer at his cottage in high spirits. The first year of his joint appointment had been strenuous; merely keeping a pace or two ahead of his students had been a ceaseless labour. Though he had worked occasionally on his poetry, he had finished and published little. Yet that little was so superior to anything else he had published so far that it might almost have been written by another poet. 'Carlo' (*The Canadian Forum*, November 1920), an affectionately humorous monologue addressed to a dog, though perhaps a little overweighted with 'academic baggage,' is pleasantly conversational in tone and quite free of borrowed trappings. A group of five short poems published in the June 1921 issue of the *Forum* included what was perhaps his best published poem to date, 'In Absentia,' the delightfully whimsical yet gently ironic caricature of an old professor briefly emancipated from time and place by a fish at the end of his line. (The poem, according to Arthur Phelps, was based on 'an old academic who frequented Bobcaygeon, whom Ned had seen wetting a line when he [Pratt] was visiting us the previous year.') So far Pratt had written nothing so spare, controlled, and imaginatively charged in almost every word, nor so fresh and evocative in its imagery. How rapidly he had advanced in a very short time may be seen by comparing this poem with two others in the group, 'Anticipations' I and II, which were earlier lyrics extracted from *Clay*. Though written not more than two years before, they seem almost to belong to another era.

These six poems were all he published in the course of eighteen months. But the new ones at least were propitious omens, and a summer at Bobcaygeon lay ahead.

16

Arcadian Adventures

Bobcaygeon, Ont.
Monday morning [September 1922]

Dear Billy,

Would you like to run up to Bobcaygeon on a holiday for one, two, three or four days ... My wife and bairn are in Toronto and I am left alone for one whole week ending Sept. 23rd. I have just shot two wild ducks less than an hour ago. What am I going to do with them? They won't keep till my return and I can't eat them all by myself. The train leaves Toronto 9.05 a.m. and 5 p.m., and leaves Bobcaygeon 6.45 a.m. and 2.45 p.m. So good connections. Great sleeping here out in the open and thoroughly screened in, not a footstep day or night to disturb dreams. I have a little garden containing, at present, sweet corn, beans, tomatoes, squash and so on, all clamouring for your stomach. An open fire place with pine stumps! Evening Smokes! Fresh Cream! Bass!

Can you come? ... If you can make it let me know by wire ... and I will meet you, with canoe, at the station. Bring some of your stuff with you to while away an evening.

Sincerely,
Ned Pratt
[to William A. Deacon]

THE BOBCAYGEON SUMMERS, especially the early ones, were golden times for Pratt, among the happiest he would ever know. Before many years had passed clouds would overcast his skies; and financial demands, not all of his own making, would compel him to mark examination scripts or teach at summer schools from one end of Canada to the other, reducing his time at the cottage to a few weeks in June, a few more in late summer, and occasional week-ends during term. There would be other good times, but none quite like the halcyon days of the early summers at Bobcaygeon. Not only was his escape from the classroom a tonic release (though he usually enjoyed his university teaching), but being free to order his time as he chose, forget the clock and the streetcar, abandon collar and tie, sleep without 'a footstep day or night to disturb dreams' (he loved his sleep but was a notoriously light sleeper) were sheer delight. A city dweller by instinct who would have languished in permanent rural seclusion, he nevertheless truly enjoyed his seasonal retreats to Bobcaygeon – provided he was not left alone there for very long at a stretch.

Not that a summer place appealed to him for its primitive rusticity; he took little pleasure in roughing it, was too fond of creature comforts to sacrifice them willingly for the dubious delights of being close to Nature. He loved the sun and fresh air, the quiet and freedom; and such deprivations as the lack of indoor plumbing he could tolerate – for a time. But mosquitoes, ants, bats, stray cats, hard beds, rustic furniture, and other such concomitants of unaffluent rusticity were his abomination. (For the same reasons he loathed picnics al fresco.) The cottage was therefore made as civilized as possible, with at least second-best beds; deep, comfortable armchairs (second-hand); ant-traps, flit-guns, and many yards of mosquito netting. To ensure the quiet and seclusion necessary for literary composition, he had a small cabin built at some distance from the cottage, where he could closet himself with his pencil stubs and cheap notebooks and a coffee pot to spur his muse. (In the early 1920s he was still, to quote Arthur Phelps, 'a novice – though progressing – in the arts of alcoholic excitement.') Since a garden was one of the usual appurtenances of a proper summer place in those days, he decided that he must have a garden too. The landward portion of his property being largely unclaimed wilderness, he shortly began, wielding his own axe and pick, to clear himself a modest plot. Here he set out to grow (to quote Phelps again) 'the largest squash ever seen in those parts – a *titan* amongst squash!' But he never realized his ambition, the stony soil defeating him year after year. Other crops, however, including strawberries and 'Irish Cobblers,' managed to flourish and were proudly displayed to visitors instead of giant squash.

And visitors there were before long: 'lads' from the University, select members of the Toronto writing fraternity as well as artists of other stripes, fellow members of several Toronto clubs he joined, and many others as the years passed and his coterie grew – a veritable menagerie. Except for a wife or two who occasionally tagged along, his guests typically were all males, although, as we shall see, there would be rare and very special times when the company was designedly more heterogeneous. (The notion hinted to me by some of my sources that Pratt may have been 'homosexually inclined' is quite unsupported by any evidence I have uncovered. My evidence suggests the contrary interpretation.) The normal visitation was an easy-going, informal affair: jaunts along the river, fishing or canoeing for some, sketching for others, and usually an outdoor barbecue, the host presiding at the stone fireplace by the lakeshore. When darkness fell and the mosquitoes rose, the scene shifted indoors, with lively talk, stories and jokes (mostly by Ned, as everyone called him by now), poker games, and more refreshment, which gradually came to include a burgeoning array of bottles. (A recollection by Adrian Macdonald, English teacher and occasional author, sheds amusing light on Pratt's temperately daring approach to his alcoholic initiation. Meeting him one day in a town near Bobcaygeon, Macdonald asked him 'what he was up to,' to which Pratt replied that having invited 'two of the boys' up for a week-end he had come to town to fetch 'a couple bottles of beer.' Macdonald added: 'It would have done your heart good to have heard the unholy glee with which he uttered the words "a couple buttles of beer".')

Sometimes, too, as R.S. Knox (in English at University College) recalled, 'After we had tramped and sketched and talked we prevailed on Ned to read some of his poems.' He was rarely averse to trying out his still unpolished lines on an intimate and responsive audience; on the contrary, this became for him almost a *modus operandi* of composition, especially of the narratives, though almost never of the more personal lyrics. He may have liked seclusion during the actual time of poetic gestation, but alone on a desert island he would have written nothing. His instincts were those of a true, original bard, an oral poet, who needed a living audience to be at his best. When there were no visitors there was, of course, Viola, sympathetic and indulgent, the ideal auditor for his poetic declamations.

And there were Arthur Phelps and his wife Lila. More congenial and helpful friends and allies Pratt could not have found, whether as a fugitive from the Methodist pulpit, aspirant to full membership in a more worldly, less rigoristic society, or as a hopeful and ambitious Canadian poet. He and Phelps had much in common. Phelps, like Pratt, had also quit the pulpit for the lecture room, first at Cornell College in Mount Vernon, Iowa (1920–1) and then at Wesley College in Winnipeg. He was also a promising poet, who might have made a lasting name for himself had he persisted. Attracted to the 'new' poetry coming into vogue in Britain and America, he had broken with the Canadian traditionalists almost from the time he wrote his first verse as a member of Edgar's group in the early years of the War. Publishing in various Canadian journals, he had won a substantial local reputation as a young avant-garde poet even before he broke the international barrier with verse in *Poetry* (Chicago), one of the first – if not the very first – Canadians to appear in its pages. Besides his *Bobcaygeon*, published as a chapbook in 1920, he had also brought out a second slim volume, *Poems*, while at Cornell College in 1921. (Pratt had reviewed it briefly in the June number of *The Canadian Forum*.) Both books had been well received, but the critic and teacher gradually came to displace the poet, and it was his old classmate and friend who went on, as he put it, to become the 'established poet.' He had early spotted Pratt's talents, long before he began 'to give us the grand stuff.' 'I prophesied then,' Phelps observed in 1958, 'that Ned would become an established poet, and that I wouldn't.' And during the summers of the early twenties he undoubtedly helped to make the prophecy come true, encouraging Pratt, giving him helpful advice and criticism, suggesting subjects for poems, 'egging him on when he felt he was out of his depth,' and occasionally 'supplying a phrase or a line or two of verse.'

They made a curiously compatible pair, each a renegade cleric turned professor in a discipline for which he had had no special training, each an aspirant to poetic honours. They took their new roles seriously, but not, to quote Phelps, '*too* seriously, because we both saw an element of incongruity if not absurdity in what we were so confidently setting out to do.' Seeing themselves in such a light, they were able to play with their new vocations and ambitions, making them the subjects of many impromptu diversions which gave them

both amusement and a degree of intellectual and imaginative stimulation. Chief among these diversions was a series of dramatic performances staged in 'The Glade' behind the cottages, where Phelps had
built a crude stone pulpit or lectern. Here, with Viola and Lila as an
amused and appreciative audience, they would take turns at 'exercising' themselves in the skills and strategies of their new roles. To cite
Phelps again:

Behind it all we were conscious of the fact that we were both beginners, as
academics and as poets. (I was no poet really, but I was poeticizing a bit.) We
would choose a subject such as 'The moon and its influences on the amorous
propensities of man,' or 'The influence of alcohol on the creatures of the
deep' – yes, *The Witches' Brew* had its start in one of these japes! – and Ned
would get up and have a go at it, sometimes in verse, sometimes in prose,
then I would, with the women around us, each an audience for the other. We
would pick a subject and play with it. We had a lot of fun, but back of it all
was the fact that we were exercising ourselves creatively and imaginatively ... They were happy, exhilarating times for both of us, and, no doubt,
good for our verbal and imaginative reflexes. Ned used to say that those
impromptu performances in the Glade did more to help him at the lectern
than all his pulpit work and university debating and suchlike. And perhaps
they did ...

The relaxed atmosphere of Bobcaygeon and the stimulating companionship of Arthur Phelps provided an ideal milieu for Pratt's creative inclinations. During term, especially in the years of his divided
allegiance to Victoria College and the School of Social Service, time
and opportunity for writing were very limited. But at the Bobcaygeon
cottage, on the shaded verandah, in his easy chair, his notebook on its
wide arm, or at his table in the little summer house, with Phelps
dropping in on him now and then, he was able to release his creative
energies and let them work or play as they would. Yet little of his new
environment was ever reflected in his poems; unlike Phelps he wrote
no vignettes of Bobcaygeon, nor 'Kawartha Lake Sketches' in the
manner of Katherine Hale. Surrounded by the blue-and-green quietude of Kawartha he returned instead to a very different world, that of
the Newfoundland outport and the waters of the North Atlantic, and
to a people who had never known any other.

According to Phelps, 'Ned wrote prodigiously' during his early summers at Bobcaygeon, 'in spite of the novel distractions of a summer place and other diversions, such as gardening and golf.' Most of the Newfoundland poems in *Newfoundland Verse* (1923) were undoubtedly written there, though it is impossible to be certain which were written precisely when. Some of those that almost certainly belong to his first Bobcaygeon summer seem to have been reworkings of verse written earlier, fragments left over from *Rachel* and *Clay* perhaps, or of other early abortive verse wisely left unpublished. An interesting illustration from this time of his reworking of earlier materials is the poem 'Loss of the Steamship Florizel,' a revision of lines appropriated from a poem that had in fact been previously published. 'Invocation,' a turgid and bombastic effusion addressed to the 'Infinite Sea,' though published shortly after the ship was lost in February 1918, had no apparent connection with that event, and may have been suggested by Wordsworth's 'Peele Castle' poem, to which it bears a crude resemblance. Now, under an explicit title, he pruned away most of the original inert mass and reshaped what remained into the brief, compact, ironic eight-line poem which first appeared in *Newfoundland Verse*.

The brooding icons of 'Sea Variations,' published a few months later (*The Canadian Bookman*, January 1922, where it was printed in curious juxtaposition with the tranquil 'Kawartha Sketches' of Katherine Hale), undoubtedly belong to the summer of 1921. This poem too suggests an earlier metamorphic stage, and may have come out of the darker sea passages of *Clay*. Out of *Rachel* almost certainly sprang another poem which Phelps would 'clearly remember' as having been written 'mostly if not entirely' that summer, 'Ned's tale of death on the ice-floes.' *Rachel*, it will be recalled, had included twenty somewhat melodramatic lines on the subject. Now, abandoning the Wordsworthian blank verse and choosing a freely varied couplet form (interspersed with quatrains), its iambs well buttressed with spondees, he reworked the whole, greatly expanded, into a vivid, swift-moving first-person dramatic narrative, almost laconic in style, full of kinetic verbs and concrete nouns – the full-blown Prattian manner almost achieved at a single stroke. By the end of the summer Phelps had heard 'passionately declaimed from our pulpit in the Glade,' almost as published in 1922, what is without doubt the finest and most durable of Pratt's shorter narratives, *The Ice-Floes*. It is not unlikely that 'The

Toll of the Bells,' a pair of grim sonnets on the same subject, was also written that summer.

But though his poetry and, on the whole, his garden flourished at Bobcaygeon, neither gardening nor writing proved to be Pratt's most significant preoccupation that summer of 1921. For some time, another of the exotic mysteries into which he had longed to be initiated had been golf. Several of his University friends were 'gentleman golfers' – Pelham Edgar, J.W. Macmillan, Malcolm Wallace, R.S. Knox, and others – all of them members of the York Downs Club, and he would have liked to join them. But the expense had deterred him. And then one week-end 'Bobby' Knox, hoping to get in a little practice, arrived at Bobcaygeon bringing his golf-kit with him. Choosing the open space across the road near the cottage, he was shortly joined by his host, who soon enquired whether he might try his hand. He did, and although, writes Knox, 'it was the first time Ned had handled a club he was straightway "caught".' Within a few days he had bought a cheap set of clubs and some balls, and soon might be seen swatting away 'oblivious of mosquitoes and everything else.' The observation by someone that Pratt 'went overboard' for anything which fully captured his fancy was never truer than of his passion for golf once he had been 'caught.' His own explanation, given in a humorous essay, 'Golfomania' (*Acta*, November 1924), was that 'when a golf novitiate purchases his first club, at that precise hour a demon enters his soul.' With some of his University friends in mind, he went on to illustrate his point:

Teachers who, in the classroom, are the mildest-mannered men possible, show incredible belligerency upon the course. I have known Old Testament exegetes and many philologists who, of all individuals, should never transgress the boundaries of exact diction, become notoriously adjectival when the ball dribbles off into a ditch after a yard of turf has been scooped up with the mid-iron. In the majority of cases, the professorial inflammation subsides upon return to domestic or academic routine ...

That autumn, back in Toronto, though still a golf novitiate, he joined the York Downs Golf Club and was soon a regular presence when the University clique performed on the greens. 'We who had played for years,' wrote Knox, 'rather patronizingly encouraged him.'

But he wanted patronizing from no one; he would play with the best or not at all. All too aware of his ineptitude, he set about mastering the game with true scientific thoroughness and appreciation. 'I made up my mind,' he wrote, 'that I would study golf in an approved and scientific fashion ... My first idea was to get hold of the most recent standard textbooks and make a thorough investigation of the principles involved.' After learning the principles and practising them in the privacy of drawing-room or kitchen, and finding that the ball 'had a most pronounced natural affinity with whatever was artistic in the room ... and would sometimes sweep it into its orbit,' he engaged an instructor with whom he worked until the greens were closed by winter.

Back at Bobcaygeon the following June he continued to practise with the same persistence, driving himself as he had done at swimming as a boy, and for much the same reasons. Watson Kirkconnell, a new colleague of Phelps at Wesley College summering at his old home in nearby Lindsay, dropped in one day to find Pratt flailing away in the heat and mosquitoes like someone pursued by the Furies. 'His mashie,' wrote Kirkconnell, 'first chewed the divots off about 100 square feet of turf; then, still operating in the same spot, it dug deeper and deeper into the sandy soil until he had unintentionally created a huge sandtrap of his own.' Nevertheless, he had his reward, as Kirkconnell admitted: 'When he came to Lindsay to have a game with me on the nine-hole course there, I devoutly wished that I had put in a similar number of hours in solitary practice.' Small wonder then, as Knox recalled, that 'within a few seasons he could beat us all in the York Downs University Group. You could be sure of a kindly word from Ned as you plodded to keep up with him. He could have patronized us, but that never occurred to him.' From then on Pratt was a habitué of the York Downs Club, or any other he happened to be living in reach of. He made it a rule, in fact, never to travel beyond convenient range of a golf-course, often accepting invitations to speak or teach only after assuring himself that he would not be housed very far from a green.

A susceptibility to 'golfomania' never left him and played an important part in shaping much of his subsequent life, social and academic as well as creative. There can be no doubt that it helped reduce the volume of his writing, as he ruefully admitted to me in 1960, pointing to his *Collected Poems* and saying (not quite truthfully), 'That's the whole of it, a life's work, less than four hundred pages. Too much golf, I daresay, and not enough midnight oil!' By how much the volume of his poetry was reduced one cannot, of course, say. Giving up the game of golf – and other gregarious pursuits – so much of what little free time he had from a busy university routine, he could hardly have had very much left over, even in summer, to devote to his writing. He often regretted that he had not more time for both golf and poetry. Friends of his sometimes affirmed that given a choice 'between writing a stirring epic and playing a good, keen game of golf,' as one of them put it, 'he would take the golf game every time!' The point is hard to dispute. The fact is that Pratt put life before writing about it; when he wrote he did so out of an enthusiasm for living rather than for writing as such. This, I think, is a primary clue to his personality and to his art. It was in his truancies from the artist's monastic cell – to play golf, grow squash, entertain his friends, carouse, and confabulate – that he found the necessary psychological aperitifs for his sessions at the Muse's table. It was this, I think, that he had in mind when he wrote that for him poetry was 'at least in part, the expression of a grand binge.' His 'binges' were orgies of living, and golf for him was a part, an important part, of the saturnalia of life.

17

Preparations for Launching –
on Troubled Seas

My first book was *Newfoundland Verse*, an attractively produced, chunky little volume ... of poems ... I had the satisfaction of seeing a few of them ... in several of the Canadian magazines ... There was no royalty here but the promotional value was far ahead of the few dollars which might have been extracted.

E.J. Pratt, 'My First Book,'
The Canadian Author and Bookman, Winter 1952–3

WHATEVER HE MAY HAVE accomplished that autumn as a neophyte golfer, the academic year following his first summer at Bobcaygeon was not a very productive one for Pratt the poet. Besides an extraordinarily heavy teaching load, an unusual set of domestic circumstances conspired to make literary activity very difficult if not impossible. But the general disposition of his ménage should perhaps first be clarified.

In the spring of that year, after the birth of her daughter, Viola had found herself too weak and ailing to cope unassisted with the new responsibilities of infant care. Consequently, her own mother, living now (since her husband's death in 1917) in a rambling, three-storey house on Davenport Road, had persuaded the Pratts to give up their small apartment on Dupont Street and move in with her, who could thus provide Viola and the baby with the care and attention they needed. It seemed to be a good arrangement, and it was, though his mother-in-law added another distracting presence to Pratt's household, now suddenly increased from two to four persons. But to aggravate the situation most of all and thrust new and distressing emotional burdens upon his spirits, his own ailing mother shortly became his chief concern and responsibility. Her left eye had that autumn developed a tumour, and her doctor in St John's (where she lived with her unmarried daughter Floss) advised her to have the necessary delicate surgery performed in Toronto. The advice was heeded and some time early in 1922 she arrived at the Davenport Road house, shortly to have the affected eye removed in a Toronto hospital. Ironically – in view of the precaution taken to have the surgery performed in a first-class institution – the pathology department inexplicably lost the excised tumour, so that no biopsy could be performed. Her surgeon surmised that the tumour had not been malignant, but it was thought prudent that she remain in Toronto until spring. Accordingly, when released from the hospital she too joined the Pratts' ménage. But as if it were not now large enough, it was shortly joined also by the sisters Pratt – Charlotte, Floss, and Nellie – taking advantage of the several spare bedrooms in the large house and the excuse of their mother's illness to pay extended visits to Toronto.

It was hardly a situation conducive to the mental equipoise and leisurely quietude Pratt needed for literary creativity, the quietude in particular. We have already noted his intense aversion to noise, even muffled sounds, when his mood or current preoccupation demanded silence. In this he could at times be annoyingly fanatical; Floss Pratt recalled his importunate shouts from the ground floor at Davenport Road to silence her already subdued voice three floors above. When silence he wanted (he didn't always, of course), 'even small sounds drove him crazy,' writes his daughter Claire: 'We could not wash dishes after meals while he was resting. He could hear me erasing pencil marks two floors away. Once when he was unwell I thought he might like someone sitting with him. I sat with a book or knitting, and he soon started to complain that he could hear me breathing.' (His well-known, later poem 'Silences,' may have a much more intimately personal significance than has usually been taken into account.) Small wonder that in a house full of loquacious women – whom he usually found irritating in the best of circumstances – he wrote little or no new verse that winter.

Most distressing for him, of course, was his mother's condition and uncertain future. But troubling him too was the knowledge that he had not told her the true state of his ministerial commitment. To

Fanny he was still her 'little preacher boy' merely on temporary leave from his real vocation. No doubt he had intended to tell her the whole truth once his appointment at the College had been confirmed, but her present condition deterred him from doing so now. It was necessary, therefore, to maintain a pretense, though he tried to do so as innocently as possible, discreetly obscuring the facts rather than engaging in explicit deceit. When she was well enough he also made a point of having her accompany him when, occasionally, he preached at some suburban church, as he still did, though far less often than previously. But knowing his utter honesty in matters of any consequence, one suspects that he suffered many pangs of conscience. By 1923 he had abandoned the pulpit altogether, but it is not known whether he ever told his mother the full truth.

By the spring of 1922 she was well enough to return to St John's and life at the house on Davenport Road returned to a state, more or less, of equilibrium – not quite, perhaps, with a year-old child at its centre. Fanny was by then sufficiently recovered to live in relative comfort almost until her death, though the sight of her undiseased eye was gradually to fail, leaving her virtually blind in the last months of her life. But the undiagnosed tumour had been malignant and eventually a cancer affected her nasal area. Her general condition by then precluded further surgery, yet, in the medical opinion of Dr Cluny Macpherson, it was from other causes that she died in December 1926. Pratt and his mother were to be together once more only, when he visited St John's briefly in 1925. His short poem 'Blind' (c1928) tenderly but unsentimentally commemorates her latter years.

What little writing he managed to do that winter seems to have been mostly revision of poems written during the previous summer. No longer now did he hastily leap into print with a new poem, as he had usually done in the days of his apprenticeship to *Acta*. A period for critical reflection and reconsideration, and if necessary rewriting, was, he now realized, an essential phase of a poem's proper evolution. As he later expressed it, he had come

to realize that presenting a poem to a magazine immediately after writing, was the same as displaying a day-old baby to the neighbours before the features took on coloring and formation. I discovered that neither editors nor neighbours react to a new-born prodigy in the same way as its parents! This took a long time to learn and many a brain child was sturdily slapped on the stern by an objective examiner and promptly sent back to the progenitor for further care and decent apparel. [He is probably exaggerating; there is no evidence of his having received *many* editorial rebuffs.]

From the summer of 1921 'Sea Variations' was published in the January 1922 number of the *Bookman* and was well received. But *The Ice-Floes*, published in *The Canadian Forum* in April, made the greatest and most favourable impression of any poem of his yet to appear. The magazine by then had attracted a quite sizable, sophisticated, and intellectual public, and while his was not a poem of intellectual sophistication, the *Forum*'s readers were, it seems, 'unusually enthusiastic.' Pratt was greatly heartened. For some time he had toyed with the idea of bringing out a booklet of verse, or even a slightly larger volume, and had hesitated between publishing *The Ice-Floes* beforehand and holding it for the book. He had decided, however, to publish it as a final trial balloon; if it rode well he would have not only a fresh verdict to present to a prospective publisher, but also the 'promotional value' of favourable publicity. Had it not he might well have lost interest in writing poetry altogether. He had worked hard at the poem and by the time he felt it was ready to be 'displayed to the neighbours' he was satisfied that it was the best he was capable of writing at the age of forty years. He was ambitious to be a poet, but he had no desire to be merely a tolerated amateur. If that was all he was destined to be, it was better to quit at once. The reception of *The Ice-Floes* seems to have convinced him that he had at least a fighting chance.

The Canadian literary world in 1922, when E.J. Pratt first began to loom significantly upon its horizon, was at last after a long period of somnolence beginning to rouse itself once more. But to what sort of life was it reawakening, a new one or merely a revival of the old one? Those who could supply the answer were divided among themselves. There were many – writers, critics, and readers – who were satisfied that Canada already had a great 'national literature'; that, in poetry at least, all the country needed to do to ensure future greatness was to perpetuate past glories by producing more and greater Bliss Carmans, Archibald Lampmans, and Duncan Campbell Scotts. Such views were not, however, unchallenged. A new breed of young writers and critics was already springing up determined to drag Canadian poetry, and literature in general, into the twentieth century. A contest between old and new was clearly in the making.

A small movement toward 'modernism' in Canadian verse had begun during the War years with experiments in free verse and imagism. By the early 1920s experimentation had advanced far enough to include cautious ventures into 'current realism' (subjects and vocabulary drawn from contemporary everyday life), political and social satire, and would soon include excursions into esoteric and metaphysical realms in the footsteps of T.S. Eliot, Edith Sitwell, Wallace Stevens, and others of that ilk. Arthur Phelps, who continued to publish in magazines during most of the twenties, was one of the innovators, who also included Raymond Knister, W.W.E. Ross, R.G. Everson, Edward Sapir, and the Group of Seven painters Lawren Harris and J.E.H. Macdonald. Yet curiously, and perhaps unfortunately, most of these young rebels either soon abandoned poetry altogether or wrote so little as to relegate themselves permanently to the ranks of the 'interesting minors.' Nor did they throw themselves into the journalistic fray which soon erupted round the Canadian muse. So long as they continued to write they were content to go on quietly practising what others argued about.

Ultimately, of course, practice is more important and productive than preaching. Yet for a time the debate carried on in the press, mainly in the little magazines, was probably as important to the development of Canadian literature as anything else that occurred in the 1920s. It certainly helped to stimulate a lively interest in Canadian writing, as well as a genuine concern to make it relevant to modern life. In the long run it probably helped also to enhance both the aesthetic and intellectual qualities of Canadian writing, though this might be harder to demonstrate.

Most important of the new magazines to furnish a vehicle for the new critical attitudes was *The Canadian Forum*. For a five-year span (1920–5), virtually alone, it provided literature in Canada not only a medium of publication, but also a critical forum which proved as effective in awakening the public to the condition and needs of Canadian literature as half-a-dozen authors' associations. *The Canadian Bookman*, founded in 1919, also began laudably enough by publishing a number of provocative essays, but in 1921 it was captured by the new-born Canadian Authors' Association and thenceforward became increasingly pro-status quo, dedicated to the proposition that what is Canadian must be good.

The Canadian Authors' Association (hereinafter designated CAA) had been conceived originally as a device to promote improvement and reform in Canada's hopelessly inadequate if not iniquitous copyright laws. Under the well-intentioned midwifery of Pelham Edgar, J.M. Gibbon, B.K. Sandwell, and a few other guardians of Canadian letters, the Association had been born at a dinner in Montreal in March 1921. At that very moment, however, what soon emerged as its perceived if not true raison d'être was foreshadowed in the symbolic act of crowning Bliss Carman Canada's first unofficial poet laureate. Thus, almost from its inception, the CAA became, at least in the eyes of the younger, more progressive writers and critics, a stronghold of extreme conservatism in literary practice and of vested interests in the publishing trade, as well as a mutual admiration club for old, established writers and those few younger ones who aspired only to join their contented ranks. This image, whether true or misleading, was all the more vividly etched on the public mind by the CAA's announced policy of 'promoting': promoting the advancement of Canadian literature by holding aloft the glories of the past; promoting sales and a national spirit by such devices as book fairs, an annual Canadian Book Week (soon the butt of much ridicule by the young dissidents), and literary tours by prominent Canadian authors (whom the dissidents denied existed); and promoting new literary talent by holding summer schools for authors in Muskoka. Branches of the Association were soon formed in most Canadian cities, including Toronto, where Pratt (conscripted by Pelham Edgar) became one of its first members, later its vice-president, and eventually, after resisting the honour for years, its president.

Not that Pratt ever subscribed to many of the views of the leading spokesmen for the CAA. For one thing, he had never had any real attachment to the 'Canadian tradition,' which was still mainly the tradition of the Group of the Sixties. Until Edgar in his poetry group had introduced him to 'the Sixties crowd,' as Pratt called them, he had known little or nothing of them. None of his Newfoundland school texts had included a single line by a Canadian poet, nor had any of his few undergraduate courses in English at Victoria College. In so far as his early influences had been Canadian – few of them had been – they had derived chiefly from the pre-War and wartime magazine poets, who, to be sure, still echoed the old refrains. His later, more intimate acquaintance with the older Canadian poets – C.G.D. Roberts, Bliss Carman, and Duncan Campbell Scott – both in their works and in the flesh, did little to arouse his enthusiasm for their verse though he sometimes found it politic to pretend otherwise, at least in public, and not always even then. In a brief critical survey of Canadian poetry, which he wrote in 1938, he generously credited Roberts, Carman, Lampman, and Scott with having given Canada a genuine poetry for the first time, but 'nature poetry only.' Furthermore, they had over-worked their material, going 'after nature in dead earnest until by the time they had finished there wasn't a recess or a ligament in her anatomy left unexposed.' They had done the job thoroughly, but the fire of poetry, he went on to add, 'is but a flickering thing at best when there is not an abundance of good solid material to burn.' This, as he saw it, was their chief defect and it was a serious one. Besides, as he wrote elsewhere, 'Nature poetry, just for itself, never appealed to me,' nor did poets who 'go mad over the way a grasshopper cocks his legs while jumping on a cabbage leaf.'

In so far then as the CAA had been created to promote the national tradition, he could never have been a very staunch supporter. Nevertheless, at the beginning at least, he seems to have been convinced, like Pelham Edgar, that an association which banded together people of similar interests, which might help to enhance the author's image and promote his sales, could be a useful and profitable kind of organization to belong to. He would soon, however, become disillusioned with both the aims and the achievements of the CAA, and begin gradually, and as unobtrusively as possible, to curtail his involvement in its activities. Yet he remained a member (chiefly, one gathers, for the sake of Pelham Edgar, who continued to believe in the CAA with religious fervour) and avoided an open break with the Toronto Branch. But for many years his connections with it were very tenuous. Yet Pratt's early associations with the CAA, his speaking on its behalf at both branch and national meetings if only occasionally, his name at the masthead of the Toronto executive for several years, meant that for some time, at least in the eyes of the many young critical gadflies, he appeared to be a member of the 'old school,' though it had to be admitted that his poetry (certainly from *The Witches' Brew* onward) suggested that he was nothing of the sort.

Far more important for the future of poetry in Canada than the activities of the CAA was the public debate on Canadian poetry that went on sporadically in the journals, especially *The Canadian Forum*. This biography is not, of course, the place to survey its history in any detail. But a few war relics from that early Canadian 'battle of the books' must be glanced at, if only to suggest something of the critical temper prevailing as Pratt prepared to launch out into the deep.

One of its first and loudest salvos was fired off by Huntley K. Gordon in an essay published in the *Forum* in the very month (March 1921) that saw the birth of the CAA. 'Canadian Poetry,' as if timed to coincide with that event, delivered a broadside at the very pantheon of deities to whom the CAA in the act of crowning Carman was already making its vows of fidelity. For Gordon had the unheard-of temerity to assail not only Carman himself, D.C. Scott, and Marjorie Pickthall (recently hailed as Canada's finest new poet), but the very godhead of Canadian poetry, Archibald Lampman. It is true that he acknowledged Lampman to be 'perhaps the truest singer and the most Canadian of our poets,' but even he was 'not of outstanding ability'; moreover, like the others, he was guilty of 'insincere ... unconvincing expression ... that destroys our claim to a distinctive poetry.' The gist of Gordon's critique was that Canadian poetry (at least in English) had been and still was derivative, imitative, and consequently minor. The sad fact was, he declared, that 'English Canada fails to produce a distinctive verse of literary value. New volumes appear continually and are, for the most part, as quickly relegated to their deserved limbo ... Only by the reality of its impression can poetry succeed, and seldom does Canadian poetry achieve reality.'

In the December issue Barker Fairley, then Literary Editor of the *Forum*, renewed his assault in a spirited critique of the CAA's first Canadian Book Week. He wrote:

We cannot say yet of any Canadian book that it expresses the strength and character of the Canadian people ... whether it be verse or prose ... But instead of facing the fact resolutely and sublimating it into an ideal for every young aspirant in letters to look up to, we belittle the noble works of poetry and literature in order to flatter ourselves that all is well and to abandon ourselves to an orgy of mutual congratulation.

He went on to accuse the CAA of making matters 'distinctly worse' by 'tacitly at least, endorsing that low standard of literary merit which is comfortable to every Canadian who possesses a fountain-pen ...' Fairley's mordant comments evoked such a spate of response, both pro and con, that the Editor at last in May called a halt to the correspondence. But by then a new series of assaults and counter-assaults had begun.

The new debate struck a fresh note, but one that was equally relevant to what had become in effect a movement for the emancipation and renaissance of Canadian literature. The debate had been launched in the April (1922) number of the *Forum* by Pratt's late officemate at Victoria College, Douglas Bush, now a postgraduate student at Harvard, but still concerned, as he continued to be, with the anaemic and languishing condition of Canadian writing. In a short, provocatively titled essay, 'A Plea for Original Sin,' employing a delicate blend of frank literalness and Swiftian irony, Bush diagnosed the primary malaise afflicting Canadian literature as, simply, puritanism:

If a man be born a Puritan, how shall he save his soul? Is it possible for a Canadian wholeheartedly, joyously, with total freedom from self-consciousness, to make an ass of himself? These questions, so far-reaching that their full import does not immediately dawn upon one, are the result of much melancholy introspection, and I think the answer to them is also the answer to the familiar query, 'Why haven't we a real Canadian literature?'

The trouble was not, as some have said, that 'we are a young country,' nor that 'we suffer from Prohibition': 'No, the evil, more seriously and deeply rooted than these, is simply that Canada is too moral.' He hastens to add that he is not suggesting that 'hitherto irreproachable citizens' go out and commit adultery or bigamy:

Heaven forbid! I refer only to the typical Canadian attitude in matters literary and artistic, to that frame of mind in a very large proportion of the reading public which is invincibly, stolidly, moral ... We are so firmly entrenched behind our rampart of middle-class morality that we are afraid, even in imagination, to look over the top. Such an atmosphere, of course, stifles artistic impulse; worse than that, it makes artistic impulse impossible.

He went on to give telling (and highly amusing but true) examples of Canadian 'super-morality.' (One wishes that space permitted giving this delightful essay in full. Only Canadian literary history could include such a document.) Bush continued:

These few scattered bits of evidence may seem trivial, but they are not; they indicate a general attitude of mind that must be the chief cause of the anaemia that pervades our literature. No one reads a Canadian novel unless by mistake ... A mass of Canadian poetry consists of apostrophes to dancing rivulets that no doubt give considerable pleasure to the author's relatives ... One can see no future for Canadian letters until Canadians learn the fine injunction to 'sin gladly ...'

As expected, Bush's plea did not go unchallenged. The *Forum*'s correspondence columns were soon delivering loud counterblasts to this 'outrageous invitation to immorality.' The essay was, in fact, so misconstrued in its intention that Bush felt constrained to write a letter himself (August 1922) explaining and clarifying his argument. In it he wrote that he had not intended to set off 'a deadly anarchistic bomb ... to shatter morals and release us all for a grand carnival of the senses.' He had designed only to place 'a modest fire-cracker' under 'the chairs of the twin Muses of Canadian literature, Sentimentalism and Insipidity.' He had wanted merely to show that 'morality and art in Canada are hand in glove, when they ought to be strangers.'

While it lasted the affair was a lively one and, to those who were not shocked by it, highly amusing. No one, we can be sure, enjoyed it more than Pratt. He had already spent a year imbibing Bush's un-Puritan views; seeing them in print must have given him, as Phelps remarked, 'convulsions of merriment.' He had no doubt added – privately – his own contribution to Bush's case: like Bush he too '*hated* Puritanism – always did' – a remark he often made. But it was not an essay he himself would have published, though he would have liked having the nerve to do so. Yet, in a very real sense, he was soon to do, in a different and more subtle way, something equally daring and, I believe, with a similar intention, an intention which Bush's essay did much to help shape in his mind. It is hardly an accident or a coincidence that the one poem in which Pratt may be said to have 'sinned gladly and gloriously' was begun within a year of the essay: *The Witches' Brew*, in which, in the form of a comic allegory, Pratt would reiterate the same 'plea.'

In 1924 the main initiative in the crusade to revive and renovate Canadian literature was seized by a group of young revolutionaries at McGill University, 'The McGill Group,' as they came to be called: A.J.M. Smith, F.R. Scott, A.M. Klein, and Leo Kennedy. With avant-garde poems of their own and critical essays that were often as militant as they were radical, the group raised up first *The McGill Daily Literary Supplement*, then *The McGill Fortnightly Review* and, when it died in 1927, *The Canadian Mercury*, to rival if not displace for a time *The Canadian Forum* as the primary vehicle of the literary insurrection in Canada. But of them, more later.

It is hard to say how much Pratt owed to the critical movement of the 1920s. Undoubtedly it had an influence, coming as it did when his poetic character was at last taking on a fixed and settled mould. But one must not claim too much for it. Though well aware of and acutely sensitive to what the new critics were saying, and the new poets doing, he was not one to fall readily in step with any new notion or new mode merely because it was new. For a time – it must have been very brief – he 'played,' as he put it, with some of the more *outré* techniques of the post-war cults, but he does not seem to have taken them very seriously. Years later, recalling the earlier time when 'this maelstrom' eddied round him, he wrote:

I have never seen the value of exclusive self-expression. There is too much implicit contempt for the reader if the poet compels him – after reading a poem – to ask, 'What is the writer thinking about? Is he attempting to describe a chimpanzee or a mushroom? Did he get paid for that line of asterisks? Do they represent personal profundities far deeper than the plummet of language can fathom – or are they just stanza divisions?'
There was a lot of that in the air ... Some of it has disappeared, for which we must thank the rational impatience of the reading public.

I was caught in this maelstrom myself. Fortunately, before I got close to the Falls I was rescued ...

His saviour, it seems, was again Pelham Edgar, who gave him 'Frost and Sandburg and [E.A.] Robinson to read instead of that damned saboteur – name of Cummings!'

But many of the new trends in poetry he generally approved, in particular a greater sensitivity and more realistic approach to contemporary life, its concerns and interests and thus a broader range of subject and theme and a language closer to that 'really used by men.' He especially welcomed a renewed interest in satire and its concomitant, humour. His attraction to the early narratives of Masefield, especially 'the Everlasting Mercy & Dauber – not the later verse,' was due, he wrote, to his 'grip on the vernacular in the telling of a story.' Unfortunately Masefield lacked humour, 'his chief defect ... and he has no satire to speak of.' His views on the 'modern movement' of the early 1920s were perhaps best expressed in a paper, 'Some Recent Trends in Modern Poetry,' which he delivered before the Women's Literary Society of Victoria College in December 1923. In it he both interpreted and defended, temperately, the 'new realism' which had brought the 'downfall of artificiality of device' and broadened 'the range of poetic theme,' thus making 'profane stretches of life ... accessible to poetic inspiration.' In a time 'when poetry is in the fierce grip of realism,' romanticism is 'the exception' in poetry. 'The "grand style" is no longer a necessity for the poet today. Even religious beliefs do not need it.' He welcomed, too, the new 'ironic element' in much of contemporary poetry. The recent war, he felt, had been the chief cause of the shift from 'the romance of the young poets at the beginning of the war' to 'the strong ... realism' that had appeared after it. He concluded his paper by reading examples of recent verse chosen to illustrate the contemporary 'extension of the field of poetry and available vocabulary; and the truth of the statement that "poetry, to become human again, must first become brutal".'

Characteristically he did not join the public debate carried on in the journals, but he followed it with occasional grunts of annoyance though more frequent chuckles of approval, if not always in 'convulsions of merriment.' But Pratt, as we know by now, was not disposed to public polemics. A truant rather than a rebel, he would go about his mildly subversive business, when necessary, of flouting the rules of the 'choric ballet,' but doing so by engaging in cautious and unadvertised misdemeanours, going his own way but not unnecessarily proclaiming the fact. He believed that Canadian poetry had to take cognizance of the new and changing in poetry, but had to adapt it rather than adopt, making it if possible, blended with the best of the old, an authentic mode of expression and communication for the individual Canadian poet's own purposes. To embrace the new without regard for either national peculiarities or individual and personal idiosyncrasies would be just as disastrous as to cling to the old without the same regard. Most Canadian poets had been doing that for too long already.

This, in general, was his stance in the great debate, which continued, between the 'traditionalists' and the 'modernists.' At times, especially in private, he bore down hard on the more ultra-modern techniques and styles, on what he saw as obscurity and what he called 'verbal gymnastics' in poetry, but he continued to be receptive toward any new mode or practice so long as it did not threaten to 'cut the lines of pleasurable and intelligible communication' between the poet and his audience: 'The artist and the audience are complementary.' He believed that the individual poet had to be *individual*; if he had genuine talent and used it intelligently to 'achieve communication' time would vindicate him. Neither striving consciously to be modern nor likewise to be Canadian would greatly help to give Canada either a healthy literature or a great one. In spite of charges sometimes brought against him of obscurity or failure to communicate in his own poetry, I think that in general the record shows that he followed his own creed and that time has proved him vindicated.

18

A Viking Raid

Here the tides flow,
And here they ebb;
Not with that dull, unsinewed tread of waters
Held under bonds to move
Around unpeopled shores –
Moon-driven through a timeless circuit
Of invasion and retreat;
But with a lusty stroke of life
Pounding at stubborn gates,
That they might run
Within the sluices of men's hearts ...
                    E.J. Pratt, from 'Newfoundland,' *Newfoundland Verse*, 1923

HE ICE-FLOES had been received enthusiastically, but re-membering his disappointment when he had offered *Clay* for publication, Pratt still hesitated to approach a publisher with a proposal for a book of poems. Besides, the quantity of verse on hand which he considered worth preserving was not great. But at Bobcaygeon in June (1922), Arthur Phelps urged him to 'put out some feelers,' and while Pratt hesitated Phelps himself wrote to Lorne Pierce, the new editor of Ryerson Press. With A.D. Watson, Pierce was preparing a new Canadian anthology, and Phelps offered him a sampling of Pratt and put in a good word for him with a man who was fast becoming the most influential young editor in Canada. Phelps was already on familiar terms with Pierce, though Pratt was not. Pierce had been briefly at Victoria College in theology, but Pratt had been deep in the sloughs of psychology and their paths had not crossed. Now he was introduced and warmly commended in a letter (5 June) from Phelps, which read in part as follows:

I am sending two sonnets ['In Memoriam,' published in *Acta* in 1919] which I regard very highly. They are by my friend Dr. E.J. Pratt of Victoria College English Department. Pratt has done a lot of verse writing but has not published much. He is one of the Canadian poets. Many who have published a good deal are *not* of the Canadian poets – the *Forum* has carried his stuff – some of it I think in the English Bookman and a piece in an American Anthology. [Phelps is mistaken about the 'English Bookman'; Pratt had published in *The Canadian Bookman*. 'The Sea-Shell' had been published in *Poets of the Future*, Boston 1917.]
    What do you think of the enclosed sonnets? Might they find a place in your anthology? They are war verse of a sort – a rather noble sort – ...

In the upper margin Phelps scribbled an afterthought: 'E.J. has a lot of stuff – lyrics etc. but I did not wish to intrude with too much upon you. The enclosed will perhaps suggest to you that he is at least worth watching.'

The letter had the desired effect: Pierce not only accepted the two sonnets, but invited something more from Pratt for the new anthology. He was flattered and exultant. He went over his scripts and selected the first section of 'Sea Variations' and his new, still unfinished 'Newfoundland' (a final stanza had yet to be added). So it was that when *Our Canadian Literature* was published later that year, more than a quarter of a century before the Old Colony became the tenth province, a Newfoundlander had the satisfaction of seeing himself classed, though in the midst of some dubious company, as 'one of the Canadian poets.'

Encouraged by Pierce's interest, Pratt worked hard during the summer of 1922 – despite the distractions of golf and other diversions – to finish enough new poems and refurbish old ones to make possible a genuine selection for the volume he was now determined to publish. The new ones were mostly short poems still mainly on Newfoundland themes, but they included some of his best: 'The Ground Swell,' 'The Shark,' 'The Fog,' 'The Drowning,' 'Newfoundland,' and 'Come

Not the Seasons Here,' this last being perhaps the finest of them all. (In *Newfoundland Verse* Pratt grouped 'Come Not the Seasons Here' with his war poems, and it may, indeed, be read as such: a picture of a landscape blighted and denatured by war, both an actual landscape and the landscape of a desolated human heart. But I have the notion, though I cannot substantiate it, that the poem was prompted by the poignant lines of *Paradise Lost*, Book III, in which Milton writes of his blindness – '... Thus with the Year / Seasons return, but not to me returns / Day, or ... vernal bloom, or Summers Rose ... etc.' – and that the primary subject of the poem is his mother's recent blindness. His grouping it with his war poems was not the only instance of his deliberately obscuring the actual origin and significance of a very personal poem.) To the summer of 1922 also seem to belong – proving that he could, when he wished, play more than one tune – the comic-satiric 'Creatures of Another Country,' as well as that curious poem of 'stealthy intrigue' (as Phelps called it), 'Magnolia Blossoms,' and probably several others. By autumn he had enough on hand to make a selection from, and sent his sheaf of manuscripts down to the editor of Ryerson Press to sound him out.

There is no record of Pierce's editorial comments, but he was sufficiently impressed to agree to publish E.J. Pratt – 'out of the goodness of his heart,' Pratt reported later, but Pierce was too good a businessman to risk his firm's capital on humanitarian grounds. According also to Pratt, Pierce was responsible for the final selection, yet all the blame for the inclusion of such things as 'The Secret of the Sea,' 'Evening,' 'The Great Mother,' and several other early amateurish pieces should not be placed on Pierce. Pratt at least acquiesced, and it was certainly he who proposed the inclusion of a portion of *Rachel* (for the sake of Robert LeDrew, in whose name the lines were inscribed) and the conclusion of *Clay* ('A Fragment of a Story'). Both had cost him too much to be wholly consigned to oblivion.

If there had been any diffidence on his part earlier, it vanished now. Emboldened he took the initiative to press not only for a handsome volume with decorations by a well-known artist, but a promise from Pierce to have the book published also by 'outside firms.' He was especially anxious to have the book published in England; he had no wish for a merely parochial audience and thus a merely local fame. There is little doubt that he already had visions of being 'among the

English poets' as well as the Canadian. For all his earlier self-doubts he was second to none in the 'chesty self-confidence' with which he offered his first regularly published volume of verse to the world. Fred Varley, member of the Group of Seven and already making a name for himself in Canada, was called on for end-paper and other decorations. But Pratt himself dictated the general style they should take: 'I would prefer,' he wrote Pierce, 'a design having the quality of spaciousness befitting ocean themes than those too closely-woven patterns with their intricacy of detail that [Wilson] MacDonald works out ...' Varley 'agreed with the suggestion.' Down on his luck, as he often was in those days despite his growing reputation as a painter, he was glad to do so. (Pratt had already been his benefactor. During the previous summer, Varley and his family having been evicted from their Toronto home, Pratt had provided them a rent-free pied à terre on the vacant lot he had recently acquired – 'for the sake of privacy' – next to his Bobcaygeon cottage. A large army tent pitched on a wooden platform supplied them at least a shelter from the elements, and the Pratt cottage the necessary domestic facilities. Not infrequently too the grocery bill to feed five extra mouths was paid out of Pratt's meagre pocket.)

Pratt was especially concerned about the public image he presented as a poet. Conscious of the connotations of pedantry and stuffiness which in many minds attach to academic titles, he cautioned Pierce to avoid 'an ugly, stiff term as "Professor"' in any 'publicity given the book.' Not only was 'the title technically incorrect'; it was, he felt, 'sufficient to stultify any poetic claims which a writer may, in all modesty, put forth.' He had no wish to be known as an 'academic poet.' Above all, he wanted no hint given of his clerical status; even the use of 'Dr' irked him: 'Just plain E.J. Pratt, or Mr. Pratt if the formality demands it.' He liked being a university man; life in a university was civilized and congenial. But he loathed the notion of having to live up to some rarefied academic ideal, especially one which in many minds (often on good grounds) was associated with pomposity, pretentiousness, and punctilio. There is little doubt that he deliberately cultivated much of the unconventional behaviour for which he came to be known, largely to exclude himself from any such class of academic.

Newfoundland Verse, as Pierce had promised, was published on 2 April 1923. To celebrate the event, the Pratts gave a grand party in their new house on Tullis Drive, the first of their many 'publication galas.' More than fifty guests were invited, including the cream of the Toronto literati, his publishers, and selected academic friends. 'All went merry as a marriage bell' until late in the evening, when the chief celebrant was suddenly stricken with severe chest pains. Food-poisoning was at first suspected, but when this proved a false diagnosis a medical consultation yielded the verdict that Pratt had suffered 'some sort of heart seizure,' fortunately a mild one. It seemed a likely diagnosis in the light of his early reputed 'heart murmur,' and he was put to bed for a month, completely at rest. He himself was not, it seems, greatly worried, though he faithfully followed his doctors' orders. But rumours of his impending demise soon spread, particularly throughout the University where there was great consternation that such brilliant promise was to be extinguished so early. Friends came round to offer their good wishes – and sometimes their condolences. One in particular Pratt recalled sitting by his bedside preparing him for 'the great experience of death.'

Lying in bed while *Newfoundland Verse* made its début on the Canadian scene, he waited impatiently for his reviews. Learning that review copies often took months to reach literary editors, he wrote Lorne Pierce (with whom he was now on terms of friendly intimacy) suggesting that if copies could be 'rushed off, the reviewers might head off the readers' ennui accompanying the temperatures of July and August.' His book would not fail for want of publicity if he could help it. He was greatly heartened on 21 April when his first review finally appeared: by the Literary Editor of *Saturday Night*, his old Victoria College classmate, W.A. ('Billy') Deacon. Pratt himself (before his illness struck) had taken the somewhat unusual step of calling on Deacon to deliver him an advance copy and ask him to review it. Deacon's response at the time had been noncommittal, though he had promised to 'have a look' at *Newfoundland Verse* and see what he could do. Nevertheless, Pratt had remained apprehensive about what Deacon might write in one of the most widely read journals in Canada. A man of many crotchets, who already after less than a year at *Saturday Night* saw himself as a species of literary arbiter, Deacon could be highly capricious in his literary judgments. Besides, as Pratt well knew, he had already decided that Canada's 'most promising new poet' was his current protégé, Wilson MacDonald. It was doubtful, therefore, whether Deacon would concede anything to the work of his on-and-off friend, Ned Pratt, which might possibly detract from the lustre he was striving to attach to his protégé's name and image. But on 21 April Deacon surprised him with a generally enthusiastic review – though, not uncharacteristically, in his literary gossip column in the same issue of the magazine he scolded Pratt (without naming him) for presuming so far as to solicit a review of his own book. (In 1966 in a letter to me Deacon wrote: 'Ned was so innocent he knew no better. I promised to look at it, no more. I did, and what I found inside jolted me.')

The long review, containing much quotation from the poems and accompanied by a large photograph of Pratt, read in part:

A new man, with the old, authentic ring to his verse! Freshness and freedom of spirit finding uncramped expression ... A background new to Canadian poetry ... Such maturity and strength and beauty are in these poems that the day of their publication is a date to be remembered in the annals of Canadian literature ... His imagery is original and arresting ... It is significant that the new poet is at his best in narrative ... As observer and recorder of things and persons in a more objective way, Dr. Pratt is distinctive ... If ... he can produce a proportionate body of work equal to, or surpassing, the best half dozen examples of his art here included, he will certainly take rank as one of our foremost poets.

Pratt was delighted; coming from Deacon it was unexpectedly generous praise for a poet other than MacDonald. Still confined to his bed, his 'heart convalescence' retarded by a bout of flu, he permitted himself the exertion of autographing and cordially inscribing a copy of *Newfoundland Verse*, which he dispatched to Deacon with a brief letter of gratitude and appreciation:

The Review tended to restore my collapsed heart more effectively than digitalis. What impressed me more favourably than anything else was the expression of your own critical integrity where side by side with your own valued appreciation you were not backward in stating an adverse judgment upon inferior work. [Actually Deacon's only 'adverse judgment' was as follows: 'The first 76 pages are markedly superior to the last 64. The latter division contains work that is, on the whole, quite ordinary.' Since the 'latter division' contained mostly early poems – with a few exceptions – his judgment was in general valid.] It's your intellectual candour no less than your literary insight that is making your column live to-day. Put the petrol on us and apply the match when necessary. There is a lot of dead timber to be consumed. God himself has special uses for flames, and a self-complacent poet makes excellent roasting.

Thanks Bill, anyway, old thing, for the generous space you gave the volume in your paper. It was more than I deserved ...

His words may seem ingratiating, but Deacon was a man whom it was politic to pet a little. Yet I have no doubt that Pratt was sincere. Besides, he had no reason yet to be annoyed with Deacon despite his open espousal of MacDonald. And perhaps *Newfoundland Verse* had changed his mind.

It had not, as Pratt later discovered, though Deacon's reply (3 May) must almost have convinced him that it had:

It was most thoughtful of you to send me this autographed copy, which I highly value. I shall treasure it against my old age, when I shall be poverty-stricken, and too old to work. Then in a moment of dire need I may sell it – a genuine first edition of Pratt – to some wealthy library for a few thousands to see me through the last years. So your act is not only courteous; it is generous, and for those thousands I thank you with all my heart ...

He went on to tell Pratt of hearing 'most encouraging reports of your sales,' suggesting that 'your pipe-dream of royalties may have something in it after all.' It was a heartening exchange when the invalid needed it most, and whether or not it helped to restore his 'collapsed heart more effectively than digitalis,' it certainly did him no harm.

After a month in bed with his reviews, which by then were many, 'all salubrious, both east and west' (to quote Pierce), Pratt was back on his feet fully recovered from the heart attack he may never have had. Viola Pratt always doubted the diagnosis, though their daughter Claire remembered hearing as a child that her father's 'bad heart' would probably carry him off before he was fifty. Whether or not it had been a 'seizure' he quickly put it behind him and by mid-May was writing in jocular vein to Lorne Pierce (whose heart had also indisposed him during the period of Pratt's convalescence):

I trust your health has improved since our hearts, a month ago, beat as one. Mine is gradually taking on normal speech though still afflicted with sibilants. Are you getting a little time to yourself, and could you run up with me for a day or two to Bobcaygeon to help me plant my Irish Cobblers? Think this question over with prayer and fasting and let me know in good time.

Pierce replied in similar vein:

I had been expecting you for a long time to confessional. I suppose your long spell of prayer and fasting has left you with very little of the taint of sin to confess.

The wholesale advise me that 'Newfoundland Verse' has excellent prospects – the 'pro' meaning 'on ahead.' Don't book your passage to Tahiti before you learn just how you stand not in spectral sovereigns but in actual dollars ... If you do not get a lift toward the Chancellorship [of the University] because of this it will have been a miscarriage of justice! ...

He added that he had asked Phelps for an article on Pratt and his book, 'which will get due prominence' in the *Guardian* (official organ of the Methodist Church and published by Ryerson).

Since Pierce could not accompany him to Bobcaygeon, he went up alone and found the Phelpses already installed there for the season. As it proved his visit was propitious for the critic and for his article, which he had promised Pierce to make 'anecdotal and interesting': a minor vagary of Pratt's provided him just the anecdote he needed for an appropriate opening. (Pratt had absent-mindedly mislaid his trouser suspenders and having called to Phelps for help without result had left on the Toronto train, the garment sustained only by a recent increase in his girth.) One anecdote led to another, so that the article when it was published on 20 June (1923) included not only a lengthy review of the book but also the first anecdotal portrait of the poet to come before the public eye, the beginning of what may be called Pratt's public 'personal legend.'

Already known around the campus as a curious and unconventional character, he now had a reputation for eccentricity which was national in scope. And similar 'portraits' soon followed. The circumstance is not without some significance in Pratt's subsequent history. There is no doubt that the 'whims and oddities' that had already made him the subject of oral anecdote had been quite spontaneous and unconscious manifestations of his temperament: his extreme absent-mindedness, his unconcern for academic and other conventions and niceties, his addiction to golf and stag parties, his poker débâcles, to mention a few general categories. But it is equally certain that once these and other idiosyncrasies had been fixed in the minds of the public and they had come to view him in such a guise, usually with appreciative amusement, he himself, wittingly or unwittingly, began to encourage the enlargement of a 'legend.' This he did by the tales and anecdotes he told of himself, many of them apocryphal in whole or in part, and by openly playing the character in which he had been cast. To 'a born actor' a role came naturally, and for him a mask was a necessary prop. But I believe that both were assumed quite without guile.

Phelps was as good as his word to Pierce: his article for the *Guardian* after disposing of the anecdotal proceeded to an interesting and sensitive appreciation of the poems. Unbiased by even 'brotherly' affection, he nevertheless could not restrain his enthusiastic admiration for most of the book, an admiration that is surely sincere. Much of what he wrote was not, of course, unique to his review, but no one, I think, said it better than Phelps, himself a poet and scholar. Here is a portion of the general preamble to his critique:

The book is true to its title. It is filled with Newfoundland. The sound of the seas around that island is in its pages; the folk of that island talk in the lines of the poems; the heart of that island cries and laughs through the print. One who is not a Newfoundlander may say this because the achievement of the book carries with it the accent of reality; the communication of the life of Newfoundland is not attempted through any unwieldly massing of cluttered detail; it is accomplished on the one hand by cannily, and sometimes seemingly grudgingly offered strokes of workmanship in the creation of mood and setting, and on the other by the presentation of certain surely fashioned and uncompromisingly proffered pictures. But ... the book is bigger than Newfoundland – ... in the sense that Hardy's Wessex is bigger than any single section of England ...

   Other reviews of *Newfoundland Verse* both preceded and followed Phelps's. Pierce sent Pratt clippings as soon as the reviews reached him; he had not been exaggerating when he had written, 'The reviews are all salubrious, both east and west.' For a book of verse in Canada its reception was nothing short of phenomenal, both in the number of full-length reviews and in the consistent and unstinted enthusiasm of them all. It was probably more than the book deserved. It is only when one considers the nature and quality of most of the verse that Canadian reviewers had had the misfortune to read in the previous decade that the genuineness and spontaneity of their enthusiasm can be understood for what it really was. One of them set the book in its proper contemporary perspective when he wrote of 'the great pleasure to pick up a volume of poems and find ... instead of the usual fifth-rate, airy, fairy stuff ... vigorous red-blooded verse.' This was the secret of *Newfoundland Verse* in 1923: the new, vigorous, virile voice that rang out in it, with 'its tang of the sea and the sounds of surf,' its 'objective utterance,' and 'unashamed realism.' Northrop Frye many years later summed up the event that *Newfoundland Verse* unquestionably was: 'The prevailing idiom in Canadian poetry when Pratt began to write was ... an idiom that was most successful in evocative nostalgia ... in fairylike fantasy, ... in wistful charm ... The noises that exploded in *Newfoundland Verse* ... rudely shattered these moods.'
   It is clear from the contemporary record that such a shattering explosion was very welcome. 'Here is a new voice,' said the Toronto *Globe*, 'with vigor and music, colour and understanding.' In two full-length columns in the London *Free Press*, 'Fanfan' (Grace Blackburn) hailed Pratt as 'A New Voice in North American Literature.' In the Montreal *Star*, S. Morgan-Powell ranked the book 'higher than any Canadian volume of verse published for some considerable time past' and went on to give 'hearty thanks' that Pratt had made 'no attempts at the wretched stuff miscalled "free Verse".' 'Ivanhoe' (W.T. Allison) in the Winnipeg *Tribune* began with the words, 'A new Canadian poet has come over the horizon. And he is not a poetaster, but one who can build the lofty rhyme.' As one who had briefly taught English at

233 A Viking Raid

Victoria College (before Pratt's time), Allison went on with more than a touch of irony (if not something sharper) to observe:

[W]e have the additional pleasure of discovering that this new poet persists in being forceful in spite of the fact that he is assistant professor of English in Victoria College, Toronto. We entertain no prejudice against this college in particular, but the wonder is that anyone in the teaching profession ... can retain the creative faculty with which nature has endowed him. But ... our new Canadian poet has been able to produce powerful verse even in the academic atmosphere, even under the aesthetic and super-critical eye of that exponent of culture, Prof. Pelham Edgar. We question very much, however, whether Poet Pratt would have been able to go on striking his lyre if he had not been born in Newfoundland. Had he been born in Ontario, academic dry-rot would probably have sapped his lyric vitality years ago.

R.S. Knox in the *Forum* praised him for his 'objective utterance' at a time when 'the fashionable cult is still of the inward vision of the poet who, turned towards himself, hearkens and bids us listen to his little soul-cries or delicately records the peculiar images which life has thrown on his moody mind.' Giving him full credit for his lyrics, Knox was nevertheless emphatic that 'the great things in the volume are ... the narratives.' *The Canadian Magazine* declared that 'There is a confidence, a solidity and substance about this work, a feeling of reserve of power, that produces interest, admiration, expectancy, and that establishes Dr. Pratt as a poet of rank.' Such was the general response – and this is but a sampling of the reviews. As the *Guardian* summed up the book's reception: 'The praise of this book has been universal. It is rarely that a poet has reaped such a harvest of commendation upon the appearance of his first book. It is rarely that a poet leaps into sunlight fully-armed as does Mr. Pratt.'

It must be added that in far-off St John's, where the exploits of Canadian poets had hitherto been quite unrecorded, their praises unsung, Pratt was no less zealously acclaimed than he had been in Canada. For the first time in the Island's history one of its native sons had been hailed a poet beyond its shores. In the St John's *Daily News* his old teacher, J. Alex Robinson, writing under the nom de plume 'Viator,' devoted him a two-column editorial 'story.' A native hero deserved much more than a review. After establishing beyond doubt his native origins, listing most of his relatives still domiciled in the Island, and recording his many scholastic attainments and his early promise of greatness as a boy at school (the last, of course, being retrospective fiction), he went on to quote the poems at length and to comment appreciatively. More apt than he knew, perhaps, is one observation toward the end of his encomium: 'Of Viking lineage he writes with that spacious freedom which is the heritage of a Viking race.' A Viking – a 'sea-raider,' an 'invader by sea' – was in a very real sense what E.J. Pratt had suddenly become in Canadian poetry, a Viking who had burst unceremoniously into the rural peace, the elfin groves, the quiet maple-leaved landscapes of Canadian poetry, which would never be quite the same again.

If *Newfoundland Verse* was, as some have said (and others have denied), an 'epoch-making' book, a granite tip breaking the placid surface of hitherto undisturbed waters, it was not because it was a notably revolutionary or 'modern' book when seen in the larger context of contemporary poetry. Looking over its contents from the viewpoint of the 1980s, one must admit that it seems unrevolutionary enough to warrant almost an outright dismissal of any claims for its epoch-making significance. Compared with new books of contemporary poetry elsewhere, Pratt's was still in many ways rather conservative reading. After all, 1923 was relatively late in the history of the 'new poetry' both in England and in America. Eliot, Pound, Amy Lowell, Sandburg, Edgar Lee Masters, E.A. Robinson, and many others of the new breed were already well established in 1923, and by no means unknown to Canadian readers. Contemporaneously with *Newfoundland Verse* had appeared Frost's *New Hampshire*, Wallace Stevens's *Harmonium*, Cummings's *Tulips and Chimneys*, Edith Sitwell's *Bucolic Comedies*, and Lawrence's *Beasts and Flowers*. Comparing Pratt's book with any of these, one can see from a glance how remote the Canadian poet actually was from the poetic radicalism both of spirit and technique already generally accepted on both sides of the Atlantic by 1923. It is only when one compares Pratt's poetry with that of his Canadian contemporaries, with, for example (to mention some of the better verse only, published that year), A.S. Bourinot's *Lyrics of the Hills*, Katherine Hale's *Morning in the West*, Florence Livesay's *Shepherd's Purse*, that one can see how 'new,' 'original,' 'virile,' and 'startling' Pratt was for his time – in Canada. If one looks back over the verse published in Canada during the preceding decade, the 'freshness,' 'vigour,' and 'resonance' of *Newfoundland Verse* are all the more apparent. Perhaps 'epoch-making' is too large a term to apply to the book, but it is not *much* too large.

... he says he will not caper ...

BOOK IV: THE NEW VOICE 1923–7

... rising pulses and the birth of pain

19

Saturnalia Observed

My Beloved Mephisto,
   If prospects be realized we shall hold our Saturnalia in the back-yards of the Allobroges – I hope – at no very far distant date ...

> Yours fraternally,
> Faust.
> E.J. Pratt to Lorne Pierce, 23 May 1923

My thesis [is] that poetry ought to be, at least in part, the expression of a grand binge, making for healthy physiological releases, where the world for a time is seen backside-up, and the poet becomes gloriously emancipated from the thralldoms of day-to-day routine ...

> E.J. Pratt to W.R. Benét, 9 September 1943

HIS ILLNESS was over and his doctors were well pleased. *Newfoundland Verse* seemed to be selling well, 'salubrious' reviews still coming in. His joint appointment at Victoria College having just been commuted to a full-time lecture-ship in English, psychology and the pulpit were now behind him forever. It is not surprising, then, that Pratt in the spring of 1923 should have looked forward to another summer at Bobcaygeon, with its opportunities for freedom and creative relaxation, in high spirits and growing self-confidence. In the words of Arthur Phelps, 'He was like a man transformed in mind and spirit ... riding high on a crest of elation that lasted all summer.' What he felt, indeed, seems to have been more than elation and confidence, rather closer to what he later described as a feeling of being 'gloriously emancipated' – in particular, from a past on which he had felt it necessary to depend, emotionally, intellectually, and poetically. *Newfoundland Verse*, for all its 'new voices' and its 'vigor and red-bloodedness,' was still very much a book that looked backward: to his own past as outport boy, student of philosophy, and Methodist preacher. It could hardly have been otherwise. But now he seems to have been eager and to have felt that he was ready and able, if not to repudiate his past, at least to put it behind him where it belonged and to face himself in new directions. Though events yet to come would further reshape both his vision and his way of life, he seems to have reached by the summer of 1923 a definitive parting of the ways, and neither he nor his poetry would ever be quite the same again.

A change of style and outlook had already been taking place in his life, as I think we have seen. His de facto escape from the ministry in 1922, his gradual acclimation to 'Pelham's vineyard,' his acquisition of new kinds of friends, as well as a summer cottage with its social and other potentialities, his growing skill in golf, his rising reputation for bonhomie and largess, were all indicative of a subtle transformation that was, if not bringing forth a 'new creature,' at least clothing him in a new guise. I say new guise rather than new man, for fundamentally he did not, I believe, really change. But there is no doubt that it was with a new sense of freedom to wear his new guise that he looked to the summer of 1923 with an enthusiasm for life and poetry such as he had never quite felt before. That his emancipation from his past was almost complete and irreversible in 1923 (not quite – it rarely is – though he seems to have believed at the time that it was) seems clear from the first-fruits of his new-found freedom: the one poem which was to engage him mind and soul throughout that summer, *The Witches' Brew*. He always insisted that the poem was written expressly to celebrate his and Viola's fifth wedding anniversary (20 August 1923): 'It was intended merely as a reading following dinner.' But all the signs indicate that anniversary or no *The Witches' Brew* or some such poem was all but inevitable in the summer of 1923.

Yet, as we know, anniversaries which provided excuses for celebration had always been signal events in Pratt's boyhood home. Such events had not, of course, been marked by saturnalian revelry, even in verse. But the idea of celebrating a wedding anniversary with a poetic Walpurgis Night was not without precedent in literature. In Goethe's *Faust* the curious Walpurgis-Night Dream, with its 'inventory' of

'shades' summoned up to speak their pieces, was expressly the celebration of the Golden Wedding of Oberon and Titania. Pratt's letter
to Pierce (quoted at the head of this chapter) suggests, moreover, that
he had been recently reading *Faust*, so that Goethe may well have
prompted the form, perhaps the idea, of the unlikely anniversary
celebration – if indeed the poem was ever intended originally to mark
that event. Whether or not, there is no doubt that his mind and
imagination were ready for a Walpurgis Night in verse, and that
signing himself 'Faust' was more than a jocular flourish. Lorne Pierce
in the role of 'Mephisto' may be hard to imagine, but for Pratt himself
that of Faust, truant philosopher and theologian, 'gloriously emancipated,' consorting with witches and angels of darkness, could scarcely
have been more appropriately chosen.

Years after *The Brew* was written Pratt recalled that his friends had
believed 'that The Witches' Brew was a psychological reaction against
the doctorate' – his dissertation on St Paul's eschatology – and that he
'had to get hell out of [his] system before [he] could do anything
worthy of serious consideration.' He neither confirmed nor denied the
notion. But even a delayed reaction seems a little unlikely more than
six years after the event. Yet the idea that the poem was a reaction
against much that the doctorate symbolized is by no means so far-
fetched. But as a psychological release the poem was not merely an
irreverent tour de force or an impulsive and spontaneous vagary. It
was partly these, but it was also, I believe, among other things, a
deliberate and conscious act of desecration and purgation, the desecration of sacred cows – puritan, Methodist, theological, academic, and
literary – and in the same act a cleansing of the Augean stables of his
mind and imagination of all the clutter that sacred cows (like any
other) inevitably accumulate about them. A passage deleted from the
original 'finished' holograph of the poem is, I think, especially illuminating. In his early 'Inventory of Hades' Pratt had included 'evangelists, / Some with brains and some without,' whom he had described
as making up

... a ragged, ghastly rout,
With Teachers of Theology
Whose straggling gowns, green and threadbare,
And musty with Eternity,
Gave off an odour like bad air.

No one in his inventory published or unpublished was transfixed with more causticity than the evangelist and the theologian.

The story of the poem's evolution is itself illuminating. Years later he gave the credit for launching it to Phelps, who, he said, suggested that he write something 'just for fun ... without any thought of fixing up society or reforming the world.' But the conception was his own. Not that the central theme (as initially conceived) – 'The true effect of alcohol / Upon the cold aquatic mind' – was spectacularly original in itself. As a boy he had often heard tall tales of the strange and wonderful antics of besotted fish. It was undoubtedly such a tale that had prompted him and Phelps, as the latter recalled, to use the theme for one of their oratorical japes in the Glade. But however he may have hit upon it as a subject for verse, once having grasped its fabulous, hyperbolical possibilities, wound himself up to its full exploitation, and found in the tempo and spirit of Hudibrastic verse the very vehicle his emancipated Pegasus needed, he found that he could not stop. Enthusiasm generated excitement, and excitement almost a kind of frenzy.

'It began,' recalled Phelps, who watched the poem grow and helped not a little its freakish evolution, 'simply as a bit of tom-foolery about inebriated fish':

But the thing caught hold of his imagination and the riotous mood he was in that summer, and wouldn't let go. It kept growing, and his excitement rose with it. I was in on it from the start and used to throw in the odd suggestion, but the poem was all Ned's just the same ... He would sit on the verandah of his cottage working away and he'd catch sight of me coming across the little road past his garden, and he'd up and yell, 'Come on! Come on! Look! I've got it! I've got it! Listen to this!' And he'd declaim a passage of *The Brew* that he'd just written, exploding with laughter. Sometimes he'd come bounding over the fence between our properties, waving a sheet of paper with his latest instalment on it, which he'd read to us with hilarious dramatic flourishes. That went on all summer ...

And so a Walpurgis Night of verse grew into a summer of Saturnalian revelry.

The poem, originally entitled *The Witches' Brew or The Immortals' Night Off (A Pot-Pourri in Verse)*, like the witches' brew itself, was concocted of wildly heterogeneous and incongruous ingredients, sacred and profane, factual and fabulous, learned and fantastical, a mélange of treasures and debris dredged up from the seabed of his brimming memory and imagination. Some of the constituent elements undoubtedly came from very personal memories: of his own initiation in the arts of brewing and concoction, his surreptitious forays 'under cover of night with a huge bag' to gather the ingredients which he boiled 'in a huge vat ... to a vile concentrate.' His witches' cauldron clearly had other sources than *Macbeth*. Even the Cretan blacksmith himself may well have been the brawny hero who had extracted a small boy's aching tooth.

But it was his reading that supplied most of the ingredients: Dante, Shakespeare and the Elizabethan dramatists (whom he was now teaching), Skelton, Hakluyt, Milton, Byron, Shelley, Melville, and others, as well as his reading in classical mythology, ancient and modern history, philosophy, and theology. Much of his oceanic lore and many of his far-flung places undoubtedly came from Frank Bullen's *Idylls of the Sea*, which he would draw on again in *The Cachalot*. Shelley's 'Peter Bell the Third' seems to have provided hints at least for Pratt's infernal sequences, in particular his celebrated 'Inventory of Hades.' Shelley had clearly anticipated it in his own catalogue of some of the tenants of Hell:

> Lawyers – judges – old hobnobbers
>   Are there – bailiffs – chancellors –
> Bishops – great and little robbers –
> Rhymesters – pamphleteers – stock-jobbers –
> Men of glory in the wars, – (Part the Third: Hell, Stanza 9)

Only the epic roll-call of 'the brands' seems to have required anything that may properly be described as original research. Both he and Arthur Phelps were still but 'dabbling our feet in the waters of inebriety,' so that their first-hand knowledge of spirituous liquors was very meagre. Pratt, accordingly, wrote to a number of distilleries requesting lists of their wares and from these devised his epic catalogue. But the rest of the poem's ingredients were already part of his mental and imaginative furniture. Yet for all the wealth of 'sources' the poem was wholly his own. Not even Coleridge ransacking the voluminous trove of his vast and promiscuous reading had gathered up and woven such a profuse array of multifarious threads into so strangely original a pattern.

By the time his wedding anniversary arrived Pratt had written nearly a thousand lines that include some of the most extraordinary verse in the English language. Unfortunately the poem in neither its original form nor the somewhat abridged 'definitive' typescript sent to Pierce in the autumn of 1923 is known to the general reader. A year later in England seeking a publisher, at the urging of certain British critics, Pratt excised so many more lines and passages that the published work was really a very different poem from that read to his friends on 20 August 1923. The chief change was that the drama of 'The Immortals' Night Off' – so his deleted subtitle had described it – was virtually eliminated, and the Immortals themselves, greatly reduced in number, relegated to mere observers. As the poem was originally written, the Shades were as central to its theme and structure as the witches, fish, and cat.

As distinct from its significance as a personal *act*, what, indeed, was its theme or underlying meaning? This is a question Pratt himself was often asked by would-be interpreters of the poem. His usual replies were either evasive ones or such declarations as that the poem 'was for me a matter of straight fun or a fantasia to let off steam'; that 'the only "didacticism" I had in mind when I scribbled that fantasy was to get away from the dead seriousness of Newfoundland Verse ... I wanted to strike a new vein'; that it was 'just a "let her go Gallagher" ... to get something out of my system'; or that 'I was "thumbing my nose at academic just-so-isms".' These are all, of course, perfectly valid answers – so far as they go. As noted, the act of writing *The Brew* had answered his need that summer to 'kick over the traces' a little, to thumb his nose at much that he wished to have done with forever. But that the poem took the form it did, especially as originally written, suggests that besides its personal, psychological, therapeutic raison d'être it may have had other ulterior ends. It has, of course, been variously interpreted by the critics, many of whose readings of the poem greatly amused Pratt, though it pleased him that they thought it significant enough to delve into. 'To have lots of interpretations,' he wrote in 1954, 'is better than to have none at all. At least it wasn't written for a Sunday School paper ...'

In a letter to me in 1968, Douglas Bush, who, it will be recalled, shared an office with Pratt in the early 1920s, undoubtedly provided the best clue to the poem's 'intention,' at least in part. He pointed out that *The Brew* 'reverberated' many of the same 'critical and satirical ideas' expressed in his celebrated *Forum* essay, 'A Plea for Original Sin.' While the essay was hardly 'the source of Ned's poem – it has no one source,' the 'reverberations' were, he thought, of 'some significance.'

There seems little doubt that Bush is right. On at least two occasions, Pratt himself, answering the familiar question, *What was The Brew intended to be?*, described it as 'a protest against a Maple Leaf psychosis which had invaded the mentality of about ten thousand writers in Canada and was rapidly getting worse.' The 'Maple Leaf' – the Canadian – 'psychosis,' as he well knew, included much more than an addiction to romantic landscapes. It included also all that Bush had meant by 'anaemia and provincialism' in Canadian literature, the root cause of which he identified as puritanism, the incapacity of Canadians to 'sin gladly.' From it had been born 'the twin muses of Canadian literature, Sentimentalism and Insipidity.' Pratt, like Bush, had it seems undertaken to place 'a modest fire-cracker' under their chairs. *The Brew* itself, quite apart from any intentional meanings, certainly paid no court to either of the twin Muses. Whatever else its comic-satiric allegory may have been aimed at, it struck most directly at the same complacent pair and all who maintained their reign. The 'cold aquatic minds' that he would jolt out of their long-established grooves of sinless incapacity are, then, Canadians in general, writers in particular. He himself had been one of them, victim indeed of even deeper 'psychoses.' His own manifesto of freedom would appear to have been also a deliberate incitement to riot. (It is perhaps significant to note that in two studies of Pratt [see Reference notes], Sandra Djwa without the benefit of Bush's suggestions arrived at a similar reading of the poem.)

Some such intention seems all the more likely when one turns from the published to the much longer, unpublished version of *The Witches' Brew*, in which the drama of 'The Immortals' Night Off' is primarily an allegory of the debilitating effects of Prohibition on the creative imagination. Since the burden of the advice given him by his British critics, on whom the significance of any such allegory was entirely lost, was 'to rid the poem of all references to Prohibition,' the original thrust of the drama was necessarily blunted if not totally thwarted in complying therewith. As originally written the role of the Immortals was to complement that of the fish – by nature incapable of 'the warm arts' of 'glad sinning' – by showing how spirits once warmed by 'holy fires' may be reduced by prohibitive decrees to the level of the piscine mentality, inert and cold, if not aquatic.

As described in the original text, the Shades of the Immortals, a motley company of historical and fictional worthies, though 'living' deep within the confines of Hades, had under the liberal laws of Satan formerly long enjoyed all the delights of sin and imaginative freedom epitomized in Hades' 'wide-open' policy of alcoholic consumption. Unfortunately for them, by an edict of Oliver Cromwell, that Puritan of Puritans who had recently usurped the Dictatorship of Hades, 'bone-dry' prohibition (and all that it symbolized) had just been extended from Ontario and other parts of Canada to include the infernal world as well. But while this and 'other repressive measures' had 'resulted in a net reduction of ... disorders' in Hades, they had also had a most subduing and chilling effect on inventive and creative proclivities. As a consequence, 'many rich and versatile natures were on the point of breaking under the enforced standardisation [sic] of tastes. Moodiness and apathy settled heavily down ...' (from one of several prose 'insets' of the original text).

To lift their spirits a little as well as to voice their pained complaint against the 'enervating decrees of the Protectorate,' the Shades compose an 'anonymous dirge called *The Lament of the Wets*,' to be sung 'every evening in the Rotunda of Hades by the national quartette.' This delightful travesty of the pastoral elegy, sung by Socrates, Ben Jonson, Columbus, and Nebuchadnezzar to musical accompaniment by Friar Tuck, Nimrod, Nero, and Ramses II, is, I think, one of the more unfortunate losses the poem suffered under the hasty excisions prompted by Pratt's British consultants. He had little choice but to let it pass into the limbo of cancelled lines, not to be published in his lifetime. It is hardly great poetry, but it is, I think, worth retrieving. Here, then, with its echoing overtones of *Lycidas*, *Adonais*, and the pastoral tradition generally, strangely blended with elements of a less funereal strain (freely translated, we are informed, 'from the original

Hindustani'), is the long-suppressed 'Lament' of the sometime 'Wets,'
for the nonce 'bone-dry' in Hades:

Come weep with us; the holy fire
That once had warmed our veins is dead;
Drowned in a vast aquatic bed.
Only the canker of desire
Survives unsatiated;
Nor shall the wisdom of this age
Concoct another beverage,
By any art, that might inspire
A taste once chlorinated.

Only the blood of fish shall flow
Through arteries that once did burn
With high-ball, cocktail and sauterne;
No more their ardours shall we know
Within our watery cloister;
The respiration of the clam
Is all that's left us now bydam,
For never shall the erotic glow
Reanimate the oyster.

No more – a voice now cries – no more,
Dear heart, that with thy rolling pin,
Welcomest the wanderer in,
Will dawn show on a stranger's floor
Thy hermit tarrying,
And vowing on his flagging knees
To mend his domesticities,
Nor shalt thou greet him at the door
With thy sweet carolling.

Farewell the honours of the toast,
The mellowed gallantries that grew
Out of a reminiscent brew;
Farewell the tavern and the host,
Farewell the jag that shot us.

For us alone – O spite accurst –
The spasms of eternal thirst;
Even now, a dry Bacchantian ghost
Faints at the epiglottis.

To summarize briefly what follows in the original text as it makes
its most pointed 'plea for original sin': the thirsty and imaginatively
debilitated Shades, their nostrils having been assailed by an 'unchal-
lengeable sniff' of the witches' liberating brew, valiantly attempt to
reach the reeking cauldron. Driven back by 'a battalion of imps,' they
retire to exchange observations on the strange behaviour of the newly
enfranchised fish. The Shade of Adam epitomizes the unlikely spectacle by observing truly that they have at last been endowed with
original sin:

If I may be allowed to quote
What Moses and John Milton wrote,
Then the behaviour of a squid
Sprang from what I and Eva did.
O Moses! Milton! that this night
Should follow from an apple bite!

The Shades decide to send Bardolph out to try his luck at filching a
quantity of the marvellous liquor. His mission succeeds: he returns
shortly with a flagon of 'hitherto untried brew,' which he shares with
his fellow Shades. The riotous scene that follows ends at last as Milton, 'who at first refused to drink but afterwards decided to do so to
vindicate his conception of liberty,' having grossly insulted Cromwell,
is borne out to the strains of a new and rather bibulous Miltonic
hymn, which he himself sings 'to the tune of Old Hundred.' The
others can only express their shocked amazement that 'the most temperate of Bards' should have undergone so utter a transformation.
Wordsworth is especially horrified:

Milton who sang of morning stars,
Loaded! and borne out by four pickups;
Joining with them in maudlin bars,
With ribald jests and vulgar hiccups.

And Adam observes with some justification,

> If he would blame me when he's dry,
> For all that I have seen to-night
> What kind of language would he try
> To fasten on me, when he's tight.

Clearly, a poet no less than a fish, taught by whatever means 'the warm arts of human sinning,' is truly 'a new creature.'

The poem does not tell whether the Cromwellian ban was thereafter lifted and the Shades permitted to feel again 'the holy fire / That once had warmed their veins.' Nevertheless, there seems little room for doubt that *The Witches' Brew* as originally written, if not as finally published, clearly made the point, both by precept and example, that 'poetry ought to be ... the expression of a grand binge,' the expression, that is, of an imagination that is not afraid to sin gladly, whether its sins be those against the dogmas of a literary tradition, or against prevailing codes that standardize behaviour as well as taste.

The Witches' Brew, 'more or less finished,' read at the Pratts' anniversary dinner, was pronounced a masterpiece by his friends, who demanded its immediate publication. He had not, he said, written it for the public at large and this was undoubtedly true of its inception. But it is also clear, despite his later protestations ('I had no intention of having it published as I thought it too inconsequential'; 'It was one of the few poems I ever wrote without any thought that it would ever be published'; 'I did not attach any literary importance to the production'), that once he began to recognize signs that the poem was shaping itself into a strange, original tour de force, he began to lavish upon it all the care and craftsmanship which he always devoted to a prospective publication. Both Phelps and Kirkconnell, who had heard much of the poem as it progressed, were strong for its immediate submission to a publisher. Pratt too was soon convinced, if in fact he needed convincing. Therefore, shortly after his return to Toronto in September he began to subject his lines to a final polishing and pruning and arranged to have a number of good typescripts made. He was dubious, however, that Lorne Pierce and Ryerson Press would be willing to risk taking on such an outrageous venture.

20

Of Publishers and Poets

I have a poem finished in which you might be interested. Both Edgar and Hooke of Victoria think it is unquestionably the best single thing I have done and are very confident of its selling qualities. It would make a little volume of fifty pages. If you would care to see it I will send it along at once.

E.J. Pratt to Lorne Pierce, November 1923

ALTHOUGH HE WAS eager to have Pierce read *The Witches' Brew* and hoped that his critical verdict would be favourable, Pratt was no longer certain that he wanted Ryerson Press to publish the book even if they were willing to do so. His dissatisfaction was not with Pierce, but with the sales and advertising department. Despite its enthusiastic reviews, *Newfoundland Verse*, after an initial spurt during May and June, had not been selling well, chiefly, he believed, because it had neither been properly advertised nor supplied to booksellers in adequate quantities.

He was not alone in his irritation. That year Ryerson had also published W.A. Deacon's collection of essays, *Pens and Pirates* (Pratt had reviewed it in the *Guardian*), Beaumont Cornell's novel *Lantern Marsh*, and Paul Wallace's collection of 'habitant tales,' *Baptiste Laroque*. By autumn Ryerson had four very unhappy authors on its hands, equally convinced of the firm's unconcern for the fate of their books in the market. Some time in October, therefore, led on by Pratt, who despite his great distaste for confrontation could summon up a fighting spirit when he felt that he suffered an injustice, they decided to call at Wesley Buildings and tackle Ryerson's Managing Director, Dr Sam Follis. Their chief target, however, was E.J.

Moore, Sales and Advertising Manager – 'that fat-head in the east of the building,' as Pratt described him – who, they were convinced, was '"out to get us" by inertia if not positive obstruction.'

It should be interjected here that Pratt's hostility toward Moore, who also sometimes doubled as an editor and proofreader, was actually motivated by more than his 'inertia' or even 'positive obstruction' in sales and advertising. Rightly or wrongly he suspected Moore of being responsible for certain unauthorized changes that had crept into the text of *Newfoundland Verse*, as well as a number of printers' errors allowed to stand after Pratt himself had carefully 'proofed the galleys.' When Deacon had written him in June blaming Moore for even worse offences against the meticulous prose of *Pens and Pirates*, Pratt believed that his own suspicions had been confirmed. As a result, replying to Deacon a few days later he had used the occasion to denigrate the hapless (and probably blameless) manager-cum-editor in what must be one of Pratt's most vituperative letters. Though not without elements of humour – mostly sardonic however – the letter not only makes very explicit his opinion of Moore; it also demonstrates that whatever demon possessed him that summer its influences were not confined to the medium of verse. That he was at the time in the midst of *The Witches' Brew* may perhaps excuse the particularly 'sulphurous' quality of the language – for the sake of which mainly I quote a portion of the letter:

With regard to Moore, since reading your letter the atmosphere of the cottage has been sulphurous. Sacré bleu! Sapristi Ciel! Damnation without Redemption! That fellow would alter the Codex Bezae if he happened to get hold of it, on the ground of archaic lettering. I am glad the Authorized Version happened to be complete before he was born and that Hebrew vowel points had been constructed before anyone thought of asking the cooperation of E.J.M. Verdammit!! Did you ever read in cold print of such presumption. Not satisfied with altering Petrarchan forms [a pair of 'disintegrated sonnets' had turned up in *Newfoundland Verse*] he must unearth the bones of sacred Herrick [quoted but mutilated in Deacon's galleys]; change constructions, punctuation! He knows as much about style as a Second Engineer in a Kansas elevator. Pierce is away just now ... but before he left he wrote me – in answer to a letter in which I protested against any fifth-rate amanuensis tinkering with my stuff – that he was going to make a rigid investigation into the various responsibilities of the house ... Moore evidently is so sore over the [personnel] readjustments of a couple of years ago that the only way he can release his feelings is by chewing up other people's manuscripts ...

Perhaps, after all, his recent 'emancipation' had indeed brought forth 'a new creature' rather than merely the old one in a 'new guise'!

The confrontation with Follis, which took place as planned, was somewhat acrimonious but without immediate results. Looking back on it later in a calmer frame of mind, Pratt seems to have regretted a little his involvement in it, chiefly because it might have pained Lorne Pierce, whose health was poor and of whom he was genuinely fond. (Pierce wrote in his diary [15 October] that he 'was chagrined' by the unpleasant affair: 'I suppose no three men [Pratt, Cornell, and Deacon] have had more done for them.') Pratt, after reviewing the case with his conscience for a month, wrote Pierce a long letter (23 November) explaining his and his friends' action, though generally defending it, and assuring Pierce that none of them blamed him for the cause of their irritation. The letter is forthright and actually retracts nothing, but it makes plain Pratt's deep concern for his friend's feelings:

Perhaps our action was ill-advised. We would not have done anything to give you anxiety or increase your cares but if we are going to meet with continuous opposition from the (as far as we are concerned) most critical part of the machinery – the Advertising and Publicity Department then we are going to govern our future contracts accordingly. I realise you have done your d—est for us and I am grateful for the enthusiastic encouragement you have given Newfoundland Verse. But I should like to know why [E.J.] M[oore] has consistently ignored that volume in his otherwise exhaustive list of new publications ...

The only thing I want to know, old chap, is – Do you candidly think that personal prejudices are working against us? You need not commit yourself if you do not want to ...

Pierce replied with politeness and restraint, but denied that the four brethren-in-arms had any valid complaints. On Newfoundland Verse he reported 'after careful investigation' that the cost of advertising it to date (29 November) would require selling all the first edition to break even. His letter, like Pratt's, was direct and forthright but not un-friendly.

Obviously relieved, Pratt replied immediately (1 December) in the old terms of banter and camaraderie, and expressed his conviction that *Newfoundland Verse* was about to be in great demand. He told of recent letters 'of warm appreciation – urging further literary activity' from a number of 'prominent critics.'

In his previous letter Pratt had briefly mentioned his new poem, *The Witches' Brew*. Though not especially eager to have Ryerson publish the book, doubtful that they would take it in any case, he saw the advantage of retaining Pierce's interest in his publishing projects. Besides, he was genuinely appreciative of Pierce's 'belief in my humble self,' and felt obligated to give Ryerson at least the opportunity of acting as Canadian agent for the 'outside publisher' he already hoped to interest in *The Brew*. His letter of 1 December continued accordingly:

I referred in my last note to a new poem which I had recently finished. Its subject and treatment are entirely new – The Witches' Brew or the Immortals Night Off in tetrameter with prose insets ... I should like it to be tried out upon one or two American and English publishers first – firms of a more aggressive character that take hold of young men.

... Edgar, [S.J.] Hooke, [W.P.M.] Kennedy, Phelps and others think it is the best, at least the most vital single thing I have done, certainly the most original. A few of the more conservative men feel a little dubious about the theme, – whether some controversy might not arise from it, but all agree as to impact and grip.

Professor [W.J.] Alexander is having an evening at his home next week where I am to present it to the staff and a few outside picked University men interested in poetry, some of whom have already seen it.

Now I know your own progressive and almost radical outlook on life and literature and I do not feel any hesitation on that score, but I want you to tell me if the Ryerson Press might feel any qualms about its publication, or whether the Canadian constituency would be interested in it. I may be raising questions without any basis whatsoever. The poem has been 'tried out' on a half-dozen of the Vic Staff and they entered whole-heartedly into the mood of it ...

But in any case, if you felt disposed – you might try to make some outside contacts first as a 'try-out.' All who have seen it suggest fantastic decoration or illustration in harmony with the framework of witchcraft in which the theme is set. It might be a work of about fifty pages which could sell for one dollar but I think illustration would be very desirable. I will send the manuscript along in a day or two.

With the best of good luck
Ned Pratt

His later account of how *The Brew* got published – 'Professor Arthur Phelps suggested that I send it to a publisher which I did, not expecting for a moment that it would be accepted. I sent it to a London publisher who to my greatest surprise decided to bring out 500 copies' – implying as it does both misgivings about the poem's merits and indifference to its fate, is quite misleading. It is true that it was an English publisher who eventually brought out *The Brew*, but not until a great many others had rejected it, and he himself had gone to England and made the rounds in person, manuscript in hand. He in fact spent more time and energy trying to place *The Witches' Brew* than any other poem he ever wrote, an experience which he remembered with distaste and consequently buried beneath an innocuous fiction. There is little doubt that despite his disclaimers he recognized the poem's latent 'epochal' significance and was firmly resolved from the outset to get it before the public.

The initial success of *Newfoundland Verse*, its acclaim by reviewers from coast to coast, meant that he returned to the College in September a not inconsiderable celebrity. 'Old Victorians' had made their name in the world of letters before, but E.J. Pratt was the first poet 'of national stature' (so the Chancellor described him) to be a member of the faculty, and accolades were heaped on him from all ranks of the academic community and beyond. He accepted them with outward befitting modesty, but he was, not unnaturally, very proud of his triumph. One practical gesture of the College administration which he heartily approved was the termination of his joint appointment and his confirmation as a regular full-time lecturer in English. His grasp of English literature might still be 'not very firm,' but unlike his more erudite colleagues he could now take heart in knowing that, in poetry at least, he was able to do more than talk about it.

He soon found, however, as invitations to address clubs and gatherings of various kinds began to pour in, that celebrity carried other responsibilities than performing in verse when the spirit moved him. Schools, service clubs, literary societies (including the Toronto Branch of the CAA), churches, and especially ladies groups of many kinds bombarded him with summonses to appear before them, both to talk about poetry and read his own. Pleased at first, even flattered, he accepted most of his invitations, but the time soon came when he rued the day that he ever allowed himself to be 'a willing draftee for the speaker's podium.' Usually he chose to read his own verse with extemporaneous comment, but occasionally, depending on his audience, he would deliver a more formal discourse from a prepared script. His scripts he used over and over, sometimes with minor changes, carefully avoiding, if possible, surrendering one for publication.

In between public engagements that autumn he continued to work on Pierce to place *The Brew* while 'the fahrenheit of the iron [was] still running high.' A few days after his previous letter (quoted above) and before Pierce had replied, he fortified his request for Pierce's help by sending him several typescripts of the poem 'To facilitate the inebriation of publishers en masse,' keeping 'at least three in "delirium tremens" at once.' Pierce accepted the 'inebriating mass of manuscripts,' promising that 'soon the publishers on both hemispheres will be, as you say, inebriated ... If you hear something that sounds like a "Whoop-ee!" it will only be another publisher gone wrong.' Pierce was as good as his word, but all his efforts proved futile. On 4 April 1924 he could still report no success, the publishers to whom he sent *The Brew* being 'certain it would not have a market.' 'We are very much down in the mouth,' Pierce added, suggesting that Pratt call on him to discuss the matter.

Pratt took the publishers' rebuffs in good humour, though he was understandably disappointed. 'I suppose, after all,' he wrote Pierce, 'publishers are the best judges of the market,' but he had not given up on *The Brew*. Pierce had assailed only American publishers; the British market was still untested and it was to 'get into England' that he longed for most. He suggested to Pierce that *Newfoundland Verse* be placed 'on the British stalls'; his name before that public might encourage publishers to take on *The Brew*. But he seems to have been already convinced that a more direct approach was probably needed. Assuring Pierce that he believed him to be 'doing his damnedest,' he went on to say that he was seriously contemplating a trip to England 'if the banks are merciful.' He did not state that a chief purpose of his trip was to place *The Brew*, but there is little doubt that it was. A week later he was writing excitedly to tell Pierce that an exhibition of Canadian books in England – a feature of the British Empire Exhibition at Wembley – was to include *Newfoundland Verse*; he hoped that British bookstores could be supplied with copies 'in case of a demand ... resulting from the Exhibit.' Since he hoped to be in England at the time, he wondered whether he might be able to take advantage of the coincidence by giving 'a few readings in clubs and churches'; he was planning to solicit some letters of introduction toward this end. If *The Brew* failed to find a publisher and he to win an international audience, inertia on his part would not be the reason.

In the same letter he also included a 'delightful little tidbit' which he was sure Pierce would appreciate. It concerned a mutual acquaintance whom so far we have encountered little more than by name: Wilson MacDonald, today but a curious footnote to the 1920s, though in 1924 the prime candidate of W.A. Deacon and a few other rash critics for 'Great Canadian Poet of the Century.' Since for nearly a decade this 'strange poet' was to be, at least in the eyes of MacDonald's few literary friends, Pratt's chief rival for poetic honours, as well as almost the only bête noire in Pratt's life, a somewhat fuller introduction should probably be included here.

'The spoiled child of disappointment,' as Pierce aptly epitomized him in 1923, MacDonald had begun with at least a faint prospect of realizing his dreams of glory as a poet. A man of many talents, he had been a precocious youth, publishing while still in his teens some not unpromising verse for a boy, for which he had been much praised by his elders. Thereafter he had gone on to win further local reputations as a pen-and-ink artist, designer, illustrator, illuminator, magician, and master of sleight-of-hand. (Pratt's earliest memory of him was as a performer of 'magic tricks' at one of Edgar's literary soirées, when MacDonald too had been, ironically enough, one of Edgar's protégés.) Since then, having published several volumes of rather tuneful, romantic verse, from which he gave frequent readings, MacDonald had achieved a measure of celebrity as a poet, and a devoted if limited circle of admirers, attracted as much by his theatrical flair and romantic figure as by his nostalgic verse. Described by another acquaintance as a man of 'gorgeous vanity ineffectively concealed under a cloak of enigma,' he was also a man of colossal conceit, fond of quoting from his own favourable reviews (some of which he was said to have written) and often repeated a story that Archibald Lampman on his deathbed (in 1899) had foretold the coming of a great poet whose description uncannily fitted Wilson MacDonald. A devout vegetarian, he nevertheless confessed a 'great weakness for cold chicken' and condemned white bread as 'poison.' He denounced tobacco as 'the greatest destroyer of sex and the coming generation,' yet consumed alcohol to 'improve the condition of his health.' He was clearly a man, as Phelps recalled him, of 'many crotchets and contradictions.'

MacDonald was nevertheless a poet of not inconsiderable talent, perhaps even a scintilla of genius, who might have carved himself a permanent niche in Canadian letters had he been as devoted to his muse as he was to his private myths and public image. His public image – part natural, part affected – was in fact unusually exotic, rather more Italian than Scots-Canadian: jet-black hair; black, flashing eyes; thin, sharp face with an olive complexion, and, when he chose, an inscrutable smile (which women, he claimed, found irresistible), 'a dark, romantic figure' (to quote a female acquaintance in 1948) characteristically dressed in a long, black cloak and a conjuror's broadbrimmed, black, felt hat. An exotic figure on the Canadian literary scene in the 1920s might well have been something Canadian poetry needed. Unfortunately, beneath MacDonald's conjuror's hat was a head filled with megalomaniac delusions, paranoiac whims, and other miscellaneous, distressing proclivities, which invariably caused him to alienate almost everyone who tried to befriend him, to denigrate any poet who seemed a likely rival or any critic who dared to be unflattering, and to damage most of his verse with gratuitous intrusions of Wilson MacDonald.

In 1924 Pratt's fame had not yet grown to the point where MacDonald could view him as a threat, so that their casual encounters had so far been amicable, even comradely. Pratt, nevertheless, was well acquainted with MacDonald's less engaging personal traits, mainly through Lorne Pierce, who, convinced like many others of the 'promise' of MacDonald's early verse, had felt it his duty to encourage him, even to offer him a publisher's helping hand. He had, in fact, taken MacDonald's latest small book of verse for publication by Ryerson Press in 1923. But the time had soon come when he rued his rash decision. The 'delightful little tidbit,' which Pratt could not forbear passing on to Pierce, would, he well knew, be acutely appreciated by Ryerson's long-suffering Editor; he had just come through his most illuminating experience of MacDonald's 'terrible egoism, conceit, and adulation-hunting' (to quote Pierce's diary), a consequence of a well-intentioned recital tour of western Canada he had arranged for Mac-Donald, mainly to publicize his new book.

MacDonald had made the tour during the previous autumn and winter, and in some places visited had attracted sizable and responsive audiences, though mostly of middle-aged women. In other places, however, chiefly by his embittered assaults on all who declined to acknowledge him 'the equal of Shelley and Keats,' he had succeeded merely in alienating former friends and creating a host of new enemies. Much of the spleen engendered by his embitterment and other trifling annoyances he had vented upon the patient and unoffending head of Lorne Pierce, accusing him of dereliction of various responsibilities financial and otherwise which he felt Pierce owed him. Their correspondence had grown increasingly acrimonious, at least on Mac-Donald's part, culminating in his threat to sever all connections with Ryerson Press, a consummation, from Pierce's viewpoint in April 1924, devoutly to be wished. The events 'out West' referred to in Pratt's letter had occurred during the ill-conceived tour. Pratt wrote:

A delightful little tidbit came into my hands a few days ago which it would be selfish to keep to myself, so I am passing it on to you. It concerns our mutual friend Wilson MacDonald and Pelham Edgar. Pelham came into my office last Thursday with a letter in his hands from W.M. – a most abusive letter in which the said W.M. asserted that when he gets back to the Queen City there is going to be war to the death between himself and the dignified Professor of English at Victoria College. Edgar said to me, 'Why Pratt, I do not even know the names of the people he is talking about or *what* he is talking about. It is enough by half to commit a fellow to a lunatic asylum.' The names of [Austin] Bothwell [teacher, editor, and journalist], [Laura] Salverson [novelist] were repeated often, and Macdonald claimed that if Edgar said one word of commendation about such a disreputable brood then MacDonald would open his seventeen inch batteries when he got back. 'Do you know what they are saying about you out here?' he asks Edgar. 'They hate you Edgar, they call you a fop, a nobody, a – – – – – – – –.' He blames

Bothwell for a dirty prank that he played on him a little while ago. Bothwell knew MacDonald for a vegetarian yet ordered a beefsteak for him at a dinner in his honour. And several of the 'literary lights' out West refuse to recognize him as the equal of Shelley or Keats. Edgar adds, 'The name of Shakespeare is just as easy to pronounce as Shelley. Why does not the damn fool bring in the Almighty as well?' Edgar did not know whether to laugh or swear when he read the letter. MacDonald is going to shake the dust of Canada off his feet, a nation of ingrates & ! ? – x ! ! – ! Edgar is getting heartily sick of him ...

I have a faint suspicion that you might regard this haphazard and inconsequential effusion as in the mad category as well ...

Pierce after managing to 'decipher most of the contents' ('You surely do write a rotten hand') digested the tidbit with much amusement but no great surprise: 'He is all that you say and more.' But turning from MacDonald to Pratt, he invited him down for a tête-à-tête – 'I have much to tell thee' – and expressed the hope that 'you are on good terms with your banker and that your trip will materialize.'

21

Shades of Egdon

Hardy ... states that it is his purpose to be vocal to tragedy – that Romance may be left to other writers with other temperaments. And so his tragic imagination is given full play ... Along this gamut then sweeps his epic lament for human misery and waste, at times querulous and wistful, at times searing with defiant reproach. Nevertheless ... there are certain values that must be asserted.

E.J. Pratt from 'Thomas Hardy,'
The Canadian Journal of Religious Thought, May–June 1924

ETWEEN APRIL 1923, when *Newfoundland Verse* appeared, and April 1924 Pratt published almost nothing. *The Witches' Brew* had occupied him all summer, and its initial revisions most of the autumn. At Pierce's request he had written a brief review for the *Guardian* (4 July 1923) of the first volume in Ryerson's new series, Makers of Canadian Literature, A.D. Watson's *Robert Norwood*. In the November number of *Acta* he had published 'The Decision,' a short, poignant lyric on the sudden death of Langford Rowell, a student-athlete at the College whom he had known, and the son of an acquaintance. The boy's death from blood-poisoning was a great shock to Pratt, and the poem, rather reminiscent of Emily Dickinson, is as much a lament for a personal friend as an act of commemoration for a College hero. From then until April 1924 he published nothing else that can be found. Nevertheless, while he 'dickered with Pierce' to place *The Witches' Brew* and Pierce resolutely assailed 'outside' publishers with the 'inebriating mass of manuscripts,' Pratt's pen was far from idle. His new ventures were, however, in a far different realm from that of sea-cats and witches. Almost as if in revulsion from the excessive mirth and absurdity of *The Brew*, he made an abrupt about-face and plunged into a world of darker moods and deeper shades.

What may be called Pratt's 'Hardy period' began in late 1923, after Arthur Phelps had sent him (given or lent) – probably at Christmas – Hardy's newest book of poems, *Late Lyrics and Earlier* (1922), with its prefatory 'Apology' for the author's 'view of life.' It lasted at least until he embarked on a British tour in June 1924. By then, in Phelps's words, 'he had imbibed at Hardy's fountain almost to the point of intoxication,' written at least ten short poems 'in Hardy's vein,' as well as a brief but discerning and appreciative scholarly essay on Hardy's thought and craft, published in the May–June number of *The Canadian Journal of Religious Thought*. It was Phelps's view, indeed, that after reading *Late Lyrics* 'Ned for a time was possessed almost by a passion to *be* a Canadian Hardy himself.'

This is undoubtedly something of an exaggeration, but the fact is that during the winter and spring of 1924 Pratt did indeed devote himself to a careful study and, for a time, to a conscious imitation of the poetic style and stance of Hardy such as he had not done with any poet before, nor would do again. Hardy, as we know, had long been a favourite author of his and had probably influenced both the form and the tenor of *Clay*. But now, whether because of his reading the new book of poems, especially its Apology, or because he was now beginning to teach Hardy, Pratt was moved to revisit the Wessex poet in a far more responsive, though not uncritical, frame of mind and imagination than his earlier reading of him had evoked. Hitherto he seems to have been mainly interested in, if not fascinated by, Hardy's grim picture of the general 'constitution of things,' and in Hardy's philosophy of 'fatalistic pessimism' and its almost unanswerable logic. Now he seems to have been more affected by the emotional and imaginative effects which Hardy creates in his poetry through his skilful exploitation of that philosophy in the context of individual, human situations, by what may be called the ironic pathos that characterizes so many of Hardy's poems. In particular, Pratt seems to have been moved to a deeper awareness of the close affinities between Hardy and himself and between the visions of life evoked by Hardy's Wessex and by his own North Atlantic Egdon. As a consequence the group of poems which he wrote that winter and spring are the most 'Hardyesque' (Pratt's own term) of all his short poems, and the essay published in *The Canadian Journal of Religious Thought* is a sympathetic and appreciative critique of Hardy's view of life by one who had seen the same spectacle if not in quite the same unfiltered light.

A Hardyesque vein is not, of course, new to Pratt's verse. *Clay*, as we saw, bears many significant resemblances to *The Dynasts*; and *Newfoundland Verse* reflects moods and responses that would not be misplaced in much of Hardy's work. An Ironic Spirit if not an Immanent Will broods over most of the sea poems in that volume. Such poems as 'The Toll of the Bells,' *The Ice-Floes*, 'The Ground Swell,' 'The Loss of the Florizel,' and 'The Drowning' all focus, in Hardyesque fashion, upon the irony of Man's predicament as a consciousness that feels and hopes yet finds 'the world / Outside the soul betray the one within,' upon the irony of what Hardy called 'the intolerable antilogy / Of making figments feel.' But one hesitates to suggest that Pratt would have written otherwise had he never read Hardy.

The new poems, however, are a different matter. These have been consciously fashioned in Hardy's image, probably the only poems of his that might be called imitations though they are more than that. The group consists of at least ten poems, two of which were left unfinished in a notebook. The others were published in various magazines shortly after they were written, though only four of them were later retrieved for book publication. It is not unlikely that several of the group were reworkings of earlier materials antedating *Newfoundland Verse*. With one or two exceptions I should not class them among his better poems, though they are generally successful in reproducing certain of Hardy's characteristic poses and effects. Space does not permit reprinting them here or examining them in any detail, but since they have not (so far as I know) been viewed before in their Hardyesque context; since also they represent an interesting and, I think, important phase in Pratt's still unfinished search for his true poetic character, at least a glance at them in probably necessary. I shall begin with the four poems which he later collected (in *Many Moods*, 1932) and are therefore best known.

'Comrades,' the first to be published (*Canadian Magazine*, April 1924), is a short, compact lyric in which, in Hardy's fashion, Pratt sets the fleeting Present over against the Eternity of the grave. Do not, he warns the comrades (or lovers), squander your words to one another on trivial exigencies that alienate and divide, for the time will soon come when you are united where there is no voice or sound:

> ...
> Do you not know that a hemlock's root
> Will enfold you together,
> Though fair be the sky
> Or foul be the weather?
> To that same bed you shall come,
> When the ear shall be deaf
> And the lips dumb;
> Where under the turf,
> Not a note shall be heard,
> From the cry of a wren
> To the thunder of surf.

Shades of Hardy are easy to detect in such lines, yet there is something about them, I think, that is uniquely Pratt.

'The Alternative' (*The Canadian Bookman*, May 1924; reprinted with revisions as 'One Hour of Life' in *Many Moods*) was probably suggested by Hardy's 'To an Unborn Pauper Child.' Pratt quotes from Hardy's poem in his essay on him to illustrate his acute awareness of 'the bitter grasp that an Ironic Fate has upon life,' that 'Birth itself is potential tragedy.' Pratt's poem, adopting the same stance and view, describes an anguished mother's last embrace of her dying new-born son, which, were it able to preserve his life,

> Could only cheat the earth to save
> The plunder for another grave –
> *For as the island mothers know,*
> *There are two ways a lad may go.*
>
> *The waters bide their time today,*
> *Death does not need a grave of clay* ...

The italicized lines (Pratt's italics), omitted from the revised version, account for its original title. In this poem Housman too seems to be hovering close by.

The other two poems in the group which Pratt republished in *Many Moods* are too well known to require quoting from here, or much in the way of commentary. 'The Drag-Irons' (*The Canadian Forum*, July 1924) gives the theme of death at sea the kind of grimly comic-ironic twist that Hardy excelled in. 'The Ritual' (*The Canadian Magazine*, October 1924), one of Pratt's best-known shorter poems, is a pair of sonnets which present two ironically contrasting pictures from the life of a ship, her birth and baptism 'beneath according skies' and her death and burial 'under revolted skies ... upon a rock.' Stylistically the least Hardyesque of the group, it nevertheless pursues its theme of 'birth as potential tragedy' with grim single-mindedness of purpose.

The four poems which Pratt published but did not retrieve were, perhaps, best left uncollected. Yet they are interesting exercises in Hardy's manner, three of the four closely reproducing one of his favourite 'lyric' forms: the short ironic narrative which depends for its chief effects on implication, suggestion, and an almost laconic style. 'The Lie' (*The Canadian Bookman*, April 1924) encapsulates in three quatrains the story of a man who by telling the truth can 'stop the ring / Of hammers on the scaffolding,' thus saving another's life, but forfeiting his own. He chooses to lie; after all,

> ... The sun that day was warm. Besides,
> He knew that no accusing sound
> Came from the body that was drowned,
> And cast up by the morning tides.

'The Frost Over-Night' (*ibid.*) is another ironic short story in capsule form: a party of travellers having survived a night of winter storm reaches the sea at last, hoping for rescue, only to find that the frost overnight has visited death upon it too –

> Had with the Master's cunning wrought no less
> A marvel than [Death's] own facsimile
> That morning by the cold waste of the sea.

'The Last Survivor' (*The Canadian Forum*, June 1924) is the story – again in three quatrains – of fifteen sealers, lost at night on an ice-floe, who valiantly play the 'merry' game with Death. All but one are beaten in the match; he alone remains 'with odds at dawn against the frost':

> ... But Death outplayed him the next night
> And beat the partner at his side
> When, in the home, she joined the fight
> Against the wind and snow and tide.

In the fourth of the published but uncollected Hardyesque poems, 'Tokens' (*The Canadian Forum*, September 1924), death at sea and grief in the home is again the narrative theme. But the poem, not particularly successful, is interesting chiefly because it draws for its sombre effects, its notes of ironic pathos, on the abundant Newfoundland folklore of signs and apparitions, natural and supernatural, presaging calamity and death. (Though a very different poem, Pratt's 'Tokens' may have been prompted by Hardy's 'Signs and Tokens,' in which he draws on the same kind of folklore from the traditions of Wessex.) A few lines will serve as illustration:

> The sea was as grey as a wild goose wing,
> And the wind like the sea was grey,
> When the bell at the Cape was heard to ring
> At the fog-blown hour of the dusk of the day.
> A wave was seen to rise in a shroud,
> A token had passed by the window in white,
> A voice in her room had called aloud,
> A robin had pecked at the fan-light ...

The wisdom of his decision not to retrieve the poem cannot, I think, be questioned.

Two other poems that seem to belong to the group were left unfinished in his small, cramped, pencilled handwriting in a 1923–4 notebook. 'The Balance Sheet,' also drawing on the lore of 'tokens,' introduces a more sombre note of fatalism than any other poem in the group. Again the theme is birth as potential tragedy, but now the tragedy is foretold even before the birth occurs. A midwife attending a woman in childbirth is convinced that a 'claw / Of foam-white fingers at the window-sill' and a voice heard in the wind are tokens of death which 'God himself [can]not undo.' She is proved right: the mother dies, though her son lives. The bereaved father, reading 'A blinding justice on the ledger-page,' believes that Providence has struck a 'bargain' with him: his wife's death has cleared the debt; his son will be spared a watery grave: 'Life for a life! a bargain? Let it be ... / A bond will be respected by the sea.' But not so. Twenty years later 'the faith of that indentured page' was broken by 'the great vandal' when, as the boy climbed the rigging of a storm-tossed ship, 'He fouled the tally when a ratline broke.'

The other unfinished poem, 'The Lee Shore' (a title Pratt used later for another poem), though much shorter, is no less grim and ironic. Consisting of twelve very imperfect lines, it depicts a bride-to-be at the hour appointed for her vows standing instead at a 'strange altar stone / And stricken at the knees.' Hardy's 'purblind Doomsters' – Pratt's 'collusion of the winds / And snow and night and fate' – have intervened to deal her grief instead of joy. He had run the gamut of Hardy's scale.

Taken together these ten poems constitute as sombre a miscellany as Pratt ever wrote, all of them, in one way and another, reflecting darkly on human mortality, on the seeming dominance of 'Crass Casualty' in human life, on the fast alliance that seems to exist between nature, especially the sea, and the Ironic Spirit. Any ray of sunlight that breaks through the gloom soon fades and any 'note of joyance' heard is soon silenced. But it was a mood Pratt could not sustain for long. Despite Hardy's undoubted attraction for him, his sense of affinity with Hardy in ways already touched on, Pratt's temperament and spiritual constitution were such that he could never become a permanent tenant of Hardy's necessitated universe.

That this is basically true is, I think, apparent from the essay, 'Thomas Hardy,' which Pratt wrote and published that spring. It is not a profoundly searching or original study; much of it indeed is superficial and obvious. But it illustrates clearly both Pratt's detailed knowledge of a large part of the Hardy canon, as well as his appreciative understanding of Hardy's most characteristic ideas. It also reveals fairly precisely how far Pratt is prepared to follow Hardy into the darkness toward which his vision leads. The essay, therefore, I think, sheds as much light on the mind of E.J. Pratt as it does on that of Thomas Hardy, and for that reason alone deserves more than a passing glance.

From the beginning it is clear that Pratt is a warm and sensitive admirer of Hardy the craftsman, and not only as a poet but as a novelist and story-teller as well. He selects for particular praise Hardy's 'fast-moving plot[s] singularly free of padding,' the 'symmetry' of design in his stories, his 'sharp and lifelike' characterizations – especially of 'peasant types' – his evocative use of landscape, and above all his subtle skill in weaving his view of life into the fabric of his fictions. To Hardy's view of life he must, of course, come before long. And here again he cannot but respond admiringly to the logic and persuasiveness with which Hardy 'forges' the 'iron chain' of causation 'around the lives of his characters,' depressing though the spectacle at times may be. Nor is Pratt prepared to admit that this is anything less than 'an unequivocal personal conviction' for Hardy: 'it would be a treasonable weakening of Hardy's outlook upon life if one ... were to explain away as an artistic device the rigidity of the Fate that broods over the Wessex woodlands and heaths ...'

Especially responsive is Pratt to the close relationship and 'determinate interaction' which Hardy sees between his characters and their 'elemental backgrounds,' between Egdon Heath, for example, 'represented as a complex system of forces,' and 'the destiny of the peasants that live upon it.' He writes, with the obvious warmth and understanding of assent:

In addition to this Natural Determinism, or perhaps as another phase of it, there are the biological processes evident in family and racial history. An act or an impulse here and there in 'Tess' is a throwback to an 'obscure strain in the D'Urberville blood,' or to some outlaw expression of ancestral days. This continuity of life with the living past and with nature is taught with all the cogency and wealth of Hardy's fund of illustration. The peasant has a relationship of marrow and blood with the soil itself.

Pratt is almost speaking for himself; his own conception of nature as a continuous 'complex system of forces' subsuming both animate and inanimate nature is virtually identical. His poem 'Newfoundland' ('Here the tides flow ...') is an obvious and familiar illustration. The flood and ebb of the tides of the sea, the flow of the blood, the rise and fall of the tides of instinct and passion – '... Along dark passages / That once were pathways of authentic fires ...' – are all of a piece in the total rhythm and pattern of nature. Like Hardy, too, he often pushes the roots of human consciousness back into a dim pre-human past, viewing it as an evolving pattern of variegated threads – many still tinged with pre-racial 'rememberings' – that link us with the primordial Unconscious. In 'Sea Variations,' for example, the waters as they 'mock our liturgy,' tearing apart 'the threads of faith,' in doing so strip

> The veilings from our eyes, and bid us cast
> Our glances on a labyrinthine past,
> ...
> To gather from a weed-grown track
> A bitter tale of dimmed rememberings ...

In 'The Ground Swell' the 'insistent note' that 'crept up from the shore / And smote upon a bedroom window-pane' is an echo of the primordial agony '... that grew / Out of the void before Eternity / Had fashioned out an edge for human grief ...' There are boundaries indeed, and the conflicts that are often concomitants of boundaries, between the human and non-human worlds – boundaries are more important to Pratt than they are to Hardy – but these exist only at the conscious and cultural levels. Even then, '... Between the temple and the cave / The boundary lies tissue thin ...'

As impressive to Pratt as Hardy's notions of biological and psychical continuity – though he cannot respond to it with equal warmth despite the poetic use he had made of it in some of his recent poems – is Hardy's conception of 'motiveless Fate,' that 'gigantic abstraction, an IT utterly uncaring and unintelligent.' In its 'developments,' Pratt writes, it may 'throw off as conscious derivatives, human beings toying with the illusion that the calculus of life [its 'balance-sheet'] will reveal a plus of happiness in relation to pain.' But this, as he recognized, merely 'constitutes the supreme irony' of Hardy's thesis:

Man is as determined as the whirling of a leaf in a gale, but he has somehow acquired this groundless belief that he is free, and the mockery of it is that he must feel the same remorse as if he were –
   'the intolerable antilogy
   of making figments feel.'
Over all action broods this universal Will. It would be more tolerable ... if IT were knowingly cruel ...

But 'impressive' though such a conception is in the context of Hardy's vision, Pratt cannot admit its 'adequacy as a view of life.' The religious prepossessions of his Methodist youth rise up between him and the ultimate bleakness of Hardy's conclusion; at least there still are grounds for regarding the case unclosed. Whether Hardy or Browning comes closer to the truth may be an unanswerable question, but it is not new. The 'ironic enigma' of Man's predicament

has always been for the human one quavering interrogation, sometimes ending upon an agonized note, sometimes uplifted into triumph;
   'He hath walled up my way that I cannot pass,
   And hath set darkness in my paths,'
for Job; the Golgotha utterance for Christ; an idiot's tale for Macbeth.

To conclude his essay Pratt turns from Hardy's pictures of 'human fate ... irrevocably sealed,' pictures 'painted in the darkest tones and hung with crepe,' to find at least a glimmer of something more cheerful and promising. He cites 'The Darkling Thrush' and the final chorus of the Pities from *The Dynasts*, and quotes (from the Apology prefixed to *Late Lyrics and Earlier*) Hardy's hope, 'forlorn' though it may be, 'a mere dream,' 'of an alliance between religion, which must be retained unless the world is to perish, and complete rationality, which must come, unless also the world is to perish ...' But it is 'from the personality of Hardy himself' that 'deliverance comes': 'We may concede the historical truthfulness of these sombre pictures ... But the way our fists are raised to support the anger of Hardy at the social prejudices that debased and exterminated Tess is at least an affirmation of the redemptive processes stirring in human hearts ...'
Especially reassuring is Hardy's sympathetic portrayal 'of the holiest forms of renunciation, of devotion in the midst of suffering,' and of that 'faithfulness of love which is unto death.' 'His power to chasten our feelings and stimulate our moral judgments is one of his silent achievements.' Having exposed Hardy's bleakest 'personal convictions' about the universe and man's fate, Pratt must show that the poet he so much admires can still believe, like himself, in 'certain values that must be asserted.'
Though Pratt wrote no more poems so consciously and obviously formed in Hardy's image as those from the winter and spring of 1924, Hardy remained one of his favourites among English poets and a

continuing influence upon his own thought and poetry and his teaching of poetry. 'Sooner or later,' I am told by old students of his from the twenties and thirties, 'Hardy was dragged into his lectures, no matter what the subject.' In 1925 *The Great Feud*, though hardly an imitation, will be partly shaped by his reading of *The Dynasts*. In 1926, asked by Victoria College to give a series of extension classes at St Catharines, he chose as his subject 'The Poetry of Thomas Hardy.' In the 1930s he edited with an appreciative critical introduction one of Hardy's novels and made 'The Convergence of the Twain,' in his own words, 'the emotional kernel – if not more' of his own *The Titanic*. During his forthcoming visit to England he will spend five days exploring 'Hardy territory,' a longer time than he will spend in any other part of Britain with the exception of London.

To visit Europe, especially the British Isles, had long been a dream of Pratt's. England and Scotland were famous for their golf greens – as well as for other things. And now there was also the urgent need for personal intercession on behalf of his new poem, unwanted it seemed on this side of the Atlantic. As luck would have it, R.S. Knox and Herbert Davis, both in the Department of English at University College and good friends of his, were planning a foray in Britain that summer – both were British and had families there – and would be happy to have him accompany them. Only the expense of the trip restrained him. He would have to borrow – and leave his wife and daughter behind him. But Viola, feeling he needed the experience, would not hear of postponement. His qualms of conscience at last suppressed – at least temporarily – and his banker proving 'merciful,' his passage was booked and his face set eagerly toward the British Isles.

22

An Unsentimental Journey

I have been to every great literary centre since I came over and have drunk deeply. I shall end that sentence right there so as to leave your imagination scope for figurative exercise ...

E.J. Pratt to Lorne Pierce, 7 August 1924

THE FOUR TRAVELLERS (Davis was accompanied by his wife) left Toronto for Montreal on 22 May, and the following day embarked for Liverpool on the Canadian Pacific liner *Montclare*. The trans-Atlantic voyage was all that Pratt had dreamed a proper ocean cruise should be, the food and prevailing air of luxury especially delighting him. He wrote Viola on board:

We have just ... finished a most marvellous dinner. The four of us sit together and we have an immense time. The weather is perfect. We spend hours on deck walking around, cultivating an appetite and the roast beef and capons disappear like magic. The steamer is very comfortable even luxurious, just suits my tastes ... Weather conditions are excellent and the prospect is ideal.

The voyage passed all too quickly and soon he was being greeted in Liverpool by his brother Arthur, who had settled in England after demobilization in 1919. Now comfortably established in Liverpool in what his father used to call 'the commercial life,' he and Maud, his bride of a few weeks, had invited Pratt to make their home his base of operations. He was glad to accept their hospitality; it would greatly ease the drain on his bank loan, and besides there were several excellent golf courses in the neighbourhood.

One of these he had soon sought out, at nearby Woolton Links, where he quickly made friends with three sporting Catholic priests. It rained almost every day, but he and his clerical friends paid scant attention to the weather. Having no galoshes in his luggage (and loath to part with any of his meagre funds for a new pair), he lined his boots with brown paper and donning a heavy mackintosh and a cloth cap which he pulled about his ears would head for the links oblivious of the elements. Knox, who had 'looked forward to the pleasure of being with him for a few days to watch his response to the Old Country,' had also stayed on in Liverpool to visit a sister who lived nearby. One day Pratt lured him to the course for a few rounds, but the weather seems to have been more pleasant on that occasion, for Knox's only recollection of it was 'Ned's thrill when he saw his first skylarks circling and singing above us.'

After a week spent mostly on the golf course Pratt set out (7 June) on the first of his exploratory forays. His first destination was Barnard Castle, his father's birthplace, on the border of Yorkshire and Durham. After a brief visit to the City of Durham to see the cathedral and castle, he arrived on 8 June at Barnard Castle, where he put up at the venerable King's Head Hotel. Here, he soon learned, young Charles Dickens had begun to write *Nicholas Nickleby* just a few months before John Pratt had been born in a house nearby. Even more exciting, and unlikely, was his meeting with an old man by the name of Sunter, reputed to have known 'all the old inhabitants' of 'the little town of four thousand ...' 'As soon as I told Sunter who I was,' Pratt reported to Viola (10 June), 'he almost fell upon my neck, crying out, "Are you actually Johnny Pratt's son?"' The following day he set out to walk, as his grandfather and his family had done long ago, the seventeen miles 'over the beautiful hills and dales' (so he described them) to Gunnerside on the Swale, the Pratts' ancestral home. It was a full day's journey, but he seems to have enjoyed it. 'This Yorkshire country,' he told Viola, 'especially these dales are so beautiful that they cannot be described. I never beheld any village more charming in its situation than Gunnerside.' The villagers gave him a warm welcome once he had made himself known, took him to see the old house where his father had lived as a boy, the chapel where he had preached his first sermon, and the cemetery 'where the Pratts for generations were buried.' Next day, after doing 'all kinds of queer stunts' (unspecified in his letter to Viola), he set out once more and arrived back at the King's Head having had enough walking to last him a long time. He stayed a day longer at Barnard Castle awaiting word from Knox about a proposed excursion into Scotland.

So far his expenses had not been great, but finances were to be a continuing, almost a guilty, anxiety to him throughout his travels. He was very conscious that they were a luxury he could ill afford. Again and again he assures Viola that 'living has not been costly so far,' that 'I am keeping well within my allowance per diem.' One senses too a feeling of guilt for having left her behind. Repeatedly he expresses the hope that 'you have a real good time with lots of leisure on your hands,' and advises her not to be 'afraid to spend a little jink once in a while to keep the days humping.' Despite the new acquaintances he constantly made, he was also lonely without the company of his familiar friends. 'This last week,' he wrote her on 10 June, 'I have been about as lonely as that Zanzibar cat [in *The Witches' Brew*] on the top of the parapet before he sprang into the Pacific ... I begin already to look forward to the time passing to board the *Montcalm* [*sic*].' (He never could remember the name of his ship, the *Montclare*, calling it variously *Montcalm*, *Montrose*, and *Montfort*.)

Two days later, the Davises having gone to the Continent, he joined Knox for a fortnight's excursion in Scotland. 'We toured central Scotland,' wrote Knox, 'stopping here and there to play golf. He was, I thought, less interested in the places visited, their scenery or history, than in golf and in the people we met.' They ended the first half of their tour with a few days at the country estate of Knox's brother-in-law at Glenisla in the county of Angus. Thence they travelled, stopping en route at Alyth, to Glasgow where Knox had a brother. Pratt, having little interest in Glasgow, parted from Knox and left for Ayr 'to spend a day looking up the monuments and memorials of Burns.' He was deeply interested in Burns, both the man and the poet, and took great delight in 'ransacking' the Alloway cottage and viewing the relics on display. He visited too the brig of Doon and the grave of Burns's father nearby. But after two days 'moping about by myself' and only a single game of golf he was glad to take a short boat trip down the Clyde to Rothesay and Dunoon. Back in Glasgow he wrote Viola an account of his exploits, which he concluded on a note that frequently recurs in his letters to her:

I am giving you a daily account of my Iliad, so you can see my geographical movements. I have decided though most emphatically that I will not take any extended trip without your Majesty and the little Princess. It is too gol darned lonely without you ... I sent Claire a post card yesterday. I hope she got it all right. Her letter to me was splendid Hindustani. I can imagine her sitting up at the table drawing those marks, bless her little neckie ...

Next day he travelled to Edinburgh and found that he had 'never visited a more beautiful city in my life': 'As soon as I arrived there I went to Holyrood and Edinburgh Castles, visited the famous Banqueting Hall of the Scottish Kings, saw the Crown jewels – the crown, the sceptres, and Stones possessed by the kings for centuries back. Queen Margaret's Chapel stood almost intact, a thousand years old nearly ...' But one day was enough for sightseeing. Next morning he was off to the golf course for 'the inevitable game of golf' with 'an Edinburgh medical student who was glad to get a partner.' His golf was continuing to improve. His new partner was 'almost a professional,' but Pratt was able to boast to Viola that he 'beat him on two holes and led on one.'

Golf rather than poetry, or even history and 'literary associations,' being clearly his ruling passion that summer, he soon cut short his Scottish tour and returned to Liverpool to witness the World Open Golf Championship at the famous Hoylake course. This was something he could not miss: 'The finest golfers in the world were to be present – Hagan, Sarazen, and Macdonald Smith ... Taylor, Vardon, Havers and a brilliant player named Duncan ...' It was, in fact, the only event of his travels which he recorded in published form:

I picked out the likely champions and dogged them around the course. The nonchalant manner in which those old timers stepped up to the tee and drove the balls with slowly rising curves two hundred and fifty yards down the middle of the fairways, with neither pull nor slice, would have brought joy to the heart of a geometrician. There was none of that agony which I had witnessed on the faces of some of my friends when addressing their Dunlops in front of the hazards on York Downs – none of that superannuated 'waggle' resembling the *rigor mortis* which takes the energy out of them before they hit. Everything was effortless rhythm and precision ...

It is doubtful whether he ever wrote with such rapturous admiration of any exhibition of the poet's art.

On 1 July he left Liverpool again, this time for the Lake District of Cumberland and Westmoreland, making Furness Abbey his base. At the hotel he struck up an acquaintance with 'a young fellow, a rural teacher,' who proved to be the very squire he needed. They decided to 'do' the Lake District together: 'It was quite fortunate for me, as he undertakes to look after tickets, hours of departure and arrival of trains and buses and he has a store of technical information that suits me very conveniently.' (Though they travelled together for three days, Pratt never learned his companion's name. 'How come?' Viola asked on his return home. 'I forgot to ask him,' was Pratt's laconic reply.)

Next day (2 July), happily accompanied by his anonymous Sancho Panza, he set out on a rapid tour, 'by train, steamer, and motor through the Wordsworth country.' This included 'a lovely cruise' on Lake Windermere to Ambleside, 'a gorgeous motor trip' through Rydal Water and Grasmere, with a brief pause at 'Wythburn Church that Wordsworth speaks of as the smallest church in England.' From there they motored up past Helvellyn and then 'down into the loveliest region I have yet seen ... Derwentwater.' Stopping for lunch at the Queen's Head Hotel in Keswick, he wrote Viola a full account of his latest travels. More personally he wrote:

I am in tip-top condition as to health, not having a headache since I came here, the only indisposition being loneliness ... I was only thinking as I returned to the Abbey Hotel last evening what I would give if some fairy could transport you and duckins to the road about one hundred yards distant. Wouldn't we have one hullabaloo of a time? However we must plan our next trip ... together ... By all means if any money comes in from any source nab it, and use it. I will not want any more. I do hope you have not gone short ... I have not done any writing since I left – too busy I guess getting up material for lectures from my trip. [I have found no record of his giving any such lectures, public ones at least.]

Returning to Furness Abbey by bus, they stopped at Grasmere to visit the cemetery, where he was much impressed by the unpretentiousness of the Wordsworth graves, 'a little rail enclosure ... very modest looking ... in a remote and unnoticed part of the cemetery.' He also called at Dove Cottage and was similarly impressed. Back at his hotel at 'about nine o'clock,' he consumed two helpings of cold roast duckling, after which, he reported, 'I went to bed and slept the sleep of the full and the just.' He took the next day off from travelling 'and went to the Golf Course and beat my last record by five shots.' 'My Brassey is improving,' he wrote Viola, 'though my mid-iron is getting weaker I think. There is some damnable compensation about this great and ancient game. If you improve on one club you correspondingly go back on another.' He decided to stay on at Furness Abbey 'over the week-end as I like the quietness and comfort of this hotel and place.'

On Monday (7 July) he returned to Liverpool, where he spent most of the following week on the Woolton Links, awaiting word from Knox and Davis about a promised excursion to Oxford and introductions to various 'literary figures' there. Word finally came and on 13 July he set out once more, joining Herbert Davis at Long Buckley. Here he spent three days, having a very peaceful time visiting small country estates and churches and playing golf in the intervals. He was much impressed by a motor visit to Naseby Ridge, 'where Cromwell defeated Charles I': 'I could imagine Cromwell's Ironsides storming down the hill on the fat shire horses overwhelming Rupert's Spanish Cavalry with sheer might. I had a beautiful view of the Midland country from the heights ...'

Arriving in Oxford on 16 July, Pratt was 'pleased' with 'the Home of Learning,' and for several days was 'busy going the rounds of the College buildings.' A formal tour planned by Knox fell through, Pratt having accepted an invitation for the same afternoon to play golf at North Oxford with a man he had met on the train. He managed, however, to visit a number of buildings that particularly interested him: St Mary's Church 'where Keble preached his sermon on National Apostasy'; Dr Johnson's room ('They tell the story that old Samuel was so poor that his shoes were worn through to his feet'), and the Bodleian Library, where a 'Latin exercise' by Queen Elizabeth I mildly piqued his curiosity.

Although the tour which Knox had planned fell through, he had the pleasure, nevertheless, of introducing Pratt to his old tutor, George

Gordon, then Merton Professor of English (later Professor of Poetry and Vice-Chancellor of Oxford University), and to J.R.R. Tolkien (best known today for his *Lord of the Rings*, then a professor at Leeds). Knox recalled the occasion thus:

[T]he three of us [Pratt, Davis, and himself] were Professor Tolkien's guests at Pembroke College where to Ned's delight we had a lively chat as we drank beer with the College porter in his lodge. We had dinner later with George Gordon and Tolkien in the Randolph Hotel, Gordon at the piano leading us in song, varied in kind – a jolly evening ...

Even more memorable for Pratt was a subsequent evening when he was guest of honour at a dinner in Gordon's house. After dinner he read *The Witches' Brew* to the company, and was delighted to find Gordon 'unreservedly enthusiastic.' 'He said,' wrote Pratt, 'it was a Julianesque production and felt certain of its success if I revised it a bit cutting out the prose explanations and digressions relating to Prohibition, which damaged the Universality of the narrative.' Gordon had thought the verse 'simply magnificent,' and had 'liked the Cat very much, calling it a zoological marvel.' Most exciting of all was Gordon's suggestion that Pratt send a revised copy to J.C. (later Sir John) Squire, editor of *The London Mercury*, who might be willing to publish it. Gordon (described by Humphrey Carpenter in his Oxford book, *The Inklings*, as 'a great intriguer') even offered to send it himself with his strong endorsement. It was a triumphant evening for Pratt. When the party broke up at two-thirty a.m. he knew that he would remember it for the rest of his life.

Anxious to strike 'while the fahrenheit of the iron was running high,' he decided to revise the poem at once. It may well be wondered why he so readily agreed to alterations which radically changed what he had intended as the definitive, authorial text of *The Brew*; and to make them by hasty deletion rather than more carefully considered revision which might have allowed him to preserve his original conception in spite of having to amputate certain portions. The reason, I think, is obvious: after so many futile attempts, publication seemed to him then a matter of 'now or never.' Besides, with only one book to his name at the age of forty-two, whose sales had been small despite its salubrious reviews and whose audience had been limited, and solely Canadian, he was impatient to publish again and to publish outside Canada. The excisions he made had been urged, after all, by a learned professor of Oxford University, who was certain that they would improve rather than damage the poem. Who was he to question such advice? With some such thoughts in his head, and visions too no doubt of international fame, he set about revising the poem in accordance with Gordon's advice, cutting out most of the prose insets, 'The Lament of the Wets,' the Milton episode, and a dozen or more 'comments' by as many miscellaneous characters. Regretful that so much pruning had been thought necessary, but delighted with the prospect of publication, he quickly delivered the mutilated manuscript to Gordon for submission to J.C. Squire. He was still fearful that it would prove too long for the *Mercury* and cautioned Viola when he wrote her not to mention its possible publication until he had been told the final editorial decision.

From Oxford he went on to Stratford-on-Avon, where he made all the usual rounds, including the Memorial Theatre, where he saw *The School for Scandal*, and Othello played by Balliol Holloway, 'a marvellously fine actor.' He was finding that time passed more quickly for him now, though he still wished that Viola was with him: 'This is a place where you must come on our next trip. If the Witches Brew [*sic*] goes ... we will have a royal time ...' One day he made 'an eight mile trip to Warwick and spent the whole afternoon in the Castle,' where he saw, without apparent excitement, 'many fine originals by Holbein, Van Dyck and Rubens.' Following that he went to Kenilworth, 'Leicester's place,' which he found 'in complete ruins with the grass growing on top of the turrets and walls.' It was all very interesting, but none of it appears to have moved him greatly if at all. His poetic instincts were quite unawakened if one can judge by the almost laconic tone of his letters and the total absence of any verse that can be linked directly with his travels, either during or after them. Golf, of course, was a different matter.

On 25 July he returned to Liverpool, where his sister Floss was now also a visitor at Arthur's house, and where he found several letters from Viola. He wrote her, reporting his exploits as usual and assuring her of his good health and careful budgeting. Their letters were still much occupied with financial matters: advice from him on what to do if she ran short and assurances from her that she was managing in reasonable comfort. He was doing his best to keep within his budget and hoped that anything that turned up could be kept as a 'contribution to the house exchequer.' (A two-dollar cheque from the *Forum* for one of his poems gave them some amusement but was gratefully received.)

He spent a week this time in Liverpool, again mostly on the golf links. Arthur and Floss went up to Burnley to visit some of their relatives – descendants of John Pratt's brother William – but he did not accompany them. Stronger then in his blood, it seems, than his Pratt consanguinity was the febrile 'virus of golf.' His three priestly golf partners had gone, but a new one, curiously another sporting Catholic cleric, had soon taken their place, as he reported to Viola:

I met a Catholic Priest on the Golf Links yesterday and became his golf partner for a couple of rounds. I took such a fancy to him or he to me that he asked me to go with him and spend two or three days at his palace near Chester sometime in August. He will show me Chester and all the historic remains there etc. I may go when I return from London if I have the time ...

He did not get to Chester, though lack of time was not the reason. His return to Liverpool at the end of August from London and several other 'ports of call' was to find him 'quite broke.'

His visit to London was now (next to golf) uppermost in his mind, and on 2 August he finally set out to make his long-awaited assault on 'the very heart of the publishing world.' Installing himself at the Grafton Hotel in Tottenham Court Road, he made his first call on J.C. Squire at the *Mercury*, who was expecting him, George Gordon having already sent along a copy of *The Brew*. The meeting proved to be most satisfactory. Squire liked the poem; *The Brew*, it seems, suited his tastes perfectly. Declaring (so Pratt reported later) that 'such high spirits are not to be resisted,' he agreed to publish the poem even if it meant 'excluding every other poet on the list.' It is not unlikely that it reminded him of another strange, new poem which he had just enthusiastically reviewed in *Mercury*: *The Flaming Terrapin* by a young South African poet named Roy Campbell. It was very probably Squire who introduced Pratt to *The Flaming Terrapin*, of which he shortly bought a copy and read. He would later write of the poem that his first reading of it was 'a great aesthetic experience, well worth I thought a trip to

England. The poem was full of power, so charged with original metaphor – and I may say, an undercurrent of philosophy which never obtruded itself, that I could [but] wonder if the young man of about 20 years could keep pace in his later development.'

It may properly be noted here that Pratt's reading *The Terrapin* in London proved to be the start of his lifelong interest in, even devotion to, Roy Campbell, whose poetry is one of the few discernible influences (other than Hardy's) on Pratt's own work. Both *The Cachalot* and *The Great Feud* were soon to reflect it, though Pratt, as he invariably did when someone suggested influences, would later deny having read *The Flaming Terrapin* before writing them. Many years later he met Campbell in person – at John Sutherland's in Montreal in 1953, when others present remarked how much alike they looked and how 'famously' they got on together – and had the pleasure of introducing him to a Canadian audience.

But in the summer of 1924 Pratt's chief interest in Campbell – apart from his interest in the poem – was to emulate him by finding a publisher who would bring out his own unusual poem in book form. Magazine publication was better than none, but he wanted another *book* to his name. If there was a publisher for a poem such as *The Flaming Terrapin* by a young poet from the colonies, there must be one for *The Brew* by another not so young. Pratt determined to find him. How many doors he knocked on or flights of stairs he climbed is not known. One, it seems, was Constable's, another Jonathan Cape's. Cape, Pratt reported, 'went into a rhapsody' over the poem, but did not wish to publish it. At last, however, he found what he sought at the house of Selwyn and Blount. As he informed Lorne Pierce, 'they accepted instantly,' contracting 'to publish One Thousand copies, cloth cover with illustrations ... to sell for one half-crown (60 cents).' (Pratt jokingly attributed Selwyn and Blount's subsequent bankruptcy to their rash decision to publish *The Witches' Brew*.) Ryerson Press, he also reported to Pierce, was to be asked to represent the English publisher in Canada. Selwyn and Blount had also agreed to 'act as English Representatives of *Newfoundland Verse*' and requested twenty copies. Pratt was elated; his trip to Britain had achieved its main goal: he was to 'get into England' as a poet after all. He had accomplished what Pierce could not and he was very pleased with himself.

The rest of his stay in London he spent happily 'seeing the sights' of 'this famous Capital'; squiring Floss round to the shops, theatres, and other 'interesting places,' she having come up to spend part of her English visit with him; and finally wearing out his only pair of boots, most of their sightseeing being done on foot. (Floss's most vivid recollection of her trip to London was Ned's heading off in the wrong direction and getting lost after a day spent 'doing' the Wembley Exhibition: 'He had no sense of direction whatsoever!')

Highly gratified with his London foray and sanguine with expectations and having left his golf clubs behind in Liverpool ('With great strength of volition [I] decided that they might possibly interfere with sight-seeing'), he determined to have a fling in Paris, though his funds were already growing so short that he would probably have to borrow to get back to Toronto. Crossing the English Channel on 16 August, he spent a week in 'Paree' having 'a whirlwind of a time.' He visited all the usual tourist attractions, but only Napoleon's tomb, it seems, made any significant impression upon him. (Napoleon had long been and remained one of his figures of endless fascination.) Unfortunately, his accounts of the 'fling' are very meagre. He explained to Viola, to whom he sent two (innocuous) postcards from Paris giving her 'a mere skeleton' of his doings, that he would tell her all in 'the calm hours after dinner and coffee next fall.' Whether he did or not we do not know. The fullest and most revealing account of his visit to Paris is thus merely the following:

I found a good companion in a man from Scotland, a Scot of Scots and an architect. He and I stayed close together all the time, visited all the places that make Paris famous from the Louvre down to a wild spot called *Ciel et Enfer* where Mephisto and his imps acted as guides to dark and sulphurous corridors and rooms. Dickson, the man just named, was a brawny Scot with a Jack Dempsey pair of arms and I felt quite reassured all the time.

Back in Bournemouth on 23 August after a night crossing on the Channel, 'during which time I slept less than thirty minutes,' he collapsed into bed at the Hotel Empress at 8.30 a.m. to sleep the clock round 'to make up for practically a week's loss of slumber.' He had had, it seems, a strenuous week in 'Paree.'

The following day he was sufficiently recovered to set out on 'a char-à-banc trip' through the Hardy country of Dorset, and other parts of southern England. Making Bournemouth his headquarters, he went first to Salisbury 'to see the famous cathedral,' and next day to Wells and Cheddar: 'The last place was one of the most picturesque sights I have ever seen. The road lay between exceptionally deep gorges and at the bottom we entered the Cheddar Caves, vast underground corridors running for nearly half-a-mile.' Next day he 'went through the New Forest and through the Dorset Moors, saw Woolbridge Manor chosen by Hardy as the scene of Tess's marriage. I spent five days in that district ...' Arriving back in Liverpool, his funds exhausted, he wrote Viola an account of his latest peregrinations and enclosed 'a little Maltese hand-made handkerchief ... bought at the Exhibition at Wembley' for three-year-old Claire.

From then until he sailed for home on 12 September he stayed in Liverpool, 'stranded' by lack of funds. Fortunately he already had his return ticket for the *Montclare*. Despite the company of Arthur, Maud, and Floss, and games of golf on the various courses in and around Liverpool, time began to drag. Not only was he lonely for his familiars; he was homesick for Toronto. On 5 September he wrote Viola:

A week from today I board the Montrose [*sic*]. By the time you get this note I shall be nearing the coast of Newfoundland or possibly steaming up the St. Lawrence. And the days can't move too quickly ...

... The steamer will probably get into Montreal about the 20th and then a day's run into Toronto. If I get in at night, you must stage a meeting with Claire in the morning. If in the morning then I must hide behind the door when I get up to the house and let her sniff me out ...

In looking over my finances for the summer, I find that I ran over my allowance somewhat on account of my London and Paris trips. I had to borrow from Art. [Floss also lent him fifty dollars.] ... Besides I have bought a suit of clothes, a mackintosh, etc. My one and only suit had become threadbare and clothing's cheap over here.

This was his last letter from England. A week later he 'set his jibs for Canada.'

In a matter-of-fact fashion he had enjoyed his summer in Britain, 'this God-intoxicated country,' as he enigmatically described it to Pierce, adding with almost the only hint of 'poetry' in any of his letters, 'Much have I voyaged since I struck this silvern isle ... been to every great literary centre ... and have drunk deeply.' Even this is an exaggeration: of the extent of both his travels and his imbibings (here, of course, emotional and imaginative rather than spirituous). The beauty and 'old-world charm' of Britain had, indeed, delighted him and he had been, in a vague, unexcited way, interested in the places and things of historical and literary importance he had seen. But hardly more than most ordinarily educated and intelligent tourists usually are. As Knox remarked, the people he met (even though he did not always learn their names) were probably of most interest to him and longest remembered – next to golf. What he called his 'Iliad' of his pilgrimage was hardly rhapsodic, quite unpoetical, almost laconic and perfunctory. He may, possibly, have written one poem during his travels, the casual and brief 'Jock O' the Links' – a golfing poem. But apart from that – and even that is uncertain – he wrote no verse during nearly four months spent in Britain. Nor did they leave any particular, identifiable impress upon his mind and imagination, nor upon his subsequent poetry, except, perhaps, for what may be reflected in his descriptions of the English countryside many years later in *Dunkirk*. Apart from stories of his meetings with Gordon and Tolkien at Oxford, and with Squire and Jonathan Cape in London, only his games of golf were recalled in later years for the entertainment of his friends. He does not seem to have had any great desire to make a second visit and never did. He certainly had no interest in settling in Britain like his brother Arthur. In all that mattered most to him, Canada, Toronto in particular, was his Land of Heart's Desire.

It was then with no regrets, on the contrary with much rejoicing, that he sailed from Liverpool on 12 September, and after a pleasant but uneventful journey arrived safely on the twenty-first 'back again in the Queen City of Diabolus.' Except for a brief holiday in the West Indies in 1937, he never left continental North America again.

23

Of Whales and Other Leviathans

We are all prone to the manufacture of myths ...
　　　　　　E.J. Pratt to the Editor of *Saturday Night*, April 1925

ELATED BY HIS London coups, Pratt did not long maintain his customary ban on premature announcements. Within a few weeks of his return most of his friends had been told of his good fortune and soon reports of the impending appearance of *The Witches' Brew* in *The London Mercury* and its more permanent publication 'later' by Selwyn and Blount were turning up as news in papers and journals in Toronto and beyond. The October issue of *Poetry* (Chicago), quoting Pratt that the poem was 'Mad as a March Hare,' elaborated the announcement by stating that the *Mercury* would 'devote the whole poetry section of one issue to the Seacat's epic inebriation.' Publication in a major British journal being a signal distinction for a Canadian author, the story received much enthusiastic comment and Pratt many (premature) congratulations.

Selwyn and Blount had indeed accepted the poem for publication in book form in England, but its appearance in Canada and hence its commercial success depended on Pratt's persuading a Canadian publisher to act as Selwyn and Blount's agent. Therefore one of his first deeds upon his return was to drop Lorne Pierce a note elaborating the arrangement made with Selwyn and Blount, requesting 'a psychic interview with your Satanic self' and expressing the hope to hear 'from you old cheese very soon.' Pierce replied on 1 October congratulating him on his successes, suggesting that Selwyn be asked to forward proofs of *The Brew* to Ryerson 'together with quotations [of price],' and inviting Pratt to 'run down some time soon ... and discuss the matter.' He added the promise 'to do all I can to help you put it over.'

Pratt was not very sanguine about the prospects of Ryerson's handling the Canadian edition. Pierce had never been enthusiastic about the poem, and its subject was certain to raise objections from other members of the firm. Besides, he was still very dubious about Ryerson's marketing practices. Accordingly he began to sound out a number of other possible publishers, chiefly Doubleday, Doran, and Gundy; and the Macmillan Company of Canada, whose enterprising young President and Managing Director, Hugh Eayrs, Pratt had recently met at the Arts and Letters Club of which both were members. He nevertheless kept the door open to Ryerson, and when page proofs of *The Brew* arrived in December he dispatched a set to Pierce with a brief note: 'Here it is: I am sure it will find favour in your eyes. Look it over and let me know what kind of "risk" you think it is.'

Pierce's reply on 15 December was not unexpected. While the Ryerson management had, he implied, enjoyed taking 'copious draughts' from the 'sparkling rim' of *The Brew*, their general feeling was 'that a publishing house so closely connected with the Methodist Church' – about to join with the Presbyterian and Congregational churches to form the United Church – 'could not very well act as Canadian distributor of it.' 'Personally,' he wrote, 'I should like very much to be able to do something for you and this book,' but hoped that Pratt would find another publisher prepared to take it on. He thought it advisable, however, that Pratt publish it anonymously: 'On page two [the title page] I should strike out your name and on page 9 [first page of the text] I should do the same kind service.' *The Brew* was clearly not a poetic offspring he wished to see publicly acknowledged by a Ryerson author. He suggested that Pratt meet him for a talk at the Arts and Letters Club very soon.

Pratt accepted Ryerson's rebuff gracefully and good-humouredly, replying (18 December) to Pierce as follows:

Sorry that the vintage proved a little too stimulating for regular consumption. I understand the situation in which you are placed, as a firm, by reason of Ecclesiastical affiliations. I think that Gundy would be willing to handle it. All I want is its appearance on such book stalls as would be interested in it. I am positive that there would be an immediate demand for a few hundred copies ...

He closed by setting a date for their luncheon meeting at the Club and signed himself 'Bacchanalianly yours.'

On the following Monday he sat in the Arts and Letters Club awaiting Pierce, but he did not come. Two days later he dropped Pratt a note of excuse and promised a meeting after Christmas. But there is no record of their confabulation, if and when it did take place. But Ryerson Press had already washed its hands of *The Brew* and, as it turned out, of E.J. Pratt.

It would probably be going too far to say that Pierce himself had done likewise; but there is little doubt that the chill which now settled upon a hitherto cordial friendship was mainly his doing. Not that Pratt had no cause to feel, if not abandoned by Pierce, at least 'let down.' Pierce had, no doubt, made some effort to persuade Ryerson to take *The Witches' Brew*, but how strongly had he urged it? His argument that the 'risk' was too great for a firm with 'ecclesiastical affiliations' might have carried more weight had he not that very month quelled all opposition at Ryerson to the firm's publishing F.P. Grove's *Settlers of the Marsh*, which most members of his Board were convinced would raise 'a storm of protest' and give the Methodist press 'a bad name throughout the Dominion.' (As it turned out their fears were well founded.) But though he was disappointed by Pierce's decision, Pratt does not appear to have felt deeply enough about the matter to have allowed it to estrange him from a close and much-valued friend. But Pierce, viewing the case in a different light, seems to have been otherwise disposed.

It was not merely that he disapproved of *The Witches' Brew* as a poem, which, to give him due credit, he had tried, even pretended, to respond to appropriately; he also deplored what he felt to be Pratt's squandering his talents on trifling, not to mention 'bibulous,' subjects. According to Arthur Phelps, Pierce while visiting him in Winnipeg earlier that autumn had

expressed his annoyance in no uncertain terms with Ned, *The Brew*, and everything connected with it. He thought Ned was prostituting himself for the sake of creating a sensation and he wanted no part of it. He had great faith in Ned's ability to write first-class stuff, but he felt that he was selling out to a popular taste for sensationalism. Lorne was dead-right, of course, on the first point – Ned's ability – but he was wrong on the second …

Pierce, it seems, had looked on Pratt not only as a potential champion in Ryerson's camp, who might bring credit, even renown, to both the firm and himself; he had seen him also as a protégé whom he might guide and shape into an embodiment of Pierce's own conception of a good, even great, Canadian poet: one in whom 'the best of the old tradition refurbished' was combined with the 'high seriousness' and 'desperate earnestness' which he felt Canadian poetry lacked. But *The Witches' Brew* and Pratt's eagerness to have it published – and under his own name – struck Pierce as singularly aberrant, a curious deviation from the poetic character which he believed to be Pratt's true one. Pratt, in short, had clearly proved himself too much the 'bucking truant with a stiff backbone' to be nurtured and guided by a tutor such as Pierce, and Pierce as a consequence, for the time being at least, 'wanted no part' (to quote Phelps) of either Pratt or his verse. It also appears (from entries in Pierce's diary, for example) that he viewed much that characterized Pratt's new 'life-style' with equal disfavour. A strict and 'pledged' teetotaller himself, he particularly deplored Pratt's gradual cultivation of 'the arts of alcoholic excitement.' He also disapproved of certain of Pratt's new friends, who, he thought, could do him no good, whose habits of life were no example to follow, whose stag party conversation was often beneath his (Pierce's) conception of high-mindedness. ('Pratt opened up on a favourite theme …,' he writes in his diary of an evening with Pratt and his friends. 'I did not enter into the talk-fest. I thought big men ought to be better employed. The conversation turned to … I came away.')

There is nothing to suggest hostility or even ill will between them during this time of estrangement; rather a cool and silent neutrality. He and Pratt still exchanged courtesies, meeting at their club or at sessions of literary groups of which they were members, and occasionally dined together with mutual friends. But for more than two years not a note or letter is on record between them, who had hitherto engaged in regular correspondence. (Their corresponding usually by letter, though both lived in Toronto, is explained by Pierce's having a serious hearing defect which made him shun the telephone whenever possible.) Nor is there mention of Pratt or his work in any of Pierce's columns in *The New Outlook*, no notice of *The Brew* when at last it was published, nor even a reference to *The Cachalot* when it appeared in *The Canadian Forum* and was loudly acclaimed by everyone else. (From his diary we know that his initial response to *The Cachalot* was little short of contemptuous.) It was early in 1927, after Pratt's return to serious themes in *The Iron Door* and *The Great Feud*, in which, as Pierce was to see it, Pratt 'lays aside cap and bells' to write again 'with desperate earnestness,' before he again so much as mentioned Pratt or his verse in print.

Pierce and Ryerson Press having turned him down, Pratt now began serious negotiations on behalf of *The Witches' Brew* with Doubleday, Doran, and Gundy. But it was soon apparent that no satisfactory arrangement could be made with them. He then turned to Hugh Eayrs, who took little time deciding that Macmillan of Canada – which, curiously enough, had just refused to touch *Settlers of the Marsh* – would publish *The Brew* in Canada simultaneously with its publication in England. This was the beginning of a mutually happy association between E.J. Pratt and Macmillan that continued until his death.

It was also the beginning of an intimate, brotherly friendship between him and 'Hughie' Eayrs, all the more welcome that winter of 1925 because of Lorne Pierce's (temporary) defection. Eayrs was of a very different nature from Pierce and in many ways from Pratt himself. There was, however, a common element in their histories: each was the son of a Yorkshire-born clergyman. (A portrait of his father, bearded and in clericals, hung for many years on Eayrs's office wall beside one of Winston Churchill inscribed by him 'For Mr. Eayrs with all the infinite respect due a publisher.') Yorkshire-born and -bred himself, a fact still emphatically proclaimed by his speech, Hugh Smithfield Eayrs had come to Canada in 1912, a fair-haired, stocky youth of eighteen, who five years later had been taken on by Macmillan of Canada as a 'promotional man' and 'Trade traveller.' (In the interval, besides holding a series of jobs, mostly in editing and publishing, he had written a biography of Sir Isaac Brock, collaborated on a novel with Thomas B. Costain, and written and published in various papers and journals innumerable short poems, which, it seems, he wisely never retrieved.) His rise in the Macmillan firm can be described only by the familiar cliché, meteoric. He was arrogant, brash, mercurial, supremely self-confident and self-assertive, but he also possessed immense charm, wit, and boyish affability, as well as genuine talent, even genius, for corporate leadership. It had soon become clear to the Macmillan hierarchy in both London and Toronto that here was no ordinary bookman. Visiting England in 1921 to see his ailing father, 'the glittering youngster' (to quote John Gray, his colleague for a decade) had called at the Macmillan headquarters in London, to come away a few days later – chummily accompanied to the railway station by Sir Frederick Macmillan – already appointed at twenty-six President of Macmillan of Canada. The incumbent, long-experienced President had, it seems, not even been consulted. It was, as John Gray observed, 'a radical decision' for the 'conservative, solid men' at the head of Macmillan to make, but one which they were never to regret.

Though very different in many ways, the personalities of Eayrs and Pratt seemed to mesh as his and Lorne Pierce's had not, for all they had in common. Pierce, ordained a Methodist minister, was a deep and earnest man, of restrained emotions and controlled energies, ab-stemious, almost ascetic, (which, being spare and angular, he looked), 'of a spirituelle expression,' to quote his biographer. Eayrs, though far from shallow or un-earnest, was almost the antithesis of Pierce: a rotund, hyperactive man, of boundless and explosive energy, neither teetotal nor 'spirituelle,' who better matched than Pierce the extro-verted, convivial side of Pratt's nature. In years to come, once Pierce had learned to take Pratt as he was – 'a dual personality,' Pierce called him, not inaccurately: 'Appollonian' and 'Dionysian' – he and Pratt would find, to their reciprocal benefit, many deep affinities between their private psyches. Eayrs, nevertheless, the perfect foil to Pierce, although twelve years Pratt's junior, retained a place that Pierce never filled among Pratt's closest confrères. Their brotherly friendship con-tinued unclouded until Eayrs's sudden and untimely death in 1940. (It should perhaps be noted that Eayrs and Pierce, fellow publishers and club members, were themselves good friends, held in mutual regard, each an admirer of the other's many though differing talents.)

Although Selwyn and Blount were now fully committed to pub-lishing *The Witches' Brew*, the project bogged down after the proofs were returned in January (1925) and Pratt heard nothing of it again for months. Nor had he, up to the end of 1924, heard anything further from J.C. Squire about the promised publication of the poem in *The London Mercury*. Nevertheless, the poem's publication by Selwyn and Blount apparently assured by Macmillan's agreement to market it in Canada, Pratt was able to turn at last to a new venture which had been simmering in his imagination for some time. He was eager to do so, for the year just ended had not been notable for new work completed. His 'output' (his usual term for published work) had comprised only the few short Hardyesque poems in magazines and the two essays, 'Thomas Hardy' and 'Golfomania.' The new project, as he told friends, was 'a tale of a whale – a *whale* of a tale.'

Many years later in letters to E.K. Brown and W.R. Benét, Pratt implied that *The Cachalot* had grown directly out of a visit he made to Newfoundland in the early summer of 1925. Such a visit he made indeed and he *was* taken to some whaling stations on the Burin Peninsula. But the poem, very much as published that autumn, had been written and 'premièred' before his trip to Newfoundland. In the same letters he mentions other experiences of whaling which contributed to the imaginative matrix out of which the poem sprang: the whale-hunt carried on at Moreton's Harbour when he had been a teacher there two decades earlier. Even so, equally if not more important, as it was for all his narrative poems and many of the others too, was his reading, in this case going back to *Peter the Whaler* and Bible stories of great leviathans and other oceanic monsters read as a boy. Long before Moreton's Harbour, 'that Leviathan whom Thou hast made to play' within the deeps was already part of his imaginative furniture.

But though he later denied having read it before writing the poem, *Moby-Dick* was undoubtedly chief among its literary progenitors. (As noted earlier, Pratt deeply resented having 'sources' suggested and 'influences' traced.) He may not have read every word of Melville's more than 500 pages, but it is obvious that he had read much of the book and knew its essentials well. For one thing, he had included Captain Ahab among the Immortals in Hades in the earliest drafts of *The Witches' Brew*. Pratt's whaling ship, the *Albatross*, is also a whaler in *Moby-Dick*, and his whale-hunters are, like Melville's, out of Nantucket, not, as one might have expected, out of Newfoundland. A number of obvious verbal echoes also occur in the poem from descriptive passages in the latter part of *Moby-Dick*. But though *The Cachalot* has often been described as 'Moby-Dick in verse' and though reading Pratt's poem, especially the magnificent catastrophic dénouement, anyone familiar with Melville almost inevitably feels a sense of déjà vu, the poem is as much an original as Melville's 'epic,' having the stamp upon it of a unique personality who was able, as he wrote, 'to incarnate' himself 'in the body of the Cachalot' and live for a time the life of a whale.

There seems little doubt, however, that it was Campbell's *Terrapin* that suggested the poem to him in 1924 (or early 1925), suggested at least the general type: a narrative having an almost mythic titan of the deep for its hero and vast panoramic vistas of oceanic time and space for its setting. This conception, embedding itself in the fertile matrix of an imagination already nurtured on memories of actual whales, perhaps too of giant squid – such sightings being not unknown in Newfoundland – as well as on the oceanic monsters of his reading early and late, was all that was needed to prompt poetic gestation. This was a common experience for him: a seedbed well prepared wanted only the implanting of the appropriate seed.

In 'a tale of a whale' Pratt had, of course, a subject which admirably suited both his creative talents and his scientific interests. It was specific, concrete, familiar (to him, though 'absolutely incredible,' he wrote, 'to people who had never seen a whale'), a subject to be treated with scientific exactitude, but which yet allowed vast scope for imaginative embellishment. 'The dramatic possibilities were enormous ... Here was material which had all the wonder of romance and yet [was] mathematically exact.' From past conversations with Newfoundland whalers he already had 'a good deal of information first hand.' Further essential facts could be had by 'digging up raw material,' for it was a subject – this provided much of its appeal for him – 'which could lend itself to research.' Actually he seems to have done little additional 'digging' beyond the books of Frank Bullen, *The Cruise of the Cachalot* (1896) and *Idylls of the Sea* (1899). The kraken (or giant squid) episode almost certainly had its source in Bullen, though it may also have owed something to C.G.D. Roberts's *The Haunters of the Silences* (1907), which, in turn, seems to have owed a large debt to Bullen. What Pratt envisaged was, in fact, a new kind of poem for him, like

Campbell's a narrative of sorts, but heavy on physical description and titanic facts, much of its 'wonder' lying in the sheer physical magnitude of its subject. Magnitude, as we know, delighted his heart.

Already provided with readymade 'titanic facts,' he had little real need for hyperbolical embellishment, yet his imagination craved it. So it was that 'Everything was drawn to huge scale and yet the [proportional] dimensions were accurate, except where they were obviously and intentionally magnified.' He admitted to 'enlarging the liver somewhat' ('... so large / The lymph-flow of his active liver, / One might believe a fair-sized barge / Could navigate along the river ...') and taking 'a few liberties with his pancreas' ('... the islands of his pancreas / Were so tremendous that between 'em / A punt would sink ...'), for which he was 'taken to task' by certain prosaic friends. In his own defence he pleaded that 'as the poem was written at the time of the discovery of insulin' (not strictly true: the discovery had been made three years earlier), he had 'manufactured' such a 'glorious pancreas' as a tribute to his friend, Dr Fred Banting, whom he had first known as a student in the psychology laboratories. Despite such liberties, he had nevertheless, he wrote, come 'at last to realize that there was a great field of relatively unexplored soil ready for poetic handling ... the field of science,' hitherto neglected 'out of a widespread and to my mind false notion that scientific or technical knowledge is unromantic.' He believed that in future 'the great subjects for the imaginative writer will come out of science and out of the humanization of science ... as the ally of the human spirit in search of its finest goals.'

In spite of the 'research' which the poem entailed, Pratt seems to have enjoyed every moment he worked on it. Indeed, it was not work, he wrote, but 'a bit of fun ... an excellent way of releasing repressions.' So writing *The Brew* had been. But the 'fun' of *The Cachalot* was different and seemed to arise from different motives and to satisfy different, more fundamental needs. As he himself described the experience some time later,

It gave me an opportunity vicariously to express my Irish love of a fight without bodily injury to myself ... an excellent way of releasing repressions ... I managed to incarnate myself in the body of the Cachalot and then for a few weeks I knew what it was to have the Pacific for a swimming pool;

to cool myself in the Arctic in the summer and to bask in [the] Caribbean in the winter, to enjoy enormous and unimpaired digestion; and to put forty-eight solid teeth into any object that looked like food ...

It is doubtful whether Pratt ever made an observation about himself which better reveals the motives for much of his behaviour, both as man and as poet. Despite its hyperbolical embellishments, having myself known Pratt, I have no reason to doubt that it faithfully reflects his feelings of actual personal involvement in the action of the poem and the deep psychic affinities he felt between himself and his titanic hero. While imputing it all to the whale, he was nevertheless, I think, giving release and expression in *The Cachalot* to the repressed life of a submerged personality within himself. There is no doubt, as others have suggested, that he was wholly 'on the side of the whale.' (What dark, lurking demon of his nether world, one wonders, may he have vanquished in the kraken?) His brief account, therefore, probably sheds more light on the 'meaning' of the poem and what he was about in writing it than many of the much more elaborate exegeses to which the poem was inevitably subjected. An American reviewer, to whom the poet was quite 'a new name,' wrote far truer than he knew: 'Mr Pratt has either been a whaler or an honorary whale, perhaps both, and he writes not with beautiful sincerity from without but with burning actuality from within.'

The poem virtually finished by mid-April, before the College clans dispersed for the long summer vacation, Pratt arranged to give his usual première of a new poem, a reading for Pelham Edgar and a small group of 'the boys.' This time a visitor from Ottawa was also included, the poet Duncan Campbell Scott, in town to address the newly-formed Poetry Society of Canada, of which Edgar was President. Since Scott was in Toronto only on 22 and 23 April, this fairly accurately dates the completion of the poem – or most of it. Not necessarily all, for Pratt's premier readings, of the narratives in particular, were often, like preliminary rehearsals of new plays, 'try-outs' of still imperfect and unfinished scripts. He was usually amenable to constructive suggestion, especially from friends like Edgar, Phelps, and Eayrs, revising lines, altering words, adding and deleting, expanding and compressing. How much his 'definitive' texts owed to the advice and suggestions of friends is impossible to say with certainty, but the debt was unquestionably great. On this occasion his audience seems to have been 'unanimously laudatory,' pronouncing his new whale of a tale superior to anything else he had yet written 'including *The Brew*.' Scott was particularly impressed, and requested a copy of the poem and permission to present it to his old friend, John Masefield, with whom he had been corresponding on and off ever since the then unknown young English poet had written him in 1903 praising his *Piper of Arll*. Scott was certain that the author of *Dauber* would take great interest in the new sea 'epic.' Pratt readily consented and a few weeks later, having made some minor revisions, dispatched a typescript of *The Cachalot* to Scott, about to leave on a trans-Atlantic tour. Pratt promptly forgot the incident, but the best advice he was to receive on how the poem might be improved was to come from John Masefield.

The Cachalot was finished – as he thought. But it was characteristic of him, as Phelps put it, 'to get wound up and be unable to stop,' or, as Pratt himself might have expressed it, to be so 'gloriously emancipated' by a poetic 'grand binge' as to crave to sustain it for as long as possible or repeat it at the first opportunity. Still aglow with the excitement and euphoria generated by *The Cachalot*, he needed only an appropriate signal to launch him upon another similar exploit in verse. That signal came in the form of a motion picture: the 1924 film based on Arthur Conan Doyle's 'prehistoric novel' *The Lost World*.

The film's Canadian première occurred on 4 April (1925) at Toronto's Regent Theatre. For days it had been heralded in the press as 'the cinematic sensation of the year,' 'the most unusual picture yet made,' in which 'the vast creatures who lived on this earth millions of years ago' are 'brought to life and made to perform before our eyes.' Newspaper advertisements and billboards, portraying a towering dinosaur in full detail, graphically confirmed the fact. Even before he had seen the film Pratt must have been feverishly agog with juvenile excitement, for he had read *The Lost World* (first published in 1912) long before, as he had done 'everything or almost' that Conan Doyle had written. He undoubtedly would have seen it whether or no; he had long been an avid movie fan, indiscriminately viewing almost anything that happened to be on the screens of the Toronto cinemas.

It is not known precisely when he saw the picture, which had a record run of three weeks in Toronto; he probably saw it more than once, as he often did a film which particularly interested him. Nor do we know how soon it was after seeing *The Lost World* that he began actually writing *The Great Feud*. Other preoccupations crowding upon him that spring and summer, including a visit to Newfoundland, he is unlikely to have had much opportunity to do more than 'dream' of 'a Pleiocene Armageddon' until much later that year. Besides, there was the 'research,' as he called it, which he always liked to do before committing himself too deeply to any poem based 'more or less on factual data.' The place of *The Great Feud* in our chronicle thus belongs to a somewhat later date than the spring of 1925. But its inception is properly noted here. As he would report a year later when the poem was nearly finished, it was 'that motion-picture ... that and *The Cachalot*, which gave me the form and technique.' As we shall see, the curious poem owes much to other sources, some of them far remote from both Conan Doyle's book and its filmed recreation, but to the latter belongs the distinction of having put 'spark to the tinder.'

Meanwhile, willingly or unwillingly, he had been drawn into a feud of a different kind, though perhaps in some ways not quite different, featuring as it did a species of literary *Tyrannosauros rex*, a revenant from the past risen up to confront a later generation.

'The Bliss Carman Controversy' of 1925 had already gone on for more than a month when Pratt joined in on 25 April. It had been touched off by Charles G.D. Roberts, another revenant who had appeared in early February to begin a triumphal progress across the nation after seventeen years in exile. Greeted by large and adoring audiences, fanfares of journalistic trumpets, and testimonial dinners, 'His Holiness, the Living Buddha of Canadian Literature' (as W.A. Deacon dubbed him), had used the occasion of a banquet in his honour given on 7 March by the Toronto Branch of the CAA to confirm the canonization of his cousin Bliss Carman by declaring him 'the greatest living lyric poet with the possible exception of Mr. W.B. Yeats.' A few days later in the Kingston *British Whig* the oracular pronouncement had been stoutly challenged by Wilson MacDonald in an article headed 'Is Carman Supreme?' Even then the affair might have gone no further had not Deacon, who no less than MacDonald delighted in 'stirring things up,' reprinted the contentious essay, accompanied by a brief provocative preface, in *Saturday Night* (28 March).

Absurd as it may seem today, an attack on Bliss Carman in 1925 was nothing short of heresy to many Canadians. Long a sentimental favourite as a poet, Carman the public figure – tall, emaciated, in his immemorial wide-awake hat (his 'Heliconian helmet,' as Pierce described it) – had grown enormously in the public imagination since his dramatic reappearance in Montreal in 1921, where, it may be recalled, he had been ceremonially 'laureled' with a wreath of maple leaves at the CAA's inaugural banquet. Elevated thus from vagabondage to laureateship, Carman had, nevertheless, taken to the road again, making several resounding national tours, and reminding Canadians that he had not yet been wholly interred in the pages of history. By 1925 he had (to quote Deacon) achieved such an 'unassailable title' as the 'All Highest of the Canadian Pantheon' as to have become in his own time a 'myth,' a 'legend,' a 'cult,' diverting thereby the limelight of public attention from 'other writers of at least equal merit' to focus upon his own 'extended and romantic physique.'

This is not the place to record the details of the journalistic feud which followed Deacon's endorsement of MacDonald's challenge. But the spate of letters to the press which thereupon erupted remains a curious and illuminating commentary on the state of Canadian poetry and the taste and sensibilities of Canadian readers in the mid-1920s. Most letters were strongly pro-Carman and anti-MacDonald and were often personally acrimonious, though a few were touched with humour and occasionally with irony. But perhaps the best of them, certainly the most temperate and reasonable, was that published on 25 April by Pratt; it was also the only one fully to support MacDonald and Deacon.

While the letter is beyond doubt an honest expression of Pratt's views on the subject – he had always scorned the notion of 'unassailable titles' or sacrosanct reputations of any kind – one strongly suspects that it was written at Deacon's urging. In both style and content it is, indeed, wholly characteristic of Pratt, but his writing it for publication is not. As we have seen, none of the *Forum*'s literary debates of the early twenties had lured him into print, nor would others yet to come. Furthermore, though Pratt was not a devotee of Carman's verse he was genuinely fond of 'dear old Bliss' himself and would not willingly have pained him. Nor could he by any stretch of imagination have been regarded as an ally of MacDonald, although, since Pratt's reputation as a poet posed as yet no threat to MacDonald, their relationship remained temperately amicable. It seems very unlikely then that Pratt's contribution to the Carman controversy was made on his own unprompted initiative. Much more probable is it that, the weight of opinion bearing heavily against MacDonald, Deacon needed at least one respected name to add to his own in the very short list of MacDonald's allies. It was the sort of thing Deacon was known to do; Pratt would be called on again to argue a case for Deacon, though not it seems in public.

Pratt's letter, nevertheless, is worth quoting in full. Not only does it express what were beyond question his views in the matter; it also illustrates his peculiar talent for cautious polemics, a case gently but firmly urged, without rancour or dogmatism:

Literary Editor, *Saturday Night*
Dear Sir,

In view of Mr Wilson MacDonald's generous inclusion of my name in one phase of the comparisons instituted by his article, there may be a touch of indelicacy on my part in making any contribution to the discussion. But disclaiming, in advance, any pretensions to rank with the well-known names quoted, I feel that his general statement is a healthy tonic for Canadian literary criticism. One of the dangers into which we are drawn today is the complacency with which we take accepted classifications. We have not gone far enough yet to satisfy ourselves with unassailable titles, and the moment we refuse to regard any writer in our midst as a legitimate problem for critical examination we are drifting into very stagnant waters. We are all prone to the manufacture of myths about our favourite authors, but granting, as we might honestly and truthfully do, a considerable basis upon which a legend might ferment in the case of Bliss Carman, yet, as you pointed out in your preface to the letter, much injustice may be done to the work of less known but equally significant writers. It might be considered sacrilege to question the place of a deity in our little world; still it must be remembered that our throne is one we build with our own hands.

E.J. Pratt.

The debate continued for another six weeks, but Pratt's support of the two assailants was not answered; nor is there any indication that it changed anyone's mind. Nevertheless, as Deacon observed in a lengthy and fair-minded essay published on 16 May in which he sought to bring the affair to a close: 'If many have been led by this discussion to procure the works of several leading Canadian poets in order to make their own comparisons ... this discussion will have been eminently worth while.'

It seems to have been a season for feuds of one kind and another. Pratt had barely emerged, unmarked, from his cautious engagement in the Carman affair, when he was plunged into another of a very different kind, one from which he was not to escape so lightly. It did not leave any permanent scars – though a temporary one on his bank account and a more or less permanent monument – but it did embroil him in a distressing altercation culminating in a summons from the courts.

This arose from the construction 'by mistake' of a pier or dock of 'monstrous proportions' on the lakefront of his Bobcaygeon property. The previous autumn, closing up the cottage for the season, he had asked a local handyman to build him by spring a 'swimming dock,' a wooden platform which, railed round with a chicken-wire bulwark, he planned to ballast to the lake bottom near the shore to provide an enclosure in which little Claire might paddle, safe from the remnants of submerged tree stumps and the danger of going beyond her depth. The discarded floor of Varley's tent would, he had thought, supply most of the timber needed; if the handyman required more he could get it from the local lumber 'magnate' and building contractor. 'A simple, inexpensive contraption was all I wanted.'

But that is not quite what he got. The handyman, misinterpreting Pratt's undoubtedly offhand and imprecise instructions, instead of building the thing himself as Pratt had thought he had described it, had placed an order in Pratt's name with the contractor for a proper 'Ontario dock,' or pier. Employing half-a-dozen carpenters and consuming vast quantities of the best materials, this the contractor had indeed built. What Pratt that spring found on his lakefront was not the 'simple, inexpensive contraption' he had envisaged, but 'a leviathan of a wharf' which, jutting far out into the lake, was big enough, so Arthur Phelps described it (with *some* exaggeration), 'to tie up an ocean liner at if one ever came into the Kawartha region.' The bill which Pratt was shortly presented was, of course, of correspondingly 'monstrous proportions.' Since he had ordered no such thing, he refused to pay and was promptly sued by the outraged contractor.

Pratt, as we know, 'loved a good fight, so long as he wasn't in it.' But this, as he saw it, was a matter of justice. Feeling that he had been tricked and was about to be robbed, he decided to fight. Having consulted his Victoria College friend, J.W. MacMillan, who as an experienced labour arbitrator was well versed in points of law, he stated his case fully to a lawyer, writing in vivid, not unemotional prose of 'this most damnedest form of trickery' in which he had been innocently involved, his 'first quarrel over property.' The lawyer was dubious, but agreed to act as his counsel when Pratt was summoned to appear at the courtroom in Lindsay, county seat for Victoria, in which county Bobcaygeon was located. But the case did not come to trial. The parties assembled and a conference between them and their counsel ended in a compromise. Pratt agreed to pay $200 and 'the magnate' to withdraw his suit for further payment. The publicity of a trial involving him in a civil action against one of the area's most popular cottagers would have done his business no good.

The outlay was still far more than Pratt had bargained for, but at least he had a dock to be proud of, though quite useless despite its size to accommodate anything larger than a small rowboat, for the water was very shallow even at the dock's farthest extremity. Yet it was by far the most imposing lakeside structure in the Kawartha region, and once the unpleasant memories associated with its construction had worn off, he came to like it, showing it off to visitors as he might have done his giant squash – had he ever grown it. Besides, it provided a pleasant promenade to stroll upon, or a sundeck for a summer afternoon's relaxation.

It is not unlikely that the experience and the financial outlay also paid him certain, small literary dividends. Though merely a surmise, it is not improbable that the exacting 'magnate,' appropriately disguised (Pratt was not called 'cautious Ned' for nothing) and, perhaps, compounded with ironic recollections of William Sclater (one-time draper of St John's), was the chief prototype of the infamous Puffsky, arch-representative of a species Pratt detested, the commercial pirate. He appears in two poems, 'The Parable of Puffsky,' better known of the two (it was published in *Many Moods* and later in *Collected Poems*), and in 'The Head of the Firm,' which remained unpublished during Pratt's life. In the latter poem he is presented as 'Puffsky, head of Fungus, Rotte and Co.,' who 'posed alike as Croesus and as Solon, / Lord of the county town by right of pelf,' an obvious allusion, it seems to me, to the magnate of local fame.

24

Sunlight and Shadows

It is almost staggering to think that one's destiny is suspended by so slight a thread, and life and death separated by almost microscopic boundaries.

E.J. Pratt to W.A. Deacon, August 1925

PRATT HAD NOT set out to make a living by his pen, but from the time he began to receive a few dollars from some of the magazines that accepted his poems he had looked forward to the day when they might help a little to 'fatten the family coffers.' In later years he often quoted approvingly Dr Johnson's dictum, 'No man but a blockhead ever wrote but for money,' and declared that the first test of literary merit was 'Is it worth hard cash?' Such things were said mostly in jest, but not wholly. Though there were other satisfactions to be derived from writing and publishing and the notice they brought him, there is no doubt that for many years he saw each of his successive books of poems as an earnest of fortune as well as of fame. Late in his life he finally acknowledged the sad fact that 'no matter how good, there is not much to be made from verse,' regretting that he had not tried his hand at more lucrative forms of writing, 'a novel, perhaps – at least *one*.' Not that his poetry made him no money; several of his books, *Brébeuf and His Brethren* and *Dunkirk* for example, were almost best-sellers in the 1940s – in Canada. But none ever reaped the harvests he continued to hope and work for even after repeated disappointments.

In the spring of 1925 the first disappointment, *Newfoundland Verse*, was already behind him, receding now as his confidence in the forthcoming *The Witches' Brew* and in his new poem, *The Cachalot*, began to rise. As we have seen, he had had high hopes for *Newfoundland Verse*. Pierce had warned him against laying out 'spectral sovereigns' in anticipation of 'actual dollars,' but his expectations had run high throughout the heady summer of 1923. And the book's initial sales while not overwhelming had indeed been encouraging enough to assure him that a second printing (the first had been of 1,000 copies) would be called for before the year was out. In anticipation of this he had sent off to Pierce a substantial 'corrigenda,' which, in a second edition, would emend typographical errors, repair 'fractured sonnets,' incorporate minor authorial revisions, and by adding 'an explanatory dedication' would, he hoped, clarify one poem which, by the 'subtlety of the lines,' had baffled many readers including Pelham Edgar. (This was the sonnet-duo – erroneously printed tripartite – 'Magnolia Blossoms,' of which the added superscription was to have been 'To a Certain Magdalen,' the poem, it would seem, having been addressed to a reformed and repentant prostitute!) As it turned out, sales of the book had ebbed dishearteningly after an initial spurt. Two years later several hundred copies still remained unsold and his corrigenda gathered dust in Pierce's office. Pratt had realized less than $100 from the sale of *Newfoundland Verse* and Ryerson Press only its costs.

   Not that Pratt himself had not done his utmost to sell the book. Following his confrontation with Follis, Ryerson's Managing Director, and having fully voiced his grievances to Pierce, he had virtually taken the advertising of *Newfoundland Verse* into his own hands, publicizing it wherever he went, ensuring its display at book fairs and exhibitions, and reading from it whenever he performed in public. He had hoped that Pierce would sponsor him on a reading tour as he had MacDonald, but Pierce had demurred, doubtless because having read the first draft of *The Witches' Brew* he had already foreseen the possibility that Pratt would not be a Ryerson author very much longer. He had had, nevertheless, a substantial number of reading engagements, especially after *The Ice-Floes* appeared in W.J. Alexander's *Shorter Poems*, prescribed in the autumn of 1924 as a high school text in Ontario. He had addressed schools not only in Toronto (such as Humberside Collegiate, where, we are told, students 'thought he looked very like a sea captain and boys who had previously thought poetry to be for little girls were noticeably impressed'), but also in several other Ontario towns and cities: in Guelph, for example, where a half-holiday was declared in his honour. Various other groups and organizations too had continued to solicit his presence, his latest engagement having taken him on 1 May to London (Ontario) where he had been welcomed to the city by a two-column feature in the *Free Press* and had addressed the local branch of the CAA on 'The Sea-faring Life.' It was probably too late to resuscitate *Newfoundland Verse*, but he believed that keeping himself in the public eye could not but improve the prospects for his forthcoming book.

The Witches' Brew, in the press at last after a long delay, was now his new hope. Though *Newfoundland Verse* had failed to fatten any coffers, it had, he believed, established him as 'one of the Canadian poets'; and having moved from Ryerson Press to Macmillan of Canada, whose sales record was known to be good, he felt justified once again to entertain 'sanguine expectations.' With a young, energetic promoter behind it like Hughie Eayrs ('bless his fat stomach') *The Brew* was almost certain to be at least a commercial success. But such a prospect was still some months away, and in the spring of 1925 he needed something more palpable than spectral sovereigns.

His financial plight had not been worse since he had joined the Department at Victoria in 1920. His salary as a university lecturer – he was still at the bottom of the ranks – was little more than it had been five years earlier. Yet the demands upon it had greatly multiplied and his summer in Britain had left him debts that had been burdensome to repay. Most of the demands were necessary enough, but others derived from something beyond strict domestic necessity, from what may be called his socio-personal or socio-psychological needs: his club life (he was a member of the Arts and Letters Club as well as most Toronto literary fraternities); his one athletic addiction, golf, a not inexpensive pastime; his increasingly more frequent stags and convivial *conversazioni*, though 'apocalyptic dinners' were still strictly limited both in number and size; and, not the least, his 'estate' at Bobcaygeon, a perennial begetter of bills for repairs and refurbishing, not to mention for structures built 'by mistake.'

To make matters more pressing he felt an urgent need to visit his mother, whom he had not seen since her return to St John's following surgery to remove her tumorous left eye and whose other eye though still sighted was now gradually deteriorating toward blindness. He greatly regretted having by-passed her on his voyage to England, regretted indeed not having visited her more often – so far only once since leaving Newfoundland in 1907. (After her death in 1926 he made amends of sorts by rewriting the record as he wished it had actually been – something he also did in other contexts – reporting to a friend who was writing about him for publication that he had visited her 'every summer until the last.') But not only was a journey to Newfoundland long and costly, it was one he could not in all conscience embark on alone. Disporting himself in Britain (and 'Paree') the previous summer, he had repeatedly consoled his wife and daughter with promises to take them on a long holiday-trip the following year. Even then he had been banking on *The Brew*: 'If the Witches Brew [*sic*] goes,' he had written from Stratford, 'we'll have a royal time.'

Financial straits were nothing new to him; he had rarely been free of them, though it was not a circumstance that had hitherto worried him noticeably. There had always been a streak of Micawber in him – mingled with his outporter's optimistic fatalism. But in the spring of 1925 it was all too apparent that, as Mrs Micawber remarked to her husband, 'Things cannot be expected to turn up of themselves. We must assist to turn them up.' Pratt did his best, but the most he could turn up that summer was a one-month appointment (during July) as a marker of school examination scripts for the Ontario Department of Education. Even so it was a welcome, if meagre, easement of his troubles, but it also marked a return to the old routine of summer jobs he had hoped was behind him forever. Though such a prospect, had he glimpsed it, would have appalled him, it was a routine that continued almost unbroken for the next twenty-five years. Never again for him would there be a long, leisurely summer at Bobcaygeon for writing, golfing, relaxing, or whatever else he fancied; rather only a few weeks in June and a few more in late August and early September. That year there would not even be a June rustication at 'Bob,' June being the only time possible for the Newfoundland excursion.

The cottage would not, however, stand idle: Deacon and his family would take it during July, though at a cut-rate rental. A further small sum could be had by letting out the house on Tullis Drive for the summer months. On his return to Toronto Pratt would take a room in one of the student residences, while Viola and Claire stayed on in St John's with his mother.

They left Toronto by train on 1 June and three days later embarked at Halifax on the SS *Rosalind* for St John's. On board was also the celebrated Arctic explorer, Captain 'Bob' Bartlett, whom Pratt remembered from his Brigus days as a tough, sea-going youth already commanding his own fishing schooner to Labrador. The simultaneous arrival of two 'native-born celebrities' caused a mild stir in the local press, *The Daily News* signalling the event with a full-length editorial headed 'Distinguished Visitors.' (Pratt, it seems, was distressed by the publicity, fearing it might prompt awkward invitations to mount the pulpit.) There were, of course, convivial reunions with his brothers, Calvert and Jim, long since prosperous businessmen of Water Street, and with a number of his old Methodist College classmates, now 'greying teachers, furrowed business men, worried trustees, and portly lawyers and justices.' It needs no telling that he enjoyed his visit with his mother most of all, though he knew it was unlikely he would ever see her again.

Much more of his holiday than he had planned was spent at Marystown, far down the Burin Peninsula. Not that he was moved by a burning passion to revisit the outport for its own sake. (To quote Viola, 'Ned had no interest whatsoever in going back to see the fishing villages again.') His reason for the trip was to visit an old Grand Bank friend, Chester Harris, medical doctor and amateur poet, whose brother had married Pratt's sister, Lottie. To reach Marystown he went to Placentia by train (which he later mildly aspersed by describing to the Toronto *Star* how he had 'beguiled the time' of a slow passage by dismounting from time to time to practise golf shots along the route!) and thence by coastal steamer to his destination. When the weather turned foul he found himself marooned there for nearly a week longer than he had planned to stay. But the time, as it proved, was well spent. Harris took him salmon fishing; on visits to nearby whaling stations, where he was able to verify some of the 'first-hand information' he had already written into *The Cachalot*; and on several medical rounds by motorboat to outlying villages along the coast. It was probably one of these 'errands of mercy' that later produced a rather grim and ironic short poem, full of omens and foreboding, 'The Doctor in the Boat,' which seems to have been unpublished in his lifetime. It was undoubtedly this outport sojourn rather than his city visit that prompted most of the series of short, usually ironic, sometimes grim, sometimes wistful lyrics which grew out of the New-foundland excursion of 1925: 'Tatterhead,' 'The Way of Cape Race,' 'Erosion,' 'Sea-Gulls,' 'The Lee-shore' (first published as 'A Lee Shore' and originally entitled 'Waiting'), and several others.

Back in St John's on 25 June he dispatched identical postcards (depicting a small, sturdy boy in sou'wester flanked by two giant codfish) to Deacon and Phelps, both at Bobcaygeon. To Deacon he wrote: 'How's this for codfish. Caught salmon last week about this size more or less (suspiciously less).' And to Phelps: 'Here's fish for you! Bet you never get anything like this in Kawartha. Glad to be out of that brawl on fiction.' He had been named with F.P. Grove and several others to a panel on Canadian fiction at the CAA convention on 27 June. By that date he was aboard the *SS Silvia* en route to Halifax, thence to Toronto and his month-long stint as a marker of examination scripts.

His month of marking turned out on the whole to be somewhat less unpleasant than he had feared. The work, to be sure, was 'monoto-nous, laborious, and soporific,' and living at the South House of Burwash Hall deprived him of many of his accustomed and much-cherished comforts and amenities. But there were enough of his famil-iars left in town, mostly fellow members of the Writers' Club (the favourite among his literary fraternities), to make up a series of lively poker games and similar convivial foregatherings. He was also fortu-nate to find a willing golf partner in a 'fellow-sufferer' (as he described himself) on the Marking Board, Adrian Macdonald, whom we have already briefly met, a young English teacher and recent author (*Cana-dian Portraits*, Ryerson 1925). (Macdonald has recalled one afternoon when he and Pratt persuaded a couple of their female colleagues on the Board to join them at the York Downs Club, but the experience was not repeated. The 'girls' proved to be 'very indifferent golfers' much to Pratt's annoyance, while much to theirs he proved to be so 'utterly preoccupied with his game' that he continued playing long after the club-house diningroom had closed, sending them home 'ex-hausted and supperless,' his promise of 'sizzling, juicy steaks when the game was over' quite unkept.) Later in the month when 'poet, philoso-pher, and orientalist,' Tom MacInnes, home from his long sojourn in China, arrived in Toronto on his first visit in thirty years, poor in health, low on funds, and dispirited because his writing had not received the recognition he believed it deserved, Pratt did his best to rally his spirits. He laid on a luncheon for MacInnes at Hart House, which led to several similar events hosted by other members of the Writers' Club, and had him up to his room at Burwash Hall for several evenings of friendly talk. When at the end of July, his marking over, Pratt headed for Bobcaygeon to rusticate until the College re-opened, he invited MacInnes to spend a few days with him and the Phelpses. 'Mac' gladly accepted the invitation; so short was he of funds that he had been living off the Deacons since his arrival in town.

Most of what was left to Pratt of his 'long vacation' he planned to spend writing, mainly some Newfoundland poems suggested by his recent visit, perhaps also making a start on the 'prehistoric extrava-ganza' that had been hatching slowly, like the dinosaur's egg, in the 'most excellent preservative' of his imagination since April past. But it is impossible to say how much he actually wrote or precisely what, though we know that at least one poem was finished, which MacInnes was one of the first to read and be given a copy of to take away with him. This was 'Tatterhead,' first published in *Acta* (January 1926), in which Pratt used again but far more succinctly and ironically now, a theme he had used in 'For Valour' (1917), the 'two lives' theme: the life of 'flowery beds of ease' contrasted with that of 'bloody seas.' Featur-ing an old Arctic explorer, it may well have been suggested to him by his recent meeting with Captain Bob Bartlett.

While Pratt wrote in his little 'summer house' nearby, MacInnes sunned himself on the spacious deck of Pratt's new leviathan of a wharf, joined by Pratt himself from time to time, declaiming lines he had just written. One afternoon, joined also by Phelps, MacInnes read aloud to them from a typescript of *The Witches' Brew*, which he had not seen before. As Phelps recalled the event: 'Tom was utterly captivated and gave us a very spirited reading ... He was, I remem-ber, particularly enchanted with the Cat ... Afterward we ceremo-nially anointed him – with a liquid suited to the occasion – and re-baptized him "Tom of Zanzibar".' (The new name was not in-appropriate for one who had discovered and rifled a small cache of liquor which Pratt had moored for safekeeping in the murky depths at the end of his dock!)

MacInnes returned to Toronto a few days later, leaving Pratt alone with his writing. But though freedom from interruption if not total seclusion was his best regime for composition, he soon felt a need for the emotional and imaginative stimuli which only a crew around him could provide. Accordingly, with the connivance of Phelps and his sister (his wife and child like Pratt's were absent 'on holiday'), he was soon laying plans for a 'gorgeous weekend' in mid-August. On the tenth he dispatched the following signal to W.A. Deacon:

Dear Billy,
We are planning one gorgeous weekend here next Saturday, 15th inst. Could you get, by hook or by crook, Roberts and [Wilson] MacDonald to come up with you, and MacInnes again if he can make it. Glad Phelps [her name was actually the Welsh *Gwlad*] is going to invite some of her *petites blondes* for a few days and it's quite possible a little moonlight dance could be executed on the grounds outside the cottage. Art is inviting you as well. Between our two cottages we could accommodate all comers. Do try to make it and *get* Roberts and Mac by all hazards. I can look after all the males.
Ned.

It should here be explained that Pratt until now had barely met C.G.D. Roberts, who, since his return in the late winter, had been travelling in Canada, mostly in the West, but was now in permanent residence – more or less – at Toronto's Ernescliffe Apartments. It is also true that Pratt had never been greatly impressed by Roberts's verse, and had been somewhat annoyed by the rather excessive national fanfare which had greeted one who had held aloof for so long from the Canadian scene. But he was well aware that 'old Charley,' despite his sixty-five years, had an underground reputation for many interesting things and was anxious to observe him at closer range. It should be explained too that Wilson MacDonald, with whom Pratt had as yet no real cause to be personally annoyed, was now, a veritable chameleon, fraternizing amicably with the recent targets of his mischievous blunderbuss, Roberts and Carman, the latter for the moment a guest at his cousin's apartment. (The curious trio were shortly to set out together for the Muskoka Assembly, that preposterous but short-lived Canadian chautauqua of the 1920s, which Pratt had so far cautiously avoided.) Carman, it seems, was not invited to the 'gorgeous weekend,' but the heterogeneity of the prospective company attests that though most of Pratt's intimates were male, he was

by no means averse to the presence of 'petites blondes' and suchlike – on appropriate occasions.

Deacon, it is known, could not attend. But how many and who
actually did, and precisely what was 'executed on the grounds outside'
or anywhere else appear to have been left unrecorded, leaving one's
imagination, as Pratt remarked on another occasion, 'scope for figurative exercise.'

Pratt's moods changed very quickly. Within a week he was writing
Deacon again, this time to express his sober reflections on an article
that Deacon had just published in *Saturday Night* (15 August), in
which he had, as Pratt put it, 're-touched ... the hoary issue of literary evaluations.' Deacon had mused darkly upon the uncertain fate of
an author's book once published: how some are destined to survive
and others to die still-born. The irony of it was that often 'the finest of
margins separates the book that is immortal from its twin that goes to
utter oblivion ...' As in nature, survival or oblivion is sometimes a
matter of mere chance, fitness or unfitness having little to do with the
case.

Soon to witness the entry into that uncertain contest of two major
new works on which he had staked so much – *The Witches' Brew* and
The Cachalot – Pratt was deeply affected by the simple truth of Deacon's words. His own to Deacon were very personal: 'It is almost
staggering to think that one's destiny is suspended by so slight a
thread, and life and death separated by almost microscopic boundaries.' For him, it seemed, much more than the fate of his poems hung
in the balance; in a very real sense, he seemed to be saying, his own
destiny, and perhaps not only as a poet, was in the balance too. What
Deacon had written reminded him of the ironic precariousness and
uncertainty of all human life and happiness, for the very reason that
his own had become so closely intertwined with the fate of his poems.
Like a parent toward his children, Pratt had come to stake his own life
and happiness on the lives of these children of his imagination. The
analogy was one he was fond of using: burning copies of his ill-fated
opus, *Clay*, was 'like strangling a child'; a new poem was like a 'day-
old child' which should not be 'displayed to the neighbours' too soon;
many a 'brain child' of his own was 'sturdily slapped on the stern' and
'promptly sent back to the progenitor.'

For all the oft-noted objectivity and detachment which he managed to achieve in the final form of most of his poems, there can be no question about Pratt's total involvement in the creative process itself. 'Incarnating' himself in the substance of a poem was not an experience unique to writing *The Cachalot*. Few poets I have ever known or studied have been more deeply and totally engaged by the act of poetic creation, or, consequently, more concerned for the fate of their work once delivered to the public. (This, of course, was something he did not admit except in unguarded, confessional moments.) His poems were rarely if ever merely academic exercises or 'intellectual constructs,' but rather, to use again his own image, flesh of his flesh, bone of his bone. And adept though he was at severing the navel cords of his poetic offspring, and though he often referred to them collectively by such ungracious terms as 'stuff' or 'output' – this was undoubtedly another feature of his protective shield – each remained a very real parcel of himself. Even those offspring which he knew were ill-favoured or misshapen, and would choose, publicly, to deny or 'forget,' retained a fond parental place in his private affections. Discussing with him in 1959 – late in his life it is true – a selection of his poems that I was editing, I was made very aware of how deeply he still felt about even minor and amateurish poems written nearly half a century earlier.

His reflections on destiny's 'slight ... thread' and life's and death's 'microscopic boundaries,' uttered mainly on the subject of his poems, soon proved to have been strangely premonitory of a blow that 'destiny' was even then poised to deal him through his actual, flesh-and-blood child. Happily, unlike his literary friends, D.C. Scott and F.P. Grove, whose private tragedies he often recalled, he did not lose his only daughter. Yet what now befell four-year-old Claire Pratt was in some ways even more agonizing to bear, because it was so prolonged and so frequently recurring and overshadowed all their lives with such ominous and continuing uncertainty. What happened was that shortly after returning with her mother from Newfoundland in early September, Claire was stricken with an illness that, though at first it baffled the doctors, was at last diagnosed as poliomyelitis.

Since at first only one of the child's legs was affected, and that not acutely, her parents though concerned were not greatly alarmed. The prognosis, they were told, was good; it was simply a matter of a little time. Time passed, but instead of improving the condition worsened. The affected leg was put in a brace, then in a cast, and the lively, healthy child, whom her father had long since determined 'to make a first-class golfer in her early teens,' was gradually transformed into a semi-cripple. She was never wholly sound of body again. Eventually a series of surgical operations would be prescribed, but these led only to worse complications: a near-fatal staphylococcic infection which not only produced innumerable abscesses but invaded her spine, affecting its growth and leading in time to further extensive (and expensive) surgery, months in plaster casts, and long periods prone in bed.

Her parents bore their anguish bravely, greatly sustained by the patience and grit of the child herself. Her father never ceased to marvel at her stubborn defiance of her misfortune; it was the kind of spirit he so much admired. Yet there is little doubt that Claire's illness was the heaviest cross he ever bore, one that was not wholly lifted from his shoulders for the rest of his life. Even during periods of relative remission – happily there were such periods of varying length when Claire was able to lead an almost normal life – the cloud was still there, casting its shadow over him. In the words of Arthur Phelps, who 'was very close to that painful drama in the early years':

It was the great tragedy of Ned's life, and make no mistake about it, it had a profound effect upon him. Not only did it make him deeply sad within but quietly grim. It ate like an organic disease quietly inside him. But for a basic resiliency in his nature, and a profound sanity, he might well have become a bitter and melancholy man – and poet. Not that he didn't have his moments of bitterness. [But] it was not Ned's way to parade his feelings. On the contrary, I would say, he made an even greater effort to put on a cheerful countenance amongst his friends – and with his family too ... He was, of course, by nature very sociable and high-spirited, but after this blow hit him his high-spiritedness became more of a defensive and protective device, and a means to help him forget and escape for a while from the deep emotional pain he suffered almost incessantly for years. Most people, I think, don't realise this – never did. But it was so ...

Phelps is undoubtedly right, though Pratt himself left few confessional records of his private sorrows. That, too, was characteristic.

It was equally characteristic that his new 'tragedy' had little immediate, obvious effect on his poetry. He in fact wrote few poems which
touch directly upon Claire's illness and these are carefully veiled expressions of the thoughts and feelings that haunted him during her
most critical years, and written retrospectively, when he could look
back with some outward detachment. He dared not attempt to exploit
his emotions at the time of their greatest turmoil. But there is no
doubt that in his poetry generally the tragic-ironic strain is deepened
thereafter, that he comes to look more closely and seriously at the
riddle of Man's existence, at the strange tragicomedy that he increasingly saw human life and history to be. He rarely wrote again in quite
the high-spirited, extravagant manner of *The Witches' Brew* and *The
Cachalot*. Only once, perhaps, did he again approach the mood and
spirit of these poems: in *The Depression Ends*, written in 1932 following,
significantly I think, Claire's recovery from one of her most critical
bouts of illness.

A National Event and Heady Wine

It is not such an exaggeration as it appears, to say that a new poem by Dr Pratt is a national event ... [But he] has too strong a brain to be perturbed by the heady wine of popularity ...

Pelham Edgar, *Willisons Monthly*, March 1926

PRATT HAD HOPED by early autumn 1925 to have finished enough new poems to make up a small volume, which Eayrs might publish in time for the Christmas trade. But the summer had proved much less productive than he had planned and it was soon apparent that the autumn term was unlikely to be any better. Besides the distracting anxieties about his daughter's illness, his teaching load had been almost doubled, a consequence of his agreeing to take on additional classes because they meant a little extra cash in his pocket. One of these was a course in English for medical students; the others ('Realism in Contemporary Poetry' and 'The Poetry of Hardy') were extramural courses offered by the College's Extension Department and required his commuting weekly by train to St Catharines. A postgraduate course, his first such assignment, though part of his 'normal' load, also added considerably to his labours, since, like all new courses he taught, it had to be got up as he went along. Prospects for a new book before Christmas grew dimmer and dimmer as the term slipped away.

His increasing involvement in CAA affairs was also consuming more and more of his time. He had joined the Toronto Branch willingly enough when Edgar had fathered it in 1922 and had been a faithful if less than zealous member ever since. But he had no wish to be anything more, partly one gathers, because a large proportion of the Toronto membership was made up of 'literary females,' a species of which he was not particularly fond – though there were some exceptions. (The picture he usually painted of them bore a close resemblance to F.R. Scott's 'Miss Crotchet': a model of 'self-unction,' 'Victorian saintliness,' and passionless virginity.) In 1924, however, Edgar, compelled to curtail his own executive duties, yet anxious to keep a hand on the helm, had manoeuvred Pratt into the First Vice-Presidency. As a consequence he had found himself increasingly enmeshed in the Branch's affairs whether he would or no.

A small incident which occurred in September 1925, one which might conceivably have resulted in his prompt un-meshing from the Toronto Branch, is all the more amusing in view of his attitude toward most literary females. Writing from Bobcaygeon simultaneously to the Branch Secretary and Clark Locke, Pratt somehow misdirected the enclosing envelopes. As a consequence Madame Secretary received a brief note from 'Ned Pratt,' affectionately addressing her as 'Dear Old Thing' – his common salutation for a very close friend – and informing her that since he was to be in Toronto for the week-end and his city house was still 'let out' he would like to spend the night with her! Her immediate response is not on record; she did, however, return the note with a tactful query. His own immediate response, we are told, was uproarious laughter, but his reply to the 'mystified' secretary was rather more restrained, even a little shamefaced: 'Many apologies for the mistake of enclosure. It was stupid of me ... Thanks for your kindness in returning the letter. I can now get in touch with the *other* mystified correspondent.' The story somehow got around, adding another whimsical touch to his image, but his reputation remained unblemished and his relationship with the Toronto Branch unimpaired.

As things turned out, Pratt found himself that autumn caught up in the Branch's affairs far more than he cared to be. With the resignation of Paul Wallace as President, Pratt as 'First Vice' fell heir to the vacant post. Loathing the prospect and casting about for a means of escape he had an inspiration: why not C.G.D. Roberts for President? He was not yet a member, but having now taken a 'permanent' address in Toronto was eligible for membership and therefore for the presidency. Calling the executive together and disavowing any desire to succeed Wallace, Pratt proposed his candidate. The executive agreed and a telegram was dispatched in quest of Roberts still junketing in some distant part of the Dominion. After a long and ominous silence, his reply arrived: 'Honour deeply appreciated. Delighted to accept.' Pratt could breathe a sigh of relief. But his deliverance proved to be largely illusory, for Roberts, elected and installed in absentia, did not return from his tour until late December so that most of the Branch's business that autumn fell to Pratt, who had stayed on as First Vice-President. He soon found himself as deeply enmeshed as if he had taken the higher office: arranging programs, recruiting speakers, planning social evenings at the Hygeia House or Mulberry Tea Rooms, and laying on dinners for distinguished visitors who usually turned up unexpectedly.

Even with Roberts's return from his autumn-long junket, Pratt's deliverance was only partial. Roberts continued to travel a good deal, though during the winter not for quite such extended periods. Pratt must have wondered at times whether his inspiration had been so brilliant after all. Nevertheless, before their co-executive year was out 'Ned' and 'Charley' had become good friends, if not perhaps quite bosom companions. Pratt found that 'the aristocratic Major' in his 'bardic accessories' (to borrow Lorne Pierce's descriptive phrases) – black-silk-beribboned pince nez, tan walking cane, fawn vest, and 'festive spats' – was after all an interesting and amusing partner. Roberts, too, seems to have found Pratt, though a rather different species of personality from himself, a congenial companion. Pratt eventually tired of him, but for nearly a decade they remained temperately close friends, exchanging informal social visits, occasionally dining out together, back-slapping each other in public, playing poker over cigars and mugs of beer and, occasionally, golf – over Pratt's (silent) objections. Roberts, who was 'no golfer' to begin with, had the disconcerting habit of dashing off the course and into the clubhouse in medias res to add a line to a poem he had been composing while he played! For Pratt there was a time and place for golf as well as for verse, but the two were very distinct. Yet whatever he may have thought of Roberts's golf or his verse, he could not but have admired his talent for poker. Adrian Macdonald recalled a game one memorable evening at Pratt's when he and Pratt were joined by Roberts and 'an impecunious artist' – unnamed but probably Alan Barr – whom they agreed to 'stake.' Roberts as usual 'cleaned us out – *all* our cash!'

Pratt's many distracting, time-devouring chores on the CAA's behalf that autumn and later need not be detailed here. How much they hindered his writing one can only conjecture. In later years looking back, his own dry verdict was that it had all been 'mostly a damnable waste of a fellow's best time.' The only chore that autumn which seems to have given him a measure of satisfaction, enough for him to remember and write of with pleasure and amusement many years later, was arranging 'a dinner and recital' for 'dear old [Bliss] Carman.' Carman had returned to Toronto in early December to give some talks at the University, and the Toronto Branch felt it should do something for him. It fell to Pratt to make the arrangements. Always the open-handed host, he not only laid on a recital and dinner (Carman, Pratt wrote with some exaggeration, 'could eat so hearty a dinner one might think he didn't expect another meal for a month'), but, Carman being almost penniless as usual, had 'the plate passed round for him' as well. As Pratt recalled the event: 'I don't know how much he netted, but I did notice a few crisp one-dollar bills covering the dimes. I said as I squeezed the amount into his hand – "Bliss, this will at least buy you a new hat" ... a rather significant remark, considering what the old hat looked like ...' – and *smelt* like, if one can believe the rest of Pratt's story!

Events, as we have seen, had frustrated his hope to have on the market by Christmas the new, small volume he had planned to entitle *The Cachalot and Other Poems*. Most of the 'other poems' being either unwritten or unfinished, the book had to wait until his multifarious distractions had subsided a little, permitting him at least occasional respites for 'creative relaxation.' This is not to say that he wrote nothing. A good deal of his 'prehistoric allegory' seems to have been roughed out during odd moments that autumn. But little if any new publishable verse appears to have been finished.

As it turned out the delay was probably fortunate: *The Cachalot* might otherwise have been published lacking eight of its best lines. What befell was this: Duncan Campbell Scott, who, it will be recalled, had earlier requested and been given a copy of the poem to deliver to his friend, John Masefield, had done as he had said he would. Pratt had quite forgotten the incident and was, therefore, pleasantly surprised when in September he received a 'lengthy and enthusiastic' letter from the English poet. Expressing his pleasure upon reading the poem and congratulating the author on 'a rousing and well-told tale,' Masefield concluded: 'The only fault, that I would suggest your thinking over ... is towards the end. It is not made clear how he (the cachalot) struck the ship and how the ship was affected. I wanted the final bang to be a little dwelt on before the blur of death takes off all the edges. Good luck and greetings.' Always amenable to constructive suggestion, Pratt reread the poem and conceded that Masefield was right. Within a few days he had added eight of the most telling lines in the whole poem:

Ten feet above and ten below
The water-line his forehead caught her,
The hatches opened to the blow
His hundred driving tons had wrought her;
The capstan and the anchor fled,
When bolts and stanchions swept asunder,
For what was iron to that head,
And oak – in that hydraulic thunder?

Satisfied that the 'fault' was mended, he wrote Masefield a warm reply of thanks and appreciation, and enclosed a copy of the new lines. As a consequence of the episode, Pratt decided that henceforth he would write his narrative poems 'stern foremost – to avoid anti-climax.' But from the random, hieroglyphical jottings that grew into the wayward drafts contained in his extant notebooks it is impossible to determine whether in fact he did or not.

His chief motive for wanting to bring out at least *The Cachalot* that autumn was, it seems, his growing apprehension that *The Witches' Brew*, soon to be published at last by Selwyn and Blount, might prove after all an egregious fiasco. It had taken so long getting into print, so much had happened since its acceptance for publication, and his subsequent writing had taken him so far from the 'absurdities' of the poem, that like champagne left too long uncorked, its former sparkle and zest had, for him at least, largely evaporated and with them much of the confidence he had felt even up to the previous spring. Perhaps remembering Deacon's dark ruminations on the 'fine margins' that separate immortality from oblivion, he had come to doubt whether *The Brew* was destined for the right side of the 'microscopic boundary.' He felt that he ought to prepare for the worst by bringing out at least *The Cachalot* – as a sort of diversionary tactic.

Hughie Eayrs was willing to publish, but the poem alone was too brief for anything more than a thin chapbook, which Pratt did not want. When in late September he learned that *The Brew* in book form was 'definitely promised' for early November, he knew that any larger volume containing *The Cachalot* was out of the question until long after *The Brew* had been delivered to 'the public surgeon.' Still, he was anxious to get *The Cachalot* into print simultaneously with *The Brew* at least in Canada. Having consulted Eayrs, who raised no objections, he sounded out *The Canadian Forum* and receiving a satisfactory offer as well as the promise of a November publication, decided to publish the poem at once.

As it turned out, Canadian readers made the acquaintance of Pratt's great whale several months before they heard of Tom of Zanzibar. *The Cachalot*, as promised, appeared in the November *Forum*, but *The Brew*, delayed once more by J.C. Squire's continuing insistence on his prior rights, was not published until it appeared, in book form only, in late January 1926, when Selwyn and Blount, and Macmillan (the Canadian publisher), having deferred to Squire three months longer, decided to publish whether or no. As a consequence the *Mercury* dropped the poem for good. Pratt did not care very much, though he felt that Squire had let him down, and the repeated announcements of its 'forthcoming appearance' in the *Mercury* required many awkward explanations. But by then the 'national acclaim' which greeted *The Cachalot* ensured that *The Witches' Brew* could not be dismissed as the ravings of an inebriated lunatic.

'National acclaim' (as Pratt himself described the phenomenon) is only a slight exaggeration, for the publication of *The Cachalot* in the November *Forum* caused a spectacle rare if not unique in Canadian publishing history: a stampede to buy. Word spread rapidly that the journal carried a new sensational poem by E.J. Pratt and every copy was sold in a day or two. (Deacon's report of the phenomenon in *Saturday Night* stated that 'hundreds of requests for copies had to be refused.') Pratt, himself, according to his report to Phelps, was 'inundated with congratulations and the most enthusiastic expressions of delight from all sorts of people.' *Newfoundland Verse* and the random pieces published since had brought him credit and a certain notability, but now, suddenly, like Byron, he was 'famous overnight.' It was a very welcome flood of sunlight in an autumn that had otherwise been, because of his daughter's illness, overcast if not quite dark.

Only Lorne Pierce, not surprisingly perhaps, was unimpressed. As yet unreconciled to his erstwhile fellow clergyman's dabbling in witches' brews, he still felt that Pratt was wasting his talents on trifling subjects. Writing in his diary on 11 November, Pierce is distinctly equivocal on the publication of *The Cachalot*, if not disdainful. Describing it coldly as 'another adjectival rhyme on a big fish,' that 'reminds me of Moby Dick,' he records that, encountering Pratt the previous evening, 'I asked him if he had any qualms in taking his cheque and he thought not. I also suggested that he now write "The Odyssey of the Shad." He liked the idea well and agreed to undertake it and dedicate it to me.' (It would seem that Pierce, whose rejoinder obviously ought to have been 'touché!,' had missed the point of Pratt's ironic reply.)

But neither Pierce's cool response to the poem nor his innuendoes seem to have affected Pratt's satisfaction with the general reception of *The Cachalot*. After all, his other doubtful critic-friend, 'Billy' Deacon, had been generous, if succinct, in his praise, calling its publication 'one of the great Canadian literary events of the year' – though within a month, in his several annual surveys of new Canadian writing, he again hailed Wilson MacDonald as 'the rising star of Canadian Poetry' and failed even to mention Pratt.

It should, perhaps, be interpolated here that this was becoming increasingly typical of Deacon's treatment of Pratt, at least in the press. Privately – so far as appears – they remained good friends, amicable if not brotherly, thanks mainly to Pratt's forebearance. But in print Deacon was beginning to display a growing ambivalence. He was not yet hostile or even openly critical, but while occasionally throwing Pratt a small bouquet (a line or two among the ephemera of his gossip column) for something such as 'a new sensational poem' that could hardly be ignored, for the permanent record he chose to write as if Pratt did not exist. Still infected with 'his "bug" about MacDonald' (as Pierce put it), he refused to consider, at least aloud, the possibility that Pratt might after all be the better poet. Pratt's growing stature in the academic community, and his popularity as a public lecturer-cum-critic also seem to have rankled with Deacon. His own foiled aspirations toward an academic post, and the University of Toronto's resolute cold-shouldering of Wilson MacDonald (which continued and for which Pratt came to be blamed by MacDonald and his few loyal allies) also undoubtedly helped to distort Deacon's view of what he called, usually with some contempt, 'the professorial class.' Pratt the professor undoubtedly disturbed his equilibrium as much as did Pratt the rival of MacDonald – maybe even more. Reporting, for example, a 'scholarly thing' on modern poetry delivered by Pratt that autumn before Edgar's new Poetry Society, Deacon can muster for his *Saturday Night* readers only a brief, ambivalent note in which sarcasm and inverse snobbery are badly disguised as bantering humour:

E.J. Pratt's address on modern English Poetry before the Poetry Society was a scholarly thing, the greatest compliment I ever heard paid to the intellectual grasp of an audience. I am proud to say that I understood the majority of his polysyllables, and recognize from 33% to 40% of his literary allusions, though some of his metaphors I could not unravel as fast as he delivered them. It was a vast subject to cover in an hour. It was nobly done, even if so compactly that some of us were mentally on the stretch trying to get it all down at one swallow.

One needs no second glance to realize that the humour is mirthless and the compliments decidedly backhanded. (Unfortunately, no copy of Pratt's script seems to be extant.)

It was, however, characteristic of Deacon that within a week of this equivocal notice, he was cordially inviting Pratt to write a book review and submit a poem for inclusion in his magazine's forthcoming Christmas Literary Supplement. It was characteristic, too, that though *The Cachalot* merited only a few lines in print, writing Pratt privately Deacon was much more expansive and congratulatory. It was equally characteristic that when Pratt complied with both requests for contributions to the Supplement, writing a brief review of Philip Sergeant's *The Courtships of Catherine the Great* and sending along several 'new and unpublished poems,' though his review appeared, the only verse to grace Deacon's Christmas Supplement – on its front page – was a poem by Wilson MacDonald.

Despite *The Cachalot*'s national acclaim, Pratt continued to be apprehensive about *The Witches' Brew*, but he need not have been concerned. Published at last toward the end of January, while it caused no stampede to buy, the poem proved to most readers of the 500 copies sold (if the reviewers provide a clue) as heady a draught as anything they had tasted in many a year – a splash of a potent 'brand of moonshine' (as one reviewer called it) on palates long accustomed to maple syrup. Even those who confessed to being 'shocked by its subject' seem to have surrendered willingly to its 'intoxication.'

Not unexpectedly there were a few reviewers who maintained a conspicuous silence and a few who chose the safety of ambivalence or ambiguity, but, so far as one can discover, no one actually assailed the poem or the poet. Pierce, of course, ignored it in his *New Outlook* columns, and Deacon in *Saturday Night* led off a brief review, devoted mostly to summary and quotation, with what a first glance seemed an accolade of almost hyperbolical extravagance: 'We have had poets of dramatic power, and with the gift of humour, and some who have had a real feeling for the sea; but never before have these qualities combined in one man to produce anything like the imaginative orgy to be found in "*The Witches' Brew*." Unique as it is in Canadian literature, I do not know in the whole realm of literature any precedent for it ...' But an 'orgy' for which there is no precedent may or may not be a good thing. Going on to rank the poem below Pratt's 'more notable work of the past,' Deacon made it quite clear that he did not view the poem as adding anything to Pratt's stature as 'one of the promising younger poets.'

Not unexpectedly too there were those who confessed themselves at a loss to determine the poem's 'meaning' or 'intention.' Was it satire? If so, on what? Was it intended to make hilarious fun of temperance and prohibition? Or was it on the contrary a vigorous if somewhat oblique blow struck on behalf of the WCTU, the Anti-saloon League, and the Ontario 'Drys'? But this was scarcely surprising in view of the mutilation and distortion the poem had suffered at the hands of Pratt's British advisers, though it might well have been the case whether or no. There were some too who wondered about the man himself who had created so unlikely a concoction. Concluded one reviewer who had praised the quality of the verse and the poem's high spirits: 'It seems odd that he should have chosen such a bibulous subject for his present poem. As he is a professor at a religious college in Toronto, a prohibition city, it looks as if Brother Pratt [he was still an undefrocked cleric] is suffering what Professor Lodge would call a suppressed complex.'

The response of most reviewers was delighted and admiring surprise – if not astonishment – mingled with whole-hearted acceptance. Even when a critic admitted his puzzlement, he was usually ready to surrender his fancy to the frolicsome diablerie of the poem. Thus, one wrote:

We must confess that we are at a loss as to what target the poet is aiming at. Our thick intellect fails to fathom his intention. Do his airy fireworks contain real explosives? Do the arrows of his wit conceal barbed darts? Is this bizarre fantasy leveled, like a gun, at some of the more solemn of our pet superstitions and taboos? Or is it all just a delightful frolic? We cannot tell. But one thing we do know; it is all fancifully absurd, inconsequential, grotesque; a masquerade of dream-begotten and gargantuan improbabilities.

The general consensus of critical opinion may be judged from the following brief but typical excerpts: 'Here is a refreshing and unfamiliar note in Canadian poetry ... a delightful imagination ... and a capacity for using words ... with captivating gusto' (Toronto *Globe*); 'No Canadian has ever written a poem of the same kind ... Our verse is frequently musical and just as often pretty ... precious and self-conscious – in fact ... feminine. But Mr. Pratt is masculine from first to last' (Toronto *Mail and Empire*); '*The Witches' Brew* is a piece of extravagance tossed off in a fit of high spirits by a highly imaginative man ... It has Aristophanic humour and a kind of imagination unique in Canadian poetry' (*The Canadian Forum*); 'Nothing here of the "lisping and vowelled purity, and lines in satin length" ... Mr. Pratt derives ... from Butler, and his cut-and-thrust style, the masculine forthrightness, the rough-and-tumble lines carry us back to "Hudibras"' (source unknown); 'We wonder ... what brand of moonshine the poet was in the habit of imbibing when he imagined and wrote this delectable fantasia ... for we would fain present a jug of it to some other of our poets, in the hope that it might enliven their flabby wits' (Hamilton *Spectator*). Others described the poem as 'delicious phantasmal poetry steeped in its own intoxication'; 'untinctured delight'; 'magnificent fooling distinguished by extraordinary gusto'; 'a weird phantasy coloured by a keen and biting sense of humour'; 'a most ingenious, pungent, and effective satire'; 'a Byronic poem.' Of the poet they declared that he had 'drawn a warm human breath across the cold and formal field of Canadian letters,' 'struck out a new line in contemporary verse,' and much more of the same kind.

Only in Britain – *The Brew* went unnoticed in the United States – were there any serious doubts about the poem. There one critic unable to find 'hidden meanings and symbolisms' in it dismissed the poem as 'a libel on the "brands" and therefore a temperance pamphlet'; another saw it as 'an advertisement but somewhat obscure'; while *The Times Literary Supplement* called it 'an original but rather pointless fantasy' in which 'if any satirical purpose underlies [the] extravaganza, it is hard to discover.'

Not unnaturally Pratt was disappointed with the poem's overseas reception. He desperately wanted to be accepted abroad as well as at home. But it was obvious that he would have to await the publication of another volume. But counterbalancing its general overseas dismissal was the poem's reception at home. So wide and enthusiastic, indeed, was his Canadian 'acclaim' that it would hardly have been surprising had his head been turned a little, but while he was very proud of his success, there is no evidence that it was. Pelham Edgar was surely right when, declaring that 'a new poem by Dr. Pratt is a national event,' he went on to add that 'Pratt has too strong a brain to be perturbed by the heady wine of popularity.'

26

Pleiocene Armageddon and Other Dreams

The method of the poem is to take an evolutionary theme and work it out in terms of an imaginary symbolism. I want to show how colossal a catastrophe if certain natural instincts and passions such as self-preservation, family and racial pride, or even a feeling of honour or adventure or the desire to possess or retain were given absolutely free rein ...

E.J. Pratt, from a 1925–6 notebook

RATT MEANWHILE pushed on with his prehistoric allegory, to which he had now given the title *The Great Feud (A Dream of a Pleiocene Armageddon)*. The going had not been easy. Besides the many demands upon his time and attention already noted, and those inevitably made upon an anxious parent by the illness of a child, the poem itself, a unique amalgam of beast epic, fantasy, allegory, science fiction and, to a degree, science documentary, gave him far more trouble than he had foreseen, its shape constantly on the verge of dissolving into amorphousness, its tone wavering between the comic if not farcical and the solemnly didactic, the 'gory stuff' (as he later called its more lurid matter) threatening to get out of hand, and the 'serious theme' disappearing in the miasmal mists of primeval swamps and enveloping clouds of recherché words whose seductions he found hard to resist. (He struggled against the seductions of recherché and recondite words for many years.)

For several weeks during February he came very close to succumbing to a rather different kind of seduction. The new object of attraction was a newspaper story of a dramatic rescue at sea, a kind of heroic action which Pratt could never resist. It had laid hold on his imagination from the moment the Toronto press, during the last week of January, had begun to publish the first sketchy accounts of almost fictive deeds being enacted on the high seas south of Newfoundland. The little British freighter, *Antinoe*, drifting helplessly in one of the worst winter storms ever recorded, had called for help. The American liner, *President Roosevelt*, had answered, and searching the snow-and-wind-swept wastes of the North Atlantic had miraculously found the small ship and set about rescuing her crew. Three days and nights the battle with the sea and storm had gone on, the *Roosevelt* herself in constant peril, losing two of her own seamen before the entire crew of the *Antinoe* was taken off just before the little vessel foundered.

To Pratt the action was 'the epitome of human courage and self-sacrifice.' No story he had ever read had so gripped his spirit and imagination. He collected copies of all the newspapers he could find and studied every account of the rescue that they contained, clipping from those that he could buy and making notes from those he could find only in libraries. Soon a new sea epic such as no one had yet attempted to write in verse had begun to shape itself in his mind. The temptation to abandon allegorical fantasies and dreams of a largely imaginary, pre-human world for something actual, immediate, and human was very great indeed. But he had struggled so far through his primeval jungle – his destination was in fact at last in view – that he determined to press on. Besides, he was still convinced of the ultimate success and worth of *The Great Feud*. The story of the *Roosevelt* and the *Antinoe* was, therefore, laid aside, but it was not forgotten.

Precisely when *The Feud* was finished is uncertain. There is no record of his giving his usual première for his friends; it was so much longer than his previous narratives that it did not lend itself to an evening's entertainment. Nor was it first 'displayed to the neighbours' in the pages of some magazine as *The Cachalot* had been, and *The Witches' Brew* had been intended to be. But finished it was by late spring or early summer, and along with *The Cachalot* and a selection of shorter pieces written since *Newfoundland Verse* assembled for publication by Macmillan under the title *The Cachalot and Other Poems*. Both the plan to include the shorter poems and the proposed title were later changed when he decided that the minor pieces were ill-suited to the company of his two titans.

As noted in a previous chapter Pratt's viewing the film of *The Lost World* in the spring of 1925 had been the spark which had ignited *The Feud* in his imagination. But there is no doubt that the tinder was already there, awaiting only the necessary spark. His writing of the poem seems to have followed what was becoming a characteristic pattern: promiscuous reading and other forms of vicarious experience having provided a fertile if temporarily dormant imaginative matrix, a single event, often unexpected and unlikely, was sufficient to impregnate it with life, which he then proceeded to nourish and enlarge with whatever additional research his subject might require. Unless a poem was straight fantasy he insisted that in 'basic particulars' it be scrupulously accurate. Occasional licence was permissible only when the context clearly showed that a liberty had been taken – usually for comic or dramatic effect. *The Great Feud* was no exception; Pratt would not, as he wrote, have some 'zoologist laughing at ... inaccuracy.' His general familiarity with past and current writing on prehistory and evolutionary biology and anthropology need not be detailed here. He was well acquainted with much of it, going back to his days in Robert Holloway's classes at the Methodist College. But how much additional research he undertook for the poem is difficult to say. The only scientific work which it seems likely he consulted at the time was F.A. Lucas's *Animals of the Past* (1922). Even that was probably a gratuitous indulgence.

Fictional treatments of the subject he also probably knew, though how many and which ones, other than *The Lost World*, cannot be identified. It is not unlikely that he knew Jack London's *Before Adam* (1907), a short novel about the 'Fire People,' 'Tree People,' and 'Folk' – anthropoidal proto-humans of the 'Mid-Pleistocene' age – and the primeval world they inhabited. London was another favourite author of his, most of whose books he had read. It is also probable that he knew C.G.D. Roberts's 'pre-historical romance,' *In the Morning of Time* (1919).

Yet for all *The Great Feud* may have owed to such books and perhaps others, and certainly to the film *The Lost World*, there seems little doubt that it owed an equally important – perhaps more important – debt to a very different kind of work. For although the poem had been prompted by a cinematic spectacular and, in the heat of *The Cachalot*'s triumphal consummation, conceived as an extravaganza featuring even more wonderful and exotic creatures than either whale or kraken, some time after he got down to serious work the poem had resolved itself into a conscious allegory having, as he frequently reiterated, 'a serious underlying theme.' Enough of the extravagant and spectacular would remain, however, not only to sustain the character of an extravanganza but also largely to obscure his ostensible theme from most of his readers and critics. For the real subject of the poem, as I think the note by Pratt quoted at the head of this chapter makes clear, was not 'the evolutionary theme' only, but war and the nature of man: the biological and psychical causes that make wars virtually inevitable. In short, far from being the mere extravaganza it was often taken for, or the Christian allegory John Sutherland made it out to be, *The Great Feud*, on one level at least, was a grim Hardyesque dramatization of the primal unconscious forces of Nature that weave the 'web Enorm' of human fate.

With this in mind I suggest that the poem also owes something, perhaps much, to Pratt's reading of Hardy, *The Dynasts* in particular. It is not, of course, in any sense an imitation of Hardy's dramatic poem, nor even, as in the 1924 'Hardy group,' an attempt to reproduce certain of Hardy's characteristic effects. Yet I think that both in its general theme and in certain particular components to be looked at shortly *The Great Feud* exhibits a number of significant parallels with *The Dynasts*. It was a poem – or drama – Pratt already knew well. His essay on Hardy published a year earlier clearly shows his familiarity with and his admiration of *The Dynasts*, which he described as 'a work so original and spacious that it can scarcely be classed under any recognized literary or philosophical index.' He quotes approvingly the final chorus of the Pities, 'who, throughout the drama have been articulating the human plea.' We know too that during the late summer and autumn of 1925, when the poem was in its early gestation period, he had had occasion to revisit Hardy in some detail for the extramural course on him which he had chosen to give at St Catharines. It may also be of some significance that in 1960, discussing *The Feud* with me (whether or not to include a portion of the poem in *Here the Tides Flow*, which I was editing), he spoke of *The Dynasts* in connection with *The Great Feud*. Arguing against including any portion of the poem, he observed that it had generally been misinterpreted, something for which he himself was undoubtedly to blame: 'I probably didn't make my intention clear enough.' He went on to explain a little of what he had had in mind. His subject, he said, was not merely 'evolution as such, but *war*,' which was 'a perennial theme.' He had wanted, he said, to show that the main causes of war are 'a natural legacy' which even the advent of Reason or Intelligence could not countervail: 'Something beyond [Reason] was necessary.' He pointed out that Hardy in *The Dynasts* had referred to this 'something' as 'the Compassions' (presumably 'the Pities'). Hardy 'took up the subject at a late stage in history, but I went back to the beginnings ... It was the same idea – but it never came across.'

The Dynasts, it will be recalled, is a vast, panoramic verse drama in which the Napoleonic Wars, that 'great feud' among the peoples of Europe, is portrayed as a random act, a 'prank,' of the 'foresightless' and 'unconscious' Will in which Man participates as portion of the universal mechanism: 'each has parcel in the total Will.' Thus Man, ironically, is party to his own bondage, for the prank, however inconsequential to the mindless Will, can only further frustrate Man's hope of that higher evolution of Consciousness which alone can free him from the 'web Enorm' of Natural Causation and its inevitable calamities. Even the emergence of Reason as an aspect of evolving Consciousness (as Pratt seems to have correctly divined from his reading of Hardy) cannot suffice to countervail the 'legacy' of Man's natural and unconscious origins and affinities. His tragedy lies in the ironic fact that, 'flesh-hinged mannikin' though he is, a puppet of the 'Prime Mover ... who pulls the strings,' he is also a mannikin 'that bleeds,' a 'figment' that 'feels.' (The theme of *The Truant* is also, of course, foreshadowed here.) Man's only hope, if there is a hope, and Hardy – as Pratt recognized in his essay – is uncertain, is that 'full Consciousness' characterized by 'Love and Light,' which are the substance of Compassion, will emerge and prevail: 'Consciousness the Will informing, till it fashion all things fair!'

While *The Great Feud* at first glance, or even upon more careful reading, may seem very remote from Hardy's epic-drama, as in many ways it is, the parallels between the two poems are extraordinarily close. And this is true not only of the central theme, but also of the pervasive determinism that shapes the action of both poems. In Pratt as in Hardy the notion that the 'viewless, voiceless Turner of the

Wheel' presides over the destinies of 'These flesh-hinged mannikins' is constantly reinforced. From the outset *The Feud* reiterates the idea that the migrations from sea to shore and from shore to land which precipitate the feud are, like the heedless movements and 'Clash of Peoples' in Hardy, the work of an impercipient but fateful force:

> It looked as if the destination
> Of all life of the stock marine
> Was doomed to be, through paths unseen,
> The most profound obliteration.

Pratt substantiates the notion by telling of the fishes' 'fear of racial doom,' of 'that strange insidious spark' which has infected them all, of 'that primal itch / For vengeance' which

> ... would expend its force
> According to an adverse Fate,
> Running a self-destroying course
> Down the blind alley of their hate.

He describes the turn of events which gives the sea its opportunity for 'the recompense / Of battle' as a 'quirk [cf. Hardy's 'prank'] that Nature flings / Into the settled scheme of things.' She it is, though 'No mortal vision may foretell / Her antics,' who breaks the 'spell' by '... a freak shifting of the odds / Within the sea-lap of the gods.' What follows is described as an 'elaborate escapade' played by 'the royal clowns of Fate.' In the background, aloof, but watching the 'great Tellurian feud,' stands the volcano 'Jurania,' which, in a later explanation of the poem, Pratt identified (still in Hardy's terms) as 'the Ironic Spirit ... preparing us for the general catastrophe.'

Like Hardy's, Pratt's viewpoint is also that of a cosmic spectator whose vision can encompass a whole vast land mass at once. Like Hardy too he conceives of that land mass, Australasia, in mythopoeic terms as a great animal or leviathan, which 'had its birth, / And vertebrated with Malay.' Hardy had seen Europe spread out beneath him 'as a prone and emaciated figure, the Alps shaping the backbone,' upon whose surface 'the peoples ... are seen writhing, crawling, heaving, and vibrating,' the armies moving 'snake-shaped, but occasionally with batrachian and saurian outlines' – not unlike the amphibians, reptiles, and other various creatures of Pratt's ancient world. The dinosaur of 'tragic birth,' Tyrannosauros Rex, who cannot distinguish friend from foe, but lays about him with indiscriminate ravage, also has his counterpart in Hardy: the 'Monster Devastation ... an unnatural Monster, loosely jointed, / With an Apocalyptic Being's shape ...'

One obvious difference between Pratt and Hardy is the seriocomic, even comic, touches which Pratt employs throughout much of the poem. Here *The Cachalot* was his model. It was that poem, he wrote, 'my first attempt to combine the serious and the comic in one production ... that gave me the cue for the Great Feud as a technique.' The poem, he felt, could properly be described as 'tragi-comedy': 'I could see life that way better than any other.' Besides, as he wrote, *The Feud* needed now and then 'a chuckle of humor' to prevent its being 'too ghastly and grim.'

One effect, however, of these recurrent chuckles of humour and the generally exuberant quality of the writing is to obscure the actual grimness of the poem's conclusion. Pratt no less than Hardy recognizes very clearly that the emergence of Reason or Intelligence cannot alone countervail the deeper and older 'natural legacies' of man's primitive origins. The behaviour of the ape, even after enlightenment, is evidence of this. As he wrote in 1954 in reply to a question about the meaning of the poem, 'Intelligence in the Ape could not prevent belligerency and destruction. A gas-chamber today is the result of an unusual intelligence ... And certainly torture is a human product.' 'Something beyond [intelligence or reason] is necessary.' What hope, then, does he see for man? So far as *The Great Feud* expresses it, not very much – or so it seems. Again he is close to Hardy. He at the end allows his propitious spirits a long, strong moment of optimism, but, as Pratt expressed it in his Hardy essay, 'Such gleams are ... not the flame of promise.' And Pratt, after 'the Ironic Spirit,' Jurania, has swept away most of his flesh-hinged mannikins beneath the deluge, leaves us only his 'female anthropoidal ape' – man after all must have an ancestor – 'cuddling her brood.' Even then, the only 'heralds' of a better day are 'Moans, / And croons, and drummings of the breast' – heralds of dawning compassion perhaps, but bearing still the taint of pain and sorrow. As he replied to his questioner in 1954, 'What happened to the ape after she returned to her brood? Well, that's another story and I had inflicted enough horror on my readers as it was.'

For all it may have owed to literary and other sources *The Great Feud* is, nevertheless, very much Pratt's own poem, a unique extravagant fantasy, which, while 'having an underlying meaning,' is first and above all a highly imaginative and often amusing adventure in hyperbolic story-telling. Despite all his assertions, both at the time and later, of the poem's 'serious intention,' one cannot but feel that his over-riding interest is in the unusual scope provided by his 'evolutionary theme' for dramatic and spectacular entertainment. Thus his materials, drawn from whatever 'sources,' are totally transformed into something audaciously original. It is doubtful whether Hardy himself would have discerned a single lineament of his own immanent visage in the scenario of Pratt's extraordinary 'Dream.' Only one reviewer, so far as I can discover, suspected a debt to the film *The Lost World*.

Pratt could probably have written a 'pre-historic fantasy' based only on the books he had read, but it would almost certainly have been a different poem. Not that it is 'based' on the film in any narrow sense. What, I think, it owes mainly to the film is the vivid realism of the spectacle presented. Reading the poem one cannot but be astonished by the sense conveyed of things actually seen, of events witnessed by human eyes which no human eye could have beheld – except in the guise of the *virtual life* that a motion picture can present. The curious fact, too, that from so vast a concourse of warring creatures there arises so little noise and clamour suggests the influence of the silent film. Throughout the poem it is the visual that is everywhere and overwhelmingly predominant. His later short poem 'Silences' is almost a kind of coda to *The Great Feud*, in which again the reptilian 'kills' are silent – as in the film.

(It is interesting to speculate on the influence of the cinema on Pratt as a narrative poet. He began, after all, when filmed entertainment was new and marvellous – and often very well done – and wrote his great narratives during its golden era. He was a film buff from his earliest days in Toronto, so that for many years his imagination, which was highly visual, was nourished almost as much on the cinema screen as on the printed page. Whether or not this fact was the reason, it is interesting to note that in his narratives his viewpoint is always that of the omniscient spectator, a cameraman behind an often cosmic lens, detached yet acutely observant, untrammelled by time or space, monarch of all he surveys, and surveyor of all that his imagination can conceive, whether the birth and global peregrinations of a great whale, the calving and vagrant progress of an iceberg, the historic pageant of the British nation culminating in Dunkirk – itself a documentary 'spectacular' – or the 'panorama' of the building of a transcontinental railway.)

The Great Feud finished, Pratt was glad to get away for a week-end at Bobcaygeon to potter in his garden and make some minor repairs before another cottage season began. Not that he expected to spend much longer at Bob than he had during the previous summer. Edgar had invited him on a motor trip to Chicago where Pelham was to attend a conference and stay on to teach summer school at the University. He had arranged for Pratt to give a recital of his poems at the conference. This safari would occupy much of June and, having accepted reappointment as a summer marker, Pratt would be compelled 'to remain in Toronto hard at it through most of July.' Deacon and his family would again take the cottage during June and part of July. Despite Deacon's ambivalence toward Pratt in public, they had so far maintained an amicable relationship in private, Pratt generously refusing to take payment for his use of the cottage and accompanying him to Bobcaygeon to see him installed there with his ménage: his wife (pregnant with their third child, soon to be born at the cottage), two small children (very audibly at an advanced stage of whooping cough), a maid, and the maid's mother.

On 8 June Pratt set out for Chicago with Edgar in his aging but still serviceable car; it was Pratt's longest journey by automobile and his first to the United States. Few details of the trip are known, except that it was leisurely with several stops en route for games of golf and a week-end of 'lavish luxury' in Detroit, where they were the presumed guests of 'a rich relative' of Edgar's, the relative later billing them for the full cost of her 'hospitality.' (The episode, once their chagrin had subsided, added another ironically amusing anecdote to their mutual repertoire.) Pratt's recital, his first of many in the United States, was, according to Edgar's report, 'a great success,' but the only correspondence to come to light in Pratt's hand from Chicago is a postcard to

Deacon saying that he had 'spent all day' at a museum 'getting acquainted with the animals of "The Great Feud".' (Deacon was already familiar with the poem. Writing in his column on 3 July during his stay at Bobcaygeon, he reported the appearance there of a 'large snapping turtle' which he had released off the end of Pratt's dock, 'thinking if such an ugly prehistoric relic bit him while in swimming it might inspire another epic fantasy like "The Feud".' But Pratt, it seems, was rather differently inspired: 'To find the brute and kill him.')

His duties for the Marking Board over by late July, Pratt was free at last to settle in at Bobcaygeon and tackle his next major project: the *Roosevelt-Antinoe* story. Suspecting that he would eventually re-tell it in his own way, he had written for copies of the New York and London papers which had carried the story. These he had already studied and now felt that he was ready to begin. He chose the 'light tetrameter' line used so successfully in *The Cachalot* and *The Feud*, but from the start he began to have, as he put it, 'troubles.' The rhythms which had swept his imagination forward in the other poems had a contrary effect on him now. The lines fell flat, the action refused to come to life, the whole spirit of the heroic rescue as he had first experienced it simply would not be evoked, and the attempt, as he said, 'fizzled': 'My metre failed and Pegasus limped. I gave it up.' But he knew that he would return to it again someday. He still believed that the great rescue deserved any immortality his verse might confer on it. But for the time being it would have to endure the mortality of newspaper prose.

His attempt to launch the new 'epic' having 'fizzled,' he turned to other less ambitious pieces, but there is no record of which poems they were. It is not unlikely that one of them – the number seems to have been small – was 'The Sea-Cathedral,' first published in *Acta Victoriana* in December that year. The poem deserves, I think, a little more attention than most of his short poems require here, since it is a particularly interesting illustration of how Pratt could be strongly influenced, even depend heavily upon, a published 'source' yet create something uniquely his own.

The source of 'The Sea-Cathedral' was, of course, Louis Noble's *After Icebergs with a Painter* (referred to earlier), his highly imaginative yet accurate account of the voyage made by Captain Knight, Pratt's grandfather, in 1859 with the American painter Frederic Edwin

Church. Pratt had long been familiar with the only book to record the exploits of one of his own kin and possessed a copy in the 1920s, probably brought with him from St John's after his 1925 visit. Possessed of a painter's eye and soul and a poet's vocabulary, Noble had written one of the most extensive and vividly detailed, if at times ecstatically rhapsodic, accounts ever published of icebergs seen close up. Pratt had often seen icebergs, but never as Noble had, close enough almost to touch, certainly to hear their 'purl / of linguals as the edges cut the sea,' and observe the minute details of their 'transcendent ... lines' and ever-changing 'festoons' of colour.

Pratt had clearly revelled in Noble's unusual pictorial and dramatic characterizations of the North Atlantic iceberg, as well as in his profusion of colourful phrases and imaginative images. Many are transferred almost intact to the poem; 'cathedral' and 'temple' are among Noble's favourite metaphors. The poem, indeed, exquisitely condenses into twenty-four lines of poetry almost the entire substance of Noble's hundred pages and more of descriptive prose. Unique to Pratt, however, is the ironic comment of his final stanza, which transforms the poem into something much more than descriptive rhapsody and removes it totally from the emotional and imaginative ambience of Noble's book. Like him Pratt sees the great cathedral of ice as epitomizing in its 'transcendent' form all the arts of man – architecture, sculpture, poetry, painting, music – a thing of beauty, majesty, and power, something to fill one with awe and admiration. But Pratt with a darker view of nature looks beyond the spectacle to the iceberg as it really is: for all its aesthetic and religious 'transcendence,' an ultimately sinister thing with a 'polar heart,' which can, though he waits for a later poem to say it, destroy a *Titanic* before being resolved once more into the primordial elements whence it came:

Within the sunlight, vast, immaculate!
Beyond all reach of earth in majesty,
It passed on southwards slowly to its fate –
To be drawn down by the inveterate sea
Without one chastening fire made to start
From altars built around its polar heart.

Nearly a decade later *After Icebergs with a Painter* was echoed in *The Titanic*, when the transmutation of Noble's

    ... facade and columns with their hint
    Of inward altars and of steepled bells
    Ringing the passage of the parallels ...

is even more radical and, for good reason, more ironic.

'The Sea-Cathedral' was long a favourite poem of Pratt's, reprinted many times and included in many a miscellaneous reading of his poems in public.

Having counted on the *Roosevelt-Antinoe* epic, now soundly dormant, to recreate his spirits during most of his six-weeks vacation, and having, it seems, disposed of other poems he had wished to work on, Pratt found himself at loose ends for the remaining weeks of his holiday. Since being at loose ends was a condition he did not enjoy, he needed something if not to interest at least to distract him. But there was nothing, not even a covey of kindred spirits to round up for a 'gorgeous weekend.' To make matters worse most of his neighbours had left, including Arthur Phelps, who had gone to attend the annual CAA convention in Vancouver. Pratt could not afford the expense and besides, as he wrote Deacon, 'I have been away enough from my family in June and July.' But surrounded by only 'mundane' things 'moving along ... slowly' and despite the presence of his small family, he was, he told Deacon, 'a bit lonely.' (He seems to have envied Deacon his larger brood, increased that summer to three. As one of eight children himself, Pratt would have liked being a more prolific paterfamilias than he was destined to be. 'Procreation is a wonderful natural gift,' he reminded Deacon, but it was one that would not bear fruit for him again.) He cheered himself a little by recalling that he could be worse off: 'with a house on a lake, a garden and a golf field not distant, and a punt these other mundane things slip by.' Deacon replied a few days later obligingly sending along 'a book to review for my early Fall Supplement to counteract the loneliness you speak of.' The book was 'an Alberta novel,' *New Furrows*, by Flora Jewell Williams, which he read without enthusiasm but dutifully reviewed as asked (*Saturday Night*, 4 December 1926). He felt, however, that the review was not '"any great shakes," as I can only accomplish anything worth while when I have the impulse to *let myself go*.' (Italics his, but how very true!) The book had generated no such impulse, nor had anything else for many days.

Pratt was thus ripe for any diversion that turned up. But it was undoubtedly the chronic precariousness of his personal finances and his still unquenchable dream of 'riches to come' which helped as much as his disconsolate mood to bestow the attraction of a lodestone and the dazzle of pure gold upon a dramatic sequence which had already begun elsewhere but which shifted its locale that summer to the village of Bobcaygeon.

Since the Pratts had first gone to summer at Bobcaygeon they had heard tales of a remarkable young man whose father had been Methodist minister there after the War. The Phelpses had got to know him, and Arthur's father had become a good friend of the Reverend Prosper Neville. He often spoke of his son, Herbert John Nelles ('Jack') Neville, as 'a good boy,' who had gone to New York while still in his teens to work for a brokerage firm, and who would no doubt soon make his fortune. He had long ago promised to do great things for his penniless father, such as buying him a house as large and splendid as the mansion owned by Bobcaygeon's wealthy lumber merchant, which they often passed as they walked together along the river bank.

By the middle 1920s stories of Jack Neville's amazing financial wizardry (he was then about twenty-three) were already being heard both in Toronto and in Bobcaygeon. And now the stories seemed proved true, for earlier that summer the huge, red-brick, gabled mansion and its large and beautiful park which he had longed for as a boy had been purchased in the young financier's name and his parents magnificently installed there. Soon, he himself and his young wife had arrived in equal magnificence aboard a luxurious motor-launch (bought from the Toronto magnate, Sir Joseph Flavelle), accompanied by an equipage befitting royalty: a peroxide blonde secretary, a nurse, several maids, a gardener, and a retinue of servants, including a Chinese cook, and a groom and liverymen to look after the stables, which soon contained more than a dozen fine horses. And the Bobcaygeon establishment was but the Nevilles' country estate. In Toronto Jack had acquired a palatial house on Whitney Avenue in fashionable Rosedale, which he had filled with handsome and costly furnishings. There could be no doubt that Jack Neville had made his fortune – somewhere, somehow.

Soon the Bobcaygeon mansion was the scene of the grandest gatherings the town had ever known. People of substance and status from

Toronto and elsewhere came to visit, were wined and dined, whisked round the lakes in the motor-launch and about the countryside in Neville's large chauffeur-driven automobile, told fabulous stories of his golden touch on the stock-market, and casually invited to entrust him with 'sure-fire investments' on their behalf. Many did so: the evidence of his magic was all too clear to resist.

Having been absent from the scene during most of the summer, Pratt had learned of the unlikely extravaganza in progress at Bobcaygeon only by report. His curiosity had been mildly piqued but he seems to have viewed it all rather sceptically – until he and Viola were invited to dine at the Neville mansion. Now he saw it all at close range and it truly seemed to be very real, and substantially based. He was, in Viola's words, 'caught at once – positively charmed.' Here was style, luxury, magnificence, abundance, hospitality, everything he could have wished for to fulfil his own ideal of a proper life-style – and all begotten by the son of an impecunious Methodist minister! Soon he found himself listening with mounting excitement to young Neville's easy talk of millions and how readily they could be come by if one had, as he did, 'inside information' and the 'right connexions.' Several of Pratt's friends had, in fact, already given Jack Neville sums of money to invest for them.

Pratt was already investing small sums here and there, now and then, and occasionally making a little profit, but nothing that could ever be called a 'killing.' He was, of course, always dreaming of one, and now at last the rainbow's end seemed to be looming into view. He had very little ready cash – he rarely did – but, once back in Toronto, he scraped together all he could lay hands on, cashed a few small bonds and an insurance policy, parted with a few possessions, and passed the proceeds over to the personable young Midas. More than this: with characteristic enthusiasm for something that had captured his imagination, and, as always, strongly moved to share his good fortune with others, convinced beyond a shade of doubt that his own was as good as made, he persuaded a number of his friends and relations to do likewise. Set up by him, in all good faith, his university friends (most of them no better off than he) were duly primed and pumped; his widowed mother-in-law talked into parting with her life's savings of several thousand dollars, and his wife's brother into investing five hundred. Ned Pratt with his knowledge of men and the world 'would certainly know whereof he spoke.' Small wonder that in the autumn of 1926 Pratt and his circle had visions of El Dorado close at hand.

The rest of the Jack Neville story took some months fully to unfold and cannot be recounted in detail here. But in so far as it affected Pratt and his friends, what followed thereafter may as well be briefly told now as later. The exigencies of strict chronology hardly warrant interrupting it *in medias res*.

Having garnered all the investments he could wring from his Toronto and Bobcaygeon 'clients,' Jack Neville departed to handle their business in person. No one was certain where he had gone, but it was assumed to be New York, where his chief 'business interests' were said to be. Before long, however, Pratt was surprised, but not unflattered, to get a letter from a well-known English duchess, who enquired whether he could vouch for one Mr John Neville who had approached her in a matter of finance and given her the name of the celebrated poet-professor as a reference. Pratt did his best to oblige. It was clear that the young broker was about his business: New York and London were both, it would seem, at his finger tips. He was surely a man who knew his way about the world of high finance.

He did indeed. In England he was following the same route he had taken in Canada: introductions to 'the best people,' a large country estate in Buckinghamshire, a chauffeur-driven limousine, and all the appurtenances of affluence and influence. Investment funds rolled in. But returns to investors seemed very slow to materialize. Soon they began to wonder and to make enquiries, especially when 'Lord' Neville, as he had begun to call himself, suddenly vanished from the British scene. Rumours began to circulate in Toronto, hints of bankruptcy proceedings, suggestions of fraud. But it was not until the following June, when stories began to 'break' in the Toronto and English papers, that panic struck the hearts of his trusting investors: Neville had disappeared again! Neville had been seen in Mexico (which had no extradition laws)! His wife had disappeared and her infant child abandoned in a Windsor hotel! The worst was confirmed when bailiffs seized the Rosedale mansion and a 'For Sale' sign appeared on the Bobcaygeon estate. The truth at last was out: Neville was an unmitigated scoundrel and his clients willing dupes.

How much he had plucked them for was never fully known, but it ran into millions. The University campus alone provided him more than a hundred thousand – including the painfully scraped-up dollars of E.J. Pratt. It was all gone – irrecoverably. So also were all his mother-in-law's savings. (She had died in March 1927 unaware of her loss, but her two sons who would have shared her cash assets were left with nothing as a consequence.) Many of Pratt's friends lost large amounts, several were quite ruined, and at least one committed suicide.

Pratt did nothing so drastic as that. Indeed, for weeks he refused to believe the lurid reports he heard and read, confident that Jack Neville could not possibly be a swindler. But at last he was forced to admit his deception. His own losses did not worry him greatly, and dashed hopes he had come to expect; he shrugged them off with ironic humour. But the distress he had helped to cause his friends was a much graver matter and for a while it hung heavy on his conscience. But since there was little he could do to make reparation, his resilient spirit soon threw off the burden. His faith in human nature had been dealt a severe blow, but it had not been obliterated. In fact, he found it hard wholly to suppress his admiration for the enterprising and daring young culprit. His deeds had been nefarious, but he had done them on a grand scale, magnificently, heroically, with flair and bold imagination. And Pratt had liked him: 'An amiable fellow – and immensely clever!' Nevertheless, speculator Pratt had learned his lesson. Thereafter he invested no more: 'No stocks! No bonds! No anything!' As he would observe, the affair had probably been providential: when the Great Crash came in 1929 he had absolutely nothing to lose!

So far as one can discover, the Neville affair did not move Pratt to poetry. But in one of his notebooks from the latter twenties there is an unfinished draft of a short story created around an unconscionable 'young Croesus' whose shady schemes and *modus operandi* are identical with those of Jack Neville down to the last theatrical flourish. Told in the first person, the story recounts in great detail, and with appropriate Leacockian touches, the talk of easy millions, the sumptuous wining and dining of prospective victims, all the visible signs of wealth, even the concern for impecunious clergymen. The tale is embellished with comic and satiric touches, but the facts, so far as they go, are the same as those in the actual history. The story breaks off before its dénouement, but enough has been written to show not only that, once the episode was over and done with, Pratt was able to look back with ironic humour at both his own trusting innocence and the young scoundrel's 'perfidity,' but also that, though verse had claimed him, he still had a hankering to write prose fiction, a fancy that would never leave him.

27

Public and Private

[With] our tendency to idolatry, we are inclined to forget that ... [those we idolize] were known to sleep, to eat, perchance to swear, to doff togas and don bathrobes ...

E.J. Pratt, foreword to *Our Great Ones*, 1932

RATT'S ROLE in the Neville affair does not seem to have been reported in the Toronto papers, though the story was fully told, including the involvement of certain unnamed Toronto professors. But this was not for lack of reporters' interest in Pratt himself as a personality, if not a 'character,' around the campus and about town. A friend of his, who remembered 'very well' his 'rise' in the twenties, has written (in a letter to me):

While it is true that a sizable public knew Ned Pratt through his published work ... by far the largest number knew him best as the subject of frequent newspaper items, personal stories of his golfing exploits, of his forgetfulness, his famous parties, and such. Many, of course, were merely of the anecdotal variety, because Ned Pratt was the sort of person to whom anecdotes stuck like barnacles to a barge. In this way as early as the middle 1920's a public legend of an unusual, but not unattractive, almost seriocomic or 'caricaturish' personality was growing up, which undoubtedly helped to publicize his poetry, but tended to make the man overshadow the poet. Perhaps in the long run this was not a bad thing. I know that Ned did nothing to discourage it ...

Ned didn't indeed. On the contrary he seems to have done much to foster it, even its serio-comic character, gladly welcoming anything, as he used to say, that 'promoted sales,' though he was actually far less calculating than he liked to pretend.

Most of the 'sketches' and 'stories' that featured him (mainly in the Toronto papers and journals, though often copied by others elsewhere), intended as they were for popular consumption, were of course superficial and anecdotal and often spiked with more than a dram of the fiction which Pratt himself was not averse to distilling. They are interesting nevertheless, both as an index to the kind of image the public formed of him and as a partial explanation of its peculiar appeal. Some of them were light-hearted, personal sketches appended to otherwise serious reviews of his poems. Phelps's anecdotal review of *Newfoundland Verse* in 1923 had been the first, but others had followed suit. A review of *Titans*, for example, ends with the following word of 'warning': 'Poetry is not the chief occupation of Ned Pratt. Neither is the teaching of English. His real business is golf. It is on the fairway that his spirits soar. A slice or a foozle breaks his heart, but a long, clean shot makes his face to shine like the sun ...' A reviewer even of *The Iron Door* (1927), which was a surprising departure from the 'ebullient gusto' of *The Cachalot* and the 'rollicking humour' of *The Witches' Brew*, cannot refrain from adding a personal vignette – if only to reassure his readers that the old Ned Pratt is still alive and well:

We cannot think, in spite of his Ode's 'high seriousness,' that Ned Pratt has really undergone a change. No man who dotes on golf and poker, who flies kites in Queen's Park on windy afternoons in spring [I have not been able to authenticate this particular eccentricity, but I have no reason to doubt it], who loves a ringside seat at a good prize-fight, who savours a chilled ale and a good cigar with the Boys at the Club, is likely to doff his spots overnight to become a permanent 'milk-white hind.'

But most of the items that built his 'legend' were quite independent of his reviews, ranging from brief, gossipy entries in the personal column to full-dress 'feature stories.' The latter were sometimes serious attempts to give accurate human interest portraits of the poet, but more often than not they comprised mostly factual trivia invested with hyperbole, sometimes more fiction than fact, but usually laughable and always innocuous: anecdotes about his 'golfomania' ('Every summer he takes two hundred golf balls with him to his cottage, [where] they become thoroughly lost in the juniper bushes ... Pratt hit upon the clever expedient of burning the bushes to recover the lost balls ... The bushes undoubtedly burned, but so did the balls.'); his absent-mindedness ('Dr. Pratt is always forgetting his rubbers or umbrella, or coming home with umbrellas [of] other people,' or 'The latest poet to have made a literary sensation in this country and in the United States is an absent-minded professor who sometimes goes to lectures wearing his wife's overcoat' (probably fictional, as was a similar story, current at the time, of his having shown up for a morning class without his trousers); his stag parties ('Though addicted to golf "Ned" Pratt's favourite recreation is probably entertaining "the lads" – though they often include prominent poets, artists, businessmen and politicians – at dinner in the Club or at home followed by poker, cigars, and a bottle or two'); or his own stories about himself ('Canada's leading poet is fond of telling stories, particularly about his early life. They are invariably comic. A favourite concerns a home-brewed cure-all he once concocted and peddled round his native Isle'). Sometimes a single bizarre incident was spun into a column-length story, such as appeared in the Toronto *Star Weekly* on 24 December 1926: 'E.J. Pratt ... is not alone a producer of Titanic poetry (the kind men stop each other to speak about at the street corners), but admits that from the golf tee he has, at least once, been responsible for a gargantuan gesture ...' The item goes on to tell an unlikely tale (but basically true) of how, 'letting drive a terrific crack ... like a cannon shot,' Pratt had made, not a hole-in-one (as he was once reported, erroneously, to have done), yet a very palpable, if unintentional, hit – 'square on the nose' of an unwary road-mender driving a team of horses. The blow knocked the man headlong into a creek, but it also obviated the necessity, and the expense, of surgery on a huge boil which had for days disfigured the aforesaid nose! Sometimes an even more expansive 'feature' accompanied by a photograph brought him the celebrity of headlines, such as one appearing in the winter of 1930 entitled (in large print) 'The Stove Was Too Big but Pratt Fixed That.' Told with much gratuitous embellishment, it is the story (again basically true) of his purchasing for his Bobcaygeon cottage a 'magnificent' second-hand stove whose installation necessitated a carpenter's not only enlarging the doorway, but also making drastic and disastrous alterations to a kitchen which had been 'a model of neatness ... arranged to the exact liking of the chatelaine.' The 'crowning touch of disaster,' however, was 'the discovery that the stove wouldn't work.' It was sold to a junk dealer for fifty cents, having cost ten dollars and the carpentry eighty-five.

It is not surprising that nourished by such stories and many others of a similar kind, most of which never got into print, a legend, a somewhat caricaturish one, should have taken root and grown, such as no literary figure (not even Leacock) had ever given rise to before in Canada. Pratt himself, with his hyperbolical if not wholly fictive stories of his own exploits, débâcles, and follies, his deliberate dramatizations of his own shortcomings, his desire to present a certain kind of character, was, as I have said, largely the author of the legend. He had long ago chosen the character he wished to play, one who was not only the opposite of all those stereotypes he detested most, but who also manifested the virtual antitheses of many of the traits which his natural inheritance, his early home environment, and his subsequent training and occupations might have been expected to bring forth. Nor can one believe that he disapproved of the touches of caricature which the legend early acquired. He was a believer in the 'truth' of caricature. In a foreword (quoted from at the head of this chapter) to a collection of linocut cartoons of Canadian historical personages, he described as a 'promising sign' of 'cultural progress' the recording of 'national biography ... through the medium of caricature.' Defining its function as the exhibition 'by controlled exaggeration' of the 'quirks and salients of human character,' he went on to write:

It does happen indeed that the only thing which posterity remembers in the life of an individual is the size and colour of his nose, when all the other features of the proprietor have disappeared in the mist. Immortality in such cases is pre-eminently the gift of the caricaturist ... For, with our tendency to idolatry, we are inclined to forget that those dynamic personalities not only thundered in Parliament and from the rostrum, but that they were known to sleep, to eat, perchance to swear, to doff togas and don bathrobes, and it is therefore fitting that, in addition to striking their official gestures in oil and marble and bronze, they should be lured into giving their unguarded intimacies in linoleum ...

There can be little doubt that Pratt wished for himself no immortality that comprised only his 'official gestures,' that did not show 'the quirks and salients ... which live longer in the public mind than the more sedate and self-conscious qualities.' If, as he wrote, 'Immortality in such cases is pre-eminently the gift of the caricaturist,' he would ensure that *his* caricaturist saw much to inscribe, and, if need be, would himself be his own.

Pratt's public image was not, of course, wholly one of caricaturish eccentricities, nor did his image and reputation depend solely on newspaper stories and the circulated anecdotes of his friends. A considerable and constantly growing, if particular, public knew him in roles where 'official gestures' and 'the more sedate and self-conscious qualities' were much more in character than 'quirks and salients.' For as time went on and his generous good nature came to be more widely known, demands for his attention, calls for his help and favours, poured in from all sides. It is hard, indeed, to conceive how he managed to do any writing at all. The siren voices of golf, poker, the cinema and theatre, and other forms of social relaxation and entertainment were distracting enough, but being constantly enmeshed in far less agreeable enterprises both public and private must have been dreadfully destructive of imaginative creativity. By nature prone (and by Methodist and maritime upbringing trained) to respond to all and sundry calls for help and favours, from the mid 1920s onward he was rarely without some extra-poetic, extra-professional chore to perform. His lingering ministerial connections invited in particular the predatory attentions of church and women's groups. As a novelist friend of his, who knew him well for many years, expressed it (in a letter to me):

Ned was ... in a way too Methodist for his own good, because the Methodist do-gooders in Toronto exploited his energies. He did all kinds of speeches and so forth for stupid women's clubs, and lacked a certain ruthlessness an artist must have in those matters if he is to survive. It would have been fatal to him had he been a novelist ...

But 'speeches and so forth' to 'stupid' clubs were by no means the full extent of the exploitation he allowed himself to suffer for years, nor were his more formal lectures and recitals. He was constantly being called on too for such gratuitous chores as giving editorial advice (having allowed his name to grace the mastheads of more journals both short- and long-lived than he could recall), judging poetry contests (a burgeoning feature of both local and national poetry groups in the twenties and thirties), handing down private critical verdicts to aspiring authors who constantly badgered him with pleas 'to be so good as to look over ... etc.,' lending support to numberless 'worthy causes,' being a sponsor of this and a patron of that, and occasionally working behind the scenes on some major project which emerged before the public in someone else's name. One instance of this last was a compendious school anthology for which he performed the whole laborious, time-devouring job of selecting the contents, though the book was published – and sold well for years – in the name of the editor who had solicited his help, without so much as an acknowledgment of Pratt's vital and excellent work, much less any remuneration for it. This was a role he came increasingly to fill; from the early 1930s to the 1950s there were few anthologies of poetry published in Canada which he did not help to make, usually without credit and, of course (for which he was sometimes thankful), without blame.

Fortunately his teaching duties were generally kept to a comfortable minimum, though they were onerous enough, especially while he found it financially necessary to continue his extension classes at St Catharines – until the late 1920s. But Pelham Edgar usually did his best not to burden his one-time protégé with more teaching than was 'desirable for a man of letters,' though he was often less considerate when it came to conscripting him for some extra-academic chore. Pratt himself usually contrived to limit his other academic services, avoiding much committee work and similar intramural duties not only by refraining from seeking them, but also, and mainly, by deliberately projecting an image of bumbling incompetence, absent-mindedness, and general impracticality. Not that he escaped them all; but it was a common judgment heard in the halls and offices of Victoria College that 'good old Ned Pratt' could add little to the efficiency of any board or committee which had 'real work to do.' There were few objections, least of all from Pratt, to the omission of his name from such official rosters. Apart, then, from attending perfunctory faculty meetings and other such traditional conclaves now and then, he was generally left to go his own way – though, of course, besides his classroom teaching such ancillary chores as monitoring examinations, marking scripts, and 'advising' students were part of his normal routine.

Yet he was by no means so free to follow his own bent as he would have liked. Even during the long summer vacation much of his 'free' time was not his own. His salary still small and his poetry bringing in next to nothing, he found it necessary to spend the greater part of each summer in some kind of supplementary employment, at first, in the twenties – as we have seen – marking high school examination scripts, and then, from the latter twenties on, teaching at summer schools in Toronto, Halifax, Vancouver, and, for more than a decade, in Kingston, Ontario. (Happily, though hardly by coincidence, he always found himself close to a good golf course, but one doubts the assertion of some of his friends that he took summer teaching appointments 'not for the money, which was always spent before it was earned, but for the sake of playing golf on a new course.') For many years too, he was glad to write, for a few cents a line, innumerable book reviews and literary columns and edit a number of texts for use in the schools. Never during more than thirty years on the Faculty of Victoria College was he granted a single session, not to mention a full year, of sabbatical or any other kind of salaried leave, apart from a few weeks now and then for an 'expenses only' recital tour. Dogged by the ironic fate that clung to him, at least in the realm of material reward, he was to have come and gone too early for any of the bounties which in later years were to lighten a little the burdens of academic life. Respectable salaries and commensurate retirement pensions, health insurance and leave entitlement, Canada Council benefactions and other such largess had not yet cast even shadows before when in 1953 he would go into honourable retirement with a testimonial dinner and a handshake.

It would, in fact, have made little difference to Pratt, materially or otherwise, had he had a larger portion of this world's goods. They would have vanished as quickly and unaccountably as did his 'allowance' each month, as well any small windfall that occasionally happened his way: a gift from Calvert ('the family Midas'), the sale of a 'Kenworthy house,' a medal of honour with a cheque attached, an honorarium for some public service or other. He was 'quite hopeless' (both his wife and banker assured me) at handling money. It was not that he was so high-minded as to be above such trivial and mundane concerns; he loved the thought of having money, longed for more, and as we have witnessed, often dreamed up ways of 'making a mint.' Yet he never repined at his lack of it, spending what little came to him joyously and often improvidently. His attitude toward money for a 'family man' was in fact almost juvenile if not irresponsible. Always he viewed it – there were still traces of the outporter in him – in terms of immediate, never deferred, satisfactions, though someone else's as often as his own. The occasional investments he made – until he had learned his hard lesson – were always short-term ones made in expectation of a quick killing.

After Jack Neville absconded with their small reserve in 1927, Viola assumed chief responsibility for manipulating the family purse-strings, and the following year herself took a job. Pratt had his own small bank account, replenished monthly, but his balance never grew, though he usually managed to remain slightly solvent. Not always, as the following excerpt from a letter to Edgar vividly demonstrates:

A cheque for fifty dollars ... was returned N.S.F. from the Royal Bank ... I didn't know how much I had with them. It turned out to be only seven dollars, but the bastards should have carried me for a few weeks ... I wrote and gave them hell – worded the remonstrations so strongly that they didn't reply. I shall try another bank.

Where his money went he rarely knew, though, in the words of a university colleague, 'there was many a sum that went to give a hand-out to a plausible mendicant or accommodate with a "temporary" loan a professed friend.' His colleague was not exaggerating. In the course of the years his *known* beneficiaries included not only bankrupt poets, painters, and other 'promising geniuses,' but proprietors of struggling 'little magazines,' impecunious students, unemployed charladies, bar-tenders, pugilists, and other miscellaneous vagabonds.

His vulnerability to both 'plausible mendicants' and 'professed friends' – at least once a professed enemy, of whom more later – lay not only in his reputation as 'an easy touch' but also in his always exuding an air of benevolent affluence. And somehow, inexplicably, he usually managed to live up to his aura. Again and again his friends have described Ned Pratt as a veritable 'walking paradox' (as one of them phrased it): though always 'broke,' he was never without money when the occasion arose. He boasted of 'loving luxury' and 'fine things,' yet his tastes were simple, and the 'luxuries' he occasionally bought were usually cheap and often tawdry. He prided himself, too, on his frugality, but while he would, for example, return as 'too expensive' a dime's worth of shoe-tacks – like his father, he was his own cobbler, after a fashion, for years – next day he might spend his last ten dollars on dinner for a 'friend' he had met for the first time. He was known, too, to drive his car (when finally he could afford one) down to the College 'to save shoe-leather' and walk home 'to save gas.'

It is not surprising that Pratt endeared himself to almost everyone who came to know him, that letters I have had from both old friends of his as well as casual acquaintances have been virtually unanimous in his praise as 'a rare and engaging character.' Selection from these letters is difficult to make, but here is how Louis MacKay, poet and classical scholar, who knew him well in the twenties and thirties, has described him:

Ned was a prince, an absolute prince, with a princely disregard for unimportant things, and a princely obstinacy about things he found important. What sticks in my memory particularly is a sort of high-spirited innocence. You couldn't imagine him doing a mean thing, not because he would have rejected it, but because it would never have occurred to him. This is perhaps one reason why he responded so naturally and immediately to the heroic – he recognized it at once, and felt at home with it.

I have known him serious, but I think gaiety is what I remember first and most about him ... I don't recall much talk about poetry, or about literature at all; we used to talk about almost everything else in the world; in particular we shared a layman's interest in science. Poetry, at least one's own poetry, was something one did, not something one talked about. You may have heard from other sources the very characteristic story ... about someone quoting a line of verse, and Ned remarking 'That's good, that's damn good. Who wrote that?' 'You did, Ned' ... He was interested in the next poem he was going to write. Those that he had written, he was through with ... He took poetry seriously; he liked doing it, and he knew he did it well; but he never took it solemnly, at least not that I ever heard. He was a great connoisseur of limericks, some of which ... display a startling virtuosity; I do not recall any of his composition, but his stag-parties were a powerful medium for the preservation of oral tradition ...

Sooner or later the recollections of all his intimates converge upon his parties and dinners, sometimes to illustrate his convivial nature – 'he loved conviviality and nothing was more enlivening than to share a glass and conversation in a company of which he became by common consent the centre' (Robert Finch) – and sometimes to reveal a trait of character more easily described than defined:

I remember one famous dinner when we were told to expect wild duck shot by Ned near his summer cottage at Bobcaygeon. We sat down to a pair of fat but pallid ducks which seemed genuine enough, except for colour, because of the pellets, which we stored at the sides of our plates. It turned out that our hunter had failed to get a duck, but rather than let the party down, he had bought two dressed from a poulterer and shot them on a fence post! (Eric Arthur)

By 1926 such convivial occasions, for which he was in many minds almost as celebrated as for his poetry, had become regular features of his social ritual – his new volume, *Titans*, published late that year, was dedicated to 'the boys of the stag parties' – though actually they were less frequent than some of his old friends have recalled. He did not, as someone has written, sit 'eternally at the table, a large cooked bird before him, congenial men around him.' Yet because so many of his friends remembered him best and happiest as the genial host this became in their minds, next to golf, his most frequent and characteristic occupation. It was certainly something he loved to do, a necessary part of the role of full-handed benefactor and disinterested patron which he coveted and would have liked to perform much oftener than he was able.

His dinner parties, as distinct from his stags, were usually occasions, gala affairs held to mark some signal accomplishment, a new book of poems, the presence of some celebrity whom he wanted his friends to meet, or merely because he hankered for another 'festive affair.' The guests might number from half a dozen intimates to fifty or more friends and peripheral acquaintances – all carefully chosen, however – crammed into living-room and dining-room of the moderate-sized house on Tullis Drive, later on Cortleigh Boulevard. These events, thanks to Viola's meticulous attention to detail, impeccable taste, and long, patient hours of preparation, were models of table elegance and dining etiquette, as well as gustatory regalement. Pratt himself, who tended to see them as *his* dinners, usually received the lion's share of the credit and the praise, but most of it was due entirely to his capable and hard-working wife in her role not only of chatelaine and hostess, but also of *chef de cuisine*.

For many years in early autumn – when again Viola was called on for valorous service behind the scenes – his entire freshman class of sixty or more students was fêted at home by Professor Pratt, and smaller groups of senior students invited in for 'a good meal' from time to time throughout the term. Often, if the group was not too large, he would take them downtown to a postprandial concert or motion picture. Few of them ever forgot these events. Here is a recollection of one, but typical of many:

I remember that Pratt took me to the first talking movie I ever saw. We had dinner at his house; afterward we went down to Loew's Uptown Theatre. The picture we saw was a silent picture that had had voices dubbed in. Ned was greatly excited about it; it caught his imagination: 'Oh, this has a wonderful future!' He could see that while it sounded rather crude to most people, a mere fad, it was a sign of things to come. We thoroughly enjoyed it and went back to his house and talked about it until the early hours of the morning ...

His stag parties, which were more frequent than his dinners, were usually – though not always – gratuitous, informal, extempore affairs, a crew of his cronies gathered up by telephone as the whim struck him. Here, for example, is how in a letter to Edgar he described one such impromptu, 'drummed up' while, teaching at summer school, he lived alone, his wife and daughter being at Bobcaygeon:

Wednesday evening ... I felt rather lonely for my old friends so I drummed up a monster stag at our house, the largest ever. That afternoon I played out a foursome at York Downs – Malcolm Wallace, J.S. MacLean, Arthur Meighen, and I, and we decided to end up at 25 Tullis Drive. I rounded up post-haste fourteen men ... We had a snack at midnight, O'Keefe's and Sandwiches and lobster (Newfoundland). We sang the national Anthem, toasted you and several other absentees. One of the jokes of the evening was the fact that all cars had to be parked up near Yonge St. The immortal red light still stands in front of Tullis Drive. 'Road under repair.' It is still there and will be for the next ten years. Wallace remarked on turning the corner that he always knew Ned's street from the red light.

The names of only three of his golf partners convey some idea of the astonishing heterogeneity of his cronies: Wallace was a professor of English at University College, a scholar and a critic; MacLean was a prominent business executive; and Arthur Meighen was, of course, the hapless, erstwhile Conservative Prime Minister – briefly twice in the 1920s – who, after his defeat by Mackenzie King in 1926, migrated from the world of politics where he had spent the previous twenty years to that of high finance in Toronto. Here he soon struck up a friendship with Pratt, 'whose salty humour and good conversation,' writes Meighen's biographer, 'were among the pleasures ... [he] savoured for the rest of his days.' Many years later Pratt would recall his eccentricities as a golfer with humour and affection: 'When he came within range of the pin he became more deliberate ... He would take a parliamentary stance and by some kind of calculus known only to himself he would assess all the factors and then strike. The pin was up there like a political opponent which had to be out-manoeuvred, not so much reached as attacked.'

Although Pratt enjoyed a 'glorious dinner,' when the guests were often of both sexes, his stags were, nevertheless, his favourite fêtes. These, when his family was at home, he would sometimes hold at a hotel or one of his clubs. But there were many times when Viola was again called on to lay 'the real foundation of the spree.' When the guests arrived, writes Claire, 'she and I would repair to the upper regions ... while the smoke and singing would drift upwards and fill the house. There were many such occasions ...' To quote R.S. Knox, a long-time regular:

It was as host to a group of his male friends that he was socially in his element. Ned puffing at his cigar and the box sent round; his stories, often against himself, laughingly told between puffs; the good talk on varying levels, the good refreshment – these were grand evenings. After dinner, for which Ned had invented a series of humorous toasts, there would generally follow the evening's sport, poker. The betting was kept within academic limits and no one was allowed to lose much. Ned, as I recollect, was seldom the winner. He had neither the poker face nor the cunning. For him and for the rest of us the game was merely the setting for the talk ...

Knox is unquestionably right about Pratt: it was the conversation that flowed at his dinners and stags that he enjoyed most. He liked to see plentiful good food and drink before him, but his appetite for neither was great. Though he deliberately created the impression of being both a gourmet and a gourmand, and at times even a carouser, he was actually none of them. As one of his early stag party regulars described him, 'Ned was an epicure in imagination only.' As Knox has said, it was the talk that mattered most to him. He had many friends whom he rarely invited to his parties, men of intellect and accomplishment, but whose presence and conversation would have killed the spirit of free and easy, often juvenilely boisterous, camaraderie which he liked to prevail at such events.

It was chiefly for this reason, rather than any lack of interest in the sex, that he usually preferred to have no women present. However frank and earthy his conversation among men, the code of an earlier Victorian-puritan era, bred deeply in him from childhood, prohibited his being anything but the decorous 'gentil knyght' in the presence of woman. But among his peers – yet not quite peers, for although his was an Arthurian Round Table, theoretically egalitarian, his role was that of the King whose chair no one else might fill – he could revel in 'jest not made for dainty ear' and talk 'not fashioned for gentle lip.' Yet, as we have seen and will see again, he was no misogynist and had many close women friends, though it is probably true that women also constituted a majority of those people whom he disliked. He could endure, though painfully, a boring male – once. But a female who bored or annoyed him – with small talk, vacuity, pretensions, hauteur, or bad verse – he could ruthlessly and unceremoniously, though without noticeable discourtesy, 'shuck off with a skill and ease that were marvellous to witness.'

This picture of Pratt in the character of convivial bon vivant does not, of course, show the whole man. There were depths and recesses within where sheltered an 'other self' (to use Viola's term), a self not unlike the sensitive, vulnerable, insecure and 'delicate' boy from the outport manse. Few, even of those who knew him best, seem to have fully perceived this other Pratt. Arthur Phelps undoubtedly did; he speaks of seeing 'allegro' and 'penseroso' personalities in the man. And Lorne Pierce distinguished an 'Apollonian' and a 'Dionysian' personality. Viola Pratt went further, describing him as 'in a sense several personalities – different personalities.' She agreed that the character he displayed to most of his friends, 'the stag party host, the "hail-fellow-well-met",' was 'very much on the surface,' though she also agreed that he depended heavily on his 'social occasions' as means of escape from 'his other self.' This other self, she admitted, was 'difficult to plumb, intangible, but very real': 'In spite of his seeming lighthearted outlook on life, he took life very seriously ... He was really a very sensitive and emotional person, with feelings that ran very deep ... Like his mother, he could cry very easily. Tears were often near the surface even when they didn't show ...' It is not surprising that he shunned by every possible device any emotional upheaval which might cause the tender, 'womanish' side of his nature to break through what he wished to be seen as a tough, masculine exterior. Highly susceptible to the sentimental, he was nevertheless undoubtedly speaking the truth when he declared, as he often did, that he *hated* sentimentality.' His 'hatred' was directed, it seems, toward a part of himself of which he was ashamed and which he felt he must conceal. Much of what is most recognizably Prattian in the style, tone, and temper of his poetry derives, I believe, from an almost obsessive anxiety to control, if not suppress, his other, susceptible self.

Though a different kind of emotional response, anger too he strove to avoid; when fully roused it was an emotion that shook him to the depths of his being, raising tempests within that both agonized and embarrassed him. Consequently he avoided if at all possible anything that might move him to anger, at least in public. He could swear royally under his breath, or, among friends, curse someone or something that deeply, genuinely vexed him. But because he could be profoundly moved, yet lacked the hardihood and sang-froid to vent his feelings, confidently and comfortably, face to face, he preferred to quell them or direct them into other channels. Better to swallow an offence, deflect it with a humorous retort, purge it by writing a vituperative letter which, more often than not, he destroyed next day. For similar reasons, though he enjoyed engaging in 'peaceful debate' with 'reasonable people,' he dreaded embroilment in even a warm argument, and became very adept at manoeuvring into a more peaceable course a conversation which threatened to brew one. Though he could – and occasionally did – wield a respectable, if reluctant, cudgel when forced to do so by something he could not dismiss, he would much rather pretend to acquiesce than run the risk of an altercation. Yet, as we know, he had 'a passion for fights' – from a safe distance. There is no doubt, as I have remarked elsewhere, that this 'passion,' as well as the apparent delight in violence which many of his poems suggest, were largely if not wholly vicarious means of rectifying the balances of his own nature. As he wrote of his cachalot whale's herculean exploits, they 'gave me an opportunity vicariously to express my Irish love of a fight without bodily injury to myself or to my colleagues.'

Knowing himself no hero, he nevertheless admired the heroic, the defiant, and the strong, though he could not but feel sympathy for those like himself, sensitive, unaggressive men, who must band together for survival or heroic action. There is little doubt that 'Ned, the stag party host' was primarily for him a role in which he could assume the outward characteristics of a kind of hero, larger than life, a focal figure, very male and very brave, without the least risk to himself or his delicate sensibilities.

28

Hymns Devout, Brickbats, and Roses

No Englishman could have written *Titans*. It was necessary that the author of
this volume should have been bred beside the unpeopled waters.

Barker Fairley, *The Canadian Forum*, February 1927

N THE AUTUMN of 1926, for the first time in nearly two
years, Pratt had no major poem 'on the stocks.' *Titans* (containing *The Cachalot* and *The Great Feud*) had gone to press,
and the *Roosevelt-Antinoe* project had been laid aside until he
felt more confident of grappling successfully with it. Having resigned
the Vice-Presidency of the Toronto Branch of the CAA and with few
short poems he was anxious to finish, he was persuaded for the first
time to accept what amounted to a commission to write verse. It had
come from his Church, the newly created United Church of Canada,
which was preparing, as a joint celebration of its own consummation
of union and the Diamond Jubilee of Canadian Confederation, a great
religious 'musical and pictorial pageant.' As the only Canadian poet of
stature who was also an ordained clergyman – though 'lapsed' as he
often reminded his friends – he was an obvious choice to write new
hymns and other verse needed for 'the massive production' ('nearly
300 persons in costume'). He protested that religious verse was no
longer his line, but Denzil Ridout, the indefatigible begetter of the
venture, was most persuasive: he had already engaged the services of
Dr (later Sir) Ernest MacMillan, Principal of the Toronto Conserva-
tory of Music, to write new tunes for any hymns which E.J. Pratt
composed.

Unlikely though it was for the poet he had become, the commission
was accepted and its execution set about with apparent energy if not

enthusiasm. But it proved to be a largely perfunctory exercise. Neither the subject nor the occasion allowed Pratt much scope for original creativity or imaginative embellishment. As he had observed shortly before, 'I can only accomplish anything worth while when I have the impulse to *let myself go.*' Such an impulse was clearly fleeting, if not wholly absent. His five hymns are probably the best of his contribution, though they add little to his reputation as a poet. The chef-d'œuvre of his hymnody, the anthem 'Thou God of All the Peoples,' written as the keystone of the entire pageant, is in fact a rather banal iteration of the doctrine of equality before God, combined with an equally banal prayer for mutual understanding among Canada's multiracial peoples. His other verse is equally lacking in celestial fire, though he generates a degree of fervour when describing, in the closing scene, a vision of the 'crowning days that are to be' when the triumph of the 'Galilean creed' has transformed Canada and the world into a utopian (mildly socialist) Christian Commonwealth of Man. (Though he was never a political zealot, his political views at the time were, and continued to be for many years, mildly socialist, views of which his church would have strongly approved. Later dubbed by some 'Red Ned,' he was in fact never so much as a fellow traveller.) Interestingly enough it is when he occasionally allows himself to touch upon the 'old fundamentals' of religion that he rises to the only heights of 'near-poetry' in the whole of his pageant verse:

> Give us the starry faith serene
>   That glows within a clouded night,
> The hold upon the things unseen,
>   The promised core of morning light
> That trust which, in a burned desire,
> Can take refinement from the fire.

The lines are almost Prattian, but such moments are few.

In both substance and craftsmanship it was all a very improbable work for the poet of *The Witches' Brew* and *Titans.* But his church seems to have thought well of it, declaring in its official organ (*The United Church Record*, April 1927) that the 'presentation' demonstrated that 'erudition and creative ability' can be 'combined to produce a popular pageant.' And not only was his verse used in the 'grand performance' at Massey Hall in March 1927 (when the author had a front-row seat), but many years later much of it was resurrected and reused by the United Church in a similar celebration.

Whether the knowledge of his mother's rapidly deteriorating health influenced his accepting the unlikely commission is not known, but it is not an improbability. His learning of her impending death coincided with his agreeing to take on the task, which he may well have seen as a last opportunity to show her that he had not wholly abandoned his covenanted calling. Whether or not she lived long enough to hear any of his new verse – being blind she could not have read it – is also unknown. She died in December, soon after publication of *Titans*.

Titans was published simultaneously in Great Britain and the United States toward the end of October, but its publication in Canada had to await the arrival of copies from England, where all the printing and binding was done. Deacon, in *Saturday Night*, reported on 30 October that 'E.J. Pratt's "Titans" is supposed to be on the Atlantic Ocean (appropriate locality) en route to Macmillans,' but it was early December before it went on sale in Toronto.

Since the publication of *The Witches' Brew* and the first appearance of *The Cachalot* (in the *Forum*), the reading public had come to expect the extravagant and the spectacular of Pratt, so that the new book came as no surprise. Nevertheless its impact on the public imagination – *The Feud*, after all, was new – was generally a resounding one. And what is most significant is that many of the reverberations, now almost for the first time, were touched off by qualities of the poetry more central to its imaginative totality than its 'vigorous, red-blooded verse,' 'delightfully daring diction,' and 'exuberant descriptions.' Though most were uncertain about the 'intention' of *The Feud*, many reviewers seem to have suddenly realized that Pratt for all his 'infinite gusto' and 'Aristophanic humour' was a far 'deeper' poet than *The Brew* or even *The Cachalot* on its first appearance had suggested. Taken along with *The Feud*, linked to it under a common, provocative title, *The Cachalot* also assumed new dimensions and these were seen to extend beyond the superficies of technique. If the critics (reviewers, that is: no one dared to write a full-dress critique of Pratt for another decade, such was the diffidence of Canadian critics to seize a new man and venture a 'definitive' assessment of him in a void) – if the critics were less titillated by grotesqueries and pyrotechnics than they had been on imbibing *The Brew*, or less admiration-struck by 'virility,' 'extravagance,' and 'expansiveness' than on first encountering *The Cachalot*, they were now (some at least) made aware, reading *Titans*, of more substantial qualities in Pratt's poetry, more conscious and appreciative of its real imaginative power, range, and depth. Though there was still in the reviewers' critiques little that can be called detached, analytical criticism, *Titans* evoked in general something more solid and specific than 'wonder, love, and praise.'

If, however, the first full review of the book to appear in Canada had been typical, its reception would have been very mixed, to say the least. W.A. Deacon, who had been first to hail *Newfoundland Verse* and, rather less unequivocally, *The Witches' Brew*, made sure to be first heard again, but this time in a screed that carefully took with one hand what it gave with the other. Pratt had been apprehensive about Deacon's reception of the book. It is true he had praised *The Cachalot* (briefly) in public when it had appeared in the *Forum* a year earlier, but had been decidedly non-committal toward *The Feud* when Pratt had allowed him to read it earlier that year. Besides, he had already taken the precaution – so it seemed to Pratt and his friends – to temper beforehand, if not forestall, any profusion of accolades which *Titans* might evoke. Having previously read both poems in the book, he was well aware of its unique contents, and must have foreseen that it would be well received. Yet he had, in effect, already proclaimed that it was not to be the most significant book of new Canadian poetry to appear in 1926. That distinction he had just laid upon a fat volume of mediocre, mostly traditional verse entitled *Out of the Wilderness*, published in October by Wilson MacDonald. In a 4,000-word review of extraordinary misjudgment, while admitting that Pratt had 'restored narrative verse to a prestige it has not enjoyed in a generation,' Deacon went on in the same breath to declare that '1926 derives its greatest distinction from the fact that it is the year of the emergence of Wilson MacDonald ... as Canada's leading poet.' More than this, he had 'taken his place in the front rank' of *all* Canadian poets, 'the first successful challenger' of the 'supremacy' of the Group of the Sixties. Deacon predicted for MacDonald 'a harvest that will raise his fame' both at home and abroad 'above that of any of his seniors.' Knowing that Deacon's mind was already made up, Pratt had little doubt that if

'Billy' deigned to write a review at all, its tone would be pitched in a very different key from the one in which he had hymned MacDonald.

A swipe at MacDonald and a benison on Pratt, quite fortuitously delivered by Douglas Bush in the *Forum* almost simultaneously with publication of *Titans*, did nothing to dispose the Literary Editor of *Saturday Night* more favourably toward either Pratt or his new book. In a brief but rather mordant critique of Canadian writing in general, Bush, in 'Making Literature Hum,' had singled out MacDonald and Pratt for special attention. 'MacDonald,' he wrote, 'abandons himself to vague, undisciplined, and rather naive emotion; his poems have ... almost no intellectual content.' Though better than many Canadian poets, he illustrates 'the vices of Canadian verse in general,' which Bush described as 'an inadequate and untutored critical instinct, a Swinburnian inclination to invertebrate rhapsodizing, or the accumulation of sounds without any particular meaning.' Pratt he had singled out as the one exception, 'whose *Cachalot* ... confirmed the author's possession of a sinewy and arresting style, and a masculine imagination at home among the elemental energies of the sea and its creatures.'

If Deacon was peeved he appears to have taken no direct action in response to Bush's broadside. But not so MacDonald. He not only waxed 'furious,' but shortly concocted a story, which he began to circulate, that Pratt, using the name 'Bush' as a pseudonym, had himself written the *Forum* article in order, as Pratt reported it to Pierce, 'to glorify myself and belittle him.' 'Of course,' Pratt continued, 'no one around here [at the University] would believe it, but what damage he could do in remoter places I can imagine. He's a desperately dangerous fellow. Some of my friends here suggested a denial of it in the *Forum*, but I refuse because it would seem as if I took his slander seriously.' It is unlikely that Deacon believed MacDonald's story: he knew Ned Pratt to be no skulker and Doug Bush no fiction. (Bush at Harvard was highly amused by the story.) Nevertheless, the invidious juxtaposition of the names MacDonald and Pratt in the widely read *Forum* undoubtedly contributed to the jaundice in Deacon's eye when he reviewed *Titans* on 18 December.

MacDonald's story, whether generally believed or not, was all the more embarrassing to Pratt because Bush's article had offended not only one irascible poet, but many of the rank-and-file of the CAA. Bush had been quite ruthless in his assault – occasioned by the Association's recent Canadian Book Week – on the entire Canadian writing community: 'As ... the echoes of mutual adulation roll comfortably from soul to soul, there arises insistently in one bosom the impolite query: "Do Canadian authors read anything?"' He had gone on to answer his question with a resounding negative, proof of which he found abundantly in 'our windy tributes to our Shakespeares and Miltons ... [of which] every year the Hallelujah Chorus seems to grow in volume and confidence.' Such 'fantastic critical comments' he had gone on to illustrate and denounce, concluding with the suggestion that since Canadian authors simply do not know enough, 'if one must have a book-week let it be turned into "a week for reading a great non-Canadian book".' The response was a prolonged wail of pain and anger, which while Pratt chuckled over it – he had, after all, been exculpated – he would never have dreamed of provoking.

Deacon, after praising the poems in *Titans* for their novelty, humour, whimsicality, and playful use of 'the technical vocabulary of the sea, and of biology,' which is 'not the stuff many poets have chosen,' went on to say that the poems' 'virility and merits of versification are worthy of more serious uses,' and wondered how long the poems would wear. He called them 'professors' poems, full of long, unusual jaw-breaking words of many syllables ...' He doubted whether 'that poor bedraggled creature, the "average" reader' would greatly enjoy Pratt's 'pendantic fooling.' He continued, his disrelish for the 'professorial class' rather plainly showing:

Dr. Pratt told me, or I should never have known it, that 'The Great Feud,' while apparently sheer extravaganza, is an allegory. Probably the professorial readers, being intellectual giants, will appreciate that aspect of the poem; but I doubt whether common folk will be conscious at all that these words are meant to bear two interpretations.

He enjoyed the poems, he said, 'in so far as I am mentally able to grasp the jokes, which must make the book a feast to a professor of English' and 'the highly educated and intellectually sophisticated'; but he could not recommend it to 'that ignorant lout, the "average reader," lest he write me a letter complaining that too many subtleties passed over his head ... and what did I recommend it for?' The two poems, he felt, were 'challenging rather than great.' But he still had hopes that Pratt would one day do better than 'he has so far done.'

Pratt was not surprised that Deacon had been less than ecstatic, but he had not expected quite so acid a point to the instrument Deacon had used, in particular to transfix *The Feud*. He was hurt. For the first time a review had cut him deeply, all the more painfully because it had come from a 'professed friend.' 'I was not expecting anything eulogistic,' he wrote, 'but God above! – he came out with a diatribe full of cavils and sneers, and the merest appreciation – if it is that – of only the humor and such minor points.' He thought it was time that 'Billy stopped playing lick-spittle to that mischief-maker W. Mac. A pity, because Bill has some good points about him.' A few weeks after the review appeared he wrote Deacon a curt but quite rancourless note thanking him for a small cheque Deacon had sent him in payment for a review he had written for *Saturday Night*, but making no mention of the 'diatribe.' On the contrary, he wished Deacon well in future issues.

His conciliatory words may have had some small effect. A fortnight later, reporting a 'Pratt Recital' at Victoria College (11 January 1927), where a 'large, enthusiastic crowd' paid a dollar a head to hear Hubert Greaves read *The Cachalot* and Pratt *The Ice-Floes* and parts of *The Feud*, Deacon waxed almost 'eulogistic' on the subject. But though he acknowledged the audience's admiration for Pratt's 'dramatic power,' 'spontaneous humor,' and 'the kinetic vigor of his lines,' he again could not resist mocking the very notion that *The Feud* contained anything deeper than 'the surface meaning.' He wrote:

Pelham Edgar presided, and said that Ned felt hurt that the reviewers had not grasped the sublimity and deep spiritual meaning underlying his spirited lines; Dean DeWitt ... reiterated the statement of the serious philosophical import of Ned's rollicking verses, and the poet himself made the same claim; but none of the three of them ventured to explain wherein lay profundities unguessed by the critics.

The tone is less contemptuous, and, to be fair to Deacon, he had a point: Pratt's 'underlying meaning' was hardly obvious, as he himself ruefully admitted more than once in the future. Nevertheless, Deacon's initial review rankled, 'a raw subject' (as Deacon later admitted) of less than amicable conversation when occasionally they encountered one another, causing a long interruption in their hitherto comradely correspondence, a temporary suspension of Deacon's membership in Pratt's inner circle, and his reimposing a levy on Deacon when next he used the Bobcaygeon cottage. It was not until late summer, after Deacon had written him a conciliatory letter ('It was your good old self that was writing,' Pratt was persuaded), that something like the old relationship was finally restored.

Pratt had, meanwhile, recovered the aid and comfort of another temporarily estranged ally. The 'deep spiritual meaning' of *The Feud*, which Deacon and others had not perceived, had been glimpsed by Lorne Pierce, convincing him, it seems, that Pratt had at last returned to 'the high seriousness' befitting his talents. This together with Pratt's recent response to his Church's call for religious verse – a call that Pierce may have helped to prompt – and almost certainly, on Pratt's side, Pierce's 'deeply understanding sympathy and brotherly support' expressed on the occasion of Fanny Pratt's death in December, had already led to a revival of the old relationship between them. Deacon's 'cavils and sneers' may also have influenced the rapprochement. Pierce had never liked Deacon well, and grew to dislike him heartily, referring to him in his diary as 'bumptious,' having 'a swelled head,' 'tyrannizing over publishers,' 'trying to be a Mencken,' 'pontificating generally,' and above all 'irritating many people with his "bug" on Wilson MacDonald.' When a year later Deacon was 'fired' as Literary Editor of *Saturday Night*, 'because of,' as Pierce records it, 'further immoralities' (which he does not specify), he could only rejoice: 'No one will lament his eclipse.'

Whatever may have been the causes of Pierce's change of heart toward Pratt, in January 1927 he was not only ready to re-embrace an errant poet – if not a redeemed sinner – but also to take up cudgels in his behalf. Feeling that Deacon's review had been 'both carping and insensitive,' he set out to 'show him a few things he had missed,' particularly in *The Great Feud*. As a consequence Pierce wrote and published one of the longest and best critical assessments of Pratt to appear so far (*The New Outlook*, 19 January 1927). He sent Pratt a copy as soon as it came out, inscribed 'My Dear Ned, It's it! Piscatorially yours.' Pratt was elated and wrote him at once: 'Your review went gloriously to my heart. It was the best account I have had ... you

363 Hymns Devout, Brickbats, and Roses

were the only reviewer who got behind the "Great Feud." You stated exactly my own purpose especially at the conclusion ... [You] see the significance of it, apart from extravaganza ...' Pierce's conclusion, following a perceptive elucidation of *The Feud* as a dramatic allegorization of the 'age-old causes' and 'senseless slaughter' of all wars prehistoric and contemporary, was to observe that the tragic truth which the poem presents is, unfortunately, one 'which men in later times seem to understand after their own great wars, remember through grief's brief day, and then forget.'

In the first half of his essay Pierce had also written brief, temperately appreciative reviews of *The Witches' Brew* and *The Cachalot*, both of which he had ignored when they first appeared. Both poems, he now felt, contained much more than 'delicious nonsense and scholarly fooling. Collectively they are a portent of a change.' He continued: 'Possibly we are too serious and solemn, and it may be a good thing that a mentor should appear who can teach us to make merry, to carry our civilization lightly, not flippantly and irreverently, but with that easy grace which we call urbanity ...' Pratt, it is clear, had good reason to rejoice over Pierce's return to his fold.

Pierce had found nothing to qualify his praise for the two poems in *Titans*. But Barker Fairley (*The Canadian Forum*, February 1927), equally sensitive to Pratt's subtler qualities, was less reticent in observing certain of his shortcomings, though quite without Deacon's acrimonious carping. *The Cachalot*, for example, he thought successful and admirable up to the point 'where humanity makes its sole appearance in the volume ... It is not that they [the whalers] are badly done. It is simply that they narrow the focus of the poem from a pre-historic horizon to the little affairs of men ...' For him *The Cachalot* has, thus, 'a broken back.' On the other hand, *The Great Feud*, 'verbose as it may at first appear, is finely balanced. It ends on the right note, a note which we feel no other poet would have struck.' Pratt's 'occasional defects of ear, his rhetorical feeling for words, his melodrama, his bad rhymes,' Fairley observes, 'are as marked as ever.' But, he adds, 'suddenly they appear as virtues, so that to tamper with them would be to detract from the vitality of the work. In this strange blend of humour and true vision there is room for a multitude of sins ...' Fairley agreed with others who had already compared Pratt with Roy Campbell, but as to which of them 'has succeeded better in avoiding the weary vision of older cultures and seeing with primal freshness, our answer must be that the Newfoundlander has it ...' It was a balanced and perceptive review and in drawing Pratt's attention to his 'multitude of sins' was probably of more value to him as a craftsman than either Deacon's jibes or Pierce's exposition.

While there were others who saw beyond the 'fun and fireworks' of *Titans* to 'depths that a casual reading fails to fathom,' who saw social satire in *The Feud* and an Aristotelian tragic hero in the cachalot whale, and in both poems 'meanings nearer akin to philosophy than poetry' (though they were not always sure what these 'meanings' were), most reviewers in Canada still clung to the safety of acclamatory cliché:

I know of no writer of verse in Canada today who is giving us precisely this fine, rich, racy, vigorous type of poetry, in which imagination has unimpeded rein ... (S. Morgan-Powell, Montreal *Star*)

Only one familiar with the sea could write this small but gorgeous book ... [which] rings in every page with the gusto which the author felt ... (Toronto *Globe*)

In originality of conception, rhyming facility, descriptive power and conduct of narrative, Edward J. Prate [*sic*] rises upon Canadian contemporary poetry like a new dawn ... ('Ivanhoe' [W.T. Allison], Winnipeg *Tribune*. Curiously, he calls the poet 'Prate' throughout his review.)

'Titans' ... contains two poems of primordial energy ... A little matter of upon-it-from-it rhyme fails to disturb the poise of this colossal cosmic circus ... (Toronto *Daily Star*)

This last reviewer surmised that *The Great Feud* had been 'inspired by the film The Lost World.' He was probably Mel Hammond, a good friend of Pratt (who may have dropped him the hint). No one else seems to have made the deduction.

Outside Canada the few reviews to appear were, as usual, less enthusiastic. Perhaps the best of them, quoted from briefly earlier, appeared in the American *Saturday Review* (4 December 1926) and was the first to suggest a 'kinship' between Pratt and Roy Campbell: 'in both cases the vast backgrounds of their Continents seem to have opened fierce vistas of heady and sometimes inspired rhetoric.' The reviewer suggested a further comparison with Masefield:

But, though as a poet he can hardly be compared with his master, in point of genuine first-hand understanding of his subject he is Masefield's superior. Mr. Pratt has either been a whaler or an honorary whale, perhaps both, and he writes not with beautiful sincerity from without but burning actuality from within.

But then, as if suddenly aware that he has been too extravagant in praise of a mere Canadian, he decides to finish him off with a mordant coup de grâce: 'It may not be (and indeed it is not) very good poetry, but it is very good whaling.' Elsewhere in the United States the Boston *Transcript* was laudatory but confined itself to platitudes, while the New York *Herald Tribune* saw the book merely as a tour de force, but praised the poet for writing with 'directness, deftness, and much humourous effect.' In England the *Times Literary Supplement* also saw the book as a tour de force, a 'remarkable' one to be sure, but felt that Pratt's 'love of words for their own sakes is his undoing. He is intoxicated by them, and much of the energy which should sustain his imagination flows violently into this verbal channel.'

In general, however, it was what Pratt called 'a good crop of reviews,' at least at home. He was disappointed again with his reception abroad and with the failure of many critics to grasp the full significance of *The Great Feud*. But he was pleased to know, as he wrote Lorne Pierce, that 'A small circle, yourself, Edgar, [Gilbert] Norwood (of Varsity), Fairley, [Merrill] Denison, see the significance of it, apart from extravaganza.' Even so, and although he 'liked fantasy with an underlying purpose,' he had already resolved to abandon the mode of 'fantasy plus extravaganza' when he wrote his next long poem. Only once would he again approach the fanciful extravagance of *Titans* and *The Witches' Brew* – in *The Depression Ends* written in 1932.

One critic to whom Pratt had sent a copy of *Titans* had raised objections which the more Pratt thought about the more he came to agree with. This was the English poet and Orientalist, Laurence Binyon. Pratt had met him at Pelham Edgar's in November 1926, just before the publication of *Titans*, when Binyon had been visiting Toronto to lecture on 'T'ang Art.' (Pratt had found him 'one of the most solemn men of my acquaintance,' but had warmed to him considerably on learning in the course of conversation that Binyon's 'youthful hero' far from being, as Pratt would have supposed, 'an archaeologist who had deciphered a new and hitherto untranslated inscription which had thrown lurid light on mummies,' was in fact 'a man whose hobby was spitting' and who would 'make bets that he could drown a fly on the wing ... and always won.') Binyon, while warmly praising much of *Titans*, had objected to parts of *The Great Feud*, in particular the long and detailed, excessively gruesome and gory description of the beasts rending each other limb from limb; and also to a similar, though briefer, description of the volcano Jurania's abdominal turmoil and anguish, in the course of which her 'insides' had been, Binyon felt, 'excessively exposed.' Both descriptions he considered to be 'overdone and unnecessarily prolonged.'

Pratt, who, as Viola later recalled it, had himself felt 'doubts and uneasiness' about both portions of the poem, shortly agreed that Binyon was right. Soon he had slashed out half the first offending section, reducing it from sixty-four to thirty-one lines, and almost the whole of the second one. Having sutured the incisions with a few new lines and phrases, he felt satisfied that the poem was unlikely to offend even the most squeamish reader. *The Great Feud* was not published again until it appeared in *Collected Poems* (1944), where the revised version became the definitive text.

With publication of *Titans* in December 1926 and its general acclaim, at least in Canada, E.J. Pratt had reached the first major rung in his climb to the front rank of Canadian poets. Nor was there any serious challenger close behind him. He was only a month or so from his forty-fifth birthday, but had, in fact, been a serious writer for little more than five or six of those forty-five years. Yet in that short span he had established himself as one of Canada's major new poets. Though still a virtual unknown elsewhere, he could now take satisfaction from knowing that whether or not he ever wrote another line of verse he was already 'amongst the Canadian poets.'

Twenty years had passed since he had arrived in Toronto from Newfoundland as 'a raw and unpolished green-horn' (as he somewhat misrepresented himself at the time) to study theology. During those years he had wandered far (both literally and figuratively), taken many 'tangential steps,' been 'perambulated' through many 'prisms.'

But the convergence of events and circumstances in his life had at last, by a curious fortuity, shaped for him a course which he could follow with a feeling of satisfaction and growing self-confidence. The death of his mother almost simultaneously with publication of *Titans* severed Pratt's last main tie with much – never all of course – of his past, with Newfoundland and his ministerial commitments. At the beginning of 1927 he was thus on the threshold of a new phase of his life and of his poetic career. There was still a tribute to be paid 'To some very dear memories,' which he soon did in *The Iron Door*. And there would, of course, always remain many 'accents' of his past from which, as he expressed it, 'one could not, and would not if he could, dissociate himself.' But his great feud with the krakens and dinosaurs of his past was over, and he had survived. More than that: he had survived with the prospect of a future which held rewards that now were his for the taking. But, as he replied when asked, anent the survivor of his great 'tellurian' feud, What happened after that?: That's another story!

... He has abjured his choric origins ...

Notes and References

If not included here, full bibliographical details of items cited (published or unpublished) may be found in the Bibliography. Letters cited are identified by writer-addressee and date; interviews by the abbreviation 'int' followed by interviewer-interviewee, and by date if more than one interview is listed in Oral Sources. Box numbers are given for unpublished items in the Pratt Collection Victoria University (PCVU). See pages 391–2 for abbreviations.

BOOK I: THE NEWFOUNDLAND PARSON'S SON

CHAPTER 1 Ancestral Roots

3   'We have seen': Spiritual State Reports, Carbonear District 1882
4   'a lamb yoked': int DGP-Macpherson
4   'a bit of the saint': int DGP-EJP
4ff. For details of the Pratt family's early history I am indebted to Mildred Claire Pratt, *The Silent Ancestors*; and int DGP-MCP.
6   'It took me': EJP-VLP 10 June 1924
7   Revival at Gunnerside; and 'He is rather': Batty, *Gunnerside Chapel* 19
8   JP as 'Boanerges': Lench, *Story of Methodism* 153
8   'My mother was': EJP-Watson Kirkconnell 19 Mar. 1941
8ff. Knight family's early history: int DGP-Macpherson, int DGP-William Knight, jr, Knight family Bible
9   WK's expeditions of 1859: Louis Noble, *After Icebergs*, passim
10   'very ingenious model': *Evening Telegram*, St John's, 7 Feb. 1964

11ff.   Knights at Halls Bay: letters of Charlotte Knight-Jane Sophia Duder, July–Nov. 1862; int DGP-William Knight, jr
13   EJP's birth and baptismal records: baptismal register, Western Bay, Newfoundland
13   Dove's 'fall from Grace': Minutes of Conference Special Committee 1893–1946
13   EJP first called 'Ned': Esther Magoon Bailey-DGP 8 June 1967

CHAPTER 2 The Outport World

14   Epigraph: quoted by Benson, 'Who's Who in Can. Lit.' 323
16   'Every village' and 'I recovered fully': untitled, unpublished script, PCVU, box 9 (variant version in Gingell 17)
17   'the bread of' and 'the waters of': 'Newfoundland,' CP2, 3
19   'stories handed down': EJP, Rachel, HTF 48
19   'Those first twenty-odd': 'Highlights in My Early Life,' in Gingell 4
21   'the impression derived': 'Memories of Newfoundland,' ibid. 9

CHAPTER 3 Childhood in an Outport Manse

23   Epigraph: 'Highlights': in Gingell 3
23ff.   EJP's illness and coddling as a child: int DGP-CCP, int DGP-EJP, int DGP-Macpherson. Macpherson, a cousin of EJP and a medical doctor, thought that Pratt had had rheumatic fever as a small child, which accounted for the 'heart murmur' reported by CCP and VLP. But Macpherson also thought that Pratt's 'delicacy' had been 'much exaggerated' by his anxious parents. EJP's own recollections were mainly of 'endless colds and coughs,' frequent incarceration indoors, and of being much medicated with his mother's home remedies.
24   'Liquids unnamed': 'To Angelina, an Old Nurse,' CP2, 54
24   'I'm sure there was': int DGP-EJP
24   'for the good of our': int DGP-FSP
25   'peaceful debate' and 'Ned loved a good fight': int DGP-CCP
26   EJP first goes to school: 'Highlights,' in Gingell 3
27   'suggesting to the mind': Levi Curtis in Reports of the Public Schools (1901)

28   'They could take off' and 'It was, of course': int DGP-CCP
28   'there was never even': int DGP-DPH
28ff. EJP's early reading: int DGP-EJP
29   'encouraged us all' and 'Ned always seemed': int DGP-CCP
30   'We got heaven and hell': interview by Hambleton, in Gingell 42
30   JP's sermon quoted: 'Sermon for the Times,' *Methodist Monthly Greeting* (May 1893) 70
30   'Adam's blighted tree,' 'ungarnered from,' etc.: shibboleths of old-time Methodist preaching
30   EJP's conversion: Twillingate District Minutes, May 1904
31   'Ned's congenital weakness': int DGP-SHS
31   'That testifying business': int DGP-FSP
31ff. 'the congregation out of' and 'We ... would creep': 'Newfoundland Types,' in Gingell 13
32   'I always hated': int J. Frank Willis-EJP
32   'Ned had a bit of': int DGP-CCP
33   'Father had high hopes': *ibid.*
34   'spring or summer': JP-Charlotte Pratt 10 Mar. 1902
35   'very aggravating' etc.: int DGP-CCP
35   'in his shovel hat': int DGP-Macpherson
35   JP and congregational dinners: *ibid.* and int DGP-CCP
36   'gaffers and the stowaways' and 'all the gaunt': *The Depression Ends*, CP2, 62
37   'Our ... congregation know': 'Circuit Echoes: St John's East,' *Methodist Monthly Greeting* (Feb. 1894), 20
37   'loved an excuse': int DGP-DPH
37   'Memories that the years': EJP, 'Magic in Everything,' *CP2*, 118
38   'salt beef': EJP, *The Cachalot* 250–1
38   EJP's first 'snowslide': 'Highlights,' in Gingell 3
38   'a lot of making do': DPH quoting her father, James Pratt, in int DGP-DPH

CHAPTER 4 To the City and Back

39   'the coldest in': JP, 'Circuit Echoes: Brigus,' *Methodist Monthly Greeting* (Feb. 1892) 98
40   'the evil covetousness': JP, 'Sermon for the Times' 70

40   JP preaches on looting: int DGP-DPH, int DGP-Macpherson
40   return of booty: *ibid.*
41   Robinson, 'brilliant promise': *Daily News*, 26 May 1923
41   'I was caught by': int DGP-EJP
41ff. EJP, 'swimming in "The Hole"' and 'Gargantuan meals': 'Memo-
      ries,' in Gingell 6
42   'the stories of old': *ibid.*
43   JP on Fortune congregation and stoning episode: Spiritual State
      Reports, Burin District, 1898
44   'We were brought up' and 'We were always': interview by Ham-
      bleton, in Gingell 43
44   'than the fragrance': 'Memories,' in Gingell 8–9
44   'a retiring, diffident sort': int DGP-Norman Guy
45   EJP's swimming exploits: CCP, 'Boyhood of EJP,' 1958; int DGP-CCP,
      int DGP-DPH, int DGP-EJP
45   'Ned would reach': CCP, 'Boyhood of EJP'
46   'With Ned, if something': int DGP-ALP
46   'used to terrify me': int DGP-EJP
47   'normally heterosexual': phrase quoted from: int DGP-Macpherson;
      confirmed: int DGP-Norman Guy, int DGP-F. Peach; W. Morley Story-
      DGP 24 Jan. 1970
48   EJP's 'troublesome' year: int DGP-CCP, who is quoted
49   'much of this stuff': 'My First Book,' in Gingell 37
49   EJP's poor examination results: *Evening Herald*, St John's, 30 Sept.
      1896, 3; *Evening Herald*, St John's, 9 Oct. 1897, 2
49   'a secret ambition': in conversation with DGP 1 June 1955
50   'in a fishing-schooner': reported by Benson, 'Who's Who' 323
51   JP castigates merchants: 'Sermon for the Times,' *Methodist Monthly
      Greeting* (May 1893) 70ff.
51   William's alienation: int DGP-CCP, int DGP-FSP, int DGP-VLP 16 Aug.
      1967
52   'His father reached': int DGP-Macpherson

CHAPTER 5 Commerce and College

54   'He looked me over': int Willis-EJP
54ff. EJP's distresses at Sclaters: int DGP-VLP 29 Oct. 1969

55 'I learned a little': EJP-EKB 2 May 1942. The tale of the corsets occurs in several contexts and several versions, such as Wells and Klinck 5–6; McGrath 15.
55 'I hated every minute': int Willis-EJP
56 'No part of' and 'I was only': comment on 'Toll of the Bells,' in Gingell 61
56 'I'm sick of it': int Willis-EJP
57 'Old John saw his': int DGP-Macpherson
57 'I never, never': int Willis-EJP
58 EJP's academic record at College: *The Collegian* files, 1900–2
58 'quiet, reserved, studious': int DGP-Norman Guy
59 'the life of the party': Clayton Pincock-DGP 27 Oct. 1966
59 On Robert Holloway: *Collegian* files, 1892–1903
59ff. Holloway and EJP: int DGP-EJP, int DGP-SHS
60 'To see through': 'Memories,' in Gingell 7
60ff. Marconi episode and quoted passages: *ibid.* 7–8
61 'Wireless had ... given' and 'trust in science': 'The Convergence of the Twain,' *Canadian Comment* (Oct. 1935) 9
61 'night and space': 'The Radio in the Ivory Tower,' *CP2*, 86
61 'For only such culture': 'Silences,' *CP2*, 78
62 'one of the most': 'Memories,' in Gingell 7
62 EJP and the backward student: int DGP-VLP 16 Aug. 1967

CHAPTER 6 Teaching, Preaching, and Peddling

64 Epigraph: untitled, unpublished script of reminiscences, PCVU box 9
64 Details of EJP's teaching duties: *Reports of Public Schools*, 1902–4, int DGP-Brett, Willis-EJP
65 'the whole caboodle': int Willis-EJP
65 'more like one': Carolyn Knight-DGP 24 Nov. 1966
65 'I used to row': EJP-EKB n.d. [1942]
65 'about its anatomy': int DGP-Brett
65 '*not* a good disciplinarian' and following quotations: *ibid.*
66 'Father was almost': int DGP-FSP
66 'I got through': letter to *The Collegian*, Sept. 1903
66ff. EJP gets first doctor, and quoted words: int Willis-EJP
67 EJP apprehends 'wreckers': Clayton Pincock-DGP 27 Oct. 1966

374 Notes and References

67 EJP as local preacher: Twillingate District Minutes, 1904
68 JP's last message: 'Victory in Death,' *Methodist Monthly Greeting* (June 1904) 12
68 'He had a bit': int DGP-EJP
68 'the coldest in memory': int DGP-Brett
68 JP's funeral delayed by ice conditions: *Daily News*, St John's, 16–28 Mar. 1904; *Evening Herald*, 18–25 Mar. 1904
69 Funeral tributes to JP: *Daily News*, St John's, 28 Mar. 1904
70 EJP's experiences at Clarke's Beach: int DGP-SHS, int DGP-EJP, int DGP-FSP, int DGP-WHP; Wells and Klinck, *Edwin J. Pratt* 10
70 '[G]o on, continue': EJP-Barbara Brett 22 Sept. 1904
71 'a wonderful funeral man': int DGP-WHP
71 'I was called on to baptize': untitled, unpublished script, PCVU, box 9
71 'I was the first': Lillian Edwards-DGP 14 July 1966
72 EJP's 'breakdown' at Clarke's Beach: int DGP-FSP, DGP-SHS, DGP-WHP; Wells and Klinck, *Edwin J. Pratt* 10
72 EJP and W.T.D. Dunn: int DGP-FSP, DGP-SHS, DGP-WHP
74 EJP and 'Uncle Billy' and quoted passages: EJP-Willis Pike 26 Jan. 1908
75 EJP and 'lung healer': quoted words from an untitled, unpublished script, PCVU, box 9. Other details: CCP, 'Boyhood of EJP'; int DGP-WHP, int Willis-EJP; Wells and Klinck, *Edwin J. Pratt* 11–13
75 'blackstrap molasses' and following: int DGP-WHP
76ff. EJP's and friends' choice of Wesleyan College and rebellion: SHS-DGP 14 July 1966; int DGP-SHS, DGP-WHP
76 Workman controversy: Sinclair-Faulkner, 'Theory Divided,' passim
77 'to know what was': int DGP-WHP
77 'even before Ned': int DGP-SHS
77 Wesleyan College declared 'out of bounds': Conference Minutes, 1907
77 'We were incredulous': int DGP-WHP
78 Details of sales trip and Pike quoted: int DGP-WHP
81 'unscrupulous young men' and following quoted passages: anon. ('An Indirect Victim')-DGP 16 May 1966
81 'as a precaution': int DGP-WHP
81ff. Details of voyage and Pike quoted: *ibid.*

BOOK II: THE WANDERING SCHOLAR

CHAPTER 7 Undergraduate of Victoria College

85   Epigraph: *Canadian Writers* 2
85   'Ned quickly fell': int DGP-WHP
85   'blood brothers': *ibid.*
85   Details of living accommodations: WHP, 'Ned Pratt: An Outsize Personality'; int DGP-SHS, DGP-WHP
86   'We have everything like that' and following: EJP-Willis Pike 26 Jan. 1908
86   Delayed payment of tuition: int DGP-SHS, DGP-WHP
86   'bitten each gold-piece': int DGP-WHP
86   Newfoundland Conference decides: Minutes of Conference Special Committee, Nov. 1907, UCAN
86   'knowing nothing about': untitled, unpublished script, DGP
87   'I am sure no one': int DGP-SHS
88   'I am very fond': EJP-Willis Pike 26 Jan. 1908
88   'quit Theology in spite': int DGP-SHS
88   'excitingly unorthodox': *ibid.*
88ff. Details on Blewett: Paterson, 'Mind of a Methodist' 5ff.
89   '[H]e saw the analysis': Paterson, 'Mind of a Methodist' 9–10
90   'Ned was caught': int DGP-SHS
90   Details of Jackson controversy: Sinclair-Faulkner 322ff.; Annie Jackson, passim; Sissons, *History of Victoria* 202, 233–40
91   Soper quoted: int DGP-SHS
91   'It seemed to me then': int DGP-EJP
92   EJP's picture in *Acta*: Oct. 1908
92   Details of the 'Bob': Sissons, *History of Victoria*, passim; int DGP-SHS, DGP-WHP
93   For a somewhat different analysis of 'A Poem on the May Examinations' as anticipating the later Pratt: see Germaine Warkentin, in Clever, *The EJP Symposium* 23–4.
95   'throwing himself to': int DGP-SHS
95   EJP 'goes out' for public speaking: int DGP-SHS, DGP-WHP
95   EJP's 'Irish lilt': Phelps, *Canadian Writers* 2
95   'one of the best contests': *Acta*, Jan. 1910
96   'he could feel at ease': int DGP-WHP

97   On Lydia Trimble: *Acta*, graduation number 1912
97ff.   EJP and Lydia Trimble: int DGP-ALP, DGP-SHS, DGP-WHP, DGP-MCP, 16 Aug. 1967; WHP, 'Ned Pratt an Outsize Personality'; Lydia Trimble Harrison-DGP 21 Apr. 1967
98   'I don't think Ned': int DGP-WHP
99   'It is engraven on the tablets' and 'to know Dr Edgar': untitled, unpublished script, DGP
99   'When I really knew him': Edgar, *Across My Path* 117
99ff.   On Pelham Edgar: Sandwell, 'Oscar Pelham Edgar' 107–11; Sissons, *History of Victoria* 220–1
100   'Pagan, or, what is the same': untitled, unpublished script, DGP
100   'We heard that there were': *ibid.*
101   'He had a method': quoted by Sandwell, 'Oscar Pelham Edgar' 108
101   'The justness of': *ibid.*
101   'Ned's eyes would shine': int DGP-ALP
102   EJP's financial hardships: int DGP-Clark Locke, DGP-L. Macaulay
103   EJP's illness and recuperation: int DGP-VLP 16 Aug. 1967

CHAPTER 8 Westward Ho!

105   'Ned's enthusiasm': int DGP-WHP
106   'plan of campaign,' etc.: EJP, 'Western Experience' 3ff.
107ff. 'I spent the first' and 'The morning': EJP-C.E. Manning 8 July 1908
108   EJP and Magoon family: Esther Magoon Bailey-DGP 8 June 1967
108ff. EJP's farming arrangements: Bailey-DGP 8 June 1967; int DGP-WHP, DGP-VLP 20 Aug. 1966
109   EJP at Belleville: Ina McCauley-DGP 6 Nov. 1969
109ff. EJP and Young Peoples' Forward Movement: int DGP-VLP 20 Aug. 1966; Love, *Stephenson*, passim
110   EJP visits Turner: Bailey-DGP 8 June 1967
110   EJP's story to a reporter: Thelma Lecocq, 'Ned Pratt – Poet.' Repeated by Wells and Klinck and by Helen McGrath.
111   'I visited most' and 'I found': reported by Dorothy Howarth in 'Poet-Professor Keen Boxing Fan' (newspaper clipping supplied by Elsie Pomeroy, source unidentified, c1949)
111   EJP at Regina Fair: Bailey-DGP 8 June 1967; int DGP-VLP 20 June 1966

111   EJP's last visit to Magoon: Bailey-DGP 8 June 1967
112   EJP trades homestead: int DGP-VLP 20 June 1966

CHAPTER 9 In Search of an Anchorage

115   EJP's engagement to Lydia Trimble: Lydia Trimble Harrison-DGP
      21 Apr. 1967; int DGP-Harrison, DGP-ALP, DGP-SHS, DGP-VLP 3 Mar.
      1967, DGP-WHP
115   EJP's transfer into Alberta Conference: *Minutes of the Alberta Meth-
      odist Conference*, 1912; *Minutes of the Newfoundland Conference*, 1912
115   Engagement broken and visit to Lydia Trimble: int DGP-VLP 3
      Mar. 1967
116   'profoundly affected': int DGP-WHP
116   'He was devastated': int DGP-ALP
117   'there was a resiliency': int DGP-SHS
117   'shy, retiring': Paterson, 'Mind of a Methodist' 26
117   'not long after': int DGP-ALP
117   EJP and Hardy: see Book IV, Chapter 21
118   EJP's eventual defection from psychology: int DGP-EJP, DGP-VLP 3
      Mar. 1967, Willis-EJP
122   'tangled up': a phrase from EJP's 'The Fog,' *CP2*, 6
122   EJP begins relationship with VLP: int DGP-VLP 3 Mar. 1967
123   EJP's prize, medal, etc.: *Acta*, graduation number, 1913
123   EJP pawns medal: many accounts by EJP, eg, Willis-EJP
123   LP quoted on ordination: LP-John Sutherland 14 Feb 1955
124   EJP's mountain-climbing: EJP, untitled, unpublished script (of talk
      given at the University of Alberta), PCVU box 9; int DGP-VLP 3
      Mar. 1967; EJP, 'Hooked'; Sissons, *Memoirs* 172–3
126   EJP's experiences in the laboratories: untitled, unpublished scripts,
      PCVU, DGP; int Willis-EJP
126   'My most vivid memory'; untitled, unpublished script, DGP
127   EJP and the Leggotts: W.E. Collin-DGP 14 Nov. 1968
127   Collin's 'full-dress study': in *The White Savannahs*
127   'oasis in the Sahara': untitled, unpublished script, DGP

CHAPTER 10 Oasis in the Sahara

130   'a group of younger': Edgar, *Across My Path* 117

130   'a post-graduate class': untitled, unpublished script, DGP
131   'the usual anthologized pieces' and following: untitled, unpub-
        lished script, PCVU, box 9
131   'When Pelham Edgar': int DGP-ALP
131ff. VLP and EJP's 'long epic': int DGP-VLP 20 Aug. 1966
132   'If Ned took a real': int DGP-Leopold Macaulay
132   'the surest sign of': preface to *Heroic Tales* ix
132   'I was just testing': int DGP-EJP
133   'The Sea-Shell,' published in *Poets of the Future: A College Anthol-
        ogy for 1916–1917* Boston 1917
135   'only playing with': int DGP-EJP
135   'the way a grasshopper': EJP-EKB [Apr. 1942]
137   Hager Whitney recalls 'première': Whitney-DGP 18 Apr. 1970
138   'the most remarkable man' and following quoted items: int DGP-EJP
139   EJP on books supplied by Edgar: *ibid.*
140   'He could sniff a joke': EJP-H.P. Gundy 24 Oct. 1961
140   Fairley on EJP's introduction to Scott: Fairley-DGP 24 July 1967
142   'Pelham was always': int DGP-EJP
143   'I owe so much': EJP-EKB [1942]

CHAPTER 11 Tangential Steps

144   'almost a member' and following account of EJP: K. May Stevenson-
        DGP 10 Jan. 1969
145ff. EJP's real estate ventures: int DGP-VLP 10 June 1967
147   'mechanistical psychologists': int Willis-EJP
147   'were determinists': int DGP-EJP
147   'Wundtianism and [its]': EJP-Desmond Pacey 12 Nov. 1956
147   'a man who could': int Willis-EJP
147   Recent commentator on Titchener: Robert Thomson, *History* 147
147   'detest[ed] "theological"': *ibid.* 146
148   'lecturing or trying': untitled, unpublished script, DGP
148   'though I had to teach': EJP-Pacey 12 Nov. 1956
148   'a deep wish ... idealism': interview by Hambleton, in Gingell 44
148   'a lucid, interesting': int DGP-Francis Vipond
149   'W.G. Smith regarded him': W.G. Scott-DGP 4 Dec. 1969
149   'That time in Psychology': int Willis-EJP
151ff. EJP and Clare Hincks: int DGP-John Griffin, DGP-Marjorie
        Hincks

151   EJP and the Binet-Simon tests: *ibid*.
152   'a mere underling': int DGP-Hincks
152   'The subject not of': EJP-John Sutherland 21 May 1954
153   'The subject of "last things"': int DGP-VLP 27 July 1968
153ff.   EJP's experiences with Smith: int Willis-EJP
154   'I'd tell him he was': *ibid*.

BOOK III: THE YOUNG POET

CHAPTER 12 Stirrings of New Notes

159   Epigraph: 'My first long poem': EJP-DGP 18 Feb. 1958
160   EJP's visit to St John's: int DGP-VLP 27 July 1968
161   'amateurish flaws': int DGP-EJP
161   'Wordsworth at a low level': EJP-Carl Klinck 13 June 1956
161ff.   The text of *Rachel* used is that published in *HTF*, which is the
       same as that privately printed in 1917.
163   'a psychological release' 'On Publishing,' in Gingell 32
164   'was very encouraging': int DGP-EJP
165   The printing of *Rachel*: EJP-Carl Klinck 13 June 1956, EJP-DGP 18
       Feb. 1958, int DGP-VLP 27 July 1968. In a letter to EKB (n.d.
       [1942]), EJP gives a somewhat different account of how *Rachel* came
       to be printed: 'Some of my friends out of their unwarranted
       enthusiasm cajoled me into publishing or rather printing it.' But
       the account given in the text, based mainly on his letter to Klinck
       (13 June 1956), is confirmed by his letter to DGP and by VLP.
165   'the next thing': EJP-Klinck 13 June 1956
165   'generally enthusiastic': int DGP-EJP
165   'didn't think much': EJP-Klinck 13 June 1956.

CHAPTER 13 Matrimony and Other Diversions

173   Octagenarian quoted: Herbert Leamon-DGP 15 Aug. 1969
173ff.   EJP's work with Clarke and Hincks, and founding of the CMHA: int
       DGP-John Griffin, DGP-Marjorie Hincks, DGP-VLP 3 Mar. 1967
174   'Ned Pratt became the first': int DGP-Griffin
175   Marriage of EJP and VLP: int DGP-VLP 3 Mar. 1967
176   'up to the house': *ibid*.
176   'the more melting arias': Claude Bissell-DGP 15 Aug. 1967

177   EJP's fondness for boxing: int DGP-VLP 3 Mar. 1967; Dorothy How-
       arth, 'Poet-Professor Keen Boxing Fan,' printed item, source un-
       known, c1949, DGP
177   'I've a passion for fights': quoted by Howarth
177   'one of the best things': int DGP-ALP
178   'The home they': introduction to *Journeying*
178   'vitally necessary': int DGP-Griffin
179ff. Details of EJP's survey: *Canadian Journal of Mental Hygiene* (Oct.
       1920) 267ff.
180   EJP teaches course for Clarke and Hincks: *CJMH* (Apr. 1919) 62ff.
180   'the only person': int DGP-Marjorie Hincks
180   EJP teaches summer course: *CJMH* (Oct. 1919)
180   'When the spirit': int DGP-VLP 18 May 1970
181   'a bear-garden': int DGP-EJP

       CHAPTER 14   Storming Parnassus

182   Epigraph: first para.: EJP-EKB n.d. [1942]; second para.: EJP-EKB 2
       May 1942
183   'I started out most ambitiously': 'On Publishing,' in Gingell 29–30
184ff. Text of *Clay* used: typescript, PCVU, box 8
190ff. 'I remember now' and 'As my salary' and 'I went home that eve-
       ning': 'On Publishing,' in Gingell 30–1. For other interesting criti-
       cal readings of *Clay* see Djwa, *EJP: Evolutionary Vision* 21–3;
       Robert Gibbs, 'A Knocking in the Clay,' *Canadian Literature*
       (Winter 1973) 50–64.

       CHAPTER 15   A Port at Last

192   'made me an offer': int DGP-EJP
192   'distinctly remember' and following: int DGP-ALP
193   'If I have any claim' and following: in *Across My Path* 117
194   'as a work of utmost': int DGP-Marjorie Hincks
194   'was greatly impressed': *ibid.*
195   'As an everyday': Douglas Bush-DGP 25 Mar. 1967
195   'The course was a survey': int DGP-H.P. Gundy 14 June 1967
197   EJP and Greaves: int DGP-ALP, DGP-VLP 27 July 1968
197   'upon the Humber's': 'To Cornie[Greaves],' unpublished poem,
       typescript in PCVU, box 7

197   Tale of EJP, Greaves, and the red sweater: Phelps, 'The Poetry of E.J. Pratt' 12

198   EJP visits Bobcaygeon and acquires cottage: int DGP-ALP, DGP-VLP 27 July 1968

198ff.   'Ned was so entranced' and 'Ned loved the place': int 18 May 1970

200   'In Absentia' based on 'an old academic': int DGP-ALP. Pratt in a comment on the poem many years later (in Gingell 56) writes: 'I did not have in mind a *particular* person ...' But ALP's account is supported by VLP.

CHAPTER 16   Arcadian Adventures

202   'a novice' and 'the largest squash': int DGP-ALP

203   Adrian Macdonald quoted: 'Memories of a Poet' (see Bibliography, manuscripts)

203   'After we had tramped': R.S. Knox-DGP 27 Sept. 1966

204   'established poet' and following: ALP in 'Profile of a Canadian Poet' (see Sources, oral)

204   'egging him on' and 'not *too* seriously': int DGP-ALP

205   'Behind it all': *ibid.*

206   ALP on *The Ice-Floes*: *ibid.*

207   'It was his first time': Knox-DGP 27 Sept. 1966

208   'I made up my mind': 'Golfomania' 9–10

208   'His mashie': Kirkconnell-DGP 15 Oct. 1966

208   'within a few seasons': Knox-DGP 27 Sept. 1966

209   'That's the whole of it': int DGP-EJP

209   'between writing a stirring epic': int DGP-ALP

209   'at least in part, the expression': EJP-W.R. Benét 9 Sept. 1943

CHAPTER 17   Preparations for Launching – on Troubled Seas

211   FP's illness and surgery: int DGP-Marjorie Hincks, DGP-Cluny Macpherson, DGP-VLP 20 Aug. 1966, 18 May 1970

211   'even small sounds': MCP-DGP 9 Feb. 1984

212   'to realize that presenting': 'My First Book,' in Gingell 37–8

213   On reception of *The Ice-Floes*: int DGP-ALP, DGP-EJP

216   EJP's 'critical survey' cited: 'Canadian Poetry' 1–10

217   For a more comprehensive study of the role of *The Canadian Forum* in relation to literary developments in the 1920s, see San-

dra Djwa, 'The *Canadian Forum*: Literary Catalyst,' *Studies in Canadian Literature* (Winter 1976) 7–25.

219 'convulsions of merriment': int DGP-ALP

219 '*hated* Puritanism': int Willis-EJP

220 Bush's essay and Pratt's *The Witches' Brew*: Douglas Bush-DGP 5 Oct. 1968 (see below 245)

220 'I have never seen': 'My First Book,' in Gingell 37

221 'Frost and Sandburg': int DGP-EJP

221 'the Everlasting Mercy & Dauber':EJP-EKB n.d. [1942]

221 'Some Recent Trends' quoted: *Acta* (Jan. 1924) 33–4

CHAPTER 18 A Viking Raid

225 The dating of 'Come Not the Seasons Here': ALP in 'The Poetry of EJP' reports its completion in the summer of 1922.

225 'stealthy intrigue': *ibid.*

225 Pierce responsible for final selection: 'My First Book,' in Gingell 38

225 EJP on decorations by well-known artist: EJP-LP 16 Jan. 1923

226 'I would prefer': *ibid.*

226 Varley at Bobcaygeon: int DGP-ALP, DGP-VLP 27 July 1968

226 'an ugly, stiff term' and following: EJP-LP 16 Jan. 1923

227 The Pratts' 'grand party' and EJP's illness: int DGP-VLP 27 July 1968

227 'rushed off, the reviewers might': EJP-LP 16 Apr. 1923

227 EJP calls on WAD: WAD-DGP 27 June 1966

228 'The Review tended to restore': EJP-WAD n.d. [27 May 1923]

229 'all salubrious': LP-EJP 21 May 1923

230 'I trust your health': EJP-LP 16 May 1923

230 'I had been expecting': LP-EJP 21 May 1923

231 ALP's article cited: 'The Poetry of EJP: An Appreciation,' *The Christian Guardian* (20 June 1923)

232 'great pleasure to pick up': 'Ivanhoe,' Winnipeg *Tribune*, 30 Apr. 1923, in Pitt 3

232 'The prevailing idiom': Frye, introduction to *CP2*, xxv ff.

232ff. Reviews cited: *Globe*, 30 Apr. 1923; *Free Press*, 1 May 1923; *Star* (Montreal), 5 May 1923; *Forum* (Knox), May 1923; *Canadian Magazine*, May 1923; *Guardian*, 23 Apr. 1923; *Daily News* (Robinson), 26 May 1923. Other reviews: *Acta* (Oct. 1923) 12–14; *Dal-*

housie Review, III, pp 266–7; *Methodist Monthly Greeting* (Aug. 1923)
6; *Times Literary Supplement* (3 July 1924)

BOOK IV: THE NEW VOICE

CHAPTER 19 Saturnalia Observed

239   'He was like a man': int DGP-ALP
241   'that the *WB* was a psychological': 'On Publishing,' in Gingell 34
241   The 'original "finished" holograph' of *WB* cited is in PCVU, box 1.
242   'just for fun': 'On Publishing,' in Gingell 34
242   'It began simply as a bit': int DGP-ALP
243   'dabbling our feet': *ibid.*
244   'was for me a matter' and following: EJP-Desmond Pacey 11 Nov.
        1954
244   'To have lots of': *ibid.*
245   Letter by Bush cited: Douglas Bush-DGP 5 Oct. 1968
245   'a protest against': EJP-Desmond Pacey 11 Nov. 1954
245   Studies by Sandra Djwa referred to: *EJP: Evolutionary Vision*
        35–49; 'The 1920s: EJP, Transitional Modern,' in Clever, *The EJP
        Symposium* 55–68. Other interesting and useful readings of *WB*:
        Wilson, *EJP*, 21 ff.; Macpherson, *Pratt's Romantic Mythology*
246ff. Unpublished text of *WB* used is a typescript sent to LP in the
        autumn of 1923 and housed in the Douglas Library, Queen's Uni-
        versity
249   EJP's 'protestations' respecting WB: 'On Publishing,' in Gingell 34

CHAPTER 20 Of Publishers and Poets

251   'that fat-head': EJP-LP n.d. [23 Nov. 1923]
251   'With regard to Moore': EJP-WAD 19 June 1923
254   'Professor Arthur Phelps suggested': 'On Publishing,' in Gingell
        34
255   EJP and responsibilities of celebrity: int DJP-EJP
255   'To facilitate the inebriation': EJP-LP 8 Dec. 1923
255   'soon the publishers': LP-EJP 12 Dec. 1923
255   'I suppose, after all' and following: EJP-LP 5 Apr. 1924
256   'in case of demand': EJP-LP 12 Apr. 1924

256   'The spoiled child': LP, diary, Douglas Library
256   'gorgeous vanity' and following: Hughes, 'Wilson MacDonald' 9–14
257   'many crotchets': int DGP-ALP
257   'a dark, romantic figure': Joan Roberts, 'Wilson MacDonald,' in Percival, *Leading Poets* 133
258   MacDonald-LP correspondence: Douglas Library, Queen's University
258   'A delightful little tidbit': EJP-LP 12 Apr. 1924
259   'decipher most of': LP-EJP 14 Apr. 1924

CHAPTER 21 Shades of Egdon

261   'he had imbibed' and 'Ned for a time': int DGP-ALP
262   'the world / Outside the soul': *The Iron Door*, *CP*2, 30. EJP uses the word 'Hardyesque' in a comment on this stanza in a letter to WAD 25 Aug. 1927.
265   Texts of unpublished poems used: notebook in PCVU, box 7
270   'Sooner or later': int DGP-Desmond Pacey, DGP-H.P. Gundy
270   'the emotional kernel': int DGP-EJP

CHAPTER 22 An Unsentimental Journey

271ff. EJP quoted throughout this chapter and where not otherwise referred: his letters to VLP: 23 May–5 Sept. 1924
272   'looked forward to the pleasure': R.S. Knox-DGP 9 Nov. 1967
274   'I picked out': 'Golfomania' 11
277   EJP and Knox at Gordon's: R.S. Knox-DGP 9 Nov. 1967
277   'He said it was a Julianesque': EJP-LP 7 Aug. 1924
279   EJP on Squire and *WB*: EJP-LP 7 Aug. 1924
279ff. 'a great aesthetic experience': unpublished script (introduction of Roy Campbell to an audience in 1953), PCVU, box 9
280   EJP on his success with a publisher and quoted passages: EJP-LP 24 Sept. 1924
283   'this God-intoxicated': EJP-LP 7 Aug. 1924

CHAPTER 23 Of Whales and Other Leviathans

284   'a psychic interview': EJP-LP 24 Sept. 1924

285   'Here it is': EJP-LP 8 Dec. 1924
286   'expressed his annoyance': int DGP-ALP
288   'lays aside cap and bells': review of *Titans: The New Outlook*
       (19 Jan. 1927) 26
289   John Gray quoted: *Fun Tomorrow* 137. I am indebted to Gray for
       much of the personal detail about Eayrs.
289   LP's biographer quoted: Dickinson, *Lorne Pierce* 40
292   EJP quoted on the writing of *The Cachalot*: 'On Publishing,' in Gin-
       gell 35–6
292   'a bit of fun' and following: untitled published item: 'Taking only
       published work into consideration ... ' (context unidentified in
       VLP's scrapbook, c1928?)
293   American reviewer quoted: *The Saturday Review* (4 Dec. 1926) 682
293   EJP on reception of *The Cachalot* at 'premier' reading: int DGP-ALP
       (quoting letter by EJP, 27 Apr. 1925)
294   Scott requests copy of poem: int DGP-ALP, DGP-VLP 27 July 1968
294   Film *Lost World* described with quoted passages: Toronto *Globe*
       files (advertisements and reviews), 30 Mar.–10 Apr. 1925
294   'everything or almost': int DGP-ALP (quoting letter by EJP)
295   'that motion picture': int DGP-ALP (quoting letter by EJP 8 Apr.
       1926)
295ff. Details of 'Carman Controversy': Kingston *British Whig* 11–14
       Mar. 1925; *Saturday Night*, 28 Mar.–16 May 1925
298ff. EJP's 'dock' of 'monstrous proportions': int DGP-ALP (quoted phrases):
       int DGP-VLP 27 July 1968; many published accounts
299   EJP's letter to a lawyer: a draft of the letter in PCVU, box 9

CHAPTER 24 Sunlight and Shadows

300   'fatten the family coffers' and 'no matter how good': int DGP-EJP
301   Corrigenda for *NV*: EJP-LP 25 May 1923
301   EJP at Humberside Collegiate: Isabel McFadden-DGP 10 July 1967
303   'every summer until the last': reported by Benson, 'Who's Who' 323
304   'greying teachers': 'Memories,' in Gingell 6
304   'Ned had no interest': int DGP-VLP 27 July 1968
304   'beguiled the time': Toronto *Star Weekly*, 15 Feb. 1930
305   Golfing episode recalled: Macdonald, 'Memories of a Poet'
306   'Tom was utterly': int DGP-ALP
308   're-touched ... the hoary issue': EJP-WAD n.d. [18 Aug. 1925]

309ff.   Details of Claire's illness: int DGP-ALP, DGP-MCP, DGP-VLP 27 July
         1968, DGP-FSP

CHAPTER 25 A National Event and Heady Wine

313   Episode of misdirected letters: EJP-Mrs Horace Parsons 22 Sept.
         1925; int DGP-VLP 20 Aug. 1966
313ff.   EJP and the CAA, election of Roberts, etc.: Mrs Horace Parsons-EJP
         26 Oct. 1925; CAA files
314   'the aristocratic major' and following: quoted by Pomeroy in *Sir
         Charles G.D. Roberts*
315   Adrian Macdonald quoted: 'Memories of a Poet.' Alan Barr was a
         Toronto painter, whose portrait of Pelham Edgar is one of his
         best known.
315   'mostly a damnable waste': int DGP-EJP
315   EJP and Carman dinner and quoted passages: EJP-H.P. Gundy 24
         Oct. 1961
316   Masefield letter quoted: from 'John Masefield ... Admirer of Cana-
         dian Bards' (source unidentified in VLP's scrapbook, c1930)
317ff.   'National acclaim' and 'inundated with': int DGP-ALP (quoting letter
         by EJP 3 Jan. 1926)
318   WAD reports on *Cachalot: Saturday Night* 5 Dec. 1925
319   EJP's address to the Poetry Society took place on 13 Oct. Deacon
         reported it on 24 Oct. 1925.
320   Reviews of *WB* cited: 'We have had poets': WAD, *Saturday Night* 6
         Feb. 1926; 'It seems odd that he': W.T. Allison, Regina *Leader*,
         date unknown; 'We must confess': G.P.W., Hamilton *Spectator*,
         date unknown; *Globe*, 19 Feb. 1926; *Mail and Empire*, date un-
         known; *The Canadian Forum*, J.F.M., Apr. 1926; 'Nothing here of
         the "lisping"': source unknown (in VLP's scrapbook); others cited:
         Manitoba Free Press, Montreal *Star*, *Acta Victoriana* (all references to
         reviews for which date or source is unknown: VLP's scrapbook).
         British critics cited: reported by EJP in Wells and Klinck, *Edwin J.
         Pratt* 24–5; *TLS*, 18 Mar. 1926

CHAPTER 26 Pleiocene Armageddon and Other Dreams

323   Epigraph: the commentary on *The Great Feud* from which this pas-
         sage is taken is included in Gingell 68.

325 'zoologist laughing at': commentary on *The Great Feud*, in Gingell
72
326ff. EJP quoted on *The Great Feud* in conversation with DGP: int DGP-EJP
328 'Jurania' as 'the Ironic Spirit': EJP-Pacey 29 Oct. 1954
329 'my first attempt to combine' and following: EJP-EKB n.d. [1942]
329 'Intelligence in the Ape': EJP-Pacey 29 Oct. 1954
330 'What happened to the ape': *ibid.*
331 'to remain in Toronto': EJP-WAD n.d. [27 May 1926]
331 EJP's Chicago trip: int DGP-VLP 27 July 1968
331 The 'rich relative' episode.: *ibid.*; Douglas Bush-DGP 25 Mar. 1967
331 Edgar's report on EJP's 'great success': WAD in *Saturday Night*, 31
July 1926
332 'spent all day': EJP-WAD 14 June 1926. Many years later in a talk
on the poem, Pratt told his audience that he had got the idea for
his dinosaur from his visit to the Chicago museum. (See Gingell,
72.) But the poem had been finished before he made his visit to
Chicago.
332 EJP's 'troubles' with RA: reported by Augustus Bridle, 'Author ...
Tells How He Got Story,' Toronto *Star*, 1 Mar. 1930
334 'I have been away enough' and following: EJP-WAD 19 Aug. 1926
334 'a book to review': WAD-EJP 22 Aug. 1926
334 'Not "any great shakes"': EJP-WAD 9 Sept. 1926
335ff. Details of the Neville affair: int DGP-ALP, DGP-VLP 27 July 1968;
Greenaway, *The News Game* 114–31. Phrases quoted: DGP-VLP
338 Draft of a story: PCVU, box 9

CHAPTER 27 Public and Private

340 'While it is true': Knox-DGP 27 Aug. 1966
341 'Poetry is not': N.W. DeWitt, 'Professor Pratt's "Titans",' *Acta*
(Dec. 1926) 33
341 'We cannot think': anon., review of *ID* (source and date unidentified in Pomeroy's collection)
342 'Every summer' and 'Dr Pratt is always' and 'The latest poet':
anon., 'The Stove Was Too Big but Pratt Fixed That,' Toronto
Star Weekly, 15 Feb. 1930
342 'Though addicted to golf' and 'Canada's leading poet': anon., untitled item beginning: 'Dr E.J. Pratt, more commonly known as
"Ned",' source and date unidentified in Pomeroy's collection, *c* 1928

343 'It does happen indeed': foreword to *Our Great Ones*

344 'Ned was ... too Methodist': Hugh MacLennan-DGP 25 Apr. 1968

346 'not for the money': Adrian Macdonald-DGP 31 Mar. 1967

347 'A cheque for fifty dollars': EJP-Edgar 26 Aug. 1932

348 'Ned was a prince': L.A. MacKay-DGP 16 July 1967

349 'he loved conviviality': Robert Finch-DGP 20 Apr. 1968

349 'I remember one famous': Eric Arthur-DGP 25 Aug. 1968

349 'eternally at the table': Paul West, *Canadian Literature*, 19 (1964) 13

350 'I remember that Pratt': int DGP-H.P. Gundy

350 'Wednesday evening': EJP-Edgar 17 July 1930

351 Meighen biographer quoted: Roger Graham, *Meighen*, III, 6

351 'When he came within range': 'On Arthur Meighen,' CBC broadcast, 11 Aug. 1960 (quoted by Graham, III, 6)

351 'she and I would repair': MCP-DGP 9 Feb. 1984

351 'It was as host': R.S. Knox-DGP 27 Aug. 1966

352 'Ned was an epicure': Adrian Macdonald-DGP 31 Mar. 1967

352 'shuck off with a skill': int DGP-VLP 27 July 1968

353 VLP quoted on EJP: int DGP-VLP 27 July 1968

CHAPTER 28 Hymns Devout, Brickbats, and Roses

355ff. EJP and the religious pageant: int DGP-VLP 27 July 1968

356ff. EJP's contributions: *A Pictorial Presentation of the United Church of Canada*, Massey Hall, Mar. 1927 [printed booklet containing complete text]; *Triumphs of the Faith: A Pictorial Presentation*, produced by Denzil G. Ridout, assisted by E.J. Pratt *et al.*, n.d. [printed booklet containing original text and additional items for a revival of the pageant in 1954]. EJP's contributions identified by VLP and by rough drafts of several hymns, etc. in PCVU, box 7

356 Details of performance of pageant: *United Church Record and Missionary Review* (Apr. 1927) 16–17

358 WAD's review of *Out of the Wilderness: Saturday Night*, 16 Oct. 1926

359 Bush quoted: 'Making Literature Hum,' *The Canadian Forum* (Dec. 1926)

359 'to glorify myself' and following: EJP-LP 20 Jan. 1927

361 'I was not expecting' and following: EJP-LP n.d. [2 Jan. 1927]

361 'Pelham Edgar presided': *Saturday Night*, 22 Jan. 1927

362 'deep spiritual meaning' and following: LP, review of *The Titans* [sic], *New Outlook* (19 Jan. 1927) 26

362   'deeply understanding sympathy': EJP-LP n.d. [2 Jan. 1927]

362   'Your review went gloriously': EJP-LP 20 Jan. 1927

364ff.   Reviews of *TS* cited: *Boston Transcript* 29 Oct. 1927; New York *Herald Tribune* 9 Oct. 1927; Winnipeg *Tribune* 13 Jan. 1927; Montreal *Star*, Toronto *Globe*, and Toronto *Star* (dates unknown: VLP's scrapbook)

365   'A small circle' and following: EJP-LP 20 Jan. 1927

365ff.   'one of the most solemn' and following on Binyon: unpublished script, PCVU, box 9. A variant version of this script is in Gingell, entitled 'Newfoundland Types (2)' 14–17.

366   Binyon's criticisms of *The Great Feud*: int DGP-VLP 27 July 1968; Wells and Klinck, *Edwin J. Pratt* 50. Quoted passages from Wells and Klinck

367   'one could not, and would not': 'Highlights,' in Gingell 4

Bibliography

The chief sources of this biography are as yet unpublished. These have been classified and listed below. The location given in each case is that obtaining at the time I used the document or a copy of it was supplied to me. Certain published items of a special nature are included under Miscellaneous Sources. Otherwise, published works used or consulted are listed under Books and Articles.

The following abbreviations have been used throughout the Sources and Notes and References:

Personal names

ALP Arthur L. Phelps
CCP Calvert C. Pratt
     (brother of EJP)
DGP author of this book
DPH Daphne Pratt House
     (niece of EJP)
EKB E.K. Brown
EJP E.J. Pratt
FP   Fanny Pratt
     (mother of EJP)
FSP Florence (Floss) Pratt
     (sister of EJP)

JP   John Pratt
     (father of EJP)
LP   Lorne Pierce
MCP Mildred Claire Pratt
     (daughter of EJP)
SHS Samuel H. Soper
VLP Viola Leone Pratt
     (wife of EJP)
WAD William Arthur Deacon
WHP William H. Pike
WK   William Knight
     (grandfather of EJP)

Titles of books of poetry by EJP

BB *Brébeuf and His Brethren* (1940)
BL *Behind the Log* (1947)

CP1 *Collected Poems*, 1st edition
     (1944)

CP2	Collected Poems, 2nd edition (1958)	RA	The Roosevelt and the Antinoe (1930)
CPA	Collected Poems, American edition (1945)	SL	Still Life (1942)
DK	Dunkirk (1941)	TLS	Towards the Last Spike (1952)
FG	Fable of the Goats (1937)	TR	They Are Returning (1945)
HTF	Here the Tides Flow (1962)	TS	Titans (1926)
ID	The Iron Door (1927)	TT	The Titanic (1935)
MM	Many Moods (1932)	VS	Verses of the Sea (1930)
NV	Newfoundland Verse (1923)	WB	The Witches' Brew (1925)

Other abbreviations

PCVU Pratt Collection Victoria University: the EJP Manuscript Collection in the E.J. Pratt Library of Victoria University, Toronto

UCAN United Church Archives in Newfoundland (St John's)

UCAT United Church Archives in Toronto (Victoria University)

SOURCES

MANUSCRIPTS

EJP, unpublished scripts: early drafts and fair copies of poems and prose works; notebooks; holographs and typescripts of talks, lectures, etc. Most of those used are in PCVU. A few are in the possession of DGP. Many of the prose scripts are untitled, repetitive, and often fragmentary. A selection of these was published in 1983 (see Books and Articles: Gingell, Susan, ed.). A typescript of the unpublished version of WB is in the LP collection in the Douglas Library, Queen's University, Kingston. Other scripts: CCP, 'The Boyhood of E.J. Pratt,' in possession of DPH; DPH, 'A Talk on Pratt for the Opening of a School,' 'The Boyhood of E.J. Pratt,' both in her possession; DPH, 'Notes on Conversations with CCP,' 'Notes on Conversations with James C. Pratt [father of DPH],' in her possession. Scripts written specially for DGP: Watson Kirkconnell, 'Memorandum'; Adrian Macdonald, 'Memories of a Poet'; Isabel McFadden, 'Recollections of Ned Pratt'; Jacob Markowitz, 'My Friend, Ned Pratt'; WHP, 'Ned Pratt, an Outsize Personality.'

LETTERS

The possessor of the original is given in brackets after each letter or collection of letters. When the recipient holds the original his or her initials are used. (1) *By EJP*: to W.R. Benét (Yale University Library), E.K. Brown (Mrs Margaret Brown and DGP), Barbara Brett (DGP), Douglas Bush (DB), W.A. Deacon (Fisher Rare Book Library, University of Toronto), Pelham Edgar (PCVU), H.P. Gundy (HPG), Watson Kirkconnell (WK), Carl Klinck (CK), C.E. Manning (UCAT), Ina McCauley (IM), Desmond Pacey (DP), Mrs Horace Parsons (DGP), Lorne Pierce (Douglas Library, Queen's University), Willis Pike (Edwin Procunier), David G. Pitt (DGP), Mildred Claire Pratt (MCP), Viola Leona Pratt (VLP), John Sutherland (Audrey Sutherland), Henry W. Wells (HWW) (2) *To EJP*: from W.A. Deacon (Fisher Rare Book Library, Toronto), Lorne Pierce (Douglas Library, Queen's University) (3) By and to various correspondents: F.E. Church to WK, Charlotte Knight to Sophia Duder, JP to WK (William Knight, jr), FP to Charlotte Pratt, JP to Charlotte Pratt (VLP), H.J.B. Woods to JP (UCAN), ALP to LP, LP to Desmond Pacey, LP to Frederick A. Stokes, LP to John Sutherland (Douglas Library, Queen's) (4) By various correspondents to DGP: 'An Indirect Victim' (pseud.), Eric Arthur, Esther (Magoon) Bailey, Harold Bennett, Claude Bissell, Edward A. Bott, Douglas Bush, W.E. Collin, W.A. Deacon, Lillian Pratt Edwards, R.A. East, Barker Fairley, Robert Finch, Northrop Frye, Lydia Trimble Harrison, Watson Kirkconnell, Carl Klinck, Carolyn Knight, R.S. Knox, Edna Lawrence, Hubert Leamon, Adrian Macdonald, Louis MacKay, Hugh MacLennan, Ina McCauley, Isabel McFadden, Jacob Markowitz, R.J.D. Morris, W.M. Mustard, Desmond Pacey, Lester B. Pearson, Arthur L. Phelps, Clayton Pincock, W.H. Pike, Maud (Mrs Arthur) Pratt, Mildred Claire Pratt, Viola Leone Pratt, Edwin Procunier, F.R. Scott, W.G. Scott, Anna Normart (Mrs C.B.) Sissons, A.J.M. Smith, S.H. Soper, May Stevenson, W. Morley Story, Audrey (Mrs John) Sutherland, Henry W. Wells, Hager H. Whitney, Healey Willan, J. Frank Willis

ORAL SOURCES

Recording of 'Profile of a Canadian Poet,' CBC Radio, 5 Feb. 1958. Recording of 'Birthday Tribute to EJP,' CBC Radio, 6 Feb. 1963. Unedited sound track of videotaped interview of EJP by J. Frank Willis, telecast by CBC-TV, 7 Feb.

1961. Recorded interviews by DGP of the following: ALP 14 June 1967; CCP 4 June 1962; DPH 12 July 1966; EJP 23 Jan. 1960; FSP 23 Nov. 1967; MCP 27 July 1968; SHS 10 June 1967; VLP 20 Aug. 1966, 3 Mar. 1967, 16 Aug. 1967, 12 July 1968, 27 July 1968, 29 Oct. 1969, 4 Jan. 1970, 18 May 1970; WHP 12 Aug. 1966; Barbara Brett 8 June 1966; Georgina French Cotton 8 Mar. 1968; John Griffin 7 June 1967; H.P. Gundy 14 June 1967; Norman Guy 28 July 1966; Lydia Trimble Harrison 2 May 1967; Marjorie Hincks 12 June 1967; William Knight, jr 3 June 1968; Clark Locke 13 Nov. 1969; Leopold Macaulay 19 Nov. 1969; Cluny Macpherson 10 June 1966; Desmond Pacey 16 Mar. 1974; Frederick Peach 8 Sept. 1970; H.G. Puddester 23 Nov. 1967; Francis E. Vipond 8 Nov. 1967

MISCELLANEOUS SOURCES

Academic Records, Office of the Registrar, Victoria University, Toronto; and Victoria University Archives. Canadian Authors' Association Records, E.J. Pratt Library, Victoria University, Toronto. Public school records and published reports, Department of Education, Confederation Building, St John's. JP, 'Last Message to My Congregation,' UCAN. JP, 'Spiritual State Reports,' Spiritual State Report Books, 1873–1904, UCAN. Methodist College (St John's) Records, UCAN. Newfoundland Methodist District Minute Books, 1877–1913, UCAN. Newfoundland Methodist Conference Minutes, 1880–1912, UCAN. Newfoundland Methodist Church Baptismal, Marriage, and Burial Registers, UCAN. Newfoundland Methodist Conference Special Committee Minutes, 1885–1912, UCAN. Life records of the Pratts of Yorkshire, Public Records Office, London, England. Gravestone inscriptions of the Pittses of Bell Island (Gordon Duff). Genealogy of the Pittses of Bell Island and St John's (Cluny Macpherson). Genealogy of the Knights of St John's (William Knight, jr). Pratt family Bible (DPH). LP, personal diary (Douglas Library, Queen's). VLP, personal diary (VLP). Elsie Pomeroy, collection of newspaper clippings on EJP (DGP). VLP, scrapbook of clippings on EJP (VLP). Methodist College *Collegian* files, UCAN.

BOOKS AND ARTICLES

Batty, Margaret, *Gunnerside Chapel and Gunnerside Folk*. Barnard Castle 1967

Benson, Nathaniel A., 'Who's Who in Canadian Literature: Edwin J. Pratt,' *The Canadian Bookman* (Nov. 1927) 323–6
Clever, Glenn, ed., *The E.J. Pratt Symposium.* Ottawa 1977
Collin, W.E., 'Pleiocene Heroics,' in his *The White Savannahs.* Toronto 1936, pp 119–44
Dickinson, C.H., *Lorne Pierce: A Portrait.* Toronto 1965
Djwa, Sandra, *E.J. Pratt: The Evolutionary Vision.* Toronto 1974
Dudek, Louis and Michael Gnarowski, eds, *The Making of Canadian Poetry.* Toronto 1967
Edgar, Pelham, *Across My Path*, ed. by Northrop Frye. Toronto 1952
Frye, Northrop, introduction to *Collected Poems of E.J. Pratt*, 2nd ed. Toronto 1958
Gingell, Susan, ed., *E.J. Pratt on His Life and Poetry* [a selection chiefly of hitherto unpublished prose scripts by Pratt]. Toronto 1983
Graham, Jean, 'Among Those Present: Dr E.J. Pratt,' *Saturday Night* (14 May 1932) 5
Graham, Roger, *Arthur Meighen: A Biography*, III. Toronto 1965
Gray, John Morgan, *Fun Tomorrow: Learning to be a Publisher and Much Else.* Toronto 1978
Greenaway, Roy, 'Herbert John Nelles Neville: Canadian Ponzi,' in his *The News Game.* Toronto 1966, pp 114–31
Harrington, Lyn, *Syllables of Recorded Time: The Story of the Canadian Authors' Association 1921–1981.* Toronto 1981
Hughes, J. Moore, 'Wilson MacDonald: The Sketch of a Personality,' *Acta Victoriana* (Feb.-Mar. 1931)
Jackson, Annie, *George Jackson: A Commemorative Volume.* London 1949
Johnson, D.W., *History of Methodism in Eastern British America*, Sackville, NB 1925
Kirkconnell, Watson, *A Slice of Canada: Memoirs.* Toronto 1967
Lecocq, Thelma, 'Ned Pratt: Poet,' *Maclean's Magazine* (15 Nov. 1944) 17–18, 24–8
Lench, Charles, *The Story of Methodism in Bonavista.* St John's 1919
Love, Christopher, *Frederick Clark Stephenson.* Toronto 1957
McGrath, Helen, 'The Bard from Newfoundland,' *Atlantic Advocate* (Nov. 1958) 13–21
Macpherson, Jay, *Pratt's Romantic Mythology: The Witches' Brew.* Pratt Lecture for 1972 at Memorial University, St John's 1972

Noble, Louis, *After Icebergs with a Painter*. New York 1861

Paterson, Morton, 'The Mind of a Methodist: The Personalist Theology of George John Blewett in Its Historical Context,' *The Bulletin*, 27 (pub. by Committee on Archives of the United Church). Toronto 1978

Percival, W.P., ed., *Leading Canadian Poets*. Toronto 1948

Phelps, Arthur L., *Canadian Writers*. Toronto 1951

- 'The Poetry of E.J. Pratt,' *Christian Guardian* (20 June 1923) 12, 19

Pierce, Lorne, introduction to *Journeying through the Year*, ed. by Viola L. Pratt. Toronto 1957

Pitt, David G., ed., *Critical Views on Canadian Writers: E.J. Pratt*. Toronto 1969

Pomeroy, Elsie, *Sir Charles G.D. Roberts: A Biography*. Toronto 1943

Pratt, E.J., *Studies in Pauline Eschatology and Its Background (doctoral dissertation)*. Toronto 1917

- 'Application of the Binet-Simon Tests (Stanford Revision) to a Toronto Public School, The' *Canadian Journal of Mental Hygiene* (Apr. 1921) 95–116

- 'Canadian Poetry: Past and Present,' *University of Toronto Quarterly* (Oct. 1938) 1–10

- foreword to *Our Great Ones*, by Jack McLaren. Toronto 1932, unpaged

- 'Golfomania,' *Acta Victoriana* (Nov. 1924) 9–13

- 'Hooked: A Rocky Mountain Experience,' *Acta Victoriana* (Mar. 1914) 286–91

- 'My First Book,' *Canadian Author and Bookman* (Winter 1952–3) 5–7

- 'Northern Holiday, A,' *The Daily News*, St John's (23 Aug. 1907) 5

- preface to *Heroic Tales in Verse*. Toronto 1941, pp v–x

- Scientific Character of Psychology, The,' *Acta Victoriana* (Mar. 1913) 300–4

- 'Thomas Hardy,' *Canadian Journal of Religious Thought* (May–June 1924) 239–48

- Western Experience, A,' *Acta Victoriana* (Oct. 1910) 3–8

Pratt, John, 'Sermon for the Times,' *The Methodist Monthly Greeting* (May, June 1893)

Pratt, Mildred Claire, *The Silent Ancestors*. Toronto 1971

Prowse, D.W., *A History of Newfoundland*. London 1896

Rowe, F.W., *Education and Culture in Newfoundland*. Toronto 1976

Sandwell, B.K., 'Oscar Pelham Edgar,' *Royal Society of Canada: Proceedings* (1949) 107–11

Sinclair-Faulkner, Tom, 'Theory Divided from Practice: The Introduction of the Higher Criticism into Canadian Protestant Seminaries,' *Studies in Religion* x, 3 (1981) 321–43
Sissons, C.B., *A History of Victoria College*. Toronto 1952
– *Nil alienum: The Memoirs of C.B.S.* Toronto 1964
Smallwood, J.R., ed., *The Book of Newfoundland*, 2 vols. St John's 1937
– and Robert D.W. Pitt, eds, *The Encyclopaedia of Newfoundland and Labrador*, I. St John's 1981
Sproxton, Birk E., 'E.J. Pratt as Psychologist, 1919–1920,' *Canadian Notes and Queries*, 14 (1974) 7–9
Sutherland, John, *The Poetry of E.J. Pratt: A New Interpretation*. Toronto 1956
Thomas, Clara and John Lennox, *William Arthur Deacon: A Canadian Literary Life*. Toronto 1982
Thomson, Robert, *The Pelican History of Psychology*. London 1968
Toque, Philip, *Newfoundland: As It Was and As It Is in 1877*. Toronto 1878
Trevelyan, G.M., *Illustrated English Social History*, IV. London 1952
Watt, F.W., 'Edwin John Pratt,' *University of Toronto Quarterly* (Oct. 1959) 77–84
Wells, Henry W. and Carl Klinck, *Edwin J. Pratt: The Man and His Poetry*. Toronto 1947
Whalley, George: *Birthright to the Sea: Some Poems of E.J. Pratt*. Pratt Lecture for 1976 at Memorial University, St John's 1978
Wilson, Milton, *E.J. Pratt*. Toronto 1969

For a comprehensive bibliography see Lila and Raymond Laakso with Moira Allen and Marjorie Linden, *E.J. Pratt: An Annotated Bibliography*. Downsview, Ont. 1980

Index

www.ingramcontent.com/pod-product-compliance
Lightning Source LLC
Chambersburg PA
CBHW030330120726
47901CB00007B/1735